Routledge Revivals

Patriotism
The Making and Unmaking of British National Identity

First published in 1989, this is the second of three volumes exploring the changing notions of patriotism in British life from the thirteenth century to the late twentieth century and constitutes an attempt to come to terms with the power of the national idea through a historically informed critique.

This volume examines how national identity has competed with alternative, more personal forms of belonging — such as Roman Catholicism, Judaism and Nonconformism — as well looking at femininity in relation to the state. Contemporary British society's capacity to create outsiders is discussed and the introductory essay shows how this may shape our misunderstanding of earlier phases of national development.

Patriotism
The Making and Unmaking of British National Identity

Volume II
Minorities and Outsiders

Edited by
Raphael Samuel

First published in 1989
by Routledge

This edition first published in 2017 by Routledge
2 Park Square, Milton Park, Abingdon, Oxon, OX14 4RN
and by Routledge
711 Third Avenue, New York, NY 10017

Routledge is an imprint of the Taylor & Francis Group, an informa business

© 1989 History Workshop Journal

The right of Raphael Samuel to be identified as the editor of this work has been asserted by them in accordance with sections 77 and 78 of the Copyright, Designs and Patents Act 1988.

All rights reserved. No part of this book may be reprinted or reproduced or utilised in any form or by any electronic, mechanical, or other means, now known or hereafter invented, including photocopying and recording, or in any information storage or retrieval system, without permission in writing from the publishers.

Publisher's Note
The publisher has gone to great lengths to ensure the quality of this reprint but points out that some imperfections in the original copies may be apparent.

Disclaimer
The publisher has made every effort to trace copyright holders and welcomes correspondence from those they have been unable to contact.

A Library of Congress record exists under LC control number: 8911366

ISBN 13: 978-1-138-21239-8 (hbk)
ISBN 13: 978-1-315-45052-0 (ebk)
ISBN 13: 978-1-138-21240-4 (pbk)

Edited by
Raphael Samuel

Patriotism: The Making and Unmaking of British National Identity

VOLUME II
Minorities and Outsiders

ROUTLEDGE
London and New York

First published in 1989 by Routledge
11 New Fetter Lane, London EC4P 4EE
29 West 35th Street, New York NY 10001

© 1989 History Workshop Journal

Phototypeset by Input Typesetting Ltd, London
Printed in Great Britain by
The Guernsey Press, Guernsey, Channel Islands

All rights reserved. No part of this book may be reprinted or reproduced or utilized in any form or by any electronic, mechanical, or other means, now known or hereafter invented, including photocopying and recording, or in any information storage or retrieval system, without permission in writing from the publishers.

British Library Cataloguing in Publication Data

Patriotism: the making and unmaking of
   British national identity.—(History
   workshop series).
   Vol. 2: Minorities and outsiders
   1. Great Britain. Patriotism, to 1987
   I. Samuel, Raphael II. Series
   323.6'5

Library of Congress Cataloging in Publication Data

Patriotism: the making and unmaking of British
   national identity.
   (History workshop series)
   Includes indexes.
   Contents: v. 1. History and politics—v. 2.
   Minorities and outsiders—v. 3. National fictions.
   1. Nationalism—Great Britain—History. 2. Nationalism
   —England—History. 3. Patriotism—Great Britain—
   History. 4. National characteristics, British.
   5. National characteristics, English. I. Samuel, Raphael.
   II. Series.
   DA44.P38 1989   320.5'4'0941   89–11366

ISBN 0–415–01302–X
ISBN 0–415–02773–X (pbk)

Contents

Notes on contributors — vii

Introduction: The 'Little Platoons' — ix
Raphael Samuel

Childhood

1. The view from Folkestone — 3
   John Field
2. I-Spy — 9
   Frank Cottrell Boyce
3. Growing up Catholic — 18
   Mary Chamberlain

Class

4. Martyrs of class — 39
   Miranda Chaytor
5. C stream on Tyneside — 43
   Dave Douglass
6. Pride and prejudice: ladies and nurses in the Crimean War — 57
   Anne Summers

Religion

7. Dare to be a Daniel — 81
   Alun Howkins
8. An Irish religion — 94
   Raphael Samuel

Women

9 The first feminism 123
  Bridget Hill

10 Women and history 140
  Olwen Hufton

11 Tommy's Sister: Women at Woolwich in World War I 144
  Deborah Thom

12 Women in the armed services, 1940–5 158
  Di Parkin

Nations within nations

13 Scott and the image of Scotland 173
  Christopher Harvie

14 The anglicisation of South Wales 193
  Tim Williams

Minorities

15 Jews in London, 1880–1914 207
  David Feldman

16 The making of black identities 230
  Winston James

17 The idea of sexual minorities 256
  Jeffrey Weeks

18 London and Karachi 270
  Hanif Kureishi

  Name index 289

  Subject index 295

Notes on Contributors

Frank Cottrell Boyce is a research student in English Literature at Keble College, Oxford.

Mary Chamberlain is the author of *Fenwomen* and *Growing Up in Lambeth* (in press). She is a convenor of the History Workshop Centre for the Study of London History.

Miranda Chaytor is a freelance writer and historian. Her 'Household and kinship: Ryton in the late 16th and early 17th centuries' appeared in *History Workshop Journal* no. 10, Autumn 1980.

Dave Douglass is a miner at Hatfield Main Colliery, South Yorkshire, and part author of *Miners, Quarrymen and Saltworkers*, an earlier volume in the 'History Workshop' series.

David Feldman is Fellow of Christ's College, Cambridge. His *Englishmen and Jews, Immigrants and Workers, 1850–1914* will shortly be published by Yale University Press. He is also co-editor (with Gareth Stedman Jones) of *Between Neighbourhood and Nation: Histories and Representations of London since 1800*, shortly to appear in the 'History Workshop' series.

John Field is Extramural Lecturer at the University of Warwick and formerly Treasurer of the Society for the Study of Labour History.

Bridget Hill is Tutor at the Open University and editor of *The First English Feminist: Reflections upon Marriage and other writings by Mary Astell*.

Alun Howkins is Lecturer in History at the University of Sussex and an editor of *History Workshop Journal*. His *Poor Labouring Men*, a study of the Norfolk farm labourer, is an earlier volume in the 'History Workshop' series.

Olwen Hufton is Professor of History at Harvard University and author of *The Poor of Eighteenth Century France, 1750–1789*. Her chapter first appeared in a History Workshop symposium published in *History Today*, May 1984.

Winston James is Lecturer at Bulmershe College, Reading; formerly at the Centre for Caribbean Studies, Goldsmiths' College, London.

Hanif Kureishi works with the Royal Court Young People's Theatre and is the writer of *My Beautiful Laundrette* and *Sammy and Rosie Get Laid*.

Di Parkin is head of the Women's Unit, London Borough of Ealing. Her chapter is drawn from her doctoral thesis, *Nation, Class, and Gender in Second World War Britain*.

Raphael Samuel is Tutor in History at Ruskin College, Oxford, and an editor of *History Workshop Journal*.

Anne Summers is Research Fellow at the Wellcome Unit for the Study of the History of Medicine, Oxford, and an editor of *History Workshop Journal*. She is the author of *Angels and Citizens: British Women as Military Nurses, 1854–1914*.

Deborah Thom is Fellow of Robinson College, Cambridge, and a convenor of the Cambridge Social History Seminar. She is currently working on the treatment of juveniles in the inter-war period.

Jeffrey Weeks works with the Council for National Academic Awards and is an editor of *History Workshop Journal*. He is also the author of *Coming Out: Sex, Politics and Society* and *Sexuality and its Discontents*.

Tim Williams has been a political secretary with both Ann Clwyd of the Labour Party and Daffyd Ellis Thomas of Plaid Cymru. His chapter is drawn from a doctoral thesis undertaken at Jesus College, Oxford.

Introduction: The 'Little Platoons'

RAPHAEL SAMUEL

I

Minorities have not normally had an easy time of it in Britain, and the recent hysteria unleashed against the gay community – at the time of writing not only clergymen but, it seems, even teachers run the risk of dismissal if they own up to being 'queer'[1] – may remind us that stigmatisation and exclusion have been their lot. Gypsies, for instance, whatever their 'raggle-taggle' appeal to fine ladies, have typically been treated as objects of fear, and the harassment meted out to travellers on their encampments (often at the hands of the very local authorities who are statutorily obliged, under the Caravan Sites Act of 1968, to give them hospitality) may serve as a token of their pariah status. In Elizabethan times, Peter Stallybrass tells us (*Patriotism*, Vol III, p. 205), they were liable to be hanged for no greater crime than the fact of being 'Egyptians', and the penalties visited on their more indigenous second cousins – the 'sturdy vagabonds' of Tudor legislation, branded with red-hot irons – were, in intention at least, hardly less severe. Three centuries after their arrival in Britain the gypsies were still very much the 'dark people'[2] of the countryside, 'foreign' in their appearance, and frightening in their ways. Flora Thompson, in *Lark Rise to Candleford*, her autobiography of an 1870s childhood, has left a vivid account of the terrors they could inspire in a young village girl:

> When they saw the gipsies they drew back behind their mother and the baby carriage, for there was a tradition that once, years before, a child from a neighbouring village had been stolen by them. Even the cold ashes where a gipsy's fire had been sent little squiggles of fear down Laura's spine, for how could she know that they were not still lurking near with

designs upon her own person? Her mother laughed at her fears and said 'Surely to goodness they've got children enough of their own', but Laura would not be reassured. She never really enjoyed the game the hamlet children played going home from school, where one of them went on before to hide and the others followed slowly, hand in hand, singing:
  'I hope we shan't meet any gipsies to-night!
  I hope we shan't meet any gipsies to-night!'
And when the hiding-place was reached and the supposed gipsy sprung out and grabbed the nearest, she always shrieked, although she knew it was only a game.[3]

The division between the 'established' and 'the outsiders'[4] has been a normal feature of national life at whatever period one chooses to look at. One might point, in early modern times, to those 'dark corners' of the kingdom, such as Wales and Lancashire, which the Reformation never reached – strongholds, according to the Puritan divines, of both heathenism and recusancy.[5] Or to the suburbs, as they grew up in the sixteenth century, in defiance of the guild regulations and outside the city walls – 'dark dennes of adulterers, murderers and theeves', as they were called by an Elizabethan writer.[6] Or to those woodland and moorland villages, so important in the geography of English nonconformity,[7] which had their origins as squatters' settlements on the waste, or encroachment on the royal forest (the expressively named Nomansland, Hampshire, is a late example, of which we are fortunate enough to have a hamlet biography).[8] Then in the eighteenth century there were the 'Little Hells' which Wesley and the early Methodist preachers set out to evangelise in the face of riotous mobs – the industrial villages of the Black Country such as Wednesbury and Darlaston; the mining camps of the Mendips and the Northumberland coalfield; the remote colonies of the Cornish fishermen where Wesley had the temerity to preach against smugglers and wreckers; the 'half-savage' settlements of the tinners.[9] Another case in point would be the 'open' villages which grew up in the wake of the agricultural revolution, in the corn-growing counties of the south and east, the home of migrant and seasonal labourers, existing in a kind of symbiotic relation with the 'closed' or 'estate' villages where parson and squire ruled.[10] Within the villages themselves, to follow the evidence which Keith Wrightson and David Levine have gathered for Tarling, there was a process of differentiation which opposed the culture of the church to that of the tavern and drove the marginal and the outsiders to the physical edges of the villages.[11] (The New Poor Law of 1834, it has been argued, was an attempt to bring these wilder aspects of village life under a more central control).[12]

Curiously, less is known about the moral topography of the nineteenth-century town than that of seventeenth- or eighteenth-century villages. It is true that the outcast poor – the 'dangerous classes', as they were known in the 1830s – have always excited attention out of all proportion to their numbers. There is a great deal of evidence in early Victorian sanitary enquiries about the 'rookeries', those lodging-house districts (usually not more than a handful of streets) which were a major focus of anxiety in the cholera outbreaks of 1832, 1849 and 1853. From these same reports it is apparent that outlaw trades expelled from more closely governed districts were taking refuge at the ragged edges of the city, like the knackers and bone boilers who formed the original kernel of West Ham. Notting Dale, West London, in later years famous as a criminal Bohemia, and later still, the earliest ghetto of the post-*Windrush* Jamaican immigrants, was originally settled by refugee pig-keepers, expelled from Marble Arch; they were joined by laundrywomen, brickmakers and gypsies.[13] In the same period (the 1840s) Newton Heath, a suburb of Manchester, seems to have developed as a refuge of the 'slink' butchers – practitioners of one of the more flourishing branches of nineteenth-century commerce, the bad meat trade.[14] We know a good deal about the floating population who settled in the neighbourhood of the markets (Mayhew's 'wandering tribes') and the 'sailortowns' which grew up on the waterfront (there is a vivid study of them by Stan Hugill[15]). Here and there more individualised profiles appear, albeit highly coloured – for instance Fordingbridge, Dorchester, the 'Adullam' of Thomas Hardy's Casterbridge, which has latterly received attention in David Edgar's excellent chronicle play, *Entertaining Strangers*.[16] The late and much regretted Professor Dyos pioneered the study of residential segregation in mid-Victorian times,[17] and there are numbers of local studies using census enumerators and Poor Law records to establish the locus of want. But it is only at the end of the century, when autobiographical testimonies thicken, that the real tribalism of the city begins to appear with frontiers invisible to the eye of the outsider (or the cartographer) but momentous to the inhabitants within, and the 'rough' and the 'respectable' defining themselves, as in the village, by relations of antagonism and difference.[18]

The Irish formed a distinct underclass in nineteenth-century towns and cities, living in ethnic streets (in Rock Row, Stockport, the centre of the 1852 riots, every single household was Irish), and clustered around their chapels, funeral parlours, and pubs. They suffered a double opprobrium, as the bearers of an alien religion and as a source of cheap labour, and their recalcitrance to authority invited the hostile attention of the Poor Law and the police. The civil war between 'Saxon' and 'Celt' (as it was called at the time of the 1868 election) became a normal feature of the mill towns of Lancashire,[19] of the great seaports of the west, and even of such remote districts as the Fife coalfield. The Irish influence in such districts (though it has not yet been chronicled for the twentieth century) was enduring. It was sufficiently unassimilated, in 1930s Liverpool, for it to form a principal base of town politics, Conservatives championing the Orange cause and Labour inheriting the Green. J. B. Priestley writes about it in his *English Journey* (1934) and it seems to have stirred up some of his less benevolent Yorkshire prejudices:[20]

> A great many speeches have been made and books written on the subject of what England has done to Ireland. I should be interested to hear a speech and read a book or two on the subject of what Ireland has done to England. If we do have an Irish Republic as our neighbour, and it is found possible to return her exiled citizens, what a grand clearance there will be in all the Western ports, from the Clyde to Cardiff, what a fine exit of ignorance and dirt and drunkenness and disease. The Irishman in Ireland may, as we are so often assured he is, be the best fellow in the world, only waiting to say goodbye to the hateful Empire so that, free and independent at last, he can astonish the world. But the Irishman in England too often cuts a very miserable figure. He has lost his peasant virtues, whatever they are, and has acquired no others. These Irish flocked over here to be navvies and dock hands and casual labourers, and God knows that the conditions of such folk are bad enough. But the English of this class generally make some attempt to live as decently as they can under these conditions: their existence has been turned into an obstacle race, with the most monstrous and gigantic obstacles, but you may see them straining and panting, still in the race. From such glimpses as I have had, however, the Irish appear in general never even to have tried; they have settled in the nearest poor quarter and turned it into a slum, or, finding a slum, have promptly settled down to out-slum it. And this, in spite of the fact that nowadays being an Irish Roman Catholic is more likely to find a man a job than to keep him out of one. There are a very large number of them in Liverpool, and though I suppose there was a time when the city encouraged them to settle down

in it, probably to supply cheap labour, I imagine Liverpool would be glad to get rid of them now.

The poor, or at any rate the 'undeserving', 'mendicant' poor, were, for some three centuries, the untouchables of British society. From the Tudor statutes against 'sturdy vagabonds' down to the abolition of the Poor Law they were the objects of administrative deterrence and repression. For the Malthusians they were an 'extra' population, increasing geometrically by reason of their improvidence and threatening to overwhelm society by their number. For the political economists, they were the idle preying on the industrious. For the social investigators of the 1830s, they were the carriers of cholera and crime. For the Social Darwinists they were nature's failures, the 'Residuum'. As Lieutenant du Cane, the Chief Inspector of HM Prisons put it, addressing the National Association for the Promotion of Social Science in 1875, 'the great mass of habitual vagrants' were 'examples of the race reverting to some inferior type from which ages of civilization and culture have raised it. The characteristics of this class are entirely those of the inferior races of mankind – wandering habits, utter laziness, absence of forethought and provision, want of moral sense, cunning, dirt, and instances may be found in which their physical characteristics approach those of the lower animals . . . or what Professor Darwin calls "our arboreal ancestors".'[21] The notion of race was even more to the fore in the thought of the eugenists, an influential current of opinion in the birth control movement of the 1920s, as also in child welfare. Under the optic of 'race hygiene', the poor were mental and moral defectives, a hereditary selection of the unfit – the 'sub-normal types' who fascinated the imagination of inter-war social investigators[22] – and whose compulsory sterilisation a Parliamentary Commission in 1933 was solemnly pondering.[23]

The desegregation of the poor, and the coming out, or partial coming out, of the disadvantaged, are among the more striking features of recent social change. Unemployment, though a personal disaster, is no longer a passport to destitution as it was when Beveridge wrote his report in 1942; nor does old age dominate the poverty statistics as it did in the days of the Booth and Rowntree surveys, or in the 'affluent society' of the 1950s. The expansion of Supplementary Benefits and the spread of private pension schemes have substantially altered the constituencies of need, and even more so the public perception of them. The slums, those dark districts which for hundreds of years haunted the British social imagination – to a greater degree perhaps than in any other country –

succumbed to the bulldozer in the comprehensive redevelopment schemes of the 1950s and 1960s; for the first time since the Cross and Torrens Acts of the 1870s the destruction of insanitary dwellings no longer figures in the charges laid upon the local authorities. Social security 'from the cradle to the grave' may be beyond the reach of an unequal society, but lip-service is paid to the Beveridge principles of 'universal coverage', and in particular to the National Health Service, even by a government which views them with ill-disguised hostility. Beyond welfare there is also the influence of voluntary associations and self-help; the 1960s witnessed a remarkable coming out of hitherto stigmatised out-groups: unmarried mothers, now supported – if only minimally – by the state as 'single parent' families; lesbians and homosexuals; the disabled; even, to a limited degree, those age-old pariahs of British society, the gypsies.

Yet British society remains peculiarly excluding to those who, for whatever reason, fail to fit in. Newcomers are typically seen as a threat, dissidents as undesirables: in everyday life, people who look 'foreign', who speak 'strange' or who smell 'funny'; in political discourse, 'the enemy within'. It is no less apt than in the past to see the disadvantaged as second-class citizens, a burden on the country, rather than human capital. The last twenty-five years have seen a remarkable increase in the categories and sub-categories of those who are constituted in some sort as outsiders. The new ethnic minorities, subject to discrimination in jobs, homes, and family rights, are an obvious case in point. And there is also the appearance of new classes of domestic alien. Public housing projects, monuments of municipal (and architectural) pride in the 1960s, are now described as festering sores, 'inward looking, culturally deprived and spiritually desolate',[24] 'ghettoes of unemployed, educationally sub-normal, and ... "problem families".'[25] There is a comparable change in attitudes to social security claimants. They are no longer seen as people in need, as in the days when old age pensions and 'family poverty' were the focus of public attention, but rather as a new class of predators – 'bacteria' on the culture, as Mrs Thatcher described them in 1978; 'dole cheats', as they are featured in the tabloid press.[26] Ever since the downturn of the economy in 1974, and the 'scroungermania' scare of 1976, welfare itself has increasingly been used in a derogatory sense, with Asians in five-star hotels, and claimants on the 'Costa del Dole' (i.e., holidaying in the Mediterranean) occupying the symbolic space of those earlier demons of the Poor Law imagination, miners buying pianos.

Despite the disappearance of the two-camp division between

rich and poor – or for that matter capital and labour – the public is being continually frightened out of its wits by new and apparently unprecedented threats to the social order.[27] Yobs go on the rampage, not only at the seaside resorts (ever since 1964, the year of the 'Mods and Rockers' panic, almost a traditional venue) but now, as the constabulary informs us, in quiet country towns – 'a huge increase of crime, and specially of violence' (Paul Johnson writes in *The Daily Telegraph*) which has made Minehead or Taunton on a Saturday night even more terrifying than 'big cities like Bristol'.[28] Soccer mobs run riot. Monsters perpetrate crime. There is a 'rising tide of violence' in the schools. Then there are the hollow-eyed figures in the hospital dying of AIDS; the drug-addicts, poisoning themselves with needles; the glue-sniffers on the estates; the muggers in the inner city. In politics there are the 'extremists', a rotating term which can cover anyone from 'irresponsible' trade union leaders holding the country to ransom, to 'bleeding heart' Labour councillors subsidising sex on the rates. Even more shadowy, though no less frequently invoked, are the 'men of violence', a term applied interchangeably to international terrorists, picket line 'bully boys' and urban mobs.

The very indeterminacy of such threats makes them the more alarming. In the past, the subversives were a clearly identifiable and therefore controllable group – Communists and their 'agents' and 'dupes', during, say, the 'unofficial strike' panics of the 1940s and 1950s; the Irish during the Fenian scare of 1867; Papists during the Exclusion Crisis of 1679–81. Today they are everywhere and nowhere, spreading from the bottom up, and from the outside in – people who go unaccountably berserk.

The hostility which such figures arouse is quite in excess of any danger which they present to public order. Socially peripheral, they are symbolically quite central in maintaining the fiction of a moral majority – those 'ordinary, decent folk' in whose name the Prime Minister speaks, that '99 per cent' of the population (according to the newspaper editorials) who, in contradistinction to the extremists, obey the dictates of common sense. The well-advertised 'public outrage' on issue after issue nicely suggests that the malefactors are other people.

The well-publicised cases of cruelty reinforce us in the comfortable belief that we are caring. The stigmatisation of crime flatters us in the belief that we are law-abiding. The fears and phobias serve as invisible reminders of what we should be, negative proofs that something called 'the nation' is still there. Thus, the 'normal' and the 'natural' are established in a whole series of antinomies opposing the 'freaks' with the orderly and self-respecting. 'Loonies' become the negative measure by which 'ordinary' people define their normality, the focus on 'extremism' serves to highlight the national virtues of moderation and reasonableness.

II

Tolerance, though it enjoys an honoured place in the pantheon of national virtues – Britain, wrote Dean Inge in 1926, was 'the merciful society' – hardly survives historical scrutiny as a distinctive national strength. It is, after all, little more than twenty-five years ago that homosexuals were being jailed for being homosexuals, and children beaten at school for being left-handed; magistrates then were still exerting themselves to 'put down' suicide; abortion was still prosecuted as a criminal offence. And one has only to think of the treatment handed out to conscientious objectors in the First World War – most notoriously, the 'crucifixion' of those who fell into the hands of the army authorities – or of the venom of the domestic campaign against 'shirkers' to remind oneself that at moments of national crisis tolerance levels are low. Here is the diary entry of a *Times* newspaperman, penned in 1916:

> The conscientious objectors, or 'Conchies' as they are contemptuously called, are very conspicuous at the tribunals. The objection they commonly make is that their religious convictions are opposed to the killing of fellow-men even in war. Such self-centered and opinionated beings, separated from the general mass by an excess of conscience, have, however sincere, something repellent about them. It is not easy to decide between those who are moved by genuinely held convictions against fighting and those who unhappily suffer from poverty of spirit. Some members of the tribunals think they are all animated solely by a desire to save their own skins. In short, that they are all rogues, charlatans and cowards.[29]

Those who celebrate the glories of 'Merrie England' or lament 'the world that we have lost' might remind themselves that sodomy was a capital offence down to 1861;[30] that runaway apprentices were liable to be publicly whipped (a familiar spectacle in the silk-weaving district of Spitalfields in the 1770s); and that women 'big with child' were trundled out of the village by purse-proud local overseers intent on keeping down rates. Labour historians, saluting the 'freeborn Englishman', might like to recall that one of the privileges won by the journeymen tailors of Westminster, after a successful agitation in 1720–1, was that of six days' public holiday a year to watch the public hangings; and that one of the rights of Scottish stonemasons, when Alexander Somerville was a boy, was that of chastising labourers who offended them.[31] Conservatives dwelling on the paternalism of Archbishop Laud or the suffering of Charles-the-Martyr might remember that William Prynne had his ears cut off for writing *Historio-Mastix*. Religious toleration may be a distinctive feature of the national polity and one of the more enduring legacies of the English civil war, yet when tempers are up, not least in the Church of England itself, it is the persecuting spirit rather than non-intervention which seems to have prior claim.

This country has not normally been kind to those who, for whatever reason, have offended against the moral order. One might consider, for example, the stigma attaching to illegitimacy,[32] or for that matter madness,[33] and those dark and guilty secrets which have inspired so many families with dread – one of the major themes of nineteenth-century literature, though it is one which historians seem curiously to have overlooked. Or one could recall the melodrama associated with the notion of the 'fallen woman', that martyr to 'old-fashioned' values; or the torments heaped at school on the 'mother's boy' or 'cissie', or the sadistic enthusiasm of schoolmasters and the Victorian paterfamilias for the whip, 'one of those ancient English traditions', noted an astonished French visitor in 1867, 'which continue because they have continued.'[34] English child-rearing typically appears as the very reverse of the permissive, the relationship of fathers and sons being especially marked by violence. Samuel Butler's *The Way of All Flesh* would be a useful corrective to those who regret the erosion of 'Victorian values'. Here, from the other side of the parent–child divide, is the account of a father who prided himself on being 'strict', Charles Humphreys, a late-Victorian bookseller who in his spare time devoted himself to Christianising the people of Peckham.[35]

> I start teaching my children very young. If a child cries you can generally tell it is in a temper or its stomach aches, etc. Of course these or similar things we would have remedied as far as possible, but should we see what we think is temper, I frown at the child and call it 'Naughty' and this may grow in a few months into a few pats on the hand. This continues and grows in extent according to the age and the circumstances; and it is astonishing how soon children learn. This continues more or less until they are about four years of age, but I always beat them in proportion to what the offence is – a little under, if any; and after two years of age, I don't beat them directly

the offence is committed. After three years of age I may leave it for a few hours, or until the next day; and talk to them as well as punish them, and tell them as best I can that it is for their good. I never beat a child in my life, in a temper, and I always cried in my heart, and sometimes outwardly, for it is a very, very fine art to beat a child properly. About four years of age, generally, they give me a cause of clear disobedience, and then I beat them until the disobedience is removed, on the principle that I have got to conquer them or they conquer me.

Ideas of national character have typically been formed by processes of exclusion, where what it is to be British is defined in relations of opposition to enemies both without and within. The discovery of such enemies is a normal condition of national life, and historians are beginning to monitor the succession of folk devils who, briefly or more enduringly, have seemed to terrify the public. Catholics occupied this symbolic space for some three centuries after the Reformation, and the belligerent Protestantism which entered so largely into the make-up of English nationalists is incomprehensible without reference to popular fears of Popery. Traces of it are still apparent in contemporary Britain (one might ponder the extraordinarily muted trade union response to the phenomenon of Solidarnosc in Poland). In 1850s England, at the height of the Ritualist controversy and in the aftermath of the Papal Aggression, it bore the character of a national passion. Edmund Gosse's memoir of his Islington childhood gives us a glimpse of its place in the domestic affections. 'A tall and bony Jersey Protestant' used to visit his street, with ropes of onion hanging round his shoulders, and a shout:

> 'Here's your rope . . .
> To hang the Pope . . .
> And a penn'orth of cheese to choke him.[36]

'My father did not eat onions', says Gosse, 'but he encouraged this terrible fellow . . . because of his "godly attitude towards the Papacy". . . .' Gosse recalls the effect of his father's teaching on his juvenile self:

> As a little boy, when I thought, with intense vagueness, of the Pope, I used to shut my eyes tight and clench my fists. We welcomed any social disorder in any part of Italy, as likely to be annoying to the Papacy. If there was a custom-house officer stabbed in a *fracas* at Sassari, we gave loud thanks that liberty and light were breaking in upon Sardinia. If there was

an unsuccessful attempt to murder the Grand Duke, we lifted up our voices to celebrate the faith and sufferings of the dear persecuted Tuscans, and the record of some apocryphal monstrosity in Naples would only reveal to us a glorious opening for Gospel energy. My father celebrated the announcement in the newspapers of a considerable emigration from the Papal dominions, by rejoicing at 'this out-crowding of many, throughout the harlot's domain, from her sins and her plagues'.[37]

Anti-alien sentiment, though only surfacing occasionally in organised political form, might nevertheless appear (if it were historically examined) a systematic feature of national life. It was very much a force in 1940, England's 'finest hour', and not the least of the elements in the national mobilisation of the time. One of its more curious by-products was the mass internment of Jews, on the grounds that they might prove Fifth Columnists for the Nazis. The blitz, too, seems to have fuelled hostility to the Jews, who were accused of hogging the shelters in the underground stations. Even George Orwell, who had put his life on the line to fight fascism, and in later years was a notable philosemite, seems to have succumbed to it. Here is an entry from his wartime diary for 25 October 1940 – some seven weeks into the blitz:

The other night examined the crowd sheltering in Chancery Lane, Oxford Circus and Baker Street stations. *Not* all Jews, but I think, a higher proportion of Jews than one would normally see in a crowd of this size. What is bad about Jews is that they are not only conspicuous, but go out of their way to make themselves so. A fearful Jewish woman, a regular comic-paper cartoon of a Jewess, fought her way off the train at Oxford Circus, landing blows on anyone who stood in her way. It took me back to the old days on the Paris Metro. Surprised to find that D., who is distinctly Left in his views, is inclined to share the current feeling against the Jews. He says that Jews in business circles are turning pro-Hitler, or preparing to do so. This sounds almost incredible, but according to D. they will always admire someone who kicks them. What I do feel is that any Jew, i.e. European Jew, would prefer Hitler's kind of social system to ours, if it were not that he happens to persecute them. Ditto almost any Central European, e.g. the refugees. They make use of England as a sanctuary, but they cannot help feeling the profoundest contempt for it. You can see this in their eyes, even when they don't say it outright. The fact is that the insular outlook and the continental outlook are completely incompatible.[38]

Xenophobic sentiments like this were, if anything, even more conspicuous in 1919, a moment of national triumph rather than disaster. There was mass agitation for the exclusion of aliens, enthusiastically supported by the government of the day, legislated in a Bill of the following year; race riots in the major seaports; shop-keepers' agitation in East London to prevent Jews from taking up shops and stalls.[39] On the right, there was the very generalised belief that the Bolshevik revolution was the result of a Jewish conspiracy – Sir Basil Thompson, head of the CID, and Sir Winston Churchill were among those who subscribed to it;[40] on the left, militant trade union leaders bent to, or even played some part in, the 'Yellow Peril' agitation of the day. In Poplar, East London, where one hundred Chinese families were domiciled in two much commented-upon streets, labour disturbances between British and Chinese seamen triggered off a wave of anti-Chinese feeling which came to a head in the disturbances of 1916, 1917 and 1919. In 1920 there was a national scare after a local magistrate spoke of the 'moral and physical' suicide of English girls consorting with Chinamen. The *Daily Express* led the way, with a sensational sleuth's reports:

YELLOW PERIL IN LONDON

VAST SYNDICATE OF VICE WITH ITS CRIMINAL MASTER

WOMEN AND CHILD VICTIMS

A Chinese syndicate, backed by millions of money and powerful if mysterious influences, is at work in the East End of London. Its object is the propagation of vice. It is succeeding only too well. The headquarters of the syndicate are known to be either in Peking or Hong Kong, but all efforts to trace the principals have proved futile . . . The underworld of London . . . teems with stories of a Chinese Moriarty, that figure of the master criminal mind made famous by Sir Arthur Conan Doyle's 'Sherlock Holmes' adventures . . . His habitat is a mean street in the East End. He is ostensibly a humble merchant, and he displays in the windows of his shop dwelling and headquarters a few packets of tea and dried vegetables so dear to the hearts of his fellow Celestials.[41]

Lord Rothermere's *Evening News*, ever racist, followed this up with an even more inflationary story:

WHITE GIRLS 'HYPNOTISED' BY YELLOW MEN
POPULAR APPEAL TO HOME OFFICE
WHAT OUR REPRESENTATIVE SAW IN PENNYFIELDS

The 'Evening News' need make no apology for printing the alarming facts about London's 'Chinatown' set out below. It is the duty of every Englishman and Englishwoman to know the truth about degradation of young white girls in this plague spot of the metropolis. IT MUST BE STOPPED. . . . The eyes of the authorities are at last open to the condition of the Chinese colony in the East End. It has become a scandal, a peril, and a plague spot. There is vice here without veneer, and the worst side of the problem is the association of white women with yellow men. Englishwomen are selling themselves to Chinamen; they are seeking out Asiatics in streets where before the war no white woman ever walked. The evil . . . is baffling the police and social workers alike. Women who have been 'rescued' and given a fresh start have relapsed and returned to their foreign masters, and have sunk lower than before. The unmarried mother with a half-caste child is only one of the several problems that are arising. And obviously this cheapening of the white woman among men who go down to the sea in ships must have reactions in the East, and in every part of the world where coloured and white races dwell side by side.

The AIDS scare may remind us of some of the ways in which minorities are constituted as outsiders, and serve as a symbolic focus for both wider anxieties and ancient fears. It resumes what to the historian – or for that matter the student of prejudice – are themes that are only too familiar. The notion that gays are their own worst enemies ('flaunting' their peculiarities rather than, like 'normal', decent Englishmen, 'keeping themselves to themselves') is of course (as the diary quotation from George Orwell may suggest) a stock-in-trade of racial innuendo, as also of class spite. Again, the pathologising of gays as perverts corresponds to the centuries-old stigmatisation of the poor as moral defectives, the carriers of contamination and disease. In another register AIDS victims appear, like the 'idle' and 'dissolute' paupers of the Poor Law imagination, not as objects of pity but as monsters of excess. Again, the notion of AIDS victims not as sufferers but as aggressors is a leitmotiv of moral panics, however disadvantaged or deprived the targets of attack (the anti-immigrant agitations of the 1960s or the anti-alien agitation which followed the Kishinev pogrom of 1903 are points of comparison which suggest themselves). One may note too, how, as in previous anti-homosexual outbursts, very deep phobias come into play: the association of sexuality, for instance, with degeneracy, and not least the notion that homosexuals have in some sense forfeited the right to be English. 'Have you considered going to live abroad?' the governor of Winchester gaol asked Peter Wildblood in 1954 when he came before him. 'People in your position often do, you know.'[43] Finally, one may note the way in which a minority, as in the Yellow Peril scare of 1919-21 or in the virulent campaign of that time against 'half-castes', occupies an imaginary space out of all proportion to its numbers. As in previous moral panics, the immediate occasion for alarm is rapidly subsumed in a whole set of anxieties, in which fears for the stability of family and home seem quite as important as the immediate issues in play.

Politically Britain may be a pluralist society, as it has been, notionally, through three centuries of representative government. Behaviourally, though, it is fearful of departures from the norm. There are appearances to be kept up, standards to be maintained, protocols to respect, routines to follow, rules and regulations to be observed, and those who fail on any of these counts are liable to be branded as undesirables. In the field of morals, if not in party politics, a national consensus is assumed to exist. In public discourse 'British characteristics' (as the Prime Minister calls them) are still spoken of as though they were generic, the 'British' as though they were a single people, 'the British way of life' as though it were organic – a natural harmony which only the malevolent would disturb, a shared condition which newcomers must adapt to.

Freedom of speech goes hand in hand with a considerable hysteria about conduct. One could refer to the simmering resentment of 'scroungers', the fear and loathing directed at homosexuals, the extraordinary venom annually visited on the Stonehenge trekkers, the periodical panics about crime; Asians arouse enormous resentment because they keep to themselves, West Indians are feared as dangerous and exotic, even – in the persona of muggers – as killers on the loose. Self-exclusion is still typically the lot of those who, for whatever reason, offend against sexual norms – as, for instance, in the hostility of the courts to lesbian mothers when the custody of children is at stake; or the violence directed against the women of Greenham Common Peace Camp. A fierce intolerance in matters of personal hygiene is one of the more enduring legacies of the sanitary movement of the nineteenth century, and it is now reaching out into the uttermost corners of national life (the current crusade against dogshit and the phobia about toxicara is a bizarre case in point). The fetishisation of quiet – a legacy of the inter-war years – has nowadays reached such a pitch as to make any form of public assembly suspect.

Britain today resembles a society under siege. Children are everywhere instructed not to speak to strangers. Pubs, once the refuge of the working man, now display warning notices against 'dirty boots' and 'travellers'. Hitch-hikers who in the 1960s (the golden age of youth travel, and 'crashing out on pads') took to the open roads are a dwindling band, mocked as 'weirdos' or feared as potential killers. 'Living for kicks' or 'doing your own thing', which in the liberal hour of the 1960s was regarded as innocently pleasurable or even the mark of a civilised society, is today on the contrary condemned as a license to depravity of all kinds. Manifestations of youth culture are interpreted as heralding the break-up of the family; street life – save when it is coralled in the shopping malls – as a threat to public order. Whereas twenty years ago open air pop concerts would draw audiences 250,000 strong, today the smallest assembly of young people – even the informal drinking party – is seen as menacing. At Basingstoke, the *Daily Telegraph* reports, police are using guard dogs to move them on after complaints from local residents:

> Prudential Assurance, which has just bought the shopping area and plans to spend £20 million refurbishing it, is anxious to prevent youths congregating there, and has told security guards to ask people to leave who do not have 'acceptable standards of behaviour'. Disinfectant is thrown over seats where teenagers have been sitting. The punks claim they only want to meet friends, but local people say they drink beer and use foul language.[44]

Security has emerged in recent years as a national obsession. The government curries favour with the electorate by promising to make society more punitive. The DHSS is continually announcing new 'clampdowns' on 'fiddlers'. The BBC, with its *Crimewatch* programme, invites the public to take a walk-on part in the battle against professional thugs. Security guards patrol commercial premises: entry phones and closed-circuit electronic systems guard housing developments and flats. Neighbourhood watches constitute themselves as amateur vigilantes: in 1982 there was one in the country; today (as the Home Office proudly announces) there are 42,000. 'Law and order' today occupies the imaginative space given in the recent past to military preparedness; the police, armed when they go into combat with criminals, riot-shielded when they engage with 'mobs', are a first line of national defence, the thin blue line holding the forces of chaos at bay.

III

Patriotism is an occasional rather than a continuous sentiment, something called up at moments of crisis, when the country seems at risk, but at other times lying fallow. It draws on prior forms of belonging and often finds expression in terms of loyalties transferred from somewhere else – for Sir Henry Newbolt ('Vitaï Lampada') the *esprit de corps* of the school playing-fields; for S. T. Coleridge ('Fears in Solitude, 1798') the peace of the domestic cot; for the soldier-poets of the First World War, a memory of country lanes. Even when it speaks the same language, the accents are wildly various. England, in one idiom, is the land of hope and glory; in another, more convivially, it is Blighty, the place where you can get a pint of wallop or a decent cup of tea. The dissonances were never more apparent than in the First World War, when the comradeship of the trenches produced one language, the sisterhood of nursing another, the *noblesse oblige* of the officer caste a third. A high-flown rhetoric of King and Country, service and sacrifice, co-existed incongruously with the soldier's dream of home:

> When this lousy war is over
> Oh, how happy I shall be
> You can tell the sergeant major
> How I'll miss him
> How I'll grieve

Nationality is only one of the ways in which people make, or cling to, a sense of themselves. In Britain, it has always had to contend with more particularistic loyalties and alternative forms of belonging. Schism and separation, though often treated as exceptional, might rather be described as organizing principles of national life, whether in the sphere of religion and politics, or that of sociability. Contemporary preoccupation with the 'North–South' divide, for instance, might alert us to regional antagonisms in the national past. (The Welsh in 1856, when the government was making strenuous attempts to put down their language, were described as 'the most immoral people in Europe, except perhaps the Swedes')[45] Or it might alert us to the opposition between centre and periphery, or 'court' and 'country', in early modern times; to the civil war between Northerners and Southerners in the medieval university of Oxford; to the role of marcher lordships in the baronial wars; or to that extraordinary mobilisation against the dissolution of the monasteries in 1536, the Pilgrimage of Grace. Popular Jacobitism might also be studied under this optic, as also the survival of the old English Catholics.

National unification, or what has recently been called 'internal colonialism',[46] may be one part of the island story. Another, which deserves more historical commentary, would be the reproduction of earlier forms of belonging. In the epoch of the industrial revolution, for instance, one might refer to the growth of local economies or indeed, in the case of such textile towns as Bolton, 'empires';[47] to the increasingly regional character of production; and to the growth of local job monopolies, the very basis of trade union organisation in such early strongholds as Sheffield. The mining districts, though integrated into the economy of the country, were demographically and culturally autarchic, inhabited (it was said of the Durham coalfields in 1853) by 'a distinct race of beings':

> Pitmen have always lived in communities; they have association only among themselves; they have acquired habits and ideas peculiar to themselves; even their amusements are hereditary and peculiar. They almost invariably intermarry, and it is not uncommon, in their marrages, to comingle the blood of the same family.[48]

When, in 1861, a Parliamentary Commission at Westminster was interviewing Northumberland miners, the services of an interpreter had to be engaged.[49]

Nineteenth-century Britain saw an extraordinary proliferation of sectarian identities, and a multiplication of subdivisions along both horizontal and vertical lines. The agricultural interest, or 'farming fraternity', was defined as a separate estate, the butt of an increasingly militant radicalism. The City and British industry developed in separate worlds, with very little traffic between them. Church and chapel contended for local hegemony. Residential segregation, and the rise of villadom, minimised face-to-face contact between the classes; so did the growth of domestic service (at the time of the 1861 Census, the largest single occupational category in the country). The public schools – largely a creation of the early and mid-Victorian years – abstracted the sons of the commercial classes and gave them the manners and the speech of a ruling caste. 'Society' and the 'season' (an invention, Leonore Davidoff has argued, of the 1830s)[50] created a marriage market for the Upper Ten Thousand. Lower down the social scale there was a civil war between the culture of 'improvement' and that of the alehouse or tavern – a division which the temperance movement, promoting 'God's beverage, water', widened into a chasm.

Locality clearly counted for more than nationality in the days when the manor and the borough were the framework of law and government. It was hardly less important in the English Civil War, when the 'county community' of gentry was the basis of mobilisation on either side – or in the case of the West Country Clubmen, of armed neutrality.[51] Towns and boroughs, down to the Municipal Reform Act of 1834, formed corporate universes on their own. Parishes, under the laws of settlement, were a primary form of belonging. Local chauvinism had been one of the bases of the guild system, where masters and journeymen combined to keep the town trade to themselves; and it was a system which the trade clubs of the early nineteenth century – and often small employers too – tried to reproduce. In the back slums, which developed as hereditary or quasi-hereditary communities of the poor, neighbouring streets were treated as foreign territory.

London had a corporate identity for some three centuries before England became a nation-state. It enjoyed a large measure of self-government (under the 'Customs' of 1192), when the idea of Parliament was unheard of. As a source of wealth it was crucial to royal finance – more so during the French Wars of Edward III than the supplies of the House of Commons. Contiguous to the royal seat of government at Westminster, yet jurisidictionally independent of it, London could shut its gates (as the Webbs note in *The Manor and the Borough*)[52] against the king and his officers. In medieval times it acted as a 'sort of unofficial mouthpiece' for discontent, allying with aristocratic factions and opposition parties within the court.[53] The barons found 'willing allies' there at the time of Magna Carta; so did Simon de Montfort during the civil war of 1265. Londoners, according to their own tradition, played a decisive role in the opposition to Edward II, creating a sworn commune to depose him, and giving 'London's liberties' a key place in the oath of allegiance to the regime which replaced him (a similar pattern appears some 75 years later, in the successful insurrection against Richard II). As well as allying with baronial factions Londoners – or at least the merchant and craft leaders who acted for them – took action on their own account, refusing the jurisdiction of the ecclesiastical courts, enlarging – or safeguarding – the City's immunities, and taking action against the monarch who threatened to abridge their privileges. Richard II's attempt to 'take the City in the royal hands' – and his deposition of its elected officers – seems to have been a major cause of his downfall. (It would be pleasant to think that some such fate awaited his latter-day successors on the Treasury Bench at Westminster.) 'Londoners', it was said at the time of the 'Customs' of 1192, 'shall have no king but their mayor.' It was an idea still current, it seems, in 1607, when the Venetian Ambassador wrote home with the following report: 'The city', he noted, 'is especially rich in the privileges enjoyed by its inhabitants, the merchant burgesses and craftsmen, from among whom twenty-five are elected, called Aldermen, who govern the City absolutely, almost as though it were an independent Republic, and neither the King nor his Ministers can interfere in any way'.[54] The power of these immunities was vividly demonstrated in 1642, when the 'Five Members' took refuge from Charles I in the City, and its oppositional potential was again realised at the start of the Civil War, when it was the march of the London apprentices who turned back the royal armies at Turnham Green. This oppositional role was crucial in the deposition of James II; it was still important in the eighteenth century, when the Common Council of the City – with William Beckford in the lead – were strong supporters of the Wilkes agitation;[55] and it played (for the last time) an important role in the Reform Bill crisis of 1831–2, when the threat of a run on the banks helped to paralyse Tory opposition.

Londoners also enjoyed – and arguably have always enjoyed – a greater degree of personal freedom than people in other areas. In the Middle Ages, London was a sanctuary for debtors, a haven for runaway serfs. In the period of the Tudor legislation against rogues and vagabonds, it was a great refuge for 'masterless men'. Runaway apprentices made their way there in the eighteenth century. So did wave after wave of refugees – among them, in the 1770s, the slaves freed under Lord Mansfield's judgement, and the first influx of Jews escaping the pogroms in Eastern Europe. The London trades in early modern times were self-governing. Even those who followed such plebeian callings as that of waterman enjoyed the status of freemen of the city. In the case of the printers' chapel, of which there is a dramatic account in Moxon's *Mechanick Exercises*[56] (1683) some of these practices lived on – or were recreated – long after the disappearance of the guilds. Workers' combinations and trade unions flourished in London a century and more before they were recognised in many other parts of the country: in Spitalfields, among the silk weavers, they were so strong that under the Act of 1773 the power of fixing wages was taken out of the hands of the employers and placed in those of the magistrates. In the nineteenth century, despite the vast increase in manufacturing activity, London escaped the severest disciplines of the industrial revolution. The aristocracy of labour – hatters, printers, coopers, journeymen tailors, shipwrights – worked in self-regulating collectivities (among the journeymen hatters, it was *illegal* for a man to see his employer alone);[57] more depressed workers like the East End cabinetmakers or the needlewomen typically worked in semi-domestic workshops or the home, subject to a high degree of self-exploitation, but free of the steam whistle of the factory or the timekeeper's iron bell.

There was clearly no unified national consciousness in the Middle Ages, when rich and poor spoke different languages and territorial allegiances were to a local lord. Chaucer's 'parfit gentil knyght', who is often taken as the prototype of the English gentleman, seems not to have had any sense of being English at all. He had fought the 'hethen in Turkye' and at Alexandria 'when it was wronne', but the loyalties he proclaims are to his liege lord and to 'cristendom'. Glimmerings of a more national consciousness have been suggested for Malory's *Morte d'Arthur*, written at the time of the Wars of the Roses, though the author himself was a lifelong baronial *frondeur*. There is a dramatic increase in national self-consciousness in the sixteenth century, with the rise of the nation state and especially (it may be) with the triumph of English as the language of literary expression in the century's last decades.

Even so, the seventeenth-century Civil War suggests that English people were still able to separate love of country from loyalty to government, while the theory of the Norman Yoke (splendidly rescued from oblivion by Christopher Hill) offered both a class interpretation of English history and an alternative version of what it was to be English: landlords were portrayed as the descendants of the Norman barons, the common people of the 'free-born' Anglo-Saxons. In Victorian racism this theory was given a sinister twist, aligned with the Aryan myth, and made into an argument for white and imperial supremacy – excellently documented in L. P. Curtis's *Anglo-Saxons and Celts*.

In the eighteenth century, when the British appeared for the first time as a military people, and the government fought a whole series of national wars, the scene seems more familiar. Yet Marlborough's Wars – to take the example of Sir Winston Churchill's most illustrious ancestor – were regarded as 'Whig wars' and bitterly opposed by many Tories. The early Hanoverians faced an avowedly disloyal Jacobite opposition. In London there was a popular Jacobite following which served as a focal point for other discontents. In Oxford University, that citadel of High Toryism, the toast of 'the King across the Water' was exuberantly drunk.

(According to T. E. Kebbel's memoirs there was still a strain of secret Jacobitism in the country Toryism of his 1830s childhood.)

On the other side of the religious and cultural divide, nonconformists – stigmatised by all kinds of civil disabilities – seem to have had a wholesome capacity for siding with the 'country's' (i.e. the government's) enemies. Many openly sympathised with the colonists in the period of the American Revolution, and they also figure frequently in the eary 1790s among the friends of revolutionary France. The fear of invasion in 1798, as at many other times in history, seems to have produced a powerful upsurge of national unity and self-consciousness, but it is by no means apparent at other times during the Napoleonic wars. 'Remember the Bastille' was a slogan chalked up during a London food riot of 1801. The wars, after all, were also the period of the Luddite risings in Nottinghamshire and the West Riding. To see the Home Office papers of the period of agitation about the Orders in Council (1811) and the upsurge of popular radicalism at the time is to imagine that England, far from being united, was on the brink of insurrection.

Religion, of course, is a far more ancient form of belonging in this country than any notion of national allegiance. As a primary definition of self it was still very much alive in late Victorian Lancashire – in the slums of Ancoats, Manchester, for example where, as census enumerators complained in 1871, the Irish poor were apt to return their nationality as 'Catholic'; or in the nonconformist suburbs, where the chapel offered itself as an all-embracing cultural universe: as Haslam Mills writes in his memoir of Ashton-on-the-Hill: 'Aunt Margaret, challenged by a sentry, would have said not "English", certainly not "British" but "Methodist".'[58]

It is a matter of infinite consequence that the Reformation, the founding moment (according to Professor Elton) in the creation of the British state, also inaugurated a historic division of the nation along confessional lines. The recusants, to follow a fascinating line of inquiry opened up by John Bossy in *The English Catholic Community* (1979), were the first English dissenters, a persecuted minority excluded from the national church and drawing strength from their separation and apartness.[59] An even more important moment was in the 1660s and 1670s, when the civil war sects began to take shape as the alternative churches of English nonconformity – denominations which, in the case of the Congregationalists and the Baptists, were to gain a mass following in the nineteenth century. Schism and separation, albeit unwillingly adopted, were principles of growth for the Wesleyan Methodists, who colonised the unchurched parts of the country, and for the breakaway and independent churches of the nineteenth century who formed 'the dissidence of dissent'. It was hardly less apparent in the Church of England itself, with the spread, on the one hand, of Evangelicalism, and on the other the rise of Ritualism. Dissent provided a fundamental idiom of political as well as religious life, one in which the relations of the individual and society (or the citizen and the state) were constructed in a conflictual sense. It was never more salient than in the late nineteenth century, when the religious divide was the basis of constituency politics.[60]

For a further source of minority identities, reference could finally be made to a social system in which – even in the high capitalism of nineteenth-century Britain – an aristocratic principle of exclusion operated at every level of the social hierarchy. The comfortable classes, for some two centuries of commercial development, defined themselves against each other rather than, or as well as, in opposition to the masses, making a fetish of gentility and building a whole lifestyle out of their imaginary distance from 'trade'. Tradesmen and clerks – as *The Diary of a Nobody* reminds us – were no less insistent upon being 'quality'. Lower down the scale one finds aristocracies of dealers among the London costermongers and 'gentlemen dockers' among the stevedores of the East and West India Docks. Here is how *Black Beauty* (1877) – and one must suppose generations of English schoolgirls – learnt to become one of the chosen few:

> There were six young colts in the meadow besides me; they were older than I was; some were nearly as large as grown-up horses. I used to run with them, and had great fun; we used to gallop all together round and round the field, as hard as we could go. Sometimes we had rather rough play, for they would frequently bite and kick as well as gallop. One day, when there was a good deal of kicking, my mother whinnied to me to come to her, and then she said: 'I wish you to pay attention to what I am going to say to you. The colts who live here are very good colts, but they are carthorse colts, and, of course, they have not learned manners. You have been well bred and well born; your father was a great name in these parts, and your grandfather won the cup two years at the Newmarket races; your grandmother was the sweetest temper of any horse I ever knew . . . I hope you will grow up gentle and good, and never learn bad ways.'[61]

Victorian Britain, though notionally an open society, was imbued by a spirit of caste, with rigid demarcations between in and out groups, and a strict order of precedence between them.

Superiors lorded it over inferiors at every status level. 'From the very summit of society to its nethermost base', wrote the nonconformist Edward Miall in 1850, 'every man feels entitled to exact for himself, or bound to pay to others, the deference appropriate to the class to which he belongs.' And again: 'The governing circle which the precision of law has rendered definite, repeats itelf, in wider and less distinct circles, down to the very bottom of society . . . each claims for itself somewhat which it regards as incommunicable to the grades beneath it.'[62]

Local status systems reproduced the grosser divisions of the wider society, while adding discriminations and exclusions of their own. At Oxford the historic division between 'town' and 'gown' was still absolute (as late as 1829, the town burghers were still having to do penance for the souls of the undergraduates murdered on St Scholastica's day), while in county society it was not considered 'etiquette' to mix with the university.[63] In the rural suburb of Hornsey, where Mrs David Greig, the butcher's wife, went to live in 1879, there were three grades of society: grade one consisted of 'the rector, Lord of the Manor, churchwardens, doctors and their ladies'; then came grade two: 'the curate, wealthy businessmen, and their ladies'; finally, there were the nonconformists, among them her own family, 'the ministers, deacons and their ladies'.[64] In the Yorkshire village of Laxton, according to one who grew up there as a clergyman's son in the 1890s, the order of precedence was demonstrated in the church. The first to approach the communion rails were always 'the squires, their ladies and their children', followed by the curate's family, the land agents and the leading farmers, followed in turn by craftsmen and labourers:

> Industry had no accepted place. The richest local family were the Andertons, who owned lime kilns and a fertiliser factory near Howden. They were neither invited to the houses of the others, nor gave any invitations; they were 'in trade'. The barrier was maintained as firmly from the one side as the other.[65]

Nineteenth-century labour, too, was divided on lines of caste. Job preserves were rampant in every department of industrial life; restrictive practices were the workers' first line of defence against capital. Between the artisan and the labourer there was a gulf quite as great as any between the classes, and the divisions between men and women (or men and boys, the first being very often the employers of the second) were even more extreme. In boilermaking, platers and their helpers, though they worked alongside each other, were different species being; the first, according to one of them, superior craftsmen, the second 'inferior beings from some remote planet'.[66] The trade unions (a minority phenomenon) were organised as closed fraternities, jealously guarding their privileges against outsiders. As the motto of the journeymen brushmakers had it:

> In love and unity we preserve our trade
> And keep out those who would our rights invade[67]

Militant partcularism was nowhere more apparent than in that sump of unskilled labour, the docks, with a hard and fast division between the 'permanent' men and the casuals – the first in regular employment, the second subject to the vicissitudes of the 'call' – and elaborate demarcations between the different classes of work. Here is how a trade union organiser describes the situation in the Liverpool docks (he is writing of the 1890s):

> Not the least of our manifold difficulties arose from the prevalence of what I can only describe as the caste system throughout the dockers' fraternity, which led to the creation of almost innumerable small clubs and societies all hostile to each other. Some ... were sick and funeral clubs. ... Quite frequently religious and political differences kept these bodies apart, and, indeed, alive. Thus the coal heavers had one society at the north end, another at the south. The leader of one was a North of Ireland Orangeman, the leader of the other an equally perfervid Irish Home Rule Catholic. The only point on which they were united was a mutual objection to mere cargo hands handling coal. Salt heavers took up the same attitudes as to the exclusiveness of their job; if you weren't one of them you couldn't touch bulk salt.[68]

Twentieth-century social change has undermined these antique divisions, narrowing differentials between skilled and unskilled, removing domestic service as a major component of privileged lifestyles, and eliminating church and chapel as loci of political and cultural division. But it has generated new forms of particularism. The rise of the Home Counties (a phenomenon which may be dated back to the 1870s), the gentrification of the southern countryside, and the spread of dormitory towns and suburbs produced, in the 1920s and 1930s, a greater degree of residential segregation than at any earlier time in national history. Inter-war Britain was honeycombed with make-believe aristocracies, each occupying (according to its own estimate) a pinnacle of social esteem. A spirit of coterie was the organising principle in the arts, pitting 'aesthetes' against 'hearties' in the universities, modernists against traditionalists in poetry and painting, minority against mass culture.[69] In the sunken middle class, families (like John Osborne's) competed with one another as to who had fallen furthest.[70] The rising middle class made a religion of their quiet. The working class developed as a separate estate, with their own political party (Labour), their own forms of shopping (the Co-ops, whose membership doubled between the wars), and to an increasing degree their own forms of holidaymaking and entertainment. In the General Strike of 1926 they were accused of holding the country to ransom. 'The regimentation to which they have submitted in order to increase their power of action has developed into a veritable tyranny', wrote Dean Inge in the immediate aftermath of the strike ' . . . It is not surprising that foreign observers . . . suspect that the working people of the towns no longer have what was called the British character.'[71]

British society has not lost its capacity to create minorities, and the autobiographies which introduce and conclude this volume show their potency in the very recent past. For each of the writers growing up in the 1950s, England, the 'real England', was somewhere else. For Miranda Chaytor, a child of the Catholic aristocracy, living in a ruinous Durham castle, it was the servants in the kitchen, listening to *Music While You Work*. For Dave Douglass, a miner's son, living a few miles away at Wardley and leading a juvenile band of terrorists through the village, it was the teachers and their pets. For Frank Cottrell Boyce, attempting to compete for 'I-Spy' in the urban wilderness, it was the ivied church and village green where children might hope to spot cormorants. John Field was even more beleaguered in the working-class enclave of Folkestone, where the wealthy had colonised the spacious walks, and foreigners had a monopoly of glamour. Finally, Hanif Kureishi evokes the two worlds of the second-generation ethnic minorities.

There is no reason to suppose that British society in the future will be any more homogenous than it was in the past. The old class blocks may be dissolving – from a nineteenth-century vantage point they look a good deal less ancient than contemporary mythologies suggest – but this seems likely to produce more differentiation rather than less. The last twenty-five years has seen a remarkable 'coming out' of previously stigmatised groups, like the disabled; a proliferation of sexual sub-cultures, such as those now under hysterical attack; and the building of a whole way of life out of alternative lifestyles or even popular music. Style aristocracies hold the passes between capitalism and the consumer; segmentation of the market encourages the growth of minority tastes. The division between public and private sector employment has emerged as a major axis of differentiation in politics and trade unionism, scything the traditional constituencies of Labour and Conservative in two. The waning of the authority of the Church of England has put the Protestant constitution into question. The emergence of regional nationalism – most spectacularly in Northern Ireland – has exposed the fragility of the United Kingdom and the uncertainty of its territorial boundaries. The diminution of class fear allows for a more competitive political system, in which interests are narrowly and more sectionally defined. 'Housing classes' (sociologists have argued) determine the pattern of immigrant settlement and the struggle for urban space, they are not less important in the English village, where holiday homes and weekend cottages drive natives to the margins. British society seems to have lost its assimilative power. The new and post-war immigrants show less desire than their predecessors to integrate. (At the last count, Britain has 106 ethnic newspapers – 33 more than last year.[72] There are now more than 200 independent black churches in this country, many of them post-immigration foundations.) It is indeed an open question whether such a thing as the British nation exists. The rich grow increasingly cosmopolitan in their operations; the poor are localised in social security ghettos. It will take more than a 'core curriculum' to restore even the fiction of a people at one with itself.

It is extremely unfortunate that neither the Labour Party nor the Conservative Party has a language of minority rights. Both subscribe to the idea of the people as a unified whole. Conservatism, even in its Thatcherite version, is always a theory – or a rhetoric – of one nation, and the scorn visited by the Prime Minister on the 'inalienable rights' of homosexuals and the readiness to discover 'enemies within' may remind us that fear of the foreigner and hatred of dissent have always been Tory passions. Labour is no less committed to collectivism. Its ideology of fair shares, and predilection for national planning leaves no imaginative space for minorities: at best they are an embarrassment, at worst those vested interests which block the true path of reform.

This volume is intended to encourage a more molecular view of the nation, and a more pluralist politics, one which starts from a recognition of diversity – diversity of need, diversity of condition, diversity, not least, of morals – and builds upon it. It suggests that the national 'we' is always in some way a fiction and that 'us' and 'them' distinctions are a normal component of national life. Such a view is not necessarily inimical to the craving for oneness. As the Conservative philosopher Edmund Burke put it: it is by our

Introduction: The 'Little Platoons' xxxv

attachment to the 'little platoons' that we become members of the great society.

Notes

1 *Guardian*, 10 March 1988; the suspension was rescinded after vigorous protest from fellow teachers.
2 W. H. Hudson, *A Shepherd's Life*, London, 1910, p. 269.
3 Flora Thompson, *Lark Rise to Candleford*, World's Classics edn, Oxford 1971, p. 24.
4 Norbert Elias and J. L. Scotson's *The Established and the Outsiders* (London, 1965), is an interesting account of the division between an old and a newly settled working-class community in recent times.
5 Christopher Hill, 'Puritans and "the Dark Corners of the Land" ', *Transactions of the Royal Historical Society*, 5th Ser., XIII, pp. 77–102.
6 Reference temporarily mislaid.
7 Alan Everitt, 'Farm labourers' in Joan Thirsk (ed.) *The Cambridge Agrarian History*, Cambridge, 1967, IV, p. 463; *The Pattern of Rural Dissent: the Nineteenth Century*, Leicester 1972.
8 H. M. Livens, *Nomansland: a Village History*, Salisbury, 1910. For some other nineteenth-century examples see Florence A. G. Davidson, *The History of Tadley*, Basingstoke, 1913; S. J. Wolff, *Ashdown Forest* (privately printed 1935; P. P. 1868–9 (4202) XIII, Appendix Part II, p. 240 and generally; Raphael Samuel, 'Village labour' in R. Samuel (ed.) *Village Life and Labour*, London, 1975, pp. 7–10.
9 John Rule, 'Wrecking and coastal plunder' in Douglas Hay et al. (eds) *Albion's Fatal Tree*, London 1975.
10 For an example see Raphael Samuel, 'Quarry roughs' in *Village Life and Labour*, pp. 141–264; on the subject generally, see Dennis R. Mills, *Lord and Peasant in 19th Century Britain*, London 1980. The reports of the 1843 and 1868–9 Royal Commissions on Women and Children in Agriculture are a mine of information on such villages.
11 Keith Wrightson and David Levine, *Poverty and Piety in an English Village; Tarling 1500–1800*, New York, 1979.
12 Keith Snell, *Annals of the Labouring Poor: Social Change and Agrarian England*, Cambridge, 1985.
13 For some contemporary accounts of the gipsies there, Henry Woodcock, *The Gipsies*, London, 1865, pp. 144–7; V. Morwood, *Our Gipsies in City, Tent and Van*, London 1885, pp. 338–40; George Sims, *Off the Track in London*, London 1911, pp. 36–7; *Illustrated London News*, lxxv (1879) p. 503. For a recent study, see Patricia Malcolmson, 'Getting a Living in the slums of Victorian Kensington', *London Journal*, I, 1, 1975. For West Ham, see Edward G. Howarth and Mona Wilson, *West Ham*, London, 1907.
14 Rawlinson, *Report to the General Board of Health*, Newton Heath, London, 1855.
15 Stan Hugill, *Sailortown*, London, 1967.
16 There is a sanitary report on the district among those submitted to the

General Board of Health in the wake of the cholera of 1849, as well as various pamphlets by the Rev. Henry Mole. Fordingbridge is the 'Mixen Lane' of *The Mayor of Casterbridge*.

17 H. J. Dyos and D. A. Reeder, 'Slums and suburbs' in H. J. Dyos and Michael Wolff (eds) *The Victorian City*, London, 1973, I, 359–88.
18 For an autobiographical account from south-west Bethnal Green, see George Acorn, *One of the Multitude*, London, 1911.
19 Neville Kirk, *The Growth of Working-Class Reformism in mid-Victorian England*, London, 1985; R. L. Greenall, 'Poplar Conservatism in Salford, 1868–1886', *Northern History* IX, 1974, pp. 123–38.
20 J. B. Priestley, *English Journey*, London, 1934, pp. 235–6. The passage is worth considering as the nether side of Priestley's 'Little Englandism' quoted in the editorial introduction to the first volume of *Patriotism*.
21 *Transactions of the National Association for the Promotion of Social Science*, London, 1876, pp. 302–3. The 'permanent segregation of habitual criminals, paupers, drunkards, maniacs and tramps' (to take the example of a text quoted in *Efficiency and Empire*, p. 120) was a leitmotif of 'enlightened' social reform over the whole period 1870–1914.
22 D. Caradog Jones, 'The social problem group', Toronto 1945 and see D. Caradog Jones, (ed.) *The Social Survey of Merseyside*, 3 vols, Liverpool 1934.
23 PP. 1934, Cmd 4485, Dept. Committee on Sterilisation. The Committee reprinted without comment an early Nazi decree on the compulsory sterilisation of the unfit – a chilling reminder of the proximity of notions of 'race hygiene' among social reformers in Britain to those which in Germany led to racial extermination.
24 Jeffrey Richards, 'The creed behind crime', *Daily Telegraph*, 16 April 1988.
25 Letter in the *Daily Telegraph*, 12 April 1988.
26 There is a quite excellent account of the turn-about in public attitudes towards welfare and the way this was orchestrated in the press, in Peter Golding and Sue Middleton's *Images of Welfare: Press and Public Attitudes to Poverty*, Oxford, 1982.
27 For a classic account see Stan Cohen, *Folk Devils and Moral Panics*, London, 1972.
28 Paul Johnson, 'The message in the bottle', *Daily Telegraph*, 9 April 1988.
29 Michael MacDonagh, *In London During the Great War*, London, 1935. This is a valuable document, reprinting the diary entries of one who was assistant editor of *The Times*. For an account of the conscientious objectors see John Rae, *Conscience and Politics*, Oxford 1970; and David Boulton *Objection Overruled*, London 1967. For the 'crucifixions' – COs who were tied to the stake in the no-mans' land at the front – see E. Sylvia Pankhurst, *The Home Front*, London, 1978, ed. pp. 310–11, 332–3. Baroness Orczy, author of *the Scarlet Pimpernel*, was the originator of the Active Service League by which women pledged never to be seen in public with any man who had refused to volunteer, see E. S. Turner, *Dear Old Blighty*, London, 1980, p. 68.

30 For sentencing policy see A. D. Harvey, 'Prosecutions for sodomy in England at the beginning of the nineteenth century', *Historical Journal*, 21, 1978.
31 Alexander Somerville, *Autobiography of a Working Man*, London, 1854, pp. 112–14
32 Ursula Henriques, 'Bastardy and the New Poor Law', *Past and Present*, 37, 1967. It is a matter of wonder that Peter Laslett's *Family Life and Illicit Love in Earlier Generations* (Cambridge 1977) has not so much as a word, so far as I can see, about the opprobrium attaching to illegitimacy. In eighteenth-century Banff women were scourged through the streets for immorality by the common hangman and frequently banished from the town: William Cyramond, *Illegitimacy in Banffshire*, Banff, 1888, p. 10 (a little book quite out of its time, full of valuable statistics and level-headed discussion). An Act of 1810 enabled justices to commit 'a lewd woman who shall have a bastard and which may be chargeable to the parish to the House of Correction for a period ranging btween six weeks and one year.' It replaced a harsher Act of James I, Henriques, *op. cit.*, p. 104.
33 Vieda Skultan, *English Madness, Ideas of Insanity, 1580–1890*, London, 1979; Elaine Showalter, *The Female Malady; Women, Madness and English Culture, 1830–1980*, London, 1987, for the use of madhouses to dispose of unwanted women.
34 Ian Gibson, *The English Vice; Beating, Sex and Shame in Victorian England and After*, London, 1978, p. 66 (quoting a French report on English education 1867). Gibson points out that 'spare the rod and spoil the child', universally attributed by Victorians to Solomon, in fact comes from Samuel Butler's satirical poem of 1664, *Hudibras, ibid*, p. 49.
35 *The Life of Charles Humphreys, Told by Himself*, London, n.d. (1900?), p. 251. Humphreys was a well known character in the London second hand book trade, wih a shop near Paternoster Row. He was an open-air preacher on Peckham Rye. Whipping, Lawrence Stone tells us (*The Family, Sex and Marriage in England 1500–1800*, Penguin 1977 edn. p. 120) was the normal method of disciplining children at home in the sixteenth and seventeenth centuries.
36 Edmund Gosse, *Father and Son*, London 1911 ed., pp. 93–4, Cf. Geoffrey Best, 'Popular Protestantism in Victorian Britain' in Robert Robson (ed.) *Ideas and Institutions of Victorian Britain*, London, 1967; E. R. Norman, *Anti-Catholicism in Victorian England*, London 1968.
37 Ibid.
38 George Orwell, 'War-time Diary, 1940' in *Collected Essays* . . . Penguin 1977, II, p. 428. See F. Laffite, *The Internment of Aliens*, London, 1940, for a protest against the xenophobia of the time, and Bernard Wasserstein, *Britain and the Jews of Europe 1939–45*, Oxford, 1979, for government opposition to the admission of jewish refugees. MI5, the British secret service, advised the Cabinet in 1938 that the refugee problem had been deliberately created by the Nazi government 'anxious to

inundate this country with Jews, with a view to creating a Jewish problem in the United Kingdom': Wasserstein, op. cit., p. 11.
39 *The Times*, 6 Feb 1919, p. 13f: 6 September 1919, p. 7c. For the upsurge of nativism generally – hardly less virulent than the contemporaneous movement in the United States, though happily, less lasting in its effects – see David [Caesarini], 'Anti-Alienism in England after the First World War', *Immigrants and Minorities* VI/I; Neil Evans, 'Regulating the Reserve Army . . . Cardiff 1919–1945', IV/2; Jacqueline Jenkinson, 'The Glasgow Race Disturbances of 1919', ibid., IV/2; Peter Fryer, *Staying Power*, London, 1984, pp. 299–313, Ron Ramdin, *The Making of the Black Working Class in Britain*, London, 1987, pp. 68–85; Neil Evans, 'The South Wales Race Riots in 1910', *Llafur*, 11/1, 1980.
40 Basil Thomson, *Queer People*, London, 1922.
41 *Daily Express*, 1 October 1920.
42 *Evening News*, 5 October 1920. The issue of 'half-castes', like that of the 'Yellow peril', exercised a peculiar fascination on the 1920s British imagination, as a focus for existential anxiety. Social workers depicted them as a whole underclass of degenerates. On this, see Paul B. Rich 'Philanthropic racism in Britain: the Liverpool University settlement . . . and the issue of the 'half-caste' children. . . .', *Immigrants and Minorities*, III/I March, 1984; and the wretched publications of the University Settlement itself, notably M. E. Fletcher, *Report of an Investigation into the Colour Problem in Liverpool*, Liverpool, 1930. See Cedric Dover, *Half Caste*, London, 1937, for a riposte by a black progressive.
43 Peter Wildblood, *Against the Law*, Penguin 1955; cf. Kenneth Plummer, *The Making of the Modern Homosexual*, London, 1981; *Sexual Stigma, an Interactionist Account*, London, 1975. On AIDS, see Simon Watney, *Policing Desire*, London, 1988; Denis Altman, *AIDS and the new puritanism*, London, 1986.
44 *Daily Telegraph*, 18 April 1988.
45 *Dublin Review*, 1856.
46 Michael Hechter, *Internal Colonialism: the Celtic Fringe in British National Development, 1536–1966*, London, 1975.
47 For a splendid account of militant particularism in the Lancashire cotton trade, see H. A. Turner, *Trade Union Growth, Structure and Policy*, London, 1955.
48 J. R. Leitchfield, *Our Coal and Coal Pits*, London, 1853, p. 197. the coalfields were a great magnet for migratory labour; what is interesting, even if one does not accept such impressionist claims as Leitchfield's, is the way their settlements acquired a reputation for closeness in a very short space of time.
49 *The Autobiography of Thomas Burt*, London, 1900, pp. 165–6. I am grateful to Brian Harrison for this reference.
50 Leonore Davidoff, *The Best Circles: Society, Etiquette and the Season*, London, 1973.
51 For the Clubmen, see Brian Manning, *The English People and the English Revolution*, Peregrine edn, 1978.

52 Sidney and Beatrice Webb, *The Manor and the Borough*, London, 1908, p. 571.
53 For a general account, see Gwyn Williams, *Medieval London: From Commune to Capital*, London, 1963. See also Ruth Bird, *The Turbulent London of Richard II*, London, 1949.
54 *Calendar of State Papers, Venetian*, p. 503.
55 Cf. *Acts of the Common Council of the City of London*, which shows it putting forward oppositional resolutions throughout the period of the American War of Independence.
56 Reprinted in A. E. Musson, *the Typographical Association*, Oxford, 1954, p. 10.
57 London School of Economics, Booth MSS, 'B' series, 'Hatters'; and for an attractive autobiographical account, Frederick Willis, *A Book of London Yesterdays*, London, 1960, pp. 104–112.
58 William Haslam Mills, *Grey Pastures*, London, 1924.
59 John Bossy, *The English Catholic Community*, London, 1979, pp. 391–401.
60 In a vast literature, Paul T. Phillips, *The Sectarian Spirit: Sectarianism, Society, and Politics in Victorian Cotton Towns*, Toronto 1982 deserves to be better known; Valentine Cunningham, *Everywhere spoken Against: Dissent in the Victorian Novel*, Oxford, 1975 is an interesting attempt to relate dissent to national literature.
61 Anna Sewell, *Black Beauty*, Puffin edn., pp. 19–20.
62 Edward Miall, *The British Church in Relation to the British People*, London, 1850, p. 123.
63 Davidoff, op. cit., p. 72
64 Mrs David Greig, *My Life and Times* (privately printed, no date) p. 33.
65 Michael Young, *The Elmhirsts of Dartington*, London, 1982, p. 15.
66 Henry Pollitt, *Serving My Time*, London, 1940, p. 57.
67 W. Kiddier, *The Old Trade Unions*, London, 1923.
68 Sir James Sexton, *Agitator*, London, 1936, pp. 109–110.
69 I am summarising here my argument in a series of articles on 'The middle class between the wars' which appeared in *New Socialist* in 1985.
70 John Osborne, *A Better Class of Person*, Penguin edn.
71 Dean Inge, *England*, London, 1926, p. 272.
72 *The Economist*, 13 August 1988, p. 28.

Childhood

1
The view from Folkestone

JOHN FIELD

Britain does not have frontier towns, but it does have the Channel ports. Dover and Folkestone in particular are both the most cosmopolitan and the most English of towns; always full of people on the move, and with a native population whose work consists often of face-to-face services to outsiders. And the outsiders – so essential to the livelihood of practically every inhabitant – are deeply and utterly resented.

I was born and brought up in Folkestone, Dover's smaller, less significant and more conservative (in every way) neighbour. Folkestone was originally little more than a fishing town, and you can still see the trawlers coming into harbour with their stock of tomorrow's chip-shop dogfish – or 'huss', as it is known locally. There are eel and whelk stalls along the seafront in summer time, but fishing is now little more than a residual trade, carried out by families who have sailed out of the harbour for generations.

Folkestone was dragged into the nineteenth century by Lord Radnor, local landowner and bigwig, who developed a rather smart and genteel tourist centre to the west of the old port. They weren't called tourists, of course: they were always 'visitors' in those days. They stayed in the large hotels up on the Leas – a cliff some 2 or 3 miles long, with a grassed walkway and a bandstand separating the large houses and hotels from the cliff edge. Apparently Lord Radnor used to employ his own policemen to keep the local children and other unwashed characters away from the Leas, lest they might disturb the promenaders. Even now, when the grandest hotel – the Metropole – is an arts centre and adult education campus, the Leas still has that exclusive quality that made it such a fit setting for Henry James.

When I grew up in the town, it was still partly stuck in the nineteenth century. We used to hang out in a cafe in the old High

Street where the working men's club was; a cobbled street which specialised in souvenirs, knickknacks, curiosities, and pubs. My local, apart from the club, was the Globe – just up an alley from the High Street, a Fremlins pub, that sold rubbery beefburgers and put seats outside in the car park during the summer. Fifty yards away was the British Lion, home of the local gilded youth, and said to be the town's oldest building.

Territoriality was important, even during the 1960s, to adolescents like myself. The High Street was very much our patch. The working men's club had been taken over by dope-smoking youngsters who had an eyehole on the door to check enquirers before they came in; any hint of a blue uniform, and toilets flushed like the Niagara Falls. The cafe was properly called the Acropolis, but we called it Archie's, after the owner's son. Archie's dad was Greek, and the two of them argued constantly in Greek; the only word any of us could understand was 'bloody', but that didn't stop the two of them being accepted entirely as good local citizens. They argued mostly about politics; Archie was certainly active in Vietnam Solidarity, and we believed he was in the International Marxist Group.

Across the road was the Earl Grey. Still very much a part of the street culture of the 1960s adolescents, the Earl Grey attracted those who were slightly less committed to smoking dope than the club's regulars. Personally I wasn't into dope at all, so although I used to hang around the High Street and used to go into Archie's more or less daily, the Earl Grey's chief attraction was the bar billiards table. Otherwise my own circle used the Globe, unless we were hunting for women. Then we used to go up the disco above the Odeon cinema (where once a policeman was defenestrated by a drink-mad soldier on his way to Northern Ireland) or even the British Lion, where Swedes and Germans tended to go.

Looking back, our territory was amazingly restricted. We scarcely used to enter pubs in the areas where we lived: either up the east end, a mixture of council estates and run-down private housing; or down at Cheriton, to the west of town, where the industrial area was, dominated by the Dormobile factory. I only used to go to Cheriton when selling *Socialist Worker*, usually so early in the morning that only the transport cafes were open.

Folkestone was a curiously divided town, one where you were more likely to hear French spoken in the street than a Scottish accent. Everyone from north of Maidstone was a Cockney, anyone from north of London a Midlander. Either way, they didn't belong. They were tourists.

I worked for two years on the buses, and I detested tourists. As a good socialist, I ought to have taken a properly internationalist view of these people, people who worked hard for eleven months so that they could enjoy a fortnight by the sea. But nobody took that view. Tourists were bums, who complained about bus fares, never had the right change, who clambered aboard red-faced and sweating with vast piles of beach umbrellas, balls, deckchairs, picnic baskets and kids. They were rude to the conductors, treated you like a servant (which, according to the company rule book, was actually what you were). Above all, tourists had more money than you, and they were enjoying themselves while you worked.

So you took your quiet and petty revenge. Older conductors would come into the staff cafe (it was not a canteen – Lord Radnor had placed some restriction on the land lease, forbidding the sale of cooked foods), bragging about the day's short-change tricks. Usually the sums involved were quite small, but sometimes it would be a matter of a pound or so – large enough to cast a brief silence over the card game at the corner table. Others would exult over a misdirection, or a rumour that some Midlanders had been beaten up for calling fishermen 'fairies'. As the fishermen wore their hair long, had earrings (so St Peter would retrieve their souls when they drowned), and even in one or two cases had female nicknames, it would be surprising if one or two unsuspecting Midlanders had not ended up in the harbour.

Midlanders, then, were our equivalent of the Irish; dull, slow, invariably fat and middle-aged, and created by God to come and annoy us and be made fools of. Londoners, on the other hand – that is anyone from the Medway to Watford – were wide boys. We all believed that the bus company had a policy of never taking on Cockneys, first because they were all strong union men, and second because they fiddled. The words 'London Transport' were enough to put any application form straight into the manager's waste bin. As it happened, we did have at least one ex-LT driver on our buses, but this didn't stop anyone believing in the ban. An older conductor showed me all the ways there were of palming money, and warned me to watch out especially for the Cockneys: 'They'd do you as soon as look at you, chav.'

Scots were simply barbarians. The only Scots we ever saw were soldiers, and stories abounded of them beating up defenceless conductors on the late-night services. One rumour went round when the King's Own Scottish Borderers were in town:

> The last time they came, they all got on the last bus to Shorncliffe and wouldn't pay their fares. Then this sergeant got on. 'What's up, laddie', he says. He went round and

collected all the money, and gave it to the conductor. Then when he sees the conductor running off tickets he picks him up and holds him out the door. 'If I see you touch that handle again, I'll drop you.'

The KOSBs were rough. That was true, not just rumour. For some reason, one daft army bureaucrat stationed them in town at the same time as the Royal Irish Rangers, and there were two weeks of mayhem. None of us dared go out of doors at night – or so we all said afterwards.

But there were outsiders in our midst, living in the town, some of them even born there. These were the old folk who came to the town to retire, relax and die. Towards these we showed no mercy. They evoked complete and utter resistance, a subterranean class war against the 'old tits', 'old twats', 'them old bastards', living in the west end along the cliff top.

I suppose most of these people in fact had little money. They were probably living on savings and a pension, and were less well off than we were with our overtime and weekend work – and fiddles. Still, they were locked in an older age when bus conductors called everyone 'sir' or 'madam' and buses ran on time, and they treated us accordingly. And, as they lived in the smart end of town, and as they all seemed to do nothing but sit in coffee lounges or bars all day, we thought them privileged. And they never ever sounded like local people.

Deliberate and cruel attempts were made to shock these members of the bourgeoisie. One old driver – Wacker – used to work to rule as soon as he got on the route between town centre and the west end. He would drive no faster than the law allowed, would stop whenever the law required, and do anything to run late. You were supposed to ring the bell once to stop, twice to pass any bus stop; so it was the conductor's job to ring the bell, a task we guarded proudly from interference by 'the public'. These old people never took any notice of what we told them, and carried on dinging as soon as we got near their stop regardless. Wacker, himself near retirement age, took huge delight in misunderstanding the clanging of the bell, and drove on to the next stop. Sometimes he'd go half a mile without stopping, the clanging becoming more furious, until one of the passengers started shouting at him.

'Did you see how red that old sod got?' Wacker would ask at the end of the route. He was a cussed old sod himself, and most of the conductors hated working with him; I managed to get on with him, partly because I used to listen to his stories about Folkestone during the War.

Everybody had their fund of stories about the 'old tits'. One driver had managed to shut the door on a dog, and driven a quarter of a mile with the dog being dragged along on its lead. These were all lapdogs – 'fanny lickers' we used to call them.

There were real foreigners as well, French, Germans, Swedes (this included Danes and Norwegians), Belgians and Dutch, but we never really took much notice of them. Hatred of the French is commonplace in Folkestone; my mother still prides herself in being able to barge young French tourists off the pavement, a kind of pre-emptive strike, as it is widely believed that if you don't shove the French, they will shove you. But as socialists, if otherwise I and my mates shared all the prejudices of the townspeople, we thought well of the French.

We thought particularly highly of the French after May 1968. There were some French Maoists living in the town at the time, and one of them – Gilles – would read translations from their newspaper every day during the May events. Leaflets and newspapers were distributed in the High Street, and we struggled through the language barrier to try and make sense of it all. Undoubtedly, this was it. It wasn't, but the French influence was real enough on the young, just passing on from a sort of fellow-travelling with the hippies.

Folkestone briefly became a byword for radicalism. We had our own riots after the May events, when the local traders and town council decided to 'clean up the High Street'. A couple of police came along, moving people away from the territories where they had habitually stood in the High Street for a couple of years. This was public space – it was *our* space – and a couple of people started to argue. The police arrested one of them, Harry Brunt, a building worker and club bouncer who was short but so broad that he had to have jackets especially made for him. Harry punched back, the police sent for reinforcements. Full scale fighting broke out. I missed it all – I was on shift.

Anywhere else, that might have been that. But for a small seaside town, Folkestone possessed an unusually politicised group of young people, enough to turn the response to the arrests into a mini Paris. Some hundreds of people fought the police, and sought out suitable targets for stoning, like the Conservative Party offices. The rioting lasted for two days, and skirmishes continued for some weeks before the High Street was safe for the tourists once more. Even then, crowds of young people were hanging around outside the cafe, smoking grass occasionally, and sometimes reading left-wing papers. I used to read *Black Dwarf* (as well as French leftist papers); Sheila Rowbotham reckons that it must have been her whom I used to buy the *Dwarf* from.

The French, who were all socialists, were okay. Actually, apart from Gilles and one or two other socialists, who spoke English, if badly, we didn't have much to do with French people. We firmly believed that all Swedish girls were permissive (despite persistent rebuffs) and that all French girls were devout Catholics (despite occasional successes). But, to be truthful, all foreigners were more or less beyond the scope of our vision. Our real perceptions of outsiders were mostly directed against the rest of the British.

2
I-Spy

FRANK COTTRELL BOYCE

During the early 1950s, first in an unassuming column of no fixed page in the *News Chronicle*, later in the *Daily Mail*, next in a succession of paperbacks of insinuating size and cheapness, finally in the secret but momentous doings of his Tribe (membership 2/6 at your newsagent's), Big Chief I-Spy began to reveal the implications of his discovery. This discovery was billed as the 'modern way' to play that ancient game 'I spy'. It was in fact an entirely new way of seeing.

It went like this. In a series of works with titles such as *Car Number Plates* and *History*, the Big Chief provided his redskins with his details of what was 'worth' seeing in particular fields of knowledge (or 'trails' as he called them).[1] A glance at the index of *People*, for instance, reveals that while a Bank of England messenger is worth seeing, your mother is not; a schoolboy is worth seeing, provided he has got his straw hat on. In this way, item by item, a canon of good, true and beautiful sights was defined. Even within this canon, however, certain decorums had to be observed. Some things, though worth seeing, were clearly not as worth seeing as others. An order of precedence had to be formulated, and the Big Chief was the man to formulate it. To assist him in this enterprise he resorted to a simple mechanism – the points system. Redskins who saw something worth seeing scored a certain number of points. Redskins who saw something more worth seeing scored more points. So there. Someone tossing the caber, for instance, was more worth seeing than a soccer match; and though, being palefaces, you might never have guessed it, a monk (thirty points) was more worth seeing than a nun (fifteen). Beyond the monks and caber tossers was a tiny elite of sights so overwhelmingly worth seeing that redskins were called upon to declare the day on which they saw one of them a 'red letter day' and report the sighting directly to the Big Chief (Wigwam-by-the-Water, London EC4), who, if he was convinced of the authenticity of your story, would send you a pen. The most frequently-mentioned member of this elite (figuring in five of the Big Chief's works) was the organ grinder. There were 1,500 points going for each book. If you won all 1,500 you were allowed to move up one place at the Council fire, wear an extra feather in your headband – colour and shape depending on which trail you had won your points on – and claim a rank. The name of the rank also varied according to trail; a high score in the area of *The Land*, for example, would make you a First Class Honours Geologist.

Throughout my boyhood, the I-Spy books remained the source of wisdom to which I referred most frequently. They were attractively laid out and well – often beautifully – illustrated. They dispensed information in manageable units. And they were cheap. The Big Chief stressed the inclusive, encyclopedic quality of the series: 'Collect all the I-Spy books', he advised, 'and you'll have a wonderful library of your own.' All knowledge (indeed all qualifications, from bushman to anthropologist to mechanic) was here. Along with the ability to distinguish between various species of tit, however, the reader also imbibed Big Chief's hierarchical view of creation. The natural world presented itself to my imagination as a great pyramid of Being, raised up on a foundation of starlings and sparrows (at five points each) and topped off with the hoopoe and bee-eater. Beyond them, at the apex, at the vanishing point of nature, the beginnings of the Great Beyond, the ghostly snowy owl and fabulous osprey (red letter birds both) hovered serenely over the rest, presided over themselves only by the Holy Spirit in the form of a dove, waiting to be spotted by a First Class Honours Saint.

It could be argued that a ten-year-old ornithologist living in Liverpool would have felt frustrated, Big Chief or no Big Chief. The exclusion of pigeons from the canon would have confirmed rather than aroused his suspicions. The importance of the Big Chief's unique contribution to this frustration should not, however, be underestimated. His was the suggestion, built into the points system, that pigeons were boring not because they were more familiar but because they were inherently inferior to, say, herons. Liverpool, like the pigeon, was at the bottom of a pyramid. Further up the social scale you got a better class of bird. The casual tone of the books – the implication that if you just stuck one in your pocket and took a stroll outside you'd run up a decent score in no time – suggested the possibility of a different Britain, somewhere over there, where this was indeed the case, a Britain teeming with things worth seeing, a proper Britain, where otters did sun themselves obligingly on handy rocks and adders were easily distinguished by the characteristic V shape on the back of the head, where the organ grinder played and the schoolboys wore straw hats.

If this fabulous land was raised as a possibility by the books on nature, it was installed as a matter of geographical fact by *History* and by *Churches*. *Churches* describes the contents of what I assumed must be the typical British church. This was an Elizabethan, possibly Jacobean, structure with bits of Norman and Saxon still showing. It may have been restored in the nineteenth century by someone mentioned in a Betjeman poem. Inside, the lines of apse and nave were complicated by objects of uncertain significance and prayer-like name – rood-screen, reredos, rector and so on: outside, a gaitered figure under the yews, ivy and the sound of bells. By definition, it was Anglican. Catholic, Methodist and, of course, Jewish, Moslem and Hindu places of worship were definitely not worth seeing. The only point of contact between my own experience of religious duties and that described by the Big Chief came on page 4. Here there was a picture of something remotely similar to my own parish church. Underneath, the caption said 'The Unusual – 20 points.' It was, in other words, about as worth seeing as one-fifth of an organ grinder.

The geography of this far and ancient land was elaborated in *History*, in the introduction to which the Big Chief insisted that redskins would find plenty of history to be going on with in their own towns and villages, directing their attention to the local castle and manor house where, perhaps, a king or so had spent the night, to the old city gates and walls, to market crosses and Tudor shambles. In particular he recommended monasteries, where 'every stone speaks of history' (*History*, 1952, p. 45), and, to show that common folk as well as nobs had history, to the stocks and other 'Punishments in the Past'. Ancient earthworks, Roman villas, Norman castles and stately homes all took their place in the venerable pageant arranged by the great and the good for the benefit of redskins of every epoch. In the proper Britain, over there, they enjoyed a visual continuity with the past of embarrassing intensity. Every day another of them gained the lemon-coloured square-topped feather of the First Class Honours Historian. In Liverpool, on the other hand, history was about as likely as the Holy Spirit.

It's important to realise that this sense that Liverpool was somehow not a part of proper Britain, that it was a place in brackets, did not grow simply out of mere resentment over lack of access to the quaint and picturesque. To feel alienated from the country described in these books was, in effect, to feel alienated from the structures of power. I have already mentioned the privileges and honours accorded to those who scored maximum points. The names of the ranks – anthropologist, geologist, archaeologist and so on – constituted an imagery by means of which the Tribe was keyed into the ideals of the professional classes and made to ape them. The power of those redskins with prestigious feathers and exalted positions around the camp fire was based precisely upon their increased access to the picturesque and the quaint. To this extent, it might be worth reading this advice (*In the Hedgerow*, 1967, p. 47) on how to use your I-Spy badge to the best advantage as a kind of potty-training in the manipulation of the old school tie: 'Wear your I-Spy badge everywhere. You'll find it an *Open Sesame* to all kinds of places.'

In part, no doubt, this feeling of exclusion derived from the fact that I was not an invited guest, not a part of the audience which the Big Chief had in mind. The habitat, hobbies and habits of the intended audience can be deduced from the contents of the I-Spy annuals that were put out in 1954–6. From these we can learn what 'Points to watch when one is choosing a pony', how to train your puppy, what to look for on your holiday abroad, or at the ballet, how to get the most out of your skiing, and, through the adventures of Jane, Peter and Nigger (the dog), how important the country code is for those who live on large farms. As the Big Chief himself put it back in 1955, 'unless you share in the doings of the Great Tribe, you miss a lot of the fun'.

It would be wrong, however, to try and explain the feelings of alienation engendered by the I-Spy books entirely in terms of this straightforward class bias. It was not a simple case of the format being so attractive that it sold the books to an audience far wider than the one that was being catered for at the level of material. For one thing, a number of measures were taken, particularly in the early 1960s, to correct this bias in the content, the most obvious being the production of a number of titles that were addressed to a more urban audience; *Road-Building, Buses and Coaches, Building* and *Everyday Machines* are a few that come to mind. It would be easy to exaggerate the effect of these reforms. The titles I have listed were not available in colour and did not stay in print as long as some of the others. Nor was there any attempt to revise the content of those volumes which cut across the town and country division. The inhabitants of the ancient market towns of the south of England still stood a better chance of becoming historians and ecclesiologists than the rest of us. The material of even these enlightened titles is often bizarre. *Town Crafts*, for instance, which was largely about the production of high-quality cricket equipment, found a space for the bookbinder and the stained-glass-window maker but not for the bespoke tailor. The early editions of *On the Pavement* and *In the Street* conjured up a Mary Poppins-like picture of jolly bustle, the limelight being hogged by knife-grinders, lamplighters, town criers, lucky sweeps, the gay sun-tanned onion seller and, inevitably, the organ grinder. *Building* was actually about the construction of brick houses. Points were going for tiles, hods and ladders but not for scaffolding or cranes. It was quite possible that a child living next door to a large urban housing project – a block of flats, or an estate of prefabs – would score only for the drains. In *People*, only eight of the seventy-odd illustrations depicted women. All non-whites were (like the hoopoe) exotic visitors. Any notion that the Big Chief might have conceived of the possibility of a non-white reader were dispelled when we came to the page on racial types. You could score for negro, indian, Indonesian and Scandinavian faces but not for Anglo-Saxons, the implication being that the reader would only have to look in the mirror to see one of these.

The fact that, even when reading those volumes which were designed with him in mind, the city child would have felt alienated, raises the possibility that the I-Spy books were alienating in form as well as content, that even the pony-riders of Tunbridge Wells and East Grinstead would have experienced some degree of dislocation and failure of recognition on reading these books. This is not to say that there was not a significant bias towards an identifiable social group. Clearly there was. Simple snobbery is not, however, the whole story. To begin with, the image of dormitory Britain we get from these books is a suspiciously literary one. The countryside, for instance, is divided not into the categories of orthodox natural history – upland and downland, or inland and coastal – but into small, easily defined, ecological niches, the little worlds that figure so largely in the literature of English childhood – ponds, for instance, as in the fond recollections of Bowling in Orwell's *Coming Up for Air*, or rock-pools (Gosse's *Father and Son*). *In the Wood* is about mixed woodland (as in Robin Hood), as opposed to the now more familiar coniferous plantations, the timber industry being left unmentioned until the last page. *In the Country* has a double-page spread about different types of windmill and a long entry describing the craft of the wheelwright. The link between the paradigm church of *Churches* and the poetry of Betjeman has already been mentioned.

The declared aim of the I-Spy books was to encourage a closer scrutiny and a greater appreciation of the environment. The environment towards which they directed their readers' attention, however, was an ideological construct, most obviously in that in effect it presented one version of one landscape as the standard or ideal. Ideology, however, is not only a matter of geographical location; it is in the eye of the beholder, and especially in the kind of use the Big Chief suggested his redskins made of their eyes. In order to understand the full effect of the I-Spy books, it is important to understand the nature of the vision they present to the eye.

In the Hedgerow (1967, p.3) opens with the admission that the hedge is not innocent, that it is an artificial (and thus ideological) barrier. This is how the Big Chief deals with the moment of its historical appearance: 'After 1700, Parliament passed Enclosure Acts which distributed land between various people. So hedges appeared to mark boundaries.' The word 'various' here covers (in the sense, 'conceals') a multitude of sins, while the use of the verb 'appears' suggests that nature obligingly burst into hedges in order to fulfil a new human need. Big Chief even goes so far as to imply that, with the passage of time, the hedge has atoned for the sin of its political origin and achieved a state of innocence. 'These artificial boundaries', he says, 'put up by man, have now been taken over by nature.' Here the fact of the hedges' physical existence, their presence as material (almost natural) objects, is stressed at the expense of their human significance. In the same way, in *People and Places*, the example which is cited of a place in which a famous movement started is Tolpuddle (fifty points). The Tolpuddle Martyrs, says the Big Chief, were 'unjustly' transported. By whom and for what remains a mystery. An unjust transportation appears to have just happened, like a hedge. The story of the martyrs is drained of its content. The writing at this point is objective in more ways than one: firstly in that it avoids taking sides; secondly in that it turns Tolpuddle into an object, a sight among other sights. In fact, Big Chief goes out of his way to advise his redskins that if they can't get to Tolpuddle, Mow Cop, cradle of Methodism, will do just as well.

History is thus presented to us not in the present effects of its past causes but in its monuments and commemorative plaques. In fact the example given at the beginning of *History* of future history being made today is a plaque commemorating the Festival of Britain, a souvenir of a staged 'event'. Indeed, the word 'souvenir' is actually used in the 1950s editions (p.5) of *Churches*, where it is applied to a maypole. The same reduction of a process to the objects that punctuate it can be seen in *Roadmaking*, a book in which the business of actually making a road is not referred to, but in which instead the bits of technology used in that process are exhibited like species of newt, items of interest for the urban nature table. In I-Spy *People*, humans are reduced to their profession (where this has a visible marker), their disability (no marks for seeing a blind man, but enter a note about how you helped him), or their ornamental qualities – exotic foreigners, people with unusual accessories (monocles and pince-nez) and 'colourful' buskers (especially organ grinders) are all high scorers. This effect is particularly pronounced in *People and Places*, which is about neither people nor places, but statues and sights. There is a terrible pathos to this eerie vision of a fossilised world, a world in which everything has become mere spectacle, a world whose inhabitants know only one emotion, the overwhelming desire to measure things. This obsession is normally accommodated by the points system, which allows the redskin to measure the relative worth of various objects. There are, however, occasions when this is simply not enough. A redskin confronted with that rare and powerful animal the wild cat, for instance, just has to count the rings around its tail (*In the Wood*, 1968, p.23).

This petrified landscape is the setting, too, for *On a Train Journey* and *In the Street*, works in which human interaction is replaced by the apparatus of social control as the object of interest. The redskin is encouraged to look for traffic lights, road signs and policemen, to choose to give his attention to those things to which he is, in fact, obliged to give it. Adorno notes something similar in his essay on *Fetish Character in Music*, where he discusses the ways in which the members of a consumer society overcome their feeling of essential impotence by miming an active decision to identify themselves with products which have in fact become inescapable.[2] The habit of seeing artifacts as magically self-contained units, miraculously untainted by the social and economic forces that produce and consume them, the tendency to evaluate objects according to their availability, the link between status and accumulated points, all these characteristics of the consumer mentality are built into the structure of the I-Spy books. Here our heroes react to one of the wonders of nature as if it was a bargain:

> Mrs Webster said, 'If I know anything about insects, that's a hummingbird-hawk-moth flying round the petunias.'
> Mrs Webster did know, and the children rushed out to score twenty-five points.

It may be no coincidence that the I-Spy books appeared at a moment in which consumerism entered a spectacular new phase. The editions of the *News Chronicle* in which the Big Chief's column first appeared are full of jokes about hip and recently over-equipped kitchens. The image of the redskin itself is worth considering in this context.

The attractions of the redskins as the image of the ideal I-Spy reader are many and obvious. The redskin is 'traditionally' sharp-eyed. The tribe is seen as the type of the organic yet hierarchical community which has always served as the natural version of the class society. But all of these requirements could have been fulfilled by, for example, the merry men of Robin Hood; and yet the Big Chief chose instead a figure that had no historical connection with the landscape through which it was supposed to travel, which it was expected to appreciate, a figure with no patriotic content. This decision was, I believe, the foundation of his greatness. By refusing to observe historical or cultural decorum he reduced all time and space to a kind of supermarket of styles and attitudes, a dressing-up box into which anyone could dip. Here he anticipated Adam Ant by some twenty years. Indeed it is impossible to read his descriptions of Fleetfoot, the ultimate redskin who drives around on a huge motorcycle called Big Four which has a canoe in place of a side-car, without thinking of the red indian and pirate imagery favoured by the New Romantics. The back cover of the first I-Spy annual shows a pair of neatly dressed young aryans gazing forlornly into an absurdly Berkshire landscape, each with a red indian head-dress plonked on his head. Once again it is impossible to look at them without thinking of the aggressive exoticism of recent youth subcultures, their use of the alien, the space age or the pantomimic as declarations of lack of connection, lack of interest (in the sense of lack of claim as well as that of lack of concern). Both the strength and the tragedy of this condition are brilliantly dramatised in a story which appears in the Big Chief's annual for 1955. It retells the adventures that befall Fleetfoot, Jack and Jill when they attempt to navigate an old canal. At every turn, they are confronted with the evidence of industrial decay. The drawbridge is rotted, the lock-keeper's house a ruin, but our heroes are not downhearted. They note the presence of this deterioration but it has no effect on them as long as they are getting their scores up. When they come across the ruined lock, Jack admits that it's 'a bit of a wreck' but whoops with delight at the thought of his twenty points. At the climax of the story, they discover that a tunnel they have entered is no longer navigable. They almost sink their canoe. As far as Jack and Jill are concerned this raises the tone of the adventure immeasurably; it is now a red-letter day and well worth writing about to the Big Chief.

Although, then, there is an extent to which the feeling of disjunction, of being marginal, which I had when I first came across I-Spy books, can be attributed to prejudice and simple-minded Little-Englandism on the part of the author, at another level it came from the fact that these works reflected and exploited the alienation experienced by all members of a consumer society, of a generation that sees the world as a shop window display. If you sincerely wish to raise the quality of the I-Spy book – after all it is by now a great British institution – it is no good tinkering about with the contents, hoping to make them reflect the reality of a multi-racial urbanised Britain more accurately. If you really want to improve I-Spy books, END CAPITALISM NOW.

Notes

1 All the I-Spy books discussed here were published in London by the Dickens Press. Although the content of each title remained substantially unrevised throughout the period discussed, there were regular changes of format and layout. I have therefore made no attempt to indicate page numbers except when discussing the contents of a particular edition of a particular title, in which case the page and year are given in the text.
2 Theodore Adorno, 'The fetish character in music and the regression of listening', in Andrew Arato and Eike Gebhardt (eds), *The Essential Frankfurt School Reader*, Oxford, Basil Blackwell, 1978, p. 288.

3
Growing up Catholic

MARY CHAMBERLAIN

I was born within the sound of my own nomenclature, too close to Our Lady's birthday to be called anything other than Mary Christina; and I come from an old English Catholic family. Mine, however, was not the easy glittered world of *Brideshead Revisited* or Antonia White, but the siege Catholicism of Walworth and Bermondsey. The Gordon riots, for all my parents knew, had happened but yesterday. They were as proud of their spiritual as of their temporal birthright. London and Catholicism merged into a single identity – heavenly cockneys.

Yet English Catholicism sat uneasily, attempting to reconcile the – sometimes barely recognised – contradictions imposed upon it with those generated from within. Catholicism was a minority religion; yet numerical weakness did not close the gaps of class or ethnic origin. Catholics might all sing the same Credo, but with very different accents. Catholicism was both international and intensely parochial. Its language and its iconography were continental but few Catholics, save the wealthy, had ever left England. To the outsider, Catholicism's looking to Rome (and to Dublin) appeared to discharge any British allegiance. Yet to be a Catholic was to be taught true patriotism; Catholicism, for all its foreign airs, was the indigenous Christianity of Britain. It secured a place in history, as well as in Heaven. For Catholics considered themselves the inheritors of the True Cross and English Catholics had never deviated from the path of righteousness.

This sense of history and universality offered, within the English context, a sense of uniqueness. The language of Catholics was that of Latin, international. A Catholic could go to mass anywhere in the world and be able to participate fully. Latin and Greek were somehow God's languages. In any case, they were ancient languages and stood in marked contrast to the Anglicans or (God forbid) the nonconformist upstarts with their inceremonial services in the vernacular which served only to emphasise their distance from God and their very parochial nature. The universality of Catholicism was of course epitomised by the Pope, the Holy Father in Rome. Catholicism crossed and looked beyond mere national borders. Rome to Catholics is what Mecca is to Islam. We sang a hymn which began 'Full in the panting heart of Rome/Beneath the Apostles' crowned dome' and ended with the chorus 'God bless the Pope, the Great, the Good'.

But, paradoxically, we considered ourselves to be fiercely nationalistic, more English than the English. We were the old English, we were the ones who had stayed true to the true English faith of Catholicism. We sang hymns commemorating the 'Faith of our Fathers', England was Our Lady's dowry, we prayed for the reconversion of England, we made pilgrimages to English shrines and, as my old school magazine of 1962 recalls:

> On the feast of the Ascension the Senior Cadettes went on an outing to West Grinstead to see the first shrine of Our Lady erected since the Reformation in England. After that we were shown the small rooms where Mass was secretly said during the reigns of Henry VIII and Elizabeth I. We also saw some relics, sacred vessels and letters written by various priest martyrs who were hanged, drawn and quartered at Tyburn . . . The Guild of Our Lady of Ransom have been arranging visits to the different parts of London, showing its Catholic origin. Some of our girls hope to go to Westminster Abbey and the Tower of London. We hope in this way to learn more of our Catholic heritage.

For English Catholics, therefore, there was a sense of tradition at one time universalist, international and, at the same time, very narrow and British. A sense of being the last survivors, the last upholders of Truth against the Infidel.

This sense of uniqueness and exclusivity was reinforced by being a numerical minority, by a tradition of persecution and, from the eighteenth to the twentieth century, the battle for Catholic enfranchisement. It emerged in outward form, taking political expression in a deeply ambiguous relationship to the state, and social expression in an aggressive manifestation of our faith. As far as English Catholics were concerned, the Reformation and the reasons for the Reformation were not of interest.

With reason and justification, Catholics were deeply suspicious of state authority. As we were the upholders of the true English faith, so were we the upholders of the true English state. The

New Testament moral 'to render unto Caesar the things that are Caesar's, and unto God the things that are God's' was often quoted, with the clear implication that if the former tried to encroach on the spiritual or temporal authority of the latter, then no allegiance was due. Catholic teaching endorsed the views that so long as the state upholds values which the Catholic church endorses, protects the rights of Catholics to practise their faith, and does not require Catholics to act against their consciences, then, even if it is a Protestant authority, Catholics have a duty to obey. But once it transgressses, then Catholics, equally, have a duty to protest and oppose. Unlike our counterparts, we had not fallen behind Henry VIII, we upheld our consciences and protested. As far as Catholics were concerned, there should be no conflict between state and church; as far as English Catholics were concerned, because of the Reformation, it was inherent in the system. Catholic loyalty to state, and to Protestant authority was, and remains, tenuous and expresses itself at many levels. The church as a pressure group acts united and formally on certain issues such as Catholic education or abortion, issues which it feels it has a collective right and duty to fight for. Using its network of parishes, it can use the priests to pronounce from the pulpits and can rally impressive support for a lobby. On issues not considered central to Catholic practice or faith but nevertheless of concern, it permits and tolerates individual action by both the laity and the clerics. Support for Irish nationalism is a case in point; Bruce Kent's involvement with CND is another, where Monseigneur Kent's argument with Cardinal Hume rested on his right and duty as a Catholic (and a priest) to oppose what in all conscience he perceived to be a fundamentally immoral political position. Victoria Gillick, who challenged the courts on the right of children under sixteen to receive contraceptive help without parental consent, was equally acting according to conscience.

At a third level, Catholic laity have engaged in political activity. Some of the Catholic political 'mafias' have been exposed of late – O'Grady and Mellish in Southwark and O'Halloran in Islington. Although there is no formal link between the church and 'its' politicians, their engagement with the political system directly is condoned; for having Catholic politicians setting an example is one way of restoring political authority in England to its rightful owners. More pragmatic Catholic politicians can be relied upon to safeguard Catholic interests. Catholic politicians have been able to rely upon informal church networks to generate and maintain support. The fact of being a Catholic engaged in active elective politics commands almost unquestioning loyalty. At school, we prayed for the election of John F. Kennedy, not because he was a Democrat, but because he was a Catholic. At home, Bob Mellish remained a political idol not because of his politics, but because he was a Catholic (and gave the prizes out at my brothers' school). Indeed, the importance of securing the Catholic vote in an election remains a priority from any politicians – Catholic and non-Catholic – in constituencies with large Catholic populations. This readymade constituency is an important element in the power-base of Catholic politicians.

The church itself, by being prepared to engage in political controversy, provided a model for political action. But it also provided more. Catholics, like many beleagured minorities, have had a long tradition of helping their own. Irish immigration in the nineteenth and twentieth centuries required the church itself to provide organisation and help to protect and settle its new parishioners. Out of this developed a tradition of social activity and protection which extended beyond the purely pastoral role of its clerics. It was an easy step to extend those links into a wider arena, into local politics and trade union activity, to offer, in return for loyalty, to fight for political ends compatible with the social and moral position of Catholics. The logical political home for many of the urban working-class Catholics is the Labour Party, for the Tories represent not only the repression of the working class, but the repression of Ireland and Catholicism.

Yet despite this ambiguous attitude to the state and politics, as Catholics we remained deeply nationalistic, even patriotic. Though the church condoned Labour politics, it was also deeply conservative. Church hierarchies were drawn, on the whole, from wealthier and better educated Catholics, distanced from many of their parishioners by class. Temperamentally they may have been Conservative, and pragmatically they cautioned patience. Social revolt would have been anathema for the church in its attempt to achieve equality and to reaffirm in the public eye the essential patriotism of Catholics. For though we felt English, the rest of England regarded us as aliens, as Papists. We endured claims of treachery (still apparent in the rhetoric of Paisley), and had to prove that we were fit and dutiful subjects of the monarch. And, as upholders of the true England, we had a right to defend it. Although our consciences might revolt against the state, the state was where we lived and sought acceptance. We had to prove our loyalty, to prove that there was no conflict between Rome and Westminster, in our actions and our deeds. Catholics were as prepared to die for their country as their Protestant comrades, even if it required fighting fellow Catholics.

Though as Catholics we desired social acceptance, we were not prepared to compromise. Our uniqueness as Catholics, our arrogance in believing that potentially we could defy the law, reinforced Protestant anxiety, which in turn led us to a militant assertion of our faith, marks of the ghetto which we were proud to bear. Unlike, for instance, Jewish culture, where there is an ethos of education, achievement and an end goal of assimilation, Catholics educated their children in order to produce better Catholics, and better priests and nuns. Catholics have never been noted for their dominance in any one field, except perhaps, in London, print and across the nation (if somewhat dubiously), crime and politics. Yet Catholic education is good and, for boys, very good. Catholic schools have some of the highest records for university places. But university and learning – scholarship – are never the end goals. That remains to produce ambassadors of the faith, better apologists, better examples. (Those Catholics who have achieved eminence in their profession are regarded as in the vanguard of the restoration, as models to the world of the innate superiority of Catholicism.)

We stuck doggedly to our own religious practices. Our services were in Latin, our prayers and prayer forms markedly different: rosaries and ejaculations (a prayer form), medals and scapulars. We wore ash on our foreheads on Ash Wednesday, we had days and times of strict fasting and abstinence, we had incense and bells, sanctuary lamps and candles. Our churches were essentially exotic and full of drama. We had statues of the Sacred Heart, statues of Our Lady trampling barefoot on a snake, amulets and guild ribbons and of course the priests' vestments bearing more affinity to the biblical Middle East than they ever did to England. We had stunning music and plain chant, processions and ritual. We had benedictions and pilgrimages, chalices and tabernacles, but above all we – and we alone – had present in our churches and ourselves the Body and Blood of Christ every time mass was consecrated. We crossed ourselves publicly every time we passed a Catholic church, or a funeral procession passed us. As girls and women, we never entered church with our arms or heads bare; the black mantilla was ever at the ready to cover ourselves in modesty and discretion. We did not encourage and barely tolerated the 'mixed' marriage. And never, ever to Jews, the conversion of whom, along with the English, we prayed for regularly.

Let me now say something on how these factors interplayed with my own background. My maternal grandmother was a seamstress, my grandfather a printer. My mother was born and bred in Walworth, as had been her parents and grandparents before her. We were English, skilled, London working-class stock. My mother's street was classified by Booth in pink, 'poor and comfortable'. As the youngest of a large Catholic family she won and was able to take up a scholarship to the Notre Dame convent in Southwark. From there she won, and was able to take up, a place at St Charles, a teacher-training college run by the nuns of the Sacred Heart. (It is now known as Digby-Stuart College and moved to Roehampton during the war, to occupy the site of the convent immortalised by Antonia White in *Frost in May*.) My mother became an infant teacher and moved from the ranks of the labour aristocracy to those of the lower middle class.

My father, on the other hand, came from Bermondsey. His father worked on the docks but died when my father was young from what would now be recognised as an 'industrial disease', pneumoconiosis caused by inhaling corn and seed dust. My father's street was classified by Booth as dark blue, 'very poor'. He left school at fourteen, but continued his education under his own steam at night school and through correspondence courses. His career had been somewhat patchy as he graduated from working with corn merchants to renting an arch under Southwark Bridge where he hoped to make his fortune through the manufacture of ladies' cosmetics. During the war he continued his education through the Armed Forces Education Service and after the war became a teacher under the two-year teacher-training programme. But when he first came to court my mother, he was perceived as a bog-hopper from the slums, having served no apprenticeship which offered him a recognisable skill.

My mother's family have always been Catholic; indeed, it was part of the family folklore that we are one of the old English Catholic families, having been Catholic since the Reformation. I am not a genealogist, and have no wish to be, so cannot vouch for the truth of that, but as a family we have preserved a number of old documents – indentures, marriage certificates, funeral bills, etc. – and those clearly show us, not only living within the same few yards of Walworth since 1819 (the date on the earliest document), but as being Catholic all that time.

In contrast to the Irish immigrant families who had settled in Bermondsey and Walworth, and to the Italian families, my own family was marked by longevity of tenure and, because they had always been skilled workers, relative wealth. Irish piety was recognised, but Irish social graces and occupations looked down upon. The Irish were perceived as a holy, but lumpen, proletariat with, inevitably, 'exceptions' among the priests and nuns, and friends.

My mother's family enshrined the tradition of English Catholics and sense of destiny. At times there was a feeling that they were the only Catholics who could claim this dual inheritance of Catholicism. This sense of family uniqueness was reinforced by the social circumstances in which they lived. They lived, in common with most other Catholic families, within a stone's throw of the church. Their exclusivity had something of a geographical ghetto. Catholics had to attend mass regularly on Sunday; good Catholics went daily. In order to receive communion, you had to fast overnight. This clearly precluded any long walk to church. There may also have been an element of protection felt in living so close and together, for anti-Catholic feelings ran high. Father Doyle, for instance, the priest at St George's responsible for the building of the cathedral in Southwark wrote in 1851:

> For us – for the Catholic church – there is a feeling of deep-seated hatred – a feeling that lies as deep as the gravel bottom over which London stands. It seems it is an English feeling – hatred of Catholicity . . . This bitter dislike is in every class – it shows itself everywhere . . . and it burns nowadays with a malignant, sulphurous flame . . . a Catholic Priest is like the prowling wolf or the crafty fox, and a show of millions of hands would be uplifted at any hour to banish us out of the country, if the thing were possible. (*The Great Link*, London, Canon Bernard Bogan, 2nd edition, 1958)

But then Catholics did not keep low profiles, either. Parades and processions through the neighbourhood marked Ascension Day and other feast days. In 1902 the South London Press reported that a Baptist minister had been distributing scurrilous anti-papist propaganda, clearly designed to inflame anti-Catholic feelings before their annual Ascension Day procession in Peckham. In the 1920s hostility was such that my mother had to be escorted to and from school by her father and in 1936 the first (and last) public meeting my mother ever attended ended in near riots after Bishop Amigo of Southwark declared that Franco was a 'good man'. Memories like this from my mother's childhood fed into a peculiarly Catholic paranoia. Hers was the long tradition of Catholicism, against the odds.

My mother's family was a close one, and a large one. Aunts, uncles, grandparents all lived within the neighbourhood and, as a South London Catholic family, it was fairly well known by the clergy as a 'good' family – as a child I can remember on many occasions strange priests recognising my mother as a 'Harris'. Those Catholic families where the son or daughter had had a 'vocation' were especially revered. There was enormous pressure put on children to consider a religious life. Those that succeeded clearly had a special blessing from God, and their families glowed in borrowed grace. Needless to say, my family produced its share of 'vocations'. My aunt joined the Little Sisters of the Poor, and one of my cousins lasted five years in a seminary, before leaving, to the great disappointment of the family.

My parents married in 1940 when my father was in the forces. My mother continued to live with her grandmother close to the church of the English Martyrs, near Surrey Square. Regular visits from the priests were part of their life. (Indeed, regular gambling sessions on Friday nights with my uncles were held, a scene my grandmother deplored, though I'm not sure whether her disapproval was for gambling *per se* or whether it was the fact that my uncles had no inhibitions about taking money from the priest when he lost.) The pastoral role of the priests was (and still is) confused with their need for a meal and also, I suspect, their need for the company of a family.

The family house was bombed during the war and the family sought refuge in the suburbs. My uncle was the first to leave and found another house in the same street for my mother and grandmother. When my family moved to the suburbs they carried with them all their class aspirations, and their class experience, and the family sense of religious destiny and uniqueness. Our house in the suburbs was one-and-a-half miles from the centre of town, and the church. Without a car, we had to walk the distance to mass on Sundays, a three-mile round trip; and, in moments of zeal, we'd do it again in the afternoon for Benediction.

Nevertheless, this pattern of pastoral visiting continued in the suburbs. The priest had transport and after the war and during the 1950s was often someone known to my mother or her family from the old days. I think, for many of these priests, the suburbs were a strange environment and my parents represented the 'old life'. Priests were always welcome in our home, they came to the back door; indeed, as a child and adolescent, one came on the family holiday with us for years. I can't imagine, though this may be distorted memory, the priests ever entering the 'posh' houses of the majority of their parishioners with the same lack of inhibition. This familiarity with the priests confirmed the family's feelings of specialness. There crept into the family ideology the notion that wealthier Catholics were somehow less Catholic: materialism, education, free thinking – how I pictured with admiration my school friends' families – had reduced their commitment to the faith.

But this was a schizophrenic attitude, for there was also a strong desire to move upwards socially. My parents had 'made it' by becoming teachers. The war had provided them with an opportunity to leave the smoke and slums of London and acquire, with little effort, an almost new 1930s semi. ('Not much of a house' was my grandmother's verdict as she was forced by my mother to abandon the larger pieces of furniture.) When my father came back from the war and took his teaching diploma under the postwar training scheme, they took out a mortgage and were able to buy the house. But there was also a fear that in moving upwards they would break their roots with a form of Catholicism that was rooted in the ghetto. It led to an authoritarian and unyielding line on Catholicism which later conflicted sharply with my own peer group ethos, and the ethos of their parents. My upbringing – though in a very different environment from that of my parents in inner London – could not be separated from their experiences. I inherited a tradition of working-class beleaguered Catholics, but had to operate within a middle-class environment which seemed to me to be far more fluid, far less restrictive, far more affluent and altogether more attractive.

Nearly half a century later, my parents still live there. Indeed, the suburb, by south London standards, was 'posh', except where we lived, in a 1930s ribbon development of mock-tudor semi-detached houses, its class level confirmed by the building, in the 1950s, of a large council estate at the end of the road, a development that was bitterly resisted at the time. Of course, my parents' house has now been 'modernised' by layers of aspiring taste and affluence and the street itself has lost its rawness as the trees and gardens have now matured. Few of the original neighbours remain, having since moved out and up or, simply, died. Yet the class composition of the street has stayed remarkably stable; lower-middle class, and a bit 'common', the families of policemen, clerks and master craftsmen.

As a child, and even now, there were very few Catholics in the street. Our home, therefore, stood out. An over-sized statue of the Blessed Virgin dominated the landing window, clearly visible from the street. The Sacred Heart guarded the hall and the lounge, as we called it. Crucifixes controlled every bed (mine was luminous and glowed in the dark) and the holy water font with which we would bless and purify ourselves was placed conveniently, though accidentally, *en route* to the only lavatory.

I thought we were perfectly normal. We thought everybody else was odd, not least our neighbours, the Baptists. I don't recall what he did, but she was a fitter for Spirella corsets which entitled her to fix the Spirella logo to the pebble-dashed front on the house. Measuring naked or near-naked ladies seemed to me a slightly dirty occupation and totally at variance with the fierceness with which they guarded their, and their children's, Sabbath. I could not understand why my friend next door could not play on that day; neither could my mother. Ignorance and incomprehension turned astonishment into pity. Yet it was with the Baptists that I denied Christ for the first and most traumatic time in my life.

When I was ten or thereabouts the school went on a trip to the Franciscan monastery at Aylesbury and I bought as a souvenir a small brown scapular. As part of the mortification of the flesh, I wore it inside my clothes until it slipped out one day while I was playing with Baptist Brenda (*what* an un-Catholic name). She asked what it was and I was far too embarrassed to explain. Instead, I made up a far more improbable excuse; the little brown bits of cloth were in fact remnants from my (dead) grandmother's dress which I wore in memory of her. Brenda was, to say the least, incredulous, not least because both grandmothers were alive and kicking. It was undoubtedly such denials – no stranger, really, than the truth – which fed into the outsider's view of the general weirdness of Catholic behaviour. But then, as a child, no more weird than the way her mother evaded ironing the handkerchiefs; she merely put them to dry flat by sticking them on the tiled walls of the kitchen. Baptist standards on handkerchiefs, I learnt from my mother, were far lower than those of Catholics.

There was no question that I should go to a Catholic school. My mother, at secondary level, dearly wanted me to go to her old school, but decided that the journey was too far (though my brothers travelled a comparable distance to go to what my parents considered the 'best' school for them, the Jesuit college in Wimbledon). It is incumbent on good Catholic parents to send their children to Catholic schools. It is a major, if not the major, responsiblity. But as well, the battle for the right to have Catholic schools was long and hard and by sending children to those schools the political fight was reinforced.

However in my suburb there was no Catholic state-aided primary school. One started later, to which my youngest brother went. My parents, therefore, had only one choice and that was to pay at a convent preparatory school, the secondary school for which was a direct-grant grammar school.

In 1951 when I was four my mother got a job at this preparatory school and I was permitted to start proper school early. It was not my first experience of school, for I had accompanied my mother when she taught at another school in Sydenham. But this job was nearer home and free tuition made up the shortfall in my mother's salary. I continued in the same school until I was seventeen. I have few coherent memories of my prep. school. My shoe bag was made out of my father's old RAF shirt, on which my father had written, in beautiful calligraphy, my name in Indian ink. (Sign writing was a skill he had picked up along the way.) My first communion was made in 1953 in a homemade white seersucker-nylon dress which later, with a coloured petticoat, doubled as a party dress. (I wanted a gingham shoe bag and a shop-bought lacey dress.) We had the communion breakfast at school at which I received my first missal in a white plastic mother-of-pearl cover, and my luminous crucifix. The same year, I lost out on the draw to crown 'Our Lady' in the May processions. I remember my confirmation, 'adopting' a black baby (for whose spiritual welfare we named, and donated, our prayers, pocket money and milk-bottle tops and for whose physical welfare, in the secondary school, we made uniforms) and praying for the missions.

My coherent memories begin in the grammar school. Within Catholic schools there are hierarchies. A convent grammar school was above that of a state-aided but non-convent Catholic school. Indeed, under the old pre-comprehensive system, Convent schools were grammar, state-aided Catholic schools were secondary modern. But convents have hierarchies; a direct-grant grammar school was clearly below a fee-paying convent, a public school. And even within those gradations, some public schools were better than others. The order of nuns clearly made a difference. My order was the Ladies of Mary, Belgian in origin, a teaching and missionary order primarily. It laid no claims to academic excellence as did orders like the Sacred Heart of the IBVM.

My school was rigidly hierarchical. At the top was Reverend Mother, head of the convent and spiritual head of the school. Beneath her was the headmistress, always a nun. Only one other nun had a degree and could therefore teach 'O' and 'A' levels. She was also the sixth-form mistress. The main body of teaching therefore was delegated to lay Catholic women. Some nuns taught lower down the school, but only art and catechism. Although the convent was administered by nuns, the priests were always paid deferential treatment. The role of confessor clearly emphasised that although the nuns' authority within the convent was autonomous, their position vis-à-vis God – and therefore their whole *raison d'être* – clearly required a man to mediate and advise. Indeed, one was continously reminded of the church hierarchy and within that the relatively lowly place held by women. Reverend Mother was clearly supreme within the convent, but she was merely part of a continuum which stretched from her to the priest, the bishop, the Pope and ultimately God.

Academically, the school was not very good. Out of a sixth form of twenty-nine – the largest ever – only eleven went to university, and that was an all-time record. None went to Oxford or Cambridge. There seemed to be an inherent fear of university. The nuns would have been far happier if we had gone, instead, to the local Catholic teacher-training college, run by the same order. In retrospect, I think it was the advent of our sixth-form nun who signalled a shift here, having herself obtained a degree. But we were not allowed to apply for Oxford or Cambridge, because none of us was considered good enough and it was regarded almost as a sin of pride to think that we were. Universities were considered on the whole to be dangerous places which taught communism, anti-Christ and philosophy. To this day, I have a fear of philosophy. The level of intellectualism was such that even in the sixth form there was no one nun capable of teaching Catholic 'apologetics' at anything like an advanced level.

There was, therefore, a heavy emphasis on the drama and ritual, the emotions and sentiments of religion with, before we left school, a retreat run by a 'hellfire and brimstone' Jesuit. The main formal teaching of Catholicism relied on learning by rote the catechism, the little red book of Catholicism.

After John XXIII the nuns changed their title from 'mother' to 'sister' and ended, in name at least, what had been a division in their order between 'mothers', teaching staff, and 'sisters', support staff. Prior to this change there had been an implication that the 'sisters', clearly less educated, were somehow incomplete nuns. I don't know how many nuns there were altogether, but there seemed to be a lot of them. I suspect that many came to do local pastoral work or to rest between missions. One nun was sent as housekeeper to the papal nuncio in Tehran. There was certainly a very regular interchange of nuns to and from the missions. All the teaching staff were required to do a period abroad and the only news of the outside world that the school magazines printed was news from the missions, mainly in Uganda. We were encouraged to support 'our' missions in every way, spiritual, practical and financial.

Although this was a day school the outside world intruded little. The cleaners and kitchen staff were lay and almost wholly Irish until 1956, when the nuns provided home and employment for some of the Hungarian refugees. But they were always Catholic. There was a censored copy of *The Times* in the school library (for I was there during the Profumo scandal) but little discussion of 'current affairs', except in the sixth form where it took the form of discussing the Catholic position on contemporary issues. The fear of communism was rife and no opportunity was ever lost – from 1956, through to the alleged infiltration of CND by communists, to Berlin and Cuba – to expose the wily and wicked ways of communists. We were permitted to hold a 'mock' election in 1964, and I stood as the Communist candidate, a position that was tolerated only to the extent that I could parody, *à la Animal Farm*, the Marxist position. It was the first research I ever did, even though it was confined to the *Encyclopedia Britannica* at the local library. The main tenet of my programme was to convert Buckingham Palace into homes for the homeless. It was not a popular programme so, despite my oratory (I was also chair of the school debating society) I came third, way ahead of the Labour candidate, close to the Liberal candidate. Our total votes, however, would have been barely sufficient to unseat the Tory candidate. The results were a fair reflection of the background and political ethos of a middle-class convent in a middle-class area.

The school was 100 per cent white. Our contact with the missions disguised its racism in a cloak of spiritual imperialism. Of course we supported French, Belgian and British imperialism for they provided the protection whereby we could pursue our aims of global conversion. The bloody battles that accompanied some of the struggles for independence in, for instance, the Congo and elsewhere were seen as evidence of the innate savagery and paganism of the Africans and other colonials. Concepts like negritude or African nationalism were never raised, and would not be found anyway in the censored copies of *The Times*.

What were the aims and objectives of convent education? The answer was provided by the 1959 issue of the School magazine.

> Education means, of course, much more than teaching academic or practical subjects. It means the development of the whole personality of the child, as a future citizen and present child of God . . . So we may [end by] ask[ing] the blessed Mother of God, and her mother, St Anne, the patroness of our school, and all those of our sisters who have gone before and are now in the eternal presence, to watch over St Anne's and pray for us, that our work may prosper and that we, our children, their parents, and all our benefactors may one day join them in praising God forever.

Essentially, we were being groomed as ambassadresses of our faith. This meant two things. Either to become a nun, and the question of 'vocations' was kept constantly on the boil – the diocesan inspector (a priest sent by the bishop to monitor the teaching of Catholicism) would annually prophesy that one girl in every class had a vocation, and usually one a year would succumb. Or it meant becoming a mother and a lady, as innocent, gentle, humble and self-effacing as Our Lady.

Ladies were recognised by their example, a combination of glowing inner grace and outward expression. Modesty was the most important attribute of that external expression – chastity of thought, speech and action. Hence the enormous emphasis on dress, posture, deportment and speech. Common speech was immodest speech. As Catholics we had to distinguish ourselves from the common girls who were not merely working class, but immoral and licentious. For ladies were not drawn from that class but the ranks of the *ersatz* aristocracy. I had elocution lessons. For many non-Catholics, of course, the aim of a girl's education was perceived by many as a cheap public school. We were required by law to take in a percentage of non-Catholic pupils, but this was always kept to a minimum.

Nuns were the epitome of a lady. Chaste at all times, they also neither smoked nor drank, they never, ever ran, never sat cross-legged; continuously swathed in black, they were essentially ephemeral asexual creatures. They glided along the corridors, trailing their very distinctive scent; they called the girls to order with a sharp clap (for they never raised their voices). If any nun was required they would be called by the ringing of a bell. It was always very tranquil and well ordered and essentially self-effacing. And we were required to behave likewise. On our monthly reports, conduct and deportment took equal place with academic work. We had to glide along the corridors, in silence. We were forbidden any physical contact with our fellow pupils, were forbidden to run (except in games), shout or sit incorrectly and our uniform – right down to our underwear – was regularly checked for transgressions. Before we went home, the headmistress would stand at the door checking our uniforms, ensuring our hats and gloves were in place, that we wore the regulation shoes and socks, and there were stiff penalties and public humiliations for those who transgressed the rules of behaviour outside (as well as inside) school. As Catholics, we had to set an example at all times. And as convent girls we had to show the world the innate superiority of convent education. We were somehow less Catholic if we were caught not wearing our hats, or eating a bag of crisps in the street.

A convent, even a day convent like mine, was an intense and enclosed world. Religion and the nuns permeated everything. Every room was dedicated to a saint. Catechism classes were daily. Every lesson would begin with a prayer and we were encouraged to write on the top of our exercise books the initials JMJ (Jesus, Mary and Joseph). At noon the angelus would ring for our devotion. There was weekly mass and Benediction. Every time we passed the chapel we were required to genuflect and make the sign of the cross, and encouraged to enter and offer a small prayer. The many statues and grottoes in the school building and grounds were constant reminders to our devotion. Grace was always said before and after meals.

We were fed on a diet of masochism, self sacrifice and devotion. It was an intense emotional experience, undiluted Catholicism. The sense of exclusivity, uniqueness and destiny was here multiplied. We were the beleaguered island. It reflected all the religious xenophobia of English Catholicism with a primitivism which would have done credit to the early mystics. Everything was offered up to God – trials, hardships, sacrifices and joy. We were told quite openly that if an outsider said that they were 'Church of England', it means 'they are nothing', godless, pagans. We prayed for the world. And we did more. We were encouraged to join a variety of religious societies, like for instance the Sodality Cell, small caucuses of committed Catholics dedicated to converting the world, through 'routine' action or 'special' action, including the 'selling of Catholic papers and leaving copies on buses and trains, carrying out the weekly communion rota'. Or we were encouraged to join the Cadettes, where we discussed the faith and 'practised defending it'. We would progress from the Cadettes to the Aspirants and thence to full membership of the Children of Mary Immaculate, where we would be consecrated to Our Lady and would be dedicated to carrying on apostolic work and leading a life worthy of one so consecrated.

We would listen in fascination to the stories of the martyrs and the grim way they met their death, or the stories of the saints and the equally grim way they achieved sanctity. (*The Times* may have been censored, but the gruesome details of the lives of the saints were repeated in every detail.) All involved quite inhuman sacrifices and I, in common I suspect with many, prayed to be given the chance to be a martyr and would lull myself to sleep dreaming of the most horrendous tortures which I would endure for the sake of God. The pitch of religious fervour was almost hysterical and engaged our fantasies and curiosity full time. It had to, for the teaching of theology was at a very simple level. Coupled with this emotion was an equally powerful imagery – statues, pictures, dreadfully sentimental prayer cards. And though the English never engaged in the ultimate gore of preserved fingers or bodies, I am sure they would had they been given the chance, for preservation of the flesh is one of the signs of sainthood.

Yet while this intensity of emotion towards God or Our Lady was encouraged, at a personal level it was discouraged. Close friendships were frowned upon, particularly those which had any physical manifestation like holding hands. Individuality was not encouraged, for we were a community and expected to work collectively for the greater good of God. Individuality was pride. Yet our emotional faculties were tuned to a high degree of loving and preparedness to make the ultimate sacrifice of life. Love was the total subsumation of self in another. And it was forever.

If you couldn't become a martyr, saint or a nun, then the convent expected you to become a mother. There was, however, no preparation in sex education or even mothercraft, though we were taught how to sew and cook. The emphasis was more on the responsibility we had, as Catholic mothers, to bring our children up according to the Faith and set an example at all times. For that reason a 'mixed' marriage would impose an intolerable burden and was to be discouraged. (Indeed, as many obstacles as possible were put to prevent such a marriage, including the extraction from the non-Catholic partner of a written promise to allow the children to be brought up as Catholics.) At school we were given hypothetical situations to discuss regarding our behaviour in a mixed marriage, and had to gauge our strength as Catholics in mock simulations – you may love the man, but could you reject him for his Protestantism?

But this was a day school, and it was the early 1960s, and we were all growing up. Try as they might, the nuns could not finally control what went on in our lives beyond the school. There were teenage parties, with the brothers of our class-mates and their friends, at which were played such distinctly un-Catholic games as sardines and postman's knock. But we were playing with Catholic boys and though, in retrospect, it was all terribly innocent, at the time we thought it was daring and shocking. But there was never any guidance to help in coming to terms with sexuality, for the models of womanhood that we had were essentially asexual.

I had particular problems with this. My parents were excessively strict and saw these secular goings on as indicative of the decadence of the middle classes. To me, they represented Enlightenment. These girls, who lived in detached houses, clearly had parents who, because of education and class, did not see the world in such beleaguered terms; who appeared to condone behaviour which was clearly at variance with the teaching of the nuns and, indeed, Catholicism. Yet they were also practising Catholics. I began to realise that even within Catholicism there was another world where liberality, free thinking, trust was apparent. I would find myself pleading with my parents to be allowed to go to these 'mixed' parties, using arguments that I hoped would appease my parents' social aspirations and simultaneously assuage their worries. They lived in large, detached houses, I would argue, called 'Silver Beeches' or 'The White House' – for to have a house identified by title not number placed them in a wholly different social category – and yet, I would say, they were good Catholics, respectable families who regularly attended mass. And though it clearly appealed in some sense to the class snobbery of my parents, when it came to the crunch, those class barriers closed up. Liberality was not their game and they were still living in the Walworth ghetto. They could not see – or perhaps saw too clearly – that there was another form of Catholicism which could perhaps manipulate a system which they, by reason of class, would be powerless to do. For though their sort might provide the Little Sisters of the Poor and even the parish priest, it was from the ranks of the middle and upper classes that the bishops and the cardinals were drawn. And they, by reason of birth and rank, were distanced from the grass roots and entrenched Catholicism.

It was quite possible for people like my mother to live their lives – from childhood to retirement – in a hermetic Catholic environment. This was the 'world' envisaged by the nuns for their 'girls' and for which they had prepared us. But the world I encountered was beyond the experience, and I suspect the imagination, of the nuns and my parents. In this world of university in the mid and late 1960s, the arguments, so carefully rehearsed for the existence of God and the innate superiority of Catholicism, appeared irrelevant, and the preparations they had given us, as women operating in this world, woefully inadequate.

Catholic teaching places a premium on purity for women. Indeed, for Catholic women, it was almost the sole *raison d'être*. The model of St Maria Goretti – who preferred to die than surrender her virginity to a soldier – was to be our guide through life. Life, however, did not conform to such dramatic principles. I, in common with most convent educated girls, left school unaware of my own sexuality and ignorant, even, of the mechanics of sexual reproduction. Simply saying 'no' was infinitely more difficult than we had been led to expect. Our 'seducers' were not, like Maria Goretti's, potentially violent rapists but charming, persuasive and intelligent men (albeit non-Catholics, Jews and atheists even). But to 'surrender' virginity before marriage was to enter into a state of mortal sin. Yet it did not seem like mortal sin . . .

I was far too embarrassed to confide in my confessor. Indeed I could admit to no one that I was even contemplating mortal sin, for this was an entirely new situation. I also knew no other Catholic women who appeared to be undergoing the same dilemma. I was isolated, and resented the fact that the only person I could - should - turn to for help and guidance was a celibate virgin priest whom I knew could only lay down the law and could not be expected to understand or sympathise with this new trauma. The firm strictures of the church which had hitherto been my guiding principles and source of strength, and which we were led to believe were a sanctuary of love and solace, now appeared cruel and neglectful and hopelessly at variance with my new world.

I had been abandoned in my hour of need. I questioned this, and I questioned particularly a definition of sin which covered what appeared to be normal behaviour, the protagonists of which were neither ogres nor devils, struck neither blind nor dumb. In other words, my first questioning of Catholicism arose not from doubts about the existence of God, for which I had all the answers, but from a growing awareness of my own sexuality. And for this there were no answers. I began to question more. I began to be more receptive to hitherto forbidden models of society, to other rationales of human behaviour, to academic disciplines I had never even heard of. Like St Paul, the answer came in a flash, at a social anthropology lecture on religion in primitive societies. Religion was a forceful way of controlling and sanctioning human behaviour. If it was true for African tribes (the same tribes I would pray for in my youth), then it was true for us. I understood that man was not made in the image of God, but God in the image of man. Sins were not divinely declared axioms, but synonyms for anti-social behaviour. They were not immutable. The dilemma I was experiencing was unnecessary, for the sin I was contemplating was not a sin *per se*, but merely a human precept for moral behaviour. Religion, in other words – and this had to include Catholicism – was a form of political control. The reward of eternal glory was opiate indeed.

It was later that the women's movement provided a particular framework for understanding and expressing these experiences. My involvement with feminism was not because, as Catholics, we were offered models of women in authority – Reverend Mother, Our Lady - but because a recognition of female sexuality was accompanied by a fundamental questioning of the models and precepts for living with which I had been provided. Being a woman was incompatible with Catholicism. I do not believe that my experience was unique. As women, therefore, we became independent of the church, and independent women. That was our first statement; and it was a political statement. But the new world we entered, high on our personal liberation, could not live up to our expectations. It became rapidly and increasingly clear that being a woman was also incompatible with the secular view on women's role. My Catholic conscience forced me to speak out against a political system which failed to uphold values and freedoms for half the population.

Although there are now Catholic women who form a feminist lobby within the church (albeit with difficulty), for women of my – and earlier generations – there was no such alternative. We had no option but to leave. Catholicism formed a total world, an elaborate edifice which had endured for centuries and lived in our souls. But once that edifice was chinked, then it appeared as resilient as an inflatable. Our whole world collapsed. We had to build it anew, in ourselves and with our sisters, our new comrades in arms. And although this all happened nearly twenty years ago, it was a profoundly formative period in the lives of many Catholic women. If the fact of being a Catholic was a political statement even more so was its rejection by Catholic women. But my name is still Mary.

Postscript

A few years ago a close friend of mine from university days was killed, along with her husband. The joint funeral was held in a small, ancient flint church in a Sussex village. Many of her old student friends came to the funeral, including myself and another, Jewish, friend called Steve. The emotions, the sentiments were shared by us all but the form, the words, the hymns and the tunes of the Anglican funeral were as alien to him as they were to me. The Jew and the Catholic could pay silent respects only.

Class

4
Martyrs of class

MIRANDA CHAYTOR

Englishness feels a fragile identity. It relies on nostalgia for emotional power, feeds off our childhood memories of smaller, less abstract forms of belonging – to a household, neighbourhood, landscape. Patriotism draws on these images (part memories, part fantasies), exploiting our homesickness; which is probably why I'm immune to it – or would like to be. But then I have no sense of being English that I can separate from my early experience of class.

My father was a baronet. I grew up in a castle in County Durham, surrounded – half a mile down the back drive, two miles up the front – by pit villages and small tenant farms. It was a very poor part of England.

In the early 1950s we had servants – a gamekeeper, woodman, boilerman, gardener, nurserymaids, nanny, a housemaid, a butler and cook. And there were animals, though many of them were dead. The gamekeeper trapped weasels and crows, nailed their corpses to a gibbet and left them to rot. Stuffed jays, stoats and salmon lived in glass cases piled to the ceiling in unvisited storerooms. A few yards from the backdoor there was a graveyard for dogs – a trim rectangle of yew hedge enclosing the remains of previous labradors whose names were recorded on headstones.

Animals belonged, but servants, who came and went from my childhood without explanation, seemed less like us; my father at the end of an immense mahogany table, my mother on one side, me on the other, picking at our lunch watched from the walls by the ancestors.

Castle, servant, ancestor – words that freeze in my throat as though in mentioning them in public I'm recording something shamefully intimate. And maybe I am, for class consciousness doesn't wait for a sense of the public political world; its unspoken significance could be felt in the nursery, providing an idiom through which ordinary childhood fears and hostility were learnt and lived out. The distress these images evoke has little to do with my adult beliefs. It was there from the start.

Occasionally, perhaps once a year, the grounds were open to 'the public'. Small boys climbed on to the battlements and peered through the nursery windows until the curtains were drawn – pale-faced, insolent, curious. In retrospect, I realise it's my face staring out I'm describing.

Class began properly at the end of the drive. It was visible in the slag heaps and pitted fields full of poisonous ragwort, the untidy fences patched with barbed wire and sheets of corrugated iron – a bleak, makeshift countryside without any people; because I was frightened to look at them when we passed in the car; because it was only the natural world that had social significance.

Local people – tenants, old men on street corners, boys from the village who impinged on our lives as poachers – were visible, but we saw them as part of the landscape; like their derelict cottages and poorly-farmed fields, they were signifiers of deprivation and hopelessness. The countryside carried their poverty; ours as well, for we twisted the meanings of both nature and class, investing them with our personal, less accountable distress.

The landscape was a metaphor for my mother's sadness. Slag heaps, wire and poisonous weeds (dangerous to horses and cattle, inhospitable to the hunt) were symbols of privation, a focus for her disappointment with the fairytale castle that failed her. She wanted more glamour and cosiness – racehorses, thatched stable yards, wistaria and geraniums in tubs, a prettier prosperity which would hide class divisions and cruelties.

But our environment was too grim to give pleasure or pamper us. We couldn't not notice the impoverished landscape, so we deformed its significance and believed it was us it deprived. Even the peacocks looked ill and bedraggled; and they disturbed our sleep with their screeching, shat on the steps and pecked the heads off the tulips. Beds of decapitated flowers showed that our surroundings bore us ill-will; there was an unending sense of things being unfairly withheld, 'we never had any decent flowers in the house'.

Such callousness made us afraid. We sensed that the neighbourhood was to blame, but because working-class people were only an aspect of nature (inhuman, immutable), their menace was felt metaphorically – carried in the bodies of animals who were credited with a fragility and disappointment like ours. The lawns were covered with rabbits dying of myxomatosis; poachers threw stones at the swan and broke its leg; the cat was caught in a trap, bit off its paw and limped home to die.

I tell myself not to exaggerate. I don't, but my memories are very selective. Englishness seems inseparable from class; and remembering class, it's images of animals – dead, imprisoned, diseased – that recur. They had a pathos to mirror our own.

Besides, their plight implied somebody's cruelty. Not ours of course; it was the outdoor servants and poachers who exploited the vulnerable. In this silent class war we maintained a bewildered timidity which protected our power. I never sabotaged the mole traps or freed the crows from their wire-netting pen (they were tempted in with a handful of corn, then left to starve). I never rescued anything, because tormented helplessness, even for a four-year-old of my class, was the only imaginable stance? I don't know.

It's said that an early awareness of social injustice, however confused, is easily turned into socialism. I don't see why this should be, though I'm thankful that's the way it's turned out. But I'm certain class frightens me today because it was frightening then. We inhabited a country so inhospitable even the ponies and donkey fell ill – with laminitis, sweet-itch and stringhalt, equine diseases whose names and prognosis (incurable) were among the first adult words of my childhood, indelibly part of myself.

With reason, perhaps, for our suffering was what made us nice – a tenacious fiction which I'd feel better forgetting. But each time I try to set down 'the facts' of what may have been an average upper-class childhood (the obsession with animals isn't untypical), some sentimental memory intrudes – our sympathy for foxes, for instance. Though we were in favour of hunting, we felt for the victim; following the hounds in her car, my mother longed to protect it, sad that the dear woolly creature didn't hide under her rug or share a thermos of soup. My history is sweetened with sentiment. Our thwarted kindliness is caught up in the narrative, inseparable from the callousness – intuited but always displaced – that our existence maintained.

It was a kindliness that erased all human life from the landscape, leaving animals to represent our complaints. Sometimes, on the way to dancing class or the dentist, we passed a black and white pony pulling a cart up the hill. Identifying with its down-trodden look, we used to drive slowly alongside, baring our teeth at the owner – a middle-aged man who sat on the back of the cart, swinging his legs. He always ignored this wordless, no doubt incomprehensible command. (Upper-class people walked if their horses seemed tired and the hill was steep.) I've almost forgotten the man, I never looked at his face; but the pony (distorted metaphor for exploitation and bullying) still recurs in my dreams.

Did it really happen? Why do I remember it like this? Why do I remember it at all? I have no sense that these images are accurate history. How could they be when we re-invent our childhoods continuously, picking out strands of the past to make sense of the way we are now? Memories are never free from the needs of the present, but they aren't fictions either – at least not fixed or predictable ones. The past may not have happened like that, but through being remembered and ordered it takes on meaning.

If I were to write about the incidents that shaped my earliest perceptions of gender, perversely (or not, for as a woman I 'really was' born on the side of the subordinate) I'd tell different, prouder stories, or the same stories in another way; by the time I was five, I could ride, skin a rabbit, collect the rent from the farms . . .

And nationality? The English (before I was nine and went to school, met foreigners, had a passport, learnt English history) were people on the wireless, in *The Archers* and *Mrs Dale's Diary* – a more reassuring southern, sunlit country than ours. But *Music While You Work* was on (and enjoyed) every morning in the kitchen while the indoor servants had coffee and the butler taught me to foxtrot. We can't have been the listeners the BBC had in mind.

5
C stream on Tyneside

DAVE DOUGLASS

11-plus

'St Patrick's, not Willowgrove!' This was to be the last period of school, the geet skuel. It stood on a bank with rolling raggy rock covered and snatcheted with grass in a little plateau, over the end of which was a steep drop of mud to an area unseen from the staffroom. The swallie was the scene of all things unallowed – crime, pain, sex and self abuse. Here was the coming of tribes, the young St Johns, the young St Albins now together as the new intake . . . the third year 'big lads' now the fourth year gaffers, last year's first years now the kings of the roost. We knaa nowts were at the bottom.

When had 'education' ever had owt ti dee wi gaanin ti skuel? An when had skuel ever had owt ti dee wi 'education'. Suddenly on the verge of puberty, of which I knew even less, here I was, a victim of it. True, the daft lads were allowed to walk around the pipes on the wall of the class at the 'bottom' school, while we did colouring and sums; the daft lads couldn't take books home, but I could; but school had never seemed to be owt more than the playground.

How did I learn to read? Ancient memories revive still the colourful three pirates, the letter-by-letter recognition before that, the sisters reading to me, the reading back and having a hug, the dressing of the little book in my mammy's spare wallpaper to make a cover, but a system of sitting and consciously learning had never been on the scene.

When the bus left little St Johns there were no divisions, we were mental, we dived from seat to seat, we fought on the floor, we fired catapults from the windows, we stamped and sang until the bus driver went on strike, then we sat in. Teachers, brought in cars, demanded we leave the bus; they were met by tickets from lackie-band finger-tightened catapults. 'I want you boys off this bus now!' and the hard Fellin lads would sing bare-faced 'Gaan yem yi bums gaan yem yi bums gaan yem yi bums gaan yem', to the tune of 'Ad Laangs Syen', and we who really needed to get home for dinner joined in from behind the shelter of the bus seats. One by one the struggling boys would be dragged from the bottom deck of the bus, until all were dancing and singing on the pavements, then the lasses upstairs would start, a few smacks from lackie-band ticket projectiles, and a more sedate, but none the less rowdy, 'EEH the driver's got the wind-up EEH the driver's got the wind-up', to the tune of 'John Brown's Body'. We were nowt if not musically inventive.

Prior to the 11-plus some people got special red forms to fill in and to work on in classes while the rest of us just got on with the three, four or five or any number of pirate books and colouring in, and endless chanting of the tables.

SMACK on the desk with the cane, and the class in line from the front:

> Ones two is two
> Two twos are four
> Three twos are six
> Four twos are eight

and in rhythm nobody it seems had taught us we went on

> Eight twos are sixteen
> Nine twos are eighteen

but the red forms were elsewhere. They weren't in the table. They were old 11-plus exam forms. Some kids had been chosen, but none of us, even the chosen ones, had ever been in an exam before.

The exam day was a special day, special clothes day, but not like the confirmation where nobody fails, but we had that yet to learn. The air in the classroom hung heavy, the teachers' expressions drawn, the school in semi-silence, and the mind runs back to years before . . . like a funeral home . . . 'You are reminded that older pupils are today sitting their 11-plus, so there will be no playing of noisy games today.'

Doon wi sat. Handed clean sheets of paper and folded pink exam papers which sat closed on the starting line. At least ah cud read, though ah niver knew huw. 'Right!' (on your marks). 'You may now start.'

English paper? English *Comp-re-hension*? Comprybloodyhension? What the hell was that? A'h luked aroond aboot ti jest, but the teacher's eyes caught mine. 'WORK' came the simple word of command, but not before a'h had seen the heeds shek in disbelief, or faces transfixed in the stare of blissful ignorance.

English comprehension . . . A little bit of a story. In my haste to understand I noticed not the list of questions beneath, or thought them another part of the test. The idea, a'h concluded, was to continue the story out of your own head. A'h was good at stories, so away a'h went page after page after page until the bell went and a'h swaggered out feeling a'hd done well, it was a good story.

When next the class reconvened, we were more at ease, until the papers came. Maths. Maths? Up until that day wi called them *sums*. Addie-ups and tek-awa's wasn't bad, but this, this was maths. It might as weel hev been double Dutch, pages of strange squiggles, odd alphabets, the object surely was to find the missing object among the random type? A'h found a few ducks, and something that looked like a gate-post, but that a'h only did to pass the time on, a'h nivor wrote it doon. Elsewhere in the class the raggy lads spent their time trying to make the people who were writing laugh. Some kids were writing; these were the well-dressed strange kids who somehow had had old exam papers previous. On reflection they had been oft times ushered into silent corners of classrooms because they 'could work on their own', or so it was said.

Failed, of course, but that wasn't too hard to bear; so had all the kiddhas, only the odd specky willie had got through, and, besplendent in badge, blazer and brief case, they were now Grammar School Kids, poshies stroke softies – being posh and soft were synonymous to us. Kevin Garfy had got through. A butt of endless bullying amusement, he was a 'mammie's lad'. Never sweared, until that is the day we all surrounded him in the yard. 'Swear or wi'l belt yee! Swear or wi'l belt yee!' 'Err!' the wriggling asthmatic poshy groaned. 'Swear!' The grips tightening round the unfortunate throat. 'Pump! Pump!' he yelled in the same instant as his eyes enlarged in the full consciousness of the foul vulgar sound of the dirty words which had come from his mouth. We buckled at the knees and generally collapsed over walls in silent body-shaking manic laughter. It was to bring years of mirth; the sight of a blazer brought the instant response 'Pump!' and renewed piss-taking and merriment.

Mind, some must have been bothered about that exam, since kids had been offered bikes, suits, or roller skates if they did well. Doing well meant the grammar school, meant the first rung out of the working class, meant a step to the private house and not the council estate. But few went, so for all but the kids gifted enough to be allowed to work on their own with the past exam papers and force-fed the educational equivalent of the queen bee nutrients, it was not to be.

Secondary modern

The maelstrom of the secondary school, the cacophony of puberty, past friendships, big boys, elder brothers and sisters and the grip of expectancy. Bunched in the new school yard, boys dived about cocking each other, hand rammed hard over your own balls, the other cupped in a crab grabbing out at another suitably defended. For those not so on guard the unexpected grab from an assailant was excruciatingly painful.

Young Teds hung around, shouldered walls, dragged at woodbine dumps held in a safety pin to extract the last drag, little eyes screwed tight against the acrid smoke.

At last the bell for the start of this first day went, we were all marched into the assembly hall, packed us at the front, eldest at the back. The rest were lined up in classes, we were as yet classless. We packed together in a knot of excitement and terror, unsegregated; we didn't know, but in a second we would be graded, some of us destined to become thick, others bright.

Names and grades read out.

'1A. Ken Lowes.' Up till now we had all thought wasells pritty much the same as each other, as good as each other, 'John Norman', 'Paul Murphy', 'William Bell', and so it went. At the end of the list MY name had not been called. I counted every line in the wood floor, I'm not one of the best, not one that the thin-faced headmaster had called 'bright'. The voices of people congratulating each other drifted around, the blood rushed to me face, friends were drifting apart, people in different classes rarely were to mix during the rest of their school lives. The tears weren't far away. Next.

'1B. Johnny Trainor, Michael Bailly, Tom Doyle.' The heart was racing, the eyes ablaze with tears, the head bowed low, a'h wasn't there either. Sick with indignity, loss of pride, my quiet opinion of myself as being quite clever.

Finally 1C. The C stung like a backhand across the face; it would be a badge of shame at school, it would be carried afterwards, it would be repeated to interested-looking personnel managers who would do a little cough or laugh out loud. 'Michael Quinn, Kathleen Mulroy, David Douglass, Thomas Dafter' (howls of laughter, 'He's in the reet class') and the rest, the bottom of the heap, the abandoned ones, the dunces, the thickies, knaa nowts.

As the newly-assigned classes milled and, confused, marched off in the directions of their new status, a teacher's shrill voice rang out, 'Right, now the rag, tag and bobtail, quick march, that means walk fast over here!'

In normal circumstances the ring of the bell meant release, it meant outside. This time it was the signal for protracted agony, as groups gathered in the yard to interrogate each other on which classes they were in, sorrowfully hanging the head, blushing with shame, greeted with sneers, the bottom of the whole school. 'Gaanin Yem', lads yelled from the turned-round position of the front seat, 'Yee kid, what class yee in?', and the admission needs must be shouted too, 'A'aa he's a C walla.' Walking towards the door, up the street, wives hingin ower the fence, 'Aye wor Kevin gorina A class yee knaa, eeeam that pleased, Ah've telt him yee wor'c hard at the skuel and thou'l nothati gaan doon the pit.' The sobs started to break before A'h got the gate open, the folks was waiting expectantly for my first day return from the seniors. I had considered lying.

Earlier, as we were drawn into the big assembly hall, I had a mental picture of me flying through the back door and shouting 'Guess which class?' I had almost rehearsed the scene. Now it was set for a different play. I slumped through the back door, swallowed against the sobs and announced my public stupidity. Nowt was said, though I sensed their disappointment. I had let them down.

We had been told in the hall that at the end of every year kids could be moved up a class or down a class. Every year in that assembly we relived the horror. Though the indignity had gone, the heart still pounded at the roll call – 2As, 2Bs, and of course us. Cs first year, second year, third year, and the misery of miseries as the fourth year began . . . Douglass 4C. In an age of scant work, the secondary school offered little enough recommendation of work; the B-stream kid was going to find it tough . . . but a C-class lifer? As teachers throughout our school lives were to remind us, 'What employer is going to take you scruffy lot?' What indeed.

A class war of sorts

The teachers, without exception, hated the C streams. We were the stupid, sometimes dirty, illiterate, violent and stubborn morass of rudeness. From the first week on, we would don the armour of thickness; they called us thick – we would show just how thick we could be. We became expert at the blank, uncomprehending stare, the painfully slow turn of the head, the deathly slow walk, the aura from head to toe that would henceforth reek of resentment. Teachers were aggressive foes, or else soft shites whom we could bait in retaliation for those who were. Once or twice a silly bastard would drift in and out of our lives who actually tried to interest us in something. Whenever they got us actually collaborating, though, the other teachers hated them, resented them, publicly argued with them and blocked the thickos getting anything which might appear too good for them.

The headmaster was a small wiry non-dialect Geordie, who at times could look searching into the dead eyes of feigned ignorance and keek like a detective for a clue of intelligent life. At other times he was capable of monumental violence, a show trial before the school, girls and teachers alike, four boys dragged from the ranks, guilty of theft in the Fellin. Dragged by the hair, the boy slipping on the floor, the head grabbing at the struggling body, cane in hand, dragged to the stage, pushed to mount it, falling against the wood edge, cry of pain, air charged with sick violence, the anger of injustice, the big thick woodwork teacher dragging two others down the hall, one fighting, the head flaying like a cavalry officer with the stick across the legs, dragging the hand out, whacking it with fearful thrusts, smacks across the side of the heads ringing throughout the hall, girls crying out loud, and mild-mannered female teachers hiding their faces in their hands. The thug woodwork teacher gripping the lapels of a boy and shaking and shaking, 'Hand out, Finnigan, hand out, take your punishment!' The lads stand, impotent and shaking with anger, tears of anger, fists clenched, 'Bastards, bastards', A collective anger, us and them. 'Bastards!' Windows would feel the edge of the vented anger, as would buildings and machines on sites. The bastards!

The cane was no. 1 instrument of control. It stood on the top of the blackboard, or it lay exposed across the top of the desk. It was used day in day out. Twice a day, three times a day, it fell, with the swoooooo, barely-audible sound of a wicked stroke, accompanied by the lick of sadism as the teacher's tongue slid from the slit of a mouth as the cane found its mark. Offences? Who needed offences? You were a thick child of the grubby working class: they were the masters and mistresses of a detention centre. Yes, others *might* have schools but this must surely be a place of penal correction. Lads would get the cane every day, lasses sometimes, less regularly. Capital offences? 'Talking'. 'Talking?' What monstrous crime is this – talking? I was later to hear a self-proclaimed Fellin teacher announce that, yes, he used the cane, because the pupils wouldn't listen to him! 'Whey the bliddy hell want ti listen ti yee?' I asked. 'An if a'h divind, are yee gaana hit me?' Of course no such outrage would be tolerated, not least coz out of school teachers can find themselves spread over pavements. Talking and laughing. 'Who laughed? Come on, own up, the boy or girl who laughed.' (Nobody laughing now, eyes flicked from side to side.) 'Right, the punishment, the whole class caned.' Line on line, girls and boys, marching down the aisle, while the adult lashed out one after the other, the first encounter with solidarity, you don't tell tales. Us and them.

The school of the classroom was one of sullen resistance, or else electric struggle, clashing the desk lid, fifty at a time, rather instantly one after the other, the sneck which held it in place being whipped away by a sudden movement of the ruler, and bang, bang, bang, before the teacher could even turn round. The teacher leaving the classroom was the abandonment of the tigers to their own devices – BEDLAM.

The nib wood pen was a deadly weapon, especially dipped in the inkwell. Terrorist armoury, the straw. We received third-pint bottles of milk as part of the legacy of the 1945 Welfare State, and straws to drink it with. The straw, filled with ink with a nib, delivered a sting and five inches of ink on any target. The air was thick with missiles as the softy teacher walks back through the door; a second of restraint, then back with the bedlam. 'STOP IT! Stop!' Words meant nowt, the pens still fly, the girls pelt inkwells, the walls become splashed, the teacher runs back and forth, grabs here and there, the kiddha throws the offending arm off, 'GERROFFIS'. Teachers from other classes then invade the class, cuff, belt and drag the pupils, 'Dare to struggle?', the struggle continues. Kiddhas out of their seats, wrestle and mock, roll on the floor, the softy teacher in tears, the class is triumphant, the head is sent for. The punishment is hard and cruel, but as the class subsides to leaders being thrashed, the heartbeat continues – a one for us. The softy and the cruel bastards knew if the head was sent for they had failed, we had won a tiny victory. A flogging might follow, but we never succumbed. They thought us little bastards; they still look back and think that. We were, too!

Geordie, a credential of resistance. It was a mark of our resistance to authority and all attempts to anglicise us. Replying to teachers' questions in 'slang', as they called it, was cheek and instantly punishable.

'Finnigan, come out here.'
'Whey?'
'What did you say?'
'That's reet.'
The teacher grabs for the cane and makes to go down the line

toward the risen militant, who leaps to his feet and puts his fists up in a boxing stance, 'Divind yee touch me mind. A'hs warn'n ye, dinnet touch me!' Walks up the line looking towards the door and flight. The teacher grabs him by the collar, the lad whips round, teeth gritted, eye narrowed in fury and, amid a continuous cheer from the class and a few 'Yahoos!', he punches the teacher full in the jaw. The jaw both fell open and leapt back of its own free will. Finnigan, a flash of black shirt and greased hair going through the door and out down the corridors to temporary freedom. His return, to some terrible fate a day or two later, was greeted by a hero's welcome, the lads of all classes lining the fence and cheering. A class kids, 'Hey, kid, that was great', 'Weel dun kiddha.'

Spontaneous collective resistance was the most exciting. Playtime a multitude of different games, quite independent of each other, kingo, football, horseback fights, tuggy. Out walks the teacher and blows the whistle. Nobody stops playing. He blows the whistle, which is echoed by the kids round the yard, but nobody stops playing. Teacher goes back into the school and returns with reinforcements carrying canes, individuals are dragged off their sport, cuffed, caned and slung along the corridors until resistance bit by bit collapses and the lines sluggishly form up to be marched off.

A race against time when one of the meedmen left the class to gaan th netty (although enforced English meant asking 'to leave the room'). Sneaking up outside the open window of the marra's class and wait till the booming voice of the teacher was in full flight, 'How baldy heed, shut ya daft hole!' Consternation from inside the class, baldy heed attempting to climb on to a hot water pipe to see who his assailant is, while the class camps up the laughter to the point of hysterics, young Teds laugh 'HAAR, HAAAR, HAAAAR'. Meantime, away like hell back to ya own class before being sighted. In winter it would be a snowball lobbed through the window, in summer a clayball, bursting like a scatter bomb on the table or floor before the shocked teacher. Most C class wallas kept ti themselves, lack of communication with teachers extended to other classes. They were the hard lads, faces could chop sticks on, heads you could nut all day without making a dint. Their weak spot was sport; non cooperation, hatred and outright violence against teachers could be diverted by holding up the bone of a football or handball match. They hated being inside, hated the indoors, hated the lessons such as they were, peered out of the windows like captive birds. Some would be illiterate on leaving school.

A-stream kids came from smaller families. Dads tended to be craftsmen engineers, welders. They actually did some schoolwork, even some homework, tended to be brainier, Cliver. No match in fights with the thickies in the C class, though certain of them gave as good as any could give them. In general Cliverness meant also softieness; hard Geordie meant hard lad, lack of accent meant softie. Geordie a badge of hardness. Taalkin posh or 'properly' or English meant collaboration, sneak, crawler, softie.

B streams were a mixture of both, straddling the other class alliances. For years I thought the class war was the battle between A streams and C streams, about snobbery at the grammar schools. It is a mind-blowing experience to learn that above grammar schools are private schools, upper class private schools, and upper upper-class 'mind ya croon's slipping' schools.

C-class wallas had problems stopping their noses running, had problems wiping their arses properly, had difficulty getting clothes to fit them, but were first with Ted gear handed down from older brothers. C-class wallas got in *real* gangs with big lads, got hammered, had knuckles like gorillas, permanently exuding a smell of melting marge and inner resentment.

Charlie Brown was our folk hero – not the later Peanuts character, who anyway is an intellectual, a creature which in later years would produce pain in the gills from forced laughter, non-comprehending humour, a sleight-of-hand humour, which wasn't at all funny, was, I was told, 'cynical humour', but was just a drawing of a dog thinking non-understandable things. Nor, wor Charlie Brown was the Ted, true a US Ted, but we imagined him, be-jeaned, drain-piped, the home-sown variety, the shrunk-in-the-bath variety, the lap a-lang length of jean material and buck stitch like a Frankenstein face into 12-inch bottom variety.

> Who walks in the class room?
> Cool and slow!

Bliddy hell, hear that, hear that, 'cool and *slow*'?

The thick wedge, walk a million foot high, bounce on the heel, swivel on the bridge, but slow variety.

> Who calls the English teacher Daddio?

'Dafter', head turns like a 78-rpm zombie, transits slowly all the class, eyes bouncing like the wedges, up down, side side, corners come to bear with the outside of a teacher's face, but ower lowe, up the heed slaw, deed slaw, eyes come fixed with the teacher's eyes in the stare that reads mutually 'THICK PIG'. 'Eh?'

> Charlie Brown, Charlie Brown
> He's a clown

'Clown Trainor', the art teacher swiping at the six-foot boy whose neck would stand the weight of a gorilla's swipe, a Mrs Doyle swipe, a loud waap around the skull. Ignored like a mite bite, the clown carries on.

> He's goona get caught, just you wait and see.
> 'Why is everybody always picking on me?'

Gerrofis, Tommy Bone, son and grandson of colliers, probably great-grandson and great-great-grandson of colliers, Heworth pit lad, 'Didn't thou call me coward', with a direct punch ti the headmaster. Throttled by the deputy, crashed again the wall, up kicking and fighting.

> Who's always goofin in the hall

Sneak up playtimes or dinner times, gives the staffroom door a kick or the buuuurrrrp fart sound with stiff fingers we have perfected as the 'gang' symbol. Then away ti fuck, down screaming the corridors the call shout trailing ahint 'meeeeeed'.

> Who's always writing on the wall?
> Who's always heading for a fall?

'This is them, the cynics', that's what the deputy head, a woodwork teacher, called us, rounding us up for the first time, class by class, dragging us out of desks, identifying our strange interstreaming relationship. Failure of any one of us to volunteer for the school sports. Football? Na. Heeders? Na. Bag race? Na. Cricket? Na. Rounders? Na. Egg and spoon? Na. Na! Sport was collaboration, games was collaboration. Run roond daft and let the teachers think they had yee? Ney chance, ney chance. Instead to stand and gourk at the hard lads, runnin round daft, while teachers twittered 'Well done'. Not for the Meedmen.

> He's gonna get caught,
> Just you wait and see.

This lad Minchella, Italian probably, some of their roots were laid in the Fellin, his name meant nowt, one o the leyds. Discovered sex, with his ma's tits hanging oota a neetgoon. Shocked us all inti laughter, saying how he'd come inti his ma's bedroom and she leaned ower and her tits fell out, first he'd seen, said ti the leyds 'A'h cud o jumped on her and shagged her!'

A quick mental resumé of what wor Ma's wes like revealed that there wes nen of us what wad shag them, *but* Toni's ma wes young, very young, the tits he assured us dinnae droop but stuck up from all clothing and attempts to hide them. A delegation was arranged to allow inspection of Toni's mam's tits, whereupon all were agreed to a grand conspiracy to have her screw the whole gang. We were halfway through the plan, with a couple of the lads already 'inadvertently' exposing themselves with colossal teenage hard-ons, when Toni got nicked for firework stealing in Fellin Square Woolworths.

> Why is everybody always picking on me?
>
> Who walks in the class room cool and slow
> Who calls the English teacher Daddio?
>
> Charlie Brown
> He's a clown
> Charlie Brown
> He's a clown
> He's gonna get caught
> Just you wait and see
>
> Why is everybody always picking on me?
>
> Who's always goofing in the hall?
> Who's always writing on the wall?
> Who's always heading for a fall?
>
> That's *me*.
> Who me?
> Yes, you.

The Meedmen, where did they come from? A slow process of initiation, led by Ben, the leader. He gathered in those who were part. We dared, together. We weren't the hardest in the school, though some were hard. We weren't the thickest; in fact we were probably the most intelligent, though we aspired to hide it from all but ourselves. We aspired to the thickness of my C-stream marras, we perfected and bettered their sullenness. We were soft really, most of us, though we hardened wasells almost to the point where we removed feeling . . . in the day time . . . wi the gang. What we became were the best screwers in the skuel, the advice centre, the set-up crowd for shags, the friends who had friends who could tak ya heed off if necessary. Among our ranks would come the heed men. But fora mock, herbit mock, meedness and herbitmock, the twin slogans and desire of wa puberty and resistance.

The strange alliance of dissent, A streams with a thicko from the C class, was an oddity of common location and a secret rarely-exposed intelligence. The meed men were *thick* but not dense. Not being dense and being in a C stream was an immediate point of conflict with the C-stream teachers, who seen any spark of intellectual ability as an assertion of 'cockyness' and of 'cleverness'.

Books

A fascination with naval history and ships took me to the adult section of the Felling Library, to browse in awe at the shelf full of navy books. Having adult books and being a C-stream walla often required hiding the books from the eyes of teachers.

As teenage fascination in the weird and unexplained took me to the shelves of flying saucers, sea monsters, man apes, abominable snowmen, the Loch Ness beast and other phenomena, so the books grew thicker. 'DOUGLASS!' The red-faced deputy-Head bellowed down the corridors, as I walked within striking distance. The book of monsters is savagely snatched from the hand, the corridor is full of inmates streaming into classes, watching, listening to the spectacle. 'Whose is *this*?', holding it like a dirty sock. 'Av borrid it.' A mocking scathing twist of a page, flick of a leaf, the cynical sneer. 'Who reads you this?' 'Ah read mesell.' 'Oh, and who taught you to do that?' 'Not yea, forra start.' That's it, book drops to the floor, to lay abused with its spine spread down the open leafs, death-like grip on the hair, a forearm across the face to ram me into the wall. The titters from fellow-inmates, enjoying someone being shown up, now stops, grudging shuffling off down the corridors staring in hate at the class enemy. Other teachers, 'Get moving', 'Mind your own business', and, sprawling, pushed and cuffed, I am precipitated to the head's office.

It was always like that, a showing-up for trying to be clever, for having a book.

At times in my last year my hidden intellectualism broke out of the sullen defiance, the ancient headteacher used to pouring his eyes into the head of an empty pool, the still waters of perfected and socially engineered non-comprehension, when from the deep of the hidden cavern it would rear, uncalled. But the violence of words and innuendo found its mark and the wee unspoken thing of verbal and intellectual challenge would rise. Aye, rise and say something, challenge something, say something.

So it was with the books again.

So it was with the insult 'The thicko with a book again.'

In my last year, at fourteen, things started to come together. I discovered a book on *Russia, the Atom and the West*. I borrowed it, in an endeavour to see what this writer would say on all. I stood in the assembly, rank and rank, the rubbish of the prayers before the forgiving Christ in a non-forgiving school. I happened to be at the edge of my line, at the back, form four, when the ever-malevolent woodwork teacher strolled and snatched the book from behind. While the whole school stood in still silence, he shouted, 'I've got a book here' and thrust it back into my hands. 'What does it say?' he demanded. I read the title quietly to the woodwork teacher standing by my side, then he walked slowly to the front of the hall. 'What do they title that book?' I read 'Russia the atom and the West.' 'What class are you in?' '4C', I replied quietly. 'What class are you in, Mr Douglass?' '4C, sir' I replied so the whole school could hear. Then he took the book and walked down the giggling lines of first- through to fourth-year kids, handing me the book, saying 'By the time you know what *that* means, you'll have run up a fine. Here, Douglass, stick to things you understand.'

The blush covered my body from head to toe. I had not even turned the first page, could not yet have answered a single question on it, thought it would be heavy even when I took it from the shelf. I had intended to struggle with it and get something from it, on the understanding that I could read, and if it was printed I could fathom the words later. I never believed at fourteen there was a book I could make *nowt* of. But it didn't end there.

I was sitting at the desk, we was doing a rare assignment set by a young teacher to ease her conscience on what we thought of capital punishment. She asked us things like that. We had a point of view, but if you got caught by other teachers you'd get ridiculed, so it was a secret and the conspiracy, the thought-provoking exercise, worked, for we all had views and wanted to write them down, bad spelling, ink-blots and all. I was into my theme of World War Two *á la* Commando Comics and a few other references about Hitler, etc. when in strode the headmaster. 'Did a boy in this class have a book about Russia?' he asked. Only one boy in that class had ever had a book about any bloody thing. Quietly I put up the hand of subservient surrender. 'Come out here', he said, whip hand ready for the fast draw of the cane (although he didn't carry it).

The eyes peered the depth, the drawbridge didn't go up in time, a sparkle was still inside from the Commando Comics and capital punishment. He drew me outside the door, and asked confidentially, 'Who gave you this?' The conspiratorial implication was clear, the commies can 'get to kids' like the bogie man of earlier years will carry you off in his sack or 'interfere' with you. 'Nobody, sir. I took it off the library shelf.' 'But who told you to take this one?' 'Nobody sir. I just fancied the title!' 'So what do you think of Russia', he asked, smirking. 'Well', I began a half-finished philosophy not yet formed; in fact only the rudimentary outline of the first thought had formed. 'They were on our side in the war, and they fought against the Germans. Now people have turned against them.' The smirk left his face, 'Who told you that?' 'Nobody. I read it.' 'Who gave you the book with that in?' The interrogation had started. 'It wasn't one book – I read a lot about the war.' 'Is someone older telling you these things?' Eventually the dialogue ran out; I didn't know who Gaitskell was, my ideas on the Bomb were confined to wanting to know how it worked, and my opening line of philosophy had been used. 'You leave that book with me, Douglass. I'll see the library gets it back, and make sure you don't have any more of them. You'll be getting the wrong impression and turning away from your religion.'

When I went back in the class I put both hands under my armpits to create the impression I had been caned for something. A political discussion with the headmaster would not be understood.

6
Pride and prejudice: ladies and nurses in the Crimean War

ANNE SUMMERS

On 21 October 1854 Florence Nightingale set off with the first official party of female military nurses for Scutari, the base hospital for the British troops engaged in hostilities against Russia in the Crimea. She had been assisted in the selection of the nurses by her close friends Mary Stanley, daughter of the Bishop of Norwich, and Elizabeth Herbert, wife of the Secretary of State at War. On leaving, she entrusted to them the task of interviewing, selecting and, where necessary, arranging the training of the candidates who might be required to reinforce the members of the original party. By the beginning of December 1854 a second nursing party was ready to leave England. The women were assembled at the house of the Secretary of State at War to hear a solemn address on the dangers and difficulties of their undertaking. 'If you behave yourselves well,' Sidney Herbert warned them, 'there will be a provision for you; if not, it will be the ruin of you.' He went on to say 'that we all went out on the same footing as hospital nurses, and that no one was to consider herself as in any way above her companions.'[1] Herbert's first warning was directed at the paid nurses in the party; the second was intended for the 'lady volunteers'. In the circumstances of the time, it was a startling remark to address to a group composed of twenty-one working women with a variety of experience in paid nursing for the sick, fifteen Roman Catholic Sisters of Mercy from Ireland, and ten 'ladies' without experience of paid employment or affiliation to any nursing institution.[2] What kind of relationship could possibly exist between these women? The disputes and antagonisms which developed between them, and the manner in which they were resolved, form the subject of this paper. Although the story of the ladies and nurses is, on the surface, a petty and even farcical episode, it is none the less one which throws a very clear light on both the organisation of civilian and military nursing in the 1850s, and the nature of class relationships between women in the nineteenth century.

Much information about hospital nursing in this period, both within the army and outside it, is widely accessible in printed histories.[3] It has to compete, however, with a welter of misconceptions born of hagiography, half-truths half-remembered from school projects on famous men and women. It therefore has to be emphasised here that British military nursing before the advent of Florence Nightingale was not just a confused affair of army wives and camp followers. The wards of general and regimental military hospitals were staffed by male orderlies, seconded from the combatant ranks, supervised by ward sergeants. They had a very little medical knowledge, were sometimes clumsy and callous, sometimes comradely and kind. No one in the army begged for female nurses to be sent out to the East in 1854. The medical officers' chief complaint was that as soon as the orderlies had gained enough experience to be really useful, they were returned to combatant duties. It was, indeed, the presence of this staff of orderlies which made it necessary to impose uniformity of rank upon the new female nurses.

In the large metropolitan hospitals at this time a clear hierarchy of nursing duties existed. Head nurses or sisters exercised a supervisory role, while nurses or ward-maids performed functions as much domestic as medical – 'the usual duties of a housemaid' – took charge of non-severe cases by day, and watched wards by night.[4] The women going out to Scutari would not be able to replicate this structure. They would find male orderlies assigned to the heavy domestic tasks there, cooking, fetching and carrying, cleaning, emptying the foul tubs; there was no room for a low grade of female nurses to perform the same functions. Nor was it possible to create a supervisory rank of nursing sisters to replace or compete with ward sergeants, for the hastily improvised female corps had no official grading within the military hospital system. The female nurses would simply have to supplement existing nursing provision in an *ad hoc* fashion, according to the differing wishes of individual hospital doctors, and priorities to be decided by the latter on the spot.[5] Clearly, it would only complicate matters if the female nurses had to be distinguished from the outset according to rank and function. Florence Nightingale had dealt with the problem of equal grading by engaging no 'lady volunteers', as such, in her original party. Those of her nurses who were not recruited from various hospitals were drawn from the religious and nursing sisterhoods, both Catholic and Anglican. Whatever their social background, all her nurses had experienced the discipline of full-time work in obedience to a female superior; this, she hoped, would make their supervision and deployment relatively easy for her.

Florence Nightingale was not a lonely pioneer in the field of nursing reform in the year 1854; nor was she the originator of the idea of a female nursing expedition to the seat of war. The question 'Why have we no Sisters of Charity?' asked in a celebrated letter to the *Times* of 14 October was either rhetorical or ill-informed. There was no scarcity of religious nursing orders in England. The problem lay in reconciling the interests of the different church groups which sponsored them, and which competed for the opportunity to cover themselves with glory in a national, rather than sectarian cause. The high church 'Catholicising' tendency of the Church of England was particularly vocal in promoting its women protegées. The Sisterhood of the Holy Cross, set up under the influence and guidance of the Rev. Pusey in 1845, and the Sisterhood of Mercy of Devonport and Plymouth, established by Pusey's friend Priscilla Lydia Sellon in 1848, between them contributed eight nursing sisters to the first war nursing party. (For convenience's sake these sisters will all be referred to as 'Sellonite' in this paper, although the two orders did not formally merge until 1856.) The Sellonites' chief experience of nursing was in the homes of the poor, especially during outbreaks of cholera in the Plymouth area in 1848, 1849 and 1853.[6] A further six nurses were supplied to the Nightingale party by St John's House Training Institution for Nurses.[7] This high church foundation had been established in 1848 following a public appeal by a group of prominent men such as the Bishop of London, W. E. Gladstone and the Rev. F. D. Maurice. It was run by an all-male council, it being 'quite clear that there are certain duties to be discharged for which these ladies by the peculiarities of their sex must be disqualified', and it was open only to Anglicans.

St John's was – very briefly – the one institution which united the ladies and nurses of the second and subsequent Crimean nursing parties, as through its agency two or three weeks' hospital training was arranged for them.[8] It was an 'open order', whose members did not take religious vows. Members were divided into three groups. First, probationers and nurses, whose training was to fit them for private and hospital work, and who were also expected to 'assist in such domestic duties of the house as may be assigned to them'. Second, the sisters, who helped to train the probationers, and visited the sick and aged poor in their homes; these paid for their own board and lodging, and did not accept any salary.

Finally, there were associate sisters, whose home ties did not permit residence, but who supported the work of the house generally. The constitution of St John's was based on a very determined confusion of the notions of social and spiritual superiority. It assumed that women of means were more spiritually endowed than working women, and deemed the former qualified to instruct the latter in the proper duties of a nurse, without themselves having to undergo any practical probation. These assumptions were fully endorsed by Mary Stanley. Early in 1854 she had published a small book, *Hospitals and Sisterhoods*, which summarised high church views on nursing reform. It was not just a question of replacing drunken Sarah Gamps with a more respectable class of women who could be trusted to cook, clean and attend to the patients' physical requirements. No matter how satisfactorily these tasks were carried out, the patients were not being properly cared for if their souls were not receiving the same degree of attention. An ordinary nurse rarely had the time to consider her patients' spiritual welfare; moreover, she was not to be credited with the capacity to steer them towards salvation. 'There must be a head nurse and an under one to each ward, as there are in London.'[9]

As we shall see, the ladies in the nursing parties which followed Florence Nightingale's trail hardly needed to be convinced that they were in every respect superior to their paid companions; but a confirmation of their existing prejudices which emanated from the world of hospital practice, and was legitimated by these new organisations of the church, was eagerly grasped by them and put to practical use.

I

We know very little of the personal histories of the ladies and nurses who served in the Crimean War hospitals. They were not recruited by War Office officials, but by the wives of government ministers. Their particulars were not systematically filed. Some of the ladies' 'war memoirs' provide interesting material, but they rarely mentioned the paid nurses by name, and frequently employ the frustrating convention of referring to members of the writers' own class as 'Miss A–' or 'Miss O–'. However, from the memoirs, from letters of application for nursing posts, from postwar testimonial letters, and from the histories of the Anglican sisterhood movement, some recognisable faces begin to emerge, and it is to be hoped that one day our acquaintance with these women will be less fragmentary than it is at present. What we have is at least enough to rescue the second and subsequent Crimean nursing parties from 'the enormous condescension of posterity'.

Florence Nightingale's gift for the sharp phrase bordered on the libellous; eagerly abetted by her most partisan and popular biographer, she has fixed Mary Stanley and her ladies in our vicarious memory as given to 'spiritual flirtation', and 'strolling about with notebooks in their hands'.[10] Most of them, however, were seriously interested in nursing, and dedicated to the work as they conceived it. Two died at their posts. Miss Clough was one of these. She joined the party, by her own admission, more for sentimental than philanthropic reasons. She wished to visit the grave at Devna of her officer sweetheart, a younger brother of Lord Panmure (the latter replaced Sidney Herbert as Secretary of State for War on the fall of the Aberdeen Government in January 1855). Together with other members of the party, she went to nurse in the General Hospital at Balaklava in January 1855, but left there in March to take charge of a regimental hospital for the Highland Brigade. She was the only woman to nurse in a regimental hospital during the war (all the other female nurses were at base hospitals well away from the front); she went to this isolated post at the request of Lord Raglan and Sir Colin Clyde, and against the opposition of both Mary Stanley and Florence Nightingale. She died there in September 1855 of 'prolonged fevers and diarrhoea'.[11]

Jane Shaw Stewart had a more professional interest in her work. She had trained in German and English hospitals before the war; immediately afterwards she investigated, as a participant observer, the working conditions of several major hospitals in London and Paris. She was a member of a wealthy landed Scottish family, and her brother was MP for Renfrewshire. She was successively superintendent of the General and Castle Hospitals at Balaklava, and of the Land Transport Corps Hospital. In 1861, reluctantly and under pressure from the dying Sidney Herbert who, with Florence Nightingale, believed her to be the only woman who could make a success of the new post, she became superintendent of female nurses at the military general hospital at Woolwich. Her period in office bore out all her predictions of disaster, and culminated in her resignation in 1868.[12]

Frances Margaret Taylor was, at twenty-two, the youngest of Mary Stanley's ladies; both ladies and nurses were supposed to be around the thirty mark. She was the daughter of a rural clergyman. At the age of sixteen or seventeen she had visited the Anglican Sisterhood of Mercy at Devonport and Plymouth, of which her elder sister was one of the first members, and worked with them in the homes of the poor suffering from the cholera outbreak of

1849. She did not subsequently choose to join the sisterhood but lived with her widowed mother in London, where she worked in hospital wards, visited the poor in their homes, and helped to found a ragged school. She underwent another period of hospital training after being selected as a military nurse. She and Mary Stanley were both received into the Roman Catholic church while in the East. After the war, she wrote a number of books, which successfully plugged a temporary gap in the family fortunes; became proprietor of *The Lamp*, a Catholic monthly periodical; and finally became Mother Magdalen Taylor, the foundress of an order called the Poor Servants of the Mother of God.[13]

These three, like Mary Stanley herself, were far from negligible women. Other ladies in their party may, indeed, have been less experienced or capable at the outset. One of the Irish nuns wrote that many of them had never seen a dead body, a statement endorsed by Fanny Taylor.[14] Such amateur status, however, can suggest absence of opportunity as much as absence of serious intent. A poignant letter of application from a Miss Nevins illustrated the plight of the lady who longed for a wider sphere of usefulness.

> I am well acquainted with every description of domestic nursing . . . often for many weeks at a time only leaving the sick room for needful refreshment and rest. I have frequently been trusted with a sick person when even the Doctor feared to depend on a regular trained nurse, and I always follow directions *implicitly* . . . I believe I have plenty of energy, and moral courage, and I hope sufficient physical to meet where required any duty, and I never break into Hysterics or fainted in my life.

She was 'some years past thirty', was 'one of a large family', and her father was 'a Country Gentleman of *small* Fortune living near Clifton' who had so far refused her permission to go to the Crimea, although her mother was willing. Her parents claimed to be worried about the danger to her health, but they may also have worried about their own in the absence of the family nurse. Another lady withdrew her application because her brother's wife had just died in childbirth, and it was henceforth her duty to bring up 'two motherless babes'. She begged to be kept in touch with the fortunes of the expedition.[15] There must have been many such ladies, whose families' expectations at once stimulated and frustrated a genuine interest in hospital work.

Of the paid nurses whom she selected for the first nursing party, Mary Stanley wrote[16]:

> I wish people who may hereafter complain of the women selected could have seen the set we had to choose from. All London was scoured for them. We sent emissaries in every direction to every likely place . . . We felt ashamed to have in the house such women as came. One alone expressed a wish to go from a good motive. Money was the only inducement.

As the paid nurses for the first two parties were hurriedly recruited in the space of barely six weeks, it is hardly surprising that they should have included a large quota of the financially desperate. Working women who had a secure livelihood were not very likely to sacrifice it for dangerous employment of uncertain duration. But financial desperation need not preclude other sentiments. Mary Stanley must have been of a very fixed cast of mind if she was unmoved by this application from Matilda Norman[17]:

> I am Soldgers Wife and my Husband is just gone out to the East . . . the Colonel been well satisfied with my Carertor thought I should be very usefull in the Regt but having heard that was being Nurses sent out I would do any thing to go for I there might be able to help him in is dieing moments I am Young and Strong and do not mind what I suffer should Sir you not think me Experienced I will try and get into a Horsepitll for a time I really do not recorse to fly to.

There were not, in this period, many models of interaction between women of different social classes. The only context in which gentlewomen were regularly and routinely brought into contact with women who were obliged to work for their living was through their employment of the latter as domestic servants. In this relationship, the working women could be re-made, if not in their mistresses' image, at least to the point where they could blend with the latter's environment and adapt to their sense of neatness, cleanliness, regularity and decorum. Domestic servants were often women who hoped to place their daughters in similar situations and who, in their own decrepit old age, might hope to be the object of their former mistresses' charity. They would be obedient, grateful women, dependent upon their employers for good references. Their mistresses, for their part, treated the women who were economically dependent upon them as weaker beings, morally as well as socially. At best, their pattern of domination was maternal as much as authoritarian; and they convinced themselves that their servants were grateful, not just for their paid employment, but for the social and moral instruction dispensed with it.

This model of relations between the classes could not contain working women of a more independent type. Hospital nurses worked for an institution rather than an individual; they had a special kind of market value arising from their willingness to perform extremely objectionable tasks; and on this account they were able, if they wished, to move fairly easily from one post to another.[18] They might be extremely diligent and efficient workers, but they were not cast in a respectful or deferential mould.

The confrontation between ladies and nurses in the Crimea was not just an unwonted conjunction of different classes of women; it was a collision of expectations in which the normal institutional arrangements of hospital work were opposed by the working assumptions and practices of the upper-class household. It may, indeed, be less true to say that Mary Stanley's ladies were influenced by the spiritual and social hierarchies embedded in the constitution of St John's House, than that the high church and sisterhood movement in hospital nursing was itself profoundly imprinted with the values of female domestic management in the households from which its acolytes and sympathisers were drawn.

II

Florence Nightingale arrived in Turkey at the beginning of November 1854 to a very mixed reception. Many of the army medical officers at Scutari were hostile to, others contemptuous of, the female nursing corps; above all, her privilege of direct communication with the Secretary at War – despite her nominal responsibility to the principal medical officer on the spot – and her association with the muck-raking *Times*, through the shared administration of its 'comforts' fund, aroused defensive suspicion. Sensitive to these stirrings, she was upset to learn that Mary Stanley had, without first ascertaining her wishes, set off from England with the second nursing party. The composition of the new group convinced her that the Herberts and Mary Stanley had been intriguing behind her back, both to reinforce the Catholic presence in the hospitals (Mary Stanley and Elizabeth Herbert were at this time moving towards conversion to Rome) and to strengthen the influence of the kind of philanthropic non-professional gentlewoman who Florence Nightingale did not consider to have any place in a hospital at all.

Her immediate reaction to the arrival of the Stanley party was to say that she had neither room nor work for them. This argument, however, could not be sustained: the second party had arrived at precisely the moment when army hospital provision was being expanded. The 'Stanleyite' presence was timely and necessary, and seems to have been genuinely welcomed by the doctors involved in setting up overflow accommodation for the sick and wounded.[19] Florence Nightingale eventually decided to accept five Irish nuns, three lady volunteers and one nurse from the Stanley party into the Scutari establishment. The rest of the new contingent cooled their heels in lodgings at Therapia until the new hospitals were opened in late January 1855.[20] On 23 January the General Hospital at Balaklava, in the Crimea itself, was re-opened and at the request of John Hall, the Inspector-General of Hospitals, a female nursing party was established there, led by the Sellonite Mother Eldress Emma Langston, of the original nursing party, and including two of Mary Stanley's ladies, Miss Clough and Jane Shaw Stewart, and a few of her nurses. A week later the rest of the Stanley party were settling into the new hospitals at Kulali, in Turkey.[21]

The migrations to Kulali and the General Hospital at Balaklava did not end the dispersion of the female nursing corps. By March Miss Clough had left Balaklava General Hospital to take charge of the regimental hospital of the Highland Brigade. Miss Shaw Stewart in mid-1855 went to introduce female nursing staff at the Castle Hospital, Balaklava; in 1856, still in the Crimea, she left the Castle to establish female nurses at the hospital of the Land Transport Corps. In autumn 1855 the work of Kulali was wound up, and Mother Bridgeman and the nuns of the Kinsale Convent of Mercy transferred from there to Balaklava General Hospital. Female nurses were also employed in two hospitals established entirely on voluntary civilian initiative at Smyrna and Renkioi in March and October 1855 respectively. Although the civilian doctors were recruited and paid on a separate basis from their military opposite numbers, the female nurses at Smyrna and Renkioi were recruited and equipped uniformly with the nurses at the military hospitals.[22]

By the spring of 1855 the female nursing experiment had already expanded beyond anything originally envisaged by Florence Nightingale. In mid-February, writing privately to Sidney Herbert, who was now out of office, she hinted that she could not effectively exercise the supervisory role with which she had been entrusted.[23] Certainly, by anathematising the Stanley party, she had made sure that misunderstandings would multiply between the different sections of the corps, and that her authority would be resented to the point of active resistance. Her persistent snubbing of Mary Stanley was, in the end, to prove extremely counterproductive for her. She refused to countenance the latter's requests for reinforcements to the Kulali nursing complement; in consequence, Mary

Stanley wrote independently to the London organisers of the nursing corps, and also turned increasingly to Lady Stratford de Redcliffe, wife of the British ambassador at Constantinople, for help. By the end of March nurses were being sent from London for Kulali, while Florence Nightingale's requests for staff at Scutari were being only partially met; and when Florence Nightingale tried to appoint the superintendent to replace Mary Stanley shortly before the latter's departure for England, Mary Stanley peremptorily returned the candidate to Scutari.[24]

These developments completely undermined Florence Nightingale's position as 'Superintendent of the female nursing establishment in the English General Military Hospitals in Turkey'. Her original commission had been effectively withdrawn within five months of her arrival in the east. Lady Stratford, whose earlier efforts with her husband to give assistance at Scutari, had provoked scathing comments from Florence Nightingale, was now put in charge of all arrangements and appointments at Kulali, and was in constant communication with the British Military Commandant in the Bosphorus.[25] The nurses at Smyrna were already under the direction of civilian doctors. Rev. Mother Bridgeman had, before leaving England, obtained recognition as sole authority over the Kinsale nuns.[26] The nursing staff who had gone out to Balaklava had placed themselves in direct communication with Inspector-General Hall and Lord Raglan, the Commander in Chief.[27] The bulk of the female nursing work of the Crimean War was, therefore, done outside Florence Nightingale's superintendence, and without reference to her ideas of professional practice. Ladies and sisters were left in full control of the organisation of nursing outside Scutari itself, and it thus became possible for them to subvert the terms on which they had originally been engaged.

III

'Fancy one's receiving people' wrote Miss Clough from Balaklava, 'in such a costume as a pepper and salt, dirty-looking, dressing-gown sort of a dress, a night cap, a blue *checked apron*, and a hospital badge across one's shoulder! Yet I feel as proud of my humble costume as many of those men are of their orders.'[28] Her attitude was unique among the ladies going to the East, who were utterly dismayed to discover that the consequence of taking up government service was to appear to all the world as domestic servants. One of the nuns in Mary Stanley's party reflected 'That ladies could be found to walk into such a costume was certainly a triumph of grace over nature.'[29] In most cases the triumph was exceedingly short-lived. Martha Nicol, who was sent to nurse at Smyrna, felt the inconveniences of the uniform before she had even left European soil, when she heard one of the orderlies 'accost one of the ladies of our party with the greatest familiarity, shouting with laughter, when she instinctively drew back, evidently thinking she was assuming a superiority which did not belong to her. I shall not repeat his conversation, which was coarse, and excessively free and easy; but it ended by his telling her, "He supposed she was hungry, and that there was a slap-up dinner waiting for her at the hotel!" '[30] The enormity of the offence lay not so much in the orderly's indirect reference to the lady's innards, but in his addressing her at all. Members of the servant class were not supposed to initiate conversations with their superiors. Domestic servants were not, indeed, supposed even to address each other before 'the ladies and gentlemen of the house' unless it were a matter of urgent necessity, when it should be 'as shortly as possible, and in a low voice'.[31] Fanny Taylor, too, felt the distress of the situation long before she reached Turkey: 'The ladies had suffered by it through the journey, for having no authority to restrain the hired nurses they were compelled to listen to the worst language, and to be treated not unfrequently with coarse insolence.'[32] Nevertheless, according to Martha Nicol 'the real evil was done to the nurses, who fancied that according to our descent in the social scale, was to be their ascent . . . the seeds of discontent and dissatisfaction were sown by their being told that we went out on the same footing'.[33]

It was more than *amour propre* which was at stake. The Stanley party was, as we have seen, refused admission to Scutari and forced to seek lodgings elsewhere, where they had not been expected, and where arrangements for domestic service had not been made. Somewhat rashly, as it might appear to a twentieth-century eye, 'Miss Stanley refused assistance from the English hotel in Therapia, thinking it best to employ the paid nurses in the household work which was to be performed.' This might have worked in St John's House, but it aroused among the paid contingent 'a strong inclination to strike work. "We are not come out to be cooks, housemaids, and washerwomen," and they dwelt considerably on Mr. Herbert's words about equality.' The next morning, after a 'kind address' by Mary Stanley, on the need for ' "Serving one another by love", each assisting to the best of her power in the work of the house as she should allot to them . . . some few of the nurses worked hard and willingly for the public good . . . most of the paid nurses performed their work with an air of infinite condescension' and one maintained her strike to the bitter end.[34] The Smyrna ladies experienced the same revolt when they established their living quarters: 'On the nurses first being asked, if they would come and work for us, they all refused, with the exception of Mrs. Gunning and Mrs. Butler; saying, "they came out as nurses, not to do housework." '[35]

The ladies considered the issue one of urgent physical necessity as well as social principle. Mary Stanley was on record as 'lamenting her inability to carry a coal-scuttle or lift a pail of water'. Fanny Taylor was amazed when one of her own rank in the party joined the group of nurses whom Mary Stanley subsequently appointed to do laundry work for the naval hospital at Therapia: 'There would be few ladies whose health would have enabled them to undertake such a labour.'[36] It was a relief to find that not all the nurses had been contaminated by the notion of equality. Some were 'hard-working, respectable and obliging'; and at Smyrna there was even a 'treasure': 'We had now seventeen nurses, one of whom, Mrs. Suter, acted as cook at our quarters . . . Not only was she kind and obliging as a servant, but she was one who thoroughly knew her place, and was never above doing anything to assist us, or add to our comforts in any and every way.'[37] However, the ladies did not wish to remain dependent upon the mere goodwill of their social inferiors. Promptly and energetically they set about altering the relative status of ladies and nurses on the spot, and redefining the conditions of the nurses' employment as laid down in London.

A simple first step was to cease wearing the same uniform. The Smyrna ladies kept to their grey dresses, but left off their 'badges', the strips of brown material bearing the name of the hospital embroidered in red. The Stanley party changed their dress. When a new party of ladies and nurses arrived at Kulali early in April, all clad alike in the noxious weeds, the welcoming ladies expressed 'our surprise and vexation' at the fact that 'the home authorities had not thought well to learn experience from those who had to struggle with difficulties on the spot'. They soon persuaded the new arrivals of their own class to follow their example in the matter of dress.[38] More far-reaching measures followed, to establish distance between the classes. The nurses were not allowed in the wards except under the ladies' supervision. This was explained with reference to the medical needs of the patients: 'Not a single one, except Mrs. Woodward, could be trusted alone. They would give things to favourite patients without the surgeons' leave, or omit to carry out his orders unless they were made to do it.' However, this measure did also bolster the ladies' own authority over the patients: 'the more external indications of our position were kept up, the more influence we had with them'. Other non-medical considerations – the prevention of too much familiarity between nurses and male patients of the same social class – provided a further powerful impulse for control.[39]

A system of supervision was devised for the nurses at Kulali which covered all their waking, as well as their working hours:

> At the ladies' Home we assembled at eight o'clock for prayers, read by our superintendent, then followed breakfast. At nine the bell for work rang. We all assembled; each lady called the nurse under her charge to accompany her to her ward, or kitchen, or linen stores (we never allowed the nurses to go out alone, unless with special permission) . . . At half-past two we dined, the ladies in one room, the nurses in another, with a lady at the head of their table. The ladies took it by turns, a week about, to superintend all the meals of the nurses. At half-past four the bell summoned us to return to the hospital . . . At seven we returned to tea: then one lady – we took it in turns – went out with the nurses for a walk; now and then, for a treat, in caiques, to the sweet waters, or Bebec. At nine the chaplain of the Church of England came and read part of the evening service. Those who wished for it took some supper ere they went to their rooms.[40]

It may well be that 'the respectable part of the nurses submitted willingly to the restrictions placed upon them, irksome though they were', but they must have seemed intolerable to many. The controls, and the behaviour required, were not, perhaps, too dissimilar from the working conditions of a domestic servant resident in a middle- or upper-class household; but the Kulali regime also bore irresistible comparisons with the one, described by Mary Stanley in *Hospitals and Sisterhoods*, which was practised at St Mary's House, Wantage.[41] This was a small sisterhood and 'house for penitents' (i.e. redeemed prostitutes), of which Mary Stanley reported:

> these poor persons require constant watchfulness. Whenever two or more are engaged in any work, some one of authority should be present, to see that the work is properly done, and to prevent improper conversation, quarrelling, or other misconduct. It is moreover at their work, and in their hours of recreation, that their various tempers are manifested; and then the watchful eye and ready word are needed, to check the evil, or foster the good feeling, as it is drawn forth. All this requires, not only many supervisors, but great tact and peculiar

qualifications. It must be carried out by those who can unite firmness with gentleness, who will be faithful to their charge in requiring obedience, while they enforce it in the spirit of love.

Since a mistress-servant model had not held good for relations between ladies and nurses, the supervisor-penitent model was introduced to replace, or strengthen it – with equal maladroitness and lack of success.

While the ladies certainly believed themselves innately qualified to exercise spiritual authority over the nurses, they also acknowledged, at some level at least, that they derived this authority from the lower classes' recognition of their social and political power. If this recognition were not forthcoming, and a position of superiority were not reinforced within the institution (household, hospital) in which work was being carried out, then spiritual influence would evaporate with disconcerting speed. 'The real mischief of the equality system' Martha Nicol asserted, was 'done . . . to the nurses, who felt themselves aggrieved at being displaced from their fancied position of "ladies"! . . . and their insolent bearing made it impossible for us to be of that help to them which we otherwise might have been.'[42] In consequence, the Wantage methods of firmness, gentleness and the spirit of love had to be supplemented, if not indeed replaced, by the wielding of economic power, the ladies' chief weapon against the nurses being the threat of dismissal with a bad character.

Almost half the nurses at Kulali were dismissed in less than eight months, and 'to our profound astonishment we found that our sending home so many gave umbrage to the authorities at home'. A request for further particulars of individual cases produced rather vague references to 'loose character and immoral habits'. The ladies did not imagine that 'the authorities would require details which were often too terrible to dwell on'. The brazen mind of the twentieth-century reader boggles. Nowhere in these particular memoirs (Fanny Taylor's) is any more specific delinquency named than drunkenness, and one declaration of atheism.[43] However, it certainly seems as if many nurses found ways of escaping their warders. They must surely have needed a greater degree of relief from unpleasant and dangerous work, and from the contemplation of continuing, irremediable human misery, than was afforded by Mary Stanley's pious routines. For all their assumed spiritual superiority, the ladies made little allowance for the pressures acting upon their presumed weaker and more childlike sisters.

Florence Nightingale, too, had her disciplinary problems. She

Ladies and nurses in the Crimean War   71

considered that the failings of many of her paid nurses reflected their lack of previous experience, and blamed 'want of care in selection – and, I may add, want of *special* knowledge in the selectors, as well as want of assiduity in testing recommendations'. At the London end of the operation, Lady Canning admitted that nurses had been engaged without appropriate previous experience. She begged the War Office to finance two or three weeks' training for more nurses at St John's House; at present she could obtain only four or five free admissions for training. The cost would not be greater than that of sending out and bringing home unsuitable nurses. Her anxiety over training stemmed from her dislike of hospital nurses as a class: 'From experience we learn to mistrust regular hospital nurses and very few of them should be engaged. There is no doubt but that household servants and private nurses after a little teaching answer best.' In short, she sympathised with the ladies' desire for lower-class women who knew their place.[44]

By the summer of 1855 Mary Stanley was back in England, and Florence Nightingale had direct control of female nursing in Scutari only. It was at this time that the ladies' view of the proper relationship between voluntary and hired nurses began to find official expression. In July an official circular 'To the Nurses about to join the Army Hospitals in the East' was printed,[45] whose preamble stated 'that the Nurses who have gone to the East, complained of being subject to hardships and rules of which they were not previously informed, and of having to do work different to what they expected' and which warned 'that none should undertake this duty who are not prepared and willing to perform every branch of work which lies within a woman's province, such as washing, sewing, cooking, housekeeping, house cleaning – all these have been in turn required from those who have already gone out, and may be again'. It would seem, however, that this warning was by itself insufficient to raise the standard of deference to authority, for in December a far lengthier set of rules and regulations were issued, which were more explicit on the subject of ladies and nurses.[46] Along with clauses on uniform, expeditions outside the hospitals, dismissals, etc., there was now an expanded clause on domestic work which included a reference to 'the cleaning of her own and the ladies' apartments', and, in case any misunderstandings should remain, clause fourteen stated:

> It having been found that some of the nurses have believed they were to be on an equality with the ladies or sisters, it is necessary they should understand that they will remain in exactly the same relative position as that in which they were

in England, and under the authority and direction of the lady superintendent or the persons acting under her.

IV

The conflicts of approach are subtle and complex. The world of ladies' philanthropy by the 1850s was one in which evangelising Christian concern and personal influence were brought to bear on total institutions as well as individual good causes. The work of Elizabeth Fry in prisons, and Louisa Twining and others in workhouses, are outstanding examples of ladies entering male-run institutions and criticising them in the light of their own religious and domestic experience. They were not concerned with, for example, the effect the New Poor Law might or might not have on the mobility of the national workforce; they did care that children were separated from mothers, that the impoverished elderly were not allowed to die with dignity, that no distinction was made between 'deserving' and reprobate elements among the destitute; they also cared greatly about the social gulf which would widen between rich and poor once institutions had totally taken over from personal relations of patronage and clientage. Their interest in hospitals, the third great institution for the dependent poor, bore all the marks of this approach. They were less concerned to ask whether a disease had been cured or an epidemic checked, than to ask whether a stay in hospital would degrade an individual or make her or him a better human being; and whether medical aid could be granted in such a way as to convince the recipients that they and their benefactors had 'alike one hope, one end, one Master'.[47]

For most of the nineteenth century, hospitals were institutions for the reception of the poor, run by members of the middle and upper classes. They combined the functions of medical care and social management no matter what developments took place in nursing training and hospital design, in antisepsis and anaesthesia. Ladies would still be wanted, in addition to nurses, because they could put the weight of social superiority behind the effort to control patients' behaviour.

> Instead of a noisy and disorderly mob, shouting to and being screamed at by the nurse, amongst whom the feeblest fare the worst, and whose readiest means of access to the doctor is often a bribe to the porter or nurse, – the presence of a lady soon produces order and quiet. In a few kind words the poor

people are shown the advantage of patiently waiting their turn.[48]

The arguments in favour of installing ladies in hospitals were very strong; nevertheless the topic was a controversial one, as can be seen from the polemic carried on in the nursing literature of the Crimean War. Its controversial character came partly from its association with the rise of Anglican sisterhoods. These were suspect, to many outside the high church movement, as a sinister development which would subvert not just the Protestant character of the Church of England, but also the sanctity of family ties and daughterly duties. The movement's defenders had to argue that ladies following a religious vocation were indispensable to the proper performance of arduous charitable work. The extreme denigration of the Crimean nurses in the ladies' memoirs may be partly attributable to the fear that if nurses from the lower classes, working on a secular, salaried basis, were considered their equals in efficiency and kindness, then the sisterhoods would lose much of the justification for their existence. Much ink was consequently spilt denying the Crimean nurses all credit for charitable instincts. The ladies alone were allowed the title 'volunteer', as if the paid nurses were mercenaries, or unthinking conscripts. The principle was passionately asserted that nursing could not be properly carried out if sullied by thoughts of material gain, and that the work would corrupt and break the character of anyone not sustained by a religious vocation.

V

I have left to the conclusion of this paper what might be thought to belong to its introduction: the consideration of what being a lady actually meant in the nineteenth century. The material I have found on the Crimean episode suggests that it is best to consider the concept in tandem with its opposite – the non-lady. The non-lady might reasonably expect to work for a livelihood. Very often she worked for a lady. She *had* to be employed, and the sign of employment was the receiving of money, although bed, board and other payment in kind might be involved. The nature of the work she actually did was rather less important than its paid status. Fanny Taylor was amazed that a lady should have had the strength to do laundry work – but she did not assume that any caste was lost thereby. Martha Nicol recorded de-lousing a soldier, and commented that if a nurse had been available at the time, she would have been deputed to do it; the work was not pleasant, but this in itself did not make it demeaning.[49] I think it would not be profitable to try to establish work demarcations between ladies and others – such as cooking and sewing and poulticing on the one hand, but not washing, scrubbing or de-lousing on the other. Exceptions would always be found. The one constant distinction remains the paid or unpaid status of the worker. The Crimean memoirs, with their labelling of ladies, and ladies only, as 'volunteers', show how fiercely this distinction was maintained.

At the heart of the matter, however, lay the great unspoken inconsistency. The mistress of the servant was herself normally the servant of some master. The money which she paid in wages was rarely hers to give; the household she supervised, not her property. The middle- and upper-class woman was herself an employee, receiving bed, board, clothing and spending money from a husband or father. She concealed this fact from herself and her servant in order to establish a pattern of control. As Martha Nicol said of her patients, 'the more external indications of our position were kept up, the more influence we had with them'. Because the situations of mistress and servant were in fact strikingly comparable, the 'real' differences between ladies and others were to be expressed, not in economic terms, but in terms of social and mental cultivation and spiritual refinement. The Crimean experiment showed how precarious such distinctions were as caste defences. Without the power of dismissal, backed up by lady organisers in London and the male doctors on the spot, the ladies could have maintained no effective separate status. In spite of this – or rather, because of this – most of the ladies bent over backwards to re-assert the validity of the *non*-economic distinctions between themselves and the non-ladies in their memoirs.

It is very hard indeed for the late twentieth-century feminist historian to read the ladies' own account of themselves with any degree of patience. Yet it has to be understood that women of great intelligence, determination and moral independence, even women who considered themselves to be campaigning for the emancipation of their own sex, subscribed to a concept of 'the lady' which we would now regard as the height of bad faith and mystification. 'The real dignity of a gentlewoman is a very high and unassailable thing, which silently encompasses her from her birth to her grave.'[50] The quotation is from Jane Shaw Stewart, but Florence Nightingale incorporated it in her writings, and it could equally well have come from the pen of Anna Jameson, Louisa Twining or Octavia Hill.[51] The oppressive and exploitative character of the concept is clear enough. But it may also have served a contrary purpose. Lady visitors pleaded for the chance to give large impersonal hospitals the 'human touch'; lady nurses protested when women patients were callously treated by male doctors.[52] They might not have done so if they had seen themselves as vulnerable employees. The ladies; consciousness of caste, of social equality with husbands and fathers, and social superiority to men lower down the social scale, may have constituted a necessary preliminary to engagement in social action, in conflict with men, in male-run institutions. An inauthentic sense of spiritual and moral superiority to domestic servants may have been a first stage towards assuming responsibility for other, disadvantaged, women. The internal contradictions of a social movement can manifest themselves in unsympathetic and even repugnant phenomena. If we are to gain a fuller understanding of the development of women's work and women's politics in the nineteenth century, we are going to have to stifle the instinctive groans and laughter, and take the ladies as seriously as they took themselves.

Notes

These themes are further elaborated in the author's *Angels and Citizens: British Women as Military Nurses 1854–1914* (Routledge 1988).

I must thank Charles Webster, David Englander and the members of the London Women's History Group and the History Workshop London Seminar for their stimulating comments on earlier drafts of the paper. The faults and conclusions remain, of course, my own.

1 J. Williams (ed.), *The Autobiography of Elizabeth Davis, a Balaklava Nurse*, London, 1857 vol. II pp. 92–3; F. M. Taylor, *Eastern Hospitals and English Nurses*, London, 1856, vol. I, p. 13.

2 E. T. Cook, *The Life of Florence Nightingale*, London, 1913, vol. I. p. 188, cites the figure of forty-seven nurses, but on p. 191 quotes Mr Bracebridge's letter with the figure of forty-six; R. Roxburgh, 'Miss Nightingale and Miss Clough: letters from the Crimea', *Victorian Studies*, vol. 13, 1969, p. 72, gives forty-one nurses; J. Williams (ed.), *Autobiography of Elizabeth Davis*, London, 1857, vol. II, pp. 94–5 gives forty-seven nurses. As the selection of the nursing parties was a largely improvised and personal affair, few formal lists of appointees were kept in the War Office records.

3 See, for example, N. Cantlie, *A History of the Army Medical Department*, London and Edinburgh, 1974; L. R. Seymer, *A General History of Nursing*, London, 1932; P. F. Anson, *The Call of the Cloister*, London, 1955.

4 J. F. South, *Facts Relating to Hospital Nurses*, London, 1857, pp. 9, 11; 'Report on the nursing arrangements of the London hospitals', *British Medical Journal*, 1874, p. 285.

5 Florence Nightingale, *Subsidiary Notes as to the Introduction of Female Nursing into Military Hospitals in Peace and War*, London, 1858, Intro-

duction, p. 23; 'no General Order or Warrant was ever issued as to the duties of the nurses'.
6 P. F. Anson, *The Call of the Cloister*, London, 1955, pp. 220–1, 239–41.
7 M. Stanley, *Hospitals and Sisterhoods*, London, 1854, pp. 42–6; R. Few, *A History of St. John's House*, London 1884, p. 6; *St. John's House, Ninth Report of the Committee for the year ending 31.3.57*; *Rules of the Training Institution for Nurses for Hospitals, Families and the Poor*, St John's House, Queen Square, Westminster, London, 1855, pp. 8–11.
8 WO 43/963, f.218; Lady Canning to B. Hawes, 30.4.55; F. M. Taylor, *Eastern Hospitals*, London, 1856, vol. I, pp. 9–10.
9 M. Stanley, *Hospitals and Sisterhoods*, London, 1854, pp. 22, 44–5.
10 C. Woodham-Smith, *Florence Nightingale*, London, 1951, p. 194.
11 R. Roxburgh, 'Miss Nightingale and Miss Clough', *Victorian Studies*, vol. 13, 1969, pp. 71–89.
12 C. Woodham-Smith, *Florence Nightingale*, London, 1951, pp. 219, 479–80; F. B. Smith, *Florence Nightingale*, London, 1982, p. 155; Lord Stanmore, *Sidney Herbert, a Memoir*, London, 1906, vol. II, p. 438; BLAdd. MS 43402 f.19, Florence Nightingale, 'Notes on Nurses'.
13 F. C. Devas, *Mother Magdalen Taylor*, London, 1927, pp. 17–35, 54–69; F. M. Taylor, *Eastern Hospitals and English Nurses*, London, 1856, vol. II. pp. 270–1.
14 Sister Mary Aloysius Doyle, *Memories of the Crimea*, London, 1897, p. 54; F. M. Taylor, *Eastern Hospitals and English Nurses*, London, 1856, vol. I, pp. 9–10.
15 WO 25/264, Bundle N.
16 E. T. Cook, *The Life of Florence Nightingale*, London, 1913, vol. I, p. 158.
17 WO 25/264, Bundle N.
18 M. Stanley, *Hospitals and Sisterhoods*, London, 1854, p. 21; J. F. South, *Facts Relating to Hospital Nurses*, London, 1857, p. 17.
19 WO 6/70, f.31, Newcastle to Raglan 11.12.54; N. Cantlie, *A History of the Army Medical Department*, London and Edinburgh, 1974, vol. II, p. 75; Lord Stanmore, *Sidney Herbert*, London, 1906, vol. I, p. 407.
20 E. T. Cook, *The Life of Florence Nightingale*, London, 1913, vol. I, pp. 188–93; Sister Doyle, *Memories of the Crimea*, London, 1897, p. 33.
21 WO 43/963 f.296. D. Fitzgerald, Purveyor to the Forces, *Confidential Report on the Nursing System in the Crimea from 23rd January 1855*, 24.12.55; J. Williams (ed.), *Autobiography of Elizabeth Davis*, London, 1857, vol. II, pp. 126–7; F. M. Taylor, *Eastern Hospitals and English Nurses*, London, 1856, vol. I, p. 100.
22 WO 43/963, f.296, Fitzgerald, *Confidential Report*, BL,Add.MS. 43 402, f.19, Florence Nightingale, 'Notes on Nurses'; F. M. Taylor, *Eastern Hospitals and English Nurses*, London, 1856, vol. II, pp. 150–2, 164; J. Shepherd, 'The civil hospitals in the Crimea', *Proceedings of the Royal Society of Medicine*, vol. 59, 1966, pp. 199–204; WO 43/963 f.218, Lady Canning to B. Hawes, 30.4.55.
23 Lord Stanmore, *Sidney Herbert*, London, 1906, vol. I, p. 414.
24 F. M. Taylor, *Eastern Hospitals and English Nurses* (3rd edition),

London, 1856, p. 344; WO 43/963 f.205, Florence Nightingale to the War Office, 2.4.55.
25 WO 43/963 f.218, Lady Canning to B. Hawes, 30.4.55.
26 F. B. Smith, *Florence Nightingale*, London, 1982, pp. 29-30.
27 J. Williams (ed.), *Autobiography of Elizabeth Davis*, London, 1857, vol. II, pp. 132-3.
28 R. Roxburgh, 'Miss Nightingale and Miss Clough', *Victorian Studies*, vol. 13, p. 76.
29 Sister Doyle, *Memories of the Crimea*, London, 1857, p. 21.
30 M. Nicol, *Ismeer or Smyrna, and its British Hospital in 1855*, London, 1856, pp. 6-8.
31 Mrs. Motherly, *The Servant's Behaviour Book*, London, 1859, pp. 12, 19, 23-4.
32 F. M. Taylor, *Eastern Hospitals and English Nurses*, London, 1856, vol. I, p. 37.
33 M. Nicol, *Ismeer or Smyrna, and its British Hospital*, London, 1856, pp. 8, 89-90.
34 Lord Stanmore, *Sidney Herbert*, London, 1906, vol. I, p. 373; F. M. Taylor, *Eastern Hospitals and English Nurses*, London, 1856, vol. I, pp. 37-9.
35 M. Nicol, *Ismeer or Smyrna, and its British Hospital*, London, 1856, pp. 85-6.
36 Lord Stanmore, *Sidney Herbert*, London, 1906, vol. I, p. 377; F. M. Taylor, *Eastern Hospitals and English Nurses*, London, 1856, vol. I, pp. 48-9.
37 M. Nicol, *Ismeer or Smyrna, and its British Hospital*, London, 1856, pp. 308-9.
38 M. Nicol, *Ismeer or Smyrna, and its British Hospital*, London, 1856, p. 91; F. M. Taylor, *Eastern Hospitals and English Nurses*, London, 1856, vol. II, pp. 13-14. By 1856, the dresses of the Smyrna ladies differed from the nurses' in both colour and quality: BL.Add.MS 43397 f.91, H. Newman to Lady Cranworth, 14.2.56; f.111, M. Parkes to Lady Cranworth, 22.5.56.
39 At Scutari the nurses were forbidden to speak to the patients except through the Sisters of Mercy; they were also forbidden to speak to the patients of Balaklava (F. M. Taylor, *Eastern Hospitals and English Nurses*, London, 1856, vol. II, p. 20; M. Nicol, *Ismeer or Smyrna, and its British Hospital*, London, 1856, p. 89; J. Williams (ed.), *Autobiography of Elizabeth Davis*, London, 1857, vol. II, pp. 112, 126-8). Mary Stanley was, if anything, even more conscious of the difficulties of disciplining the nurses into impersonality in their relations with the sick and wounded than was Florence Nightingale.
40 F. M. Taylor, *Eastern Hospitals and English Nurses*, London, 1856, vol. I, pp. 162-3.
41 F. M. Taylor, *Eastern Hospitals and English Nurses*, London, 1856, p. 353; M. Stanley, *Hospitals and Sisterhoods*, London, 1854, p. 54-5.
42 M. Nicol, *Ismeer or Smyrna, and its British Hospital*, London, 1856, pp. 89-90.

43 F. M. Taylor, *Eastern Hospitals and English Nurses* (3rd edition), London, 1856, vol. II, pp. 19–20, 117–18; vol. I, pp. 13–21.
44 WO 43/963 f.232, Florence Nightingale to B. Hawes, 1.5.55; f.218, Lady Canning to B. Hawes, 30.4.55.
45 Printed in J. Williams, (ed.), *Autobiography of Elizabeth Davis*, London, 1857, vol. II, pp. 217–23.
46 WO 43/963 f.235.
47 F. M. Taylor, *Eastern Hospitals and English Nurses*, London, 1856, p. 356; see also F. Prochaska, *Women and Philanthropy in 19th Century England*, Oxford, 1980, and A. Summers 'A home from home – women's philanthropic work in the nineteenth century' by S. Burman, (ed.), *Fit Work for Women*, London, 1979, pp. 33–63.
48 Warrington Haward, 'Ladies and hospital nursing' in *Contemporary Review*, XXXIV, 1878–9, pp. 494–5.
49 M. Nicol, *Ismeer or Smyrna, and its British Hospital*, London, 1856, p. 63.
50 BL,Add.MS 45774 f.25, J. Shaw Stewart to F. Nightingale, 16.3.57; Florence Nightingale, *Subsidiary Notes as to the Introduction of Female Nurses to Military Hospitals*, London, 1858, p. 6.
51 '. . . you might teach and refine them and make them cleaner by merely going among them.' Octavia Hill, 'A few words to volunteer visitors among the poor' in O. Hill, *Our Common Land*, London, 1877, pp. 59–60.
52 Anna Jameson, *Sisters of Charity*, London, 1855, pp. vi–viii; R. Few, *A History of St John's House*, London, 1884, pp. 20–5.

Religion

7
Dare to be a Daniel

ALUN HOWKINS

How we sang it, loud and proud in Sunday school and chapel:

> Standing by a purpose true, heeding God's command,
> Honour them, the faithful few, Hail to Daniel's Band.
> Dare to be a Daniel, dare to stand alone,
> Dare to have a purpose firm, dare to make it known.

I don't think one of us really knew what it was about, but we were somehow separate; some like Ian Baggett, even thought they were chosen. I found it more difficult. I was 'chapel' not through direct family but through a powerful grandmother and spiritual adoption. My mother and father were carelessly infidel, at best glad to have me out of the house on Sundays, at worst fiercely sceptical. 'Don't you come that creeping Jesus stuff here', was quite sufficient martyrdom for an eleven or twelve-year-old aspiring boy-preacher.

Yet chapel still looms large in memories of my Bicester childhood - or does it? To what extent have I reconstructed my own past on the basis of my reading and talking to old chapel people in the last few years? The rural working class provide few respectable radical antecedents, but chapel was one. Where, though, does the historical end and the personal begin? If I am honest I don't really know. What follows is an attempt at working some of it out.

I find I wrote in 1975 that 'the individual in a sect begins his experience of belief with his face set firmly against the world'. Grounded in a reading of historical sources from Oxfordshire, Norfolk and Sussex, and mixed with 'theory' derived from the sociology of religion, such a statement makes, and indeed made, sense when I first began to follow my trade as an historian. At one level within my own world it was also true. The dissenters and Methodists of my small market-town childhood were often set firmly against the world. Some had been conscientious objectors, 'conchies', in the then so-recent war. A lot of slightly younger men refused to do national service or went into the Non-Combatant Corps (NCC). The angry story was still told of the Congregational minister who in the 1920s had waited his turn to speak at the Armistice Day service at the war memorial and said 'I stand here as an unrepentant pacifist'. 'It was like a sonic boom' writes Bicester's local historian, himself a lifelong Methodist.

At the end of our very respectable terrace lived the even more respectable Newby family – a father and two spinster daughters. Every morning Mr Newby, who was on the staff of the local high-class grocers (they 'purveyed' cheese and sherry to the gentry), set off for work, dressed in a Homburg hat and stiff white collar. But it was not the hat that set the Newbys against the world, nor only the fact that they were Brethren. In the winter of 1945, in an act of what can only be described as supreme Christian charity, the daughters had collected money to 'feed starving German babies'. My mother, whose whole life was based on a generous 'live and let live' philosophy derived from the awful poverty of her own childhood, never forgave them. Years later she would still get angry because my father's wounds and the pictures of Dachau seemed unable to shake the Newby sisters' faith.

The 'pacifism' which led the Newbys to 'love their enemies' and to hold mysterious 'tea meetings' for soldiers from the Non-Combatant Corps on Sunday afternoons was of an old fashioned kind. Its base was not in any theory of proletarian internationalism but in Gladstone's 'non-conformist conscience'. The same spirit which prompted 'old John Morley', Gladstone's biographer, to vote against war in August 1914 fed my town's CND group in the late 1950s and early 1960s. This was not the CND of youth and Aldermaston (although some of us longed for it to be, and Ian Baggett went to youth meetings with a guitar) but a Godly and very earnest movement. It was more akin to nonconformist 'pro-Boer' sentiment in the South African War than any 'long haired' youth culture of jazz and black jumpers. Many of the older members of our chapel would have responded to the defiant tones of the 'rebel' Methodist preacher who told a Norfolk congregation in 1899 that the war 'was unrighteous, without justification in morals or diplomacy'. A few might have gone further, like John Smith of Yarmouth, who compared the Boers with Cromwell's army and evoked all the powerful and separate history of nonconformity when he wrote, 'It is common for the jingoes to sneer at their psalm singing and praying; so Claverhouse and his dragoons sneered at the old Scottish Covenanters, and the Royalists at Cromwell and his Ironsides'.

For these reasons, 'our' CND was also much more outside the mainstream of local life than its successor today. Although meetings were held, letters written to the local press and even street leafleting tried on one dismal Easter Saturday, we remained part of chapel – odd, embattled and in the end sealed off. We never even managed to convince anybody that the fact that Upper Heyford was eight miles away meant anything other than jobs, a decline in sexual morals and an increase in road accidents.

There were other problems, though, that put us outside, that created us as a world apart. Mr Newby's hat was indicative of the terminal respectability which inflicted much of nonconformity. Dissenters were nothing if not decent, or thought they were. 'Half-sixers' an old and infidel Norfolk labourer called them – people who thought they were better than you. Certainly they were usually better off than my family, and friends (or some of them) acquired through chapel meant a modest social advance for me. (Nothing, though, compared with later socio/sexual advances made via the left!) Tradesmen, clerks, teachers led our local nonconformist sects and even the working people among them tended to be of the 'better sort'. There were also local and mildly spectacular examples of Weber's 'Protestant ethic', which produced scorn as well as envy, and further stressed chapel's special place. The Richards family (Brethren) moved from the upper end of the working class to being the owners of two or three shops within less than twenty years by dint of Godliness, thrift, hard work, and being the best bakers in North Oxfordshire. My best friend's father was a classic reformed drunkard (Jehovah's Witness). We all thought him a pain in the arse and preferred the unreformed grandad, but his life was certainly changed for the better, for a time at least.

This kind of separation was also present historically. Zacchariah Everitt, 'a confirmed poacher', was converted in Norwich Castle gaol in the 1850s. When he came out of prison, determined to preach the word, he found his whole family literally ranged against him on Norwich's Chapel fields saying that he had gone mad and was bringing disrepute on them. Robert Key, who missioned East Anglia for the Primitive Methodists in the 1830s, had the saved and self-educated working man's contempt for those who had not seen the light: 'A more wild, rough, uncultivated lot I think it would be difficult to find in the back woods settlement of America or the wilds of Africa'. George Rix, another self-educated labourer and trade unionist, constantly delivered homilies to his unenlightened fellows: 'Brethren wake up', he urged the labourers in 1881, 'resolute to do your duty, eat and drink less, read and think more'. A year earlier he had been yet more specific: 'Unite for mutal intercourse, instruction and information. Knowledge is power. Leave off smoking and tippling, and get to reading, thinking and acting and there is for the working classes of old England a brighter and better day.'

Tippling was another problem. Drink, in my childhood and youth, was an essential part of working-class life. The pub dominated the socialising of my parents and their friends, and my father's work as an agricultural engineer frequently took him into pubs even during the day. I first drank at Harry Dine's pub at fourteen years of age – the pub was so empty that Harry would serve anyone!

But chapel was different. At its Sunday school and youth clubs temperance was preached. True, the extremes of Victorian temperance propaganda had gone, but drink, and probably more importantly, pubs, were frowned on. In my early teens the lads (and a few girls) who snuck off halfway through youth club to drink cider and halves of light mild in the back passage of 'The Bell' were quietly lectured on their return. Those who persisted, as I did, were eventually asked, very politely, to leave the club. Temperance not only physically separated chapel people but set up cultural barriers between them and their peers. Not to drink was seen as 'unnatural' (unless you were ill) and therefore claims not to take the odd drop were seen as lies. All believed that temperance concealed secret drinking. 'Corse, they bloody buys it at the grocers don't they' was the standard response. Indeed, drinking at home was a real sin in my parents eyes; it was sneaky and uncontrolled. And, instead of beer they drank sherry, a vile liquid consumed in vast quantities, 'for medicinal purposes' as 'they said' behind drawn curtains.

The notion of 'hypocrisy' was central to non-chapel working-class analysis. 'Lie and cheat all through the week and go to church on Sunday' was applied to all chapel tradespeople. Their (hugely exaggerated) personal fortunes were always amassed (it was said) by fiddling working people while adopting pious expressions. This was especially so of chapel people who owned shops. A well-known local chapel worthy genuinely (and rightly) admired by his congregation and many outside it was known as 'fiddler' to my parents and their circle because in his drapers shop (it was alleged) you always had to watch your change, the length of elastic or the number of buttons sold to you. But they couldn't win either way. My first employer, a corner-shop keeper and Methodist who was generous to a fault (especially with credit when times were hard) was said to be 'too soft for his own bloody good', a failing which was blamed on his religion, although he was a member of the same congregation as the notorious 'fiddler'. Again, historically this idea was a very powerful one. Time and again nonconformist trade unionists or friendly society officials faced charges of 'fiddling the books' coming (I fear) as much from working-class distrust of the outsider as the not-infrequent Tory propaganda. George Rix felt compelled on presenting the labourers' union accounts in Norfolk in 1885 to add in his defence and the defence of another small tradesman on the committee. 'You see brethren, neither my shop, nor Mr. Hubbards cockle cart, is filled with goods bought with your district funds.'

Certainly chapel people could be 'close'. In the early nineteenth century the village of Long Crendon, about eight miles from my town, was rent by bitter divisions between the Baptists and the Church of England. So deep were the divisions within the village that 'there were church Shops and Chapel shops, and people buying groceries would go out of their way to patronise one from their own religion'. Nineteenth-century visitation returns show similar inclinations to 'look after your own'. From Chipping Norton in Oxfordshire in 1854 the vicar reported that 'there is a positive premium on Dissent in the fact of the chief employers of the people being Dissenters and almost openly preferring those of their own denomination'. In my youth my shopkeeper employer often relied on a slightly larger Methodist grocer for help when things were a bit short, sending me on the trades bike for half a pack of sugar or tea to see him through until a 'proper' order could be sent to the wholesalers. Then the goods would be returned, again by me on the trades bike.

Pushed out from the areas of socialising by their temperance beliefs and often their own perceptions of righteousness, chapel people created a separate social world. Even in the late 1950s and early 1960s there was something at the chapel most nights of the week. Sunday school and young people's fellowships marked Sunday, and youth club marked Friday, but in between there were Scouts, Guides, Cubs and Brownies as well as a debating society. The latter was a source of political education, where the rebel faction – myself, Ian Baggett, Ray Brigden and 'Pablo' Castle – battled with the moderates on issues like conscription, nationalisation, sexual rights, and ageism in general. In 1961 I led a team from the chapel to a regional final in Bexhill where we were beaten by a 'public school team' – perhaps they weren't, but Les Blackman, our mentor, CND'er and reader of advanced poetry, agreed with us that they were.

For non-rebel factions there was more still. There were at least two or three concerts a year which required endless rehearsals – proceeds went to the chapel building fund, the missionaries and to other 'good works'. Any successful entertainment was also carted around neighbouring chapels as a sign of our superior skill and ability. This was especially important as our chapel had, in the 1940s and early 1950s, produced a nationally famous harmonica band 'The Red Rythmics' whose name came from their red berets and ties rather then any affiliation with the Soviet Union. This band, which had played in the Albert Hall, on the wireless and even appeared in 1956, on TV, was a source of enormous pride in the chapel and a cross which we, the youth, had to bear since we could never be that good but were constantly urged to follow their example. Ian Baggett's CND songs and the attempts by Ray and I to start the second folksong revival were not enough.

This alternative world, which by my youth was often simply a slightly sad and moralised version of the 'real' one, had, in the eighteenth and nineteenth centuries been a vibrant and powerful popular centre. As the Anglican Rector of Scarning in Norfolk, Augustus Jessop, wrote in the 1880s:

> Explain it how we will, and draw our inferences as we choose, there is no denying it that in hundreds of parishes in England the stuffy little chapel by the wayside has been . . . the only place where the peasantry have enjoyed the free expression of their opinions, and where, under an organisation elaborated with extraordinary sagacity, they have kept up a school of music, literature, and politics, self supporting and unaided by dole or subsidy – above all a school of eloquence in which the lowliest has become familiarised with the ordinary rules of debate, and has been trained to express himself with directness, vigour and fluency.

To those who joined Daniel's band here was a genuinely alternative and all but complete society. It provided an alternative hierarchy to the outside world, through which the lowliest could rise and which demanded different and accessible criteria; another leadership who often spoke the language of the poor and middling sort; and another set of values by which to judge the members of the wider society. Like the European socialist parties of the Second International or the Communist parties of the Third, at its most extreme the chapel provided a total society which the member only needed to leave to go to work.

The scope of this society can only be sketched here. For the member of a small town chapel in the 1880s, there was often something every night of the week as well as 'day' events on Sundays and sometimes on Saturdays, especially as Saturday half-closing came to more and more of the lower middle class. Some activities were directly religious; prayer meetings, discussion circles of some kinds, preaching meetings and the class meetings of the Wesleyan Methodist or Love Feast of the Primitive Methodists all fell into this category. Some were intermediate. Many chapels ran young men's (and later young women's) associations. Christian Endeavour and the Wesley Guild, for example, were both places of Christian argument and discussion. However, even without the rebel faction that took over the Wesley Guild, in my town Christianity was interpreted widely even in the 1890s. 'Almost everybody, from very early youth was encouraged in (public speaking)', wrote E.E.Kellett; 'lads of seventeen or eighteen not only spoke at literary societies but were often utilised as local preachers.' The Methodist memorialist of my town, Sid Hedges, took his skills early on from Wesley Guild to anti-blood sports platform – not a popular cause in the 1930s in the heart of one of the country's greatest hunts.

Finally there were those activities which were religious only in the broadest possible sense. Concerts of sacred song, organ recitals and penny readings often appear as truly social events whose content just happened to be religious. E.E.Kellett again on 'lantern shows': 'It was as exciting as a Hollywood film to hear a missionary describe, perhaps with "advantages" his hairbreadth escapes, and fantastic adventures.' Chapel bands, the forerunner of Bicester's 'Red Rythmics' and possibly our vaguely ecumenical carol singings and 'peace' evenings, were firmly in this area. The Lewes Wesleyan Gospel Temperance Mission Brass Band, founded in 1896, was composed only of 'total abstainers and Christians' and played only 'sacred music' but provided instruments and tuition (like the 'Red Rythmics'). Connection with the chapel in these kinds of institutions and meetings often became difficult to maintain. The Eastbourne Temperance Mission Band (Wesleyan Methodist) was clearly a bit like the Howkins, Baggett, Brigden 'Gospel folk singers'. Having been founded and supported by the chapel at their early gigs, they proceeded to get bookings elsewhere with unsuitable organisations like the Oddfellows. Remonstration followed, rules were invoked but eventually the band (or its members) were expelled.

Covering all three categories were the ubiquitous bazaars, fetes, tea meetings, sales of work, etc, which had to support the chapel at home and abroad. Sometimes religious, usually not, the very organisational meetings for these 'great events' were in themselves social occasions, albeit with a firm business overtone (for some at least). As the Haywards Heath Wesleyans recorded in their minutes, 'Bazaar monies . . . together with the proceeds of the Sale and the Ships[?] together with some further monies . . . be invested in the Lewes Co-operative Benefit Society.'

Simply to list the organisations which met in a chapel is to invoke a total society. At Eastbourne (a big chapel admittedly) in the 1890s, as well as a Wesley Guild, a Temperance lodge, the (failed) brass band and all normal religious meetings including Sunday schools and missions, there was the Wesleyan Womens Provident Slate Club, Rechabites, Pleasant Sunday Afternoon Group, Sisters of Phoenix Womens Total Abstainers Union, Workers Slate Club, a Band of Hope, and a Young People's Association. They also provided a Young Men's Reading Room 'for young men aged 14 years and upwards'. Similar lists could be made time and time again for literally thousands of chapels throughout these islands.

But, perhaps crucially, chapel could support its members' physical as well as spiritual needs. 'Look after your own' is the other side of the working-class tradition of solidarity and chapel communities in formal as well as informal ways did just that. George Rix again giving advice from the respectable to the rough working class: 'It was the imperative duty of every young man to make himself a member of a good sick benefit society and he would strongly recommend them to join the N. Tuddenham Friendly Society with its no fines, or fees, no public house meetings, no great guns to pander to or be alarmed at.'

Aspects of chapel were almost Masonic (again a cause of anger among outsiders), and the minute books of many chapels show the extent to which being an insider gave contact with some who were social superiors and could 'help out'. Eastbourne, a wealthy urban bourgeois chapel but with a poor fringe, had a 'Poor Fund' which helped poor and deserving members of the chapel. In 1892 a Mr Owen, 'who had recently left the town to go to Wales' was deemed needy and 5 shillings sent to him. On occasions the fund helped poor members to emigrate. In September 1889 Mr J. Richards had £2 'from the poor fund' at Eastbourne to 'assist him in Australia'. More usual was temporary help because of misfortune, as in 1905 when 'a special grant of 30/-' was made to Mr. Knight 'who had recently lost his daughter through a bicycle accident, and was himself upon the club', or semi-regular payments to the chapel's poor in winter. In 1902 'The Superintendent asked for the names of deserving cases for Christmas gifts a number of which had been handed to him for disposal' and in the following year he 'presented a list of proposed recipients for a number of half crowns which had been given for distribution'. In 1906 a wealthy member gave 'an order' of coal for the poor of the chapel. Again the list was scrutinised and the deserving selected.

In a sense it was like the Masons, though it was probably the informal links which worked most powerfully – a word here, a message there, automatic links on moving to a new town, even a new town in Canada or Australia where emigrants were encouraged to contact the chapel as soon as they landed. Within my world, selective trading and employment have been mentioned but it went deeper than that. Friendships, love and marriage all came from the chapel, and although real discipline in these matters had gone by my childhood and youth, elements remained. This was especially true of groups like the Brethren or the Jehovah's Witnesses. Young people from both were untouchable, even to us Methodists. I remember twins, beautiful girls, for whom I nurtured a deep fourteen-year-old's passion but who were Brethren and so would not even speak to me at school. Endogamy was still, I think, the norm, even within the Methodism of my youth – few married out, although some married in.

Now I pause. Those twins bring back suddenly the other side of that closed society. 'Daniel's band', like Cobbett's eighteenth century, is easily romanticised. As Cobbett selected from his youth so I have been selecting from mine, and again, like Cobbett, I am selecting my history in accord with *my* view of my youth. The chapel was, as one writer has called it, 'a disciplined society', and discipline was often strict, especially in those who wanted to rise through the hierarchy. The local preachers' meeting at Mattishall in Norfolk in 1842 reprimanded or removed from the preaching plan local preachers for 'going to America without informing his wife', boxing his son's ears too soundly, 'wasting time sitting in public house' and 'agitating the Bawdeswell Society'. The complexities of these sorts of situation appear in the Maidstone Circuit minutes of 1857.

> The reason of there being no collection or very little class moneys at Braybourne Lee is owing to clerical intolerance and want of firmness in the man at whose house we preach. The clergyman of the above named place has offered the man at whose house we preach coals. Blankets and soup if he would turn us out and although he and his wife are members with us we are not allowed to preach in his house.

After discussion the man, but not his wife, was expelled.

Doctrinal problems seldom seem to have been a reason for expulsion, at least after the 1850s. Occasionally, especially on new circuits, where one assumes a fiercer enthusiasm burned, there were problems. The Maidstone Circuit of the Primitive Methodists was new in the 1840s. In 1852 personal animosity, broken friendships and doctrinal differences led to the expulsion of one half of the congregation by the other half at Lenham Heath. Earlier Bro. H. Smart had been taken off the plan for 'neglect of the means of Grace'.

Such splits were rare as the century progressed. Indeed it is a salutary comment on the romanticisation of 'chapel consciousness' that most cases of expulsion contained in minute books refer either to financial or sexual affairs. A case from Haywards Heath stands halfway between doctrine and money. In September 1892 the minutes record:

> That the names of Marshall Coppard, Mary Coppard and Ann Coppard be removed from our roll of membership on the ground that they still persist in opening their shop for sale on Sunday, though the evil and inconsistency of their conduct has affectionately been pointed out.

At the same time Marshall Coppard lost his job as chapel cleaner.

The hypocrisy of much chapel belief in the eyes of my parents and many like them is borne out by the large number of expulsions from membership or loss of preaching credentials for financial problems. Here we see the unedifying spectacle of the Church of Christ's poor expelling men and women for essentially failing to perform successfully in the world of Mammon. These were not men or women who absconded with funds (although there were such cases) but members whose business dealings outside the chapel had got into difficulties. In the Lewes Circuit minutes we find in October 1884 'it was thought desirable from Brother Stevens Embarrassed position financially to drop his name from the plan for the present'. Or again at Lewes in 1897, 'The Chairman reported that Mr. Peart had been unable to meet the demands of his creditors and therefore sent in his resignation, which was accepted.' Even Kent in the 1840s could find time to take Sister Cleavers name 'off the plan' for debt. She was however restored within less than a year and continued to serve the cause for Kent Primitive Methodism for many years.

Sexual behaviour was another reason for expulsion, and one which was as obvious (perhaps more obvious) in the early stages of a chapel's life. In Mattishall in Norfolk in 1842 a committee was set up to investigate a case of a sister who had been jilted by a brother. The committee reported 'It is the opinion of this committee that both Mr. A and Miss B. have been wrong in their courting affairs and they are recommended to bury and suppress their grievances and sincerely repent and do better in future.' On the Retford (Notts) Wesleyan Circuit in 1839 John Pearson lost his preaching credentials 'for having married a person not at all religious' and in 1840 the Mansfield Primitive Methodist Circuit expelled Thomas Ward for 'improperly associating with Mrs Wild and being with her in the fields and on the railway at a late hour'. There was obviously a rash of un-Godly Romeos that year, as W. Clarke admitted 'he took freedoms with Fanny Hopkinson and that he put his arm round Mary Ball once'.

The double standard was the most frequent source of the scorn in which many working people held chapel folk. There were endless stories (all libellous and certainly not repeatable) of the sexual doings of this or that deacon or lay preacher. Indeed such calumnies have a long and dishonourable tradition. The Pepys collection contains numerous versions of the anti-Puritan ballad known usually as 'Preaching for Bacon' in which, under the guise of Godliness, a Puritan minister eats the food of, and has 'his wicked way' with, another man's wife. The ballad was reprinted frequently in the eighteenth century when the Puritan nearly always becomes a Methodist.

To move now towards some sort of conclusion. The chapel of my youth was in many ways a separate society. Its institutions reinforced the half-remembered history which told of past persecutions but also of past victories for the chosen.

> On my comrades, see the signal, waving in the sky,
> Reinforcement now appearing, Victory is nigh,
> Hold the Fort for I am coming,
> Jesus answers clear.
> Send the watchword back to heaven,
> Victory is near.

The embattled fort ultimately relieved, Daniel's Band fighting giants in the world's wilderness were historical images which were constantly reinforced by the institutions and relationships of 'chapel folk'. Clubs, meetings, friendships, marriage, all came from the chapel. The lived world of human experience was one in which separateness and closure confirmed and dominated thought. Even if you 'moved out' to battle the world, as generations of nonconformist politicians and trades unionists did you remained 'peculiar' in the sense of Watt's great hymn:

> We are a garden walled around,
> Chosen and made peculiar ground.

Yet chapel was, I think, not unusual in this. The whole of my childhood was divided into groups, of an informal as well as a formal kind. Chapel was perhaps only the most extreme. Political parties at local level often had the same clannish closed world, especially the Labour Party. In my town there was a minute Labour presence which was more like the embattled fort than the bigger sects – we were truly 'Daniel's Band'. And we talked in the same way about these groups as we did about chapel. You were a 'Labour' man or woman, you came from a 'Labour family'. Indeed the ethos of Bicester Labour Party was too like the chapel in all sorts of ways for many of us, but that's another story, or essay . . .

But I must beware. Chapel separateness also meant it was narrow and bigoted. Its sense of its own history not only gave it great strength, but also a conviction that it was always right which stifled discussion and prevented change. Younger chapel members who 'stayed inside' found this increasingly difficult in the 1960s, when pressure from their peers on many issues, but especially those to do with personal sexuality and Left politics, brought clashes with the older leadership. I left, bloody but unbowed, in a clash with one such figure of the 'line' to be taken by our hitherto successful debating team. To him it was certainly nothing: to me is was like Tom Paine seeing the light (though I'd never heard of Tom Paine then). We were to debate on contraception rights and wrongs. I, with all the fervour of youth, effectively wanted to advocate 'free love' (as we in Bicester still called it). My real religious faith was residual and private now, but the institution remained. In a public and angry clash the battle was fought out and I lost. I saw myself then as a victim of religious bigotry and persecution. That was dramatic in the way a teenager sees the world, but in the end I must never forget that in some ways I was right and they were wrong. The closed world of chapel gave enormous advantages to its members but by the twentieth century there was a high price to pay.

Bibliographical notes

This piece, for a number of reasons, was written without notes, but some indication is offered here. The manuscript materials quoted come from the East Sussex Record Office, Kent Record Office, the Bodleian Library and the collection of Mr Cyril Jolly in Norfolk. Throughout, sometimes concealed use is made of local newspapers.

Anyone who has ever worked on English nonconformity must owe an enormous debt to its own literature. The autobiography almost becomes a nonconformist form. Too many to mention inform this piece, but I select, for the reason that it is quoted, E. E. Kellett's *As I Remember* (London, 1936). There is also a debt to be paid to local history. Journals like the *Transactions of the Thoroton Society* which provided an article by B. J. Briggs and the Nottinghamshire material, and record societies like the Buckinghamshire Record Society which provided the material on Long Crendon, are vital to this piece. Finally, if you want the 'other side', Sid Hedges – chapel worthy, youth leader, creator of the 'Red Rythmics' and author of 126 books – gives an account of Bicester in *Bicester Wuz a Little Town* (Bicester (where else), 1968). The book is sometimes marred by silly rhymes in mock dialect, but it is a smashing account of the town, especially in the 1900s. It is also the product of chapel, with its strengths and weaknesses.

8
An Irish religion

RAPHAEL SAMUEL

Back-street Catholicism

The Catholic church in the second half of the nineteenth century pursued a double mission. It reached out in its proselytising work of conversion to the well-born and the rich – those especially who had come within the Puseyite orbit. At the same time it served as a national church of the Irish poor, planting its chapels and schoolrooms in the close quarters and the narrow streets, seeking out the Irish in the workhouse, the children's orphanage and the reformatory,[1] ministering to the Irish soldier in his barracks[2] and the Irish prisoner in his cell.[3] Between, on the one hand, the Catholic yeomen and the farmers of Broughton in the Fylde and, on the other, the Irish Catholic poor – market people, washerwomen, labourers – congregating together in belligerent fidelity, the contrast in religious sensibility, as in nationality and social station, was as great as any separating church and chapel among the Protestants.

The great wave of the Irish immigration coincided in years with the Romeward movement among the Tractarians, and the Catholic revival to which Newman gave the name of 'Second Spring'. Indeed, it may be said to have engulfed it, and never more obviously so than during the cholera of 1849, when Newman and St John were sent to administer the last sacraments to the cholera victims at Walsall and Bilston – 'everyone crying as if we were going to be killed'[4] – while the London house of the Oratory was employed on a similar mission among the poor Irish hop-pickers of Kent.[5]

The Irish poor were for half a century the great support of the church, and it was the increase in their numbers, especially in the decades following the Famine, which was responsible for the multiplication of Catholic missions and schools. So close, indeed, was the association that the church, which gratefully acknowledged their role as 'eminent propagandists of the faith',[6] sometimes treated 'Catholic' and 'Irish' as interchangeable terms. The appearance of a settled body of Irish in any place was generally a signal for the planting of a Catholic mission to begin. Protestant missionaries, who suffered their persecutions in the street, were accustomed to classify the Irish indiscriminately as 'Romanists', whose 'superstition' and 'ignorance' it was one of their painful duties to meet – one missionary even complained of 'Papist charwomen' at a London hospital, biasing the patients against the influence of 'Bible instructions'.[7] For working people, too, like the colliers at Airdrie who struck work in 1854 'until the Catholic miners were dismissed',[8] the religion of the newly-arrived immigrants might appear as distinctive a peculiarity as their race; the Roman Catholic church, a London street sweeper told Mayhew, was 'a Irish religion' which, as he explained, he 'wasn't to be expected to understand'.[9] The Irish, for their part, rejoiced in the equation and seem to have sought out occasions on which it might be displayed.[10] During the taking of the 1871 Census in Ancoats, for example, a batch of returns was found to have been completed at a local public house – 'the House of Commons for Ireland' – in which religion and social status were interestingly confused: 'Numbers of papers were found filled up in the same handwriting, and the occupation of almost all of them returned as Catholic.'[11]

The Irish stood in a hereditary relationship to their religion. Faith and nationality, hallowed by persecution, reciprocated one another's claims, and in the harsh conditions of his exile, stigmatised alike by religion and by race, the partnership was persistently renewed. Samuel Bamford describes the scene in 1819 when the Rochdale and Middleton people, on their way to Peterloo, stopped their procession at Newtown, just outside Manchester.

> we were welcomed with open arms by the poor Irish weavers, who came out in their best drapery, and uttered blessings and words of endearment, many of which were not understood by our rural patriots. Some of them danced, and others stood with clasped hands and tearful eyes, adoring almost, that banner whose colour was often their national one, and the emblem of their green island home. We thanked them by the band striking up, 'Saint Patrick's day in the morning'. They were electrified; and we passed on, leaving these warm-hearted suburbans capering and whooping like mad.[12]

Religious spirit among the street folk whom Mayhew wrote about ran high, and they entered keenly into the subject of their faith. 'I don't go much among the English street-dalers', said one, 'They talk like haythens'; and he went on to say that he was 'almost glad' to have no 'childer' because of the way that in England they were allowed to run wild: 'They haven't the fear of God or the saints. They'd hang a praste – glory to be to God! they would.'[13] Another, who crossed himself repeatedly as he spoke, claimed to be more tolerant. He had 'nothing to say' against 'Protistints' ('I've heard it said "It's best to pray for them" '), and he observed that the 'Protistint gintlemen and ladies' among his customers 'sometimes . . . talk to me kindly about religion'. But he referred with contempt to the spiritual state of his fellow-costers among the English ('The street-people that call themselves Protistants are no riligion at all'), and as for the Protestant 'gintlemen and ladies', he mused upon the possible fate awaiting them 'in another worruld': 'I can't say what their lot may be . . . for not being of the true faith. No, sir, I'll give no opinions – none.'[14]

The Irish in England defended the church when under attack with something of that primitive violence which made it dangerous, in the more inflammatory parts of rural Ireland, for a bailiff to serve his writ or for a landlord to reside. The 'rough' elements in the congregation were ready, and indeed eager, to avenge whatever insults were offered to their priests or to the honour of the church – 'the roughest the readiest', a London priest told Booth.[15] Father Gavazzi, the celebrated apostate, received almost as stormy a reception from the Irish of Wolverhampton as from those of Tralee, 'vast numbers of Papists' taking up every approach to the Corn Exchange where he was due to lecture, and the authorities becoming so alarmed that soldiers were summoned from Birmingham and an additional force of police from Stafford.[16] The notorious Baron de Camin, an alleged ex-Dominican monk, lecturing with his wife Lavinia at the Mechanics' Institute, provoked a civil war in Wigan, centering upon the rival churches of St Catherine's and St Patrick's in the Scholes[17]; three years later, when his lectures provoked riots in Bradford, 'One side . . . vented their rage on the windows of St. Marie's chapel and schools, breaking about 400 squares of glass, and the other side threatened to attack the Parish Church.'[18]

At such times as these – and in the manufacturing towns of Irish settlement religious and racial disturbances were contiguous possibilities which the lightest affray might provoke – the primal solidarities of the community were engaged. The children of the immigrant poor – 'chiefly noisy, unwashed young Hibernians', in the unenthusiastic description of a schools inspector,[19] 'very rough and obstreperous', as even their own priests sometimes felt constrained to complain[20] – seem to have shared the combativity of their parents. They might be called upon to defend their very homes against attack, as at Barrack Yard, Wigan, where on the third night of the de Camin rioting in 1859 a mob of English workmen and colliers were 'gallantly resisted by a handful of boys and girls, who showered stones upon the attacking party' and were compelled for a time to retreat[21]; and they seem to have been no less ready to take part in the tumults of the street, as at Failsworth in 1868,[22] and Tredegar in 1882.[23] The turbulent Irishwoman, with her sleeves tucked up, and her apron full of stones,[24] or, flourishing her rolling pin in battle,[25] was as distinguished a presence in the Irish mob as the labourer with his shillelagh. And when the chapel bells pealed their alarms, and the narrow streets echoed to the 'No Popery' cry, the Irishman was ready, with a stone in his hand, an iron stick or cudgel[26] – sometimes, indeed, as at Ashton-under-Lyne and Staleybridge in 1868, fortified by pistols[27] – to defend his church, as he was wont to do his street, with an impulsive belligerence which the clergy themselves found it impossible to restrain.

However lowly and inferior their position in English society, the Irish maintained an exalted notion of their own religion and a sovereign contempt for the 'haythen' with whom they were surrounded. Town missionaries, seeking to enlighten their darkness, found them 'warm antagonists of truth' – 'Generally they refuse to take a tract, or to listen to any remarks that may be made for their benefit'[28]; the 'pleasing testimonies' which they were able occasionally to record, where an isolated believer had been persuaded to accept a tract or to listen to a reading of the Bible, were apt to collapse under the intervention of a religious member of the family or a visit from the priest.[29] Distrust of Protestantism was, like the faith itself, inveterate, and might survive even a formal separation from the church. An Irish tinker girl, who admitted to George Borrow that she was 'clane unsettled about religion', and whose family had discarded the Catholic symbols of faith,[30] was nevertheless indignant at the suggestion that she might join the Methodists:

> I have been at their chapels at nights and have listened to their screaming prayers, and have seen what's been going on outside the chapel after their services, as they call them, were over – I never saw the like going on outside Father Toban's chapel, yere hanner![31]

The sorrowing note of a Birmingham town missionary suggests

that even among those whom the evangelical found seemingly complaisant, there remained still a loyalty, furtive but persistent, to the ancient faith:

> In one house that I entered a man & his wife were sitting opposite each other with short pipes in their mouths smoaking & playing at cards, the woman was very much ashamed to see me & shuffled the cards up to hide them. The man seeing he was detected in his hypocrisy for he remembered as well as I did the conversation we had together the week before, and the way in which he had spoken of the religion of the Bible, speaking of it in the highest terms. He said, I won't deceive you. I am not a Protestant, I am a Roman Catholic and if you should run a spear into me I will not change the religion I believe. I said I had a good tract which would suit him if he would promise to read it. He said he would and I left with him a tract on the Wrath of the Soul. I asked the woman if she would not be happier reading some good book than playing at cards, she confessed she should, but when I proposed burning the cards she said they were borrowed.[32]

It seems that rush-bearing at Manchester was brought to an end in the 1820s because the Irish, 'taking offence at some orange-coloured lillies adorning a rush-cart', fell upon the hapless dancers accompanying the carts from the outlying townships and dispersed them — a proceeding which was repeated on subsequent occasions until the visits of the rush-carts ceased.[33] It is an extreme case, but one which illustrates a general truth, for the merest symptom of Protestant activity seems to have been treated by the Irish as a national affront, and to have provoked them, individually or collectively - and often with a reckless disregard of the consequences — to riot.

In Garibaldian times, the 'low Irish' of the London rookeries made the Papal cause vociferously their own, attacking all who ventured to express Italian sympathies, and turning Hyde Park into an arena of religious war. On two successive Sundays some thousands of Irish labourers and costermongers, 'easily observable by dress and feature',[34] poured out their wrath upon the working-men Garibaldians, the contest centering symbolically upon a struggle for mastery of the 'Redan' — a mound of rubbish where the Garibaldians had planned to hold a meeting. The disturbances spread from Hyde Park to the Irish quarters of the metropolis. On Monday 6 October, for example, after the second Sunday of the fighting at Hyde Park, the neighbourhood of Gray's Buildings, Marylebone, a famous Irish rookery, was kept in a state of disturbance throughout the day by threatening assemblies of labourers, while at night, when 'a large number of Irish labourers, who usually assemble against the hoarding between Field-lane and Victoria-street, got up a discussion upon the respective merits of Garibaldi and the Pope' ('levies of young and old from Saffron hill' later joining in), the rioting was taken up by the dangerous classes in one of their classical haunts. On Wednesday night, at Tothill Street, Westminster, another riot took place, 'originating in a drinking saloon' with the cry of 'Up with the Pope, down with Garibaldi' and cut and injured some Guards taking part in the affray 'so seriously . . . that they had to be taken to Westminster Hospital for surgical assistance'. Drink, in short, far from damping down the ardour of the Irishman, served rather to inflame it, and he was ready to call out as lustily for the Pope in 1862 as he was for the Fenians five years later.[35]

The second and third generation of the immigrants seem to have shared a good deal of the belligerent fidelity of the first. The walls of the Irish home continued to be adorned by a free intermixture of sacred and patriotic subjects, as they had been when Mayhew described them in the middle of the century.[36] 'Often', Joe Toole recalls of the Salford Irish homes of his childhood, 'did I see a picture of the Saviour on one wall and one of J. L. Sullivan, the bare-knuckle fighter, opposite.'[37] For the Home Rule canvasser, indeed, they served indiscriminately as insignia of national support: 'If they see a picture of St. Patrick, or the Pope, or Robert Emmet, they assume they are in an Irish house of the right sort.'[38] On St Patrick's Day itself, religion and nationality continued to meet in explosive combination with the drink, as a missionary in the East End of London prudently acknowledged:

> Tuesday (St. Patrick's Day). The Irish dock labourer is rampant to-day, and anyone who wishes to be involved in a serious row could not do better than broach the subject of Evangelical religion. I wisely refrain to-day and confine my efforts to railway men at Millwall.[39]

The spiritual inheritance of the children included a vivid recollection of national wrong. James Sexton, for example, growing up in St Helens, where his parents kept a stall in the open market, served his political apprenticeship when, as a boy, he accompanied his father and grandfather in their 'missionary' activity among the Irish navvies at work on a nearby railway, to whom they administered the Fenian oath. His mother had been born in Warrington, but her parents had experienced the terrible aftermath of the Irish rebellion of 1798 – 'the days when the pitch-cap and gibbet were the certain fate of any priest caught celebrating Mass, as they were of the peasant who dared to take up arms against injustice'; for a young boy of the second generation, to whom the memory was handed down, it still served to define the moral atmosphere of the home:

> The story of those days of terror was handed on to the children of all who endured their agony; it spread all over the world, and engendered in the mind of every Irishman and Irishwoman who heard it hatred – bitter and boundless hatred – of everything connected with the Briton and the British. That, so far as my mind was concerned, was my principal political and spiritual inheritance.[40]

Tom Barclay, recalling a Leicester Irish childhood of the 1860s, describes the militant religion which he took with him to the workshop: 'Protestant hymns disgusted me, and I actually used to spit out to cleanse my mouth if I thoughtlessly had been singing a strain caught from some pious shop-mates.' As a child he had been made familiar with the heritage of national struggle. 'My father was a Limerick man, and we were often hearing of the hero Patrick Sarsfield, and the women of Limerick who fought and repelled the English during the siege of that city.' A quite ordinary scuffle with the children at the other end of the yard took on, for him, the epic quality of an historical national drama:

> One day the kids from the other end of the court, or 'yard' as we called it, attacked us under Bill, their leader, and broke a pane of glass and thrust a rod through: unable to get out, or fearful of a spanking if we did, we scuttled upstairs and threw cinders from the chamber window on Billy and his pals: they battered the door, and we retaliated as we could. My imagination went to work: Billy was King William and we were the Irish: it was the siege of Limerick being in some mysterious manner enacted over again.[41]

George Lansbury remembered the Irish boys at his school in Bethnal Green as being 'all "Fenians" ';

> consequently, when the wall of Clerkenwell prison was blown down and three Irish martyrs executed in Manchester because a police officer was accidentally killed, very great excitement prevailed in our classes and playground. The teachers tried to make us understand how wicked the Irishmen had been on both occasions, but my Irish friends would have none of it, and when a few months later T. D. Sullivan's song *God Save*

Ireland came out, we boys were shouting it at the tops of our voices every playtime.[42]

In Clerkenwell, where the Irish and Italians occupied adjacent quarters, and fought between each other, the name of Garibaldi was perpetuated as a ritual challenge in the children's games of the street:

> the small boys and lads . . . seem to have had plenty of excitement as a result of perennial faction-fighting between the Catholic Irish and the 'patriot' Italians who occupied another quarter . . . 'Garibaldi? or the Pope?' 'The Pope? or Garibaldi?' were opening challenges in many a scrimmage . . . The Irish Catholics would bash you if you were for Garibaldi, the patriot Italians would 'bash' you if you declared for the Pope.[43]

'Faith and fatherland', in short, found their defenders in the tenement streets of East and Central London, and in the back streets of Bradford and the Scholes, as well as in Ireland itself.

The Irish brought with them into the country a complex of popular devotional practices, whose warmth and externality were often contrasted with the more reserved tradition of worship which prevailed among the English. The Irish might carry the signs of religious privilege about their person – the scapular,[44] the crucifix,[45] the picture of Mary[46] – blessed by the priest for members of the congregation and worn close to the heart; he crossed himself devoutly at the mention of each holy name.[47] The 'rude representation of the Crucifixion'[48] and the show of sacred pictures upon the wall made the mysteries of the faith a commonplace feature of the immigrant family home – 'the adoration of the shepherds', as Mayhew remarked in an Irish lodging house near Drury Lane, 'watched on the other side of the fireplace by a portrait of Daniel O'Connell',[49] 'the very staircase', as he writes of another house he visited, 'having pictures fastened against the wooden partition'.[50] The rosary served as a focus and discipline of prayer, an instrument of domestic piety by which the spiritual exercises of the church were reproduced in a kindred ceremonial of the home:

> before going to bed we all knelt down, and after a supper of Indian meal, on the bare uneven brick floor and recited the Rosary, father leading off: one Our Father to ten Hail Mary's: one of the prayers spoken fifty times by the help of a string of beads: and we arose feeling good and comforted and strengthened for the morrow's work.[51]

Personal prayer seems to have provided a religious comfort and consolation of the simplest and most elemental kind, as it did for the Irish crossing-sweeper who was, Mayhew records, 'a very melancholy-looking man' who could not understand the Mass but who prayed to the saints every night 'for a blissin', and to rise me out of my misery'[52]; or the travelling packman who came to the Franciscans in Wales, an elderly man 'with a sad and weary-looking face' who 'thought he should like to learn a few prayers . . . as he was getting old and did not feel very strong'.[53]

The Irish language, 'the tongue in which they both think and pray',[54] provided one continuing association. Some of the immigrants from the West of Ireland knew no other tongue,[55] and for many, especially among the women, it remained a primary cultural resource.[56] When the new Catholic cemetery was opened at Kensal Town, for example, in 1858,

> A very large number of the poorer class of funerals at that time were those of emigrants from the West of Ireland, all speaking the Irish language . . . chattering among themselves and collecting the money for the payments of their relations' funerals.[57]

Even those who had ceased to use the Irish in everyday life might revert to it in moments of high feeling. 'When they began to get elevated', a stonemason remarked of the Irish harvesters who spent their Saturday nights at a public house in Mosston, Surrey, 'they always started to talk in their own native tongue, and I noticed it was generally the women who commenced.'[58] Tom Barclay's memoir indicated the way in which it might serve as a common bond of nationality and faith. His mother, whose people were O'Reilly's, and who had been brought up 'in the wilds of County Mayo', could 'sing and recite a goodly number of old Irish songs and poems', a solace amidst the hardship and penury of life in a Leicester back court:

> She was not permitted, even had she the money and leisure, to indulge in beer and dominoes of an evening like my father; her consolation was an old Irish lamentation or love song and the contemplation of the sufferings of 'Our Blessed Lord' and his virgin mother.

She was held to be 'quite exceptional' among her fellow-country women in that she could 'read Dr. Gallacher's sermons in Irish', and it was her custom to read them aloud to her neighbours on Good Friday: 'It did them good to hear a . . . sermon . . . in the first language they ever spoke.'

How she who read English with difficulty could read these
sermons, though in Roman characters, with their
transliteration nearly as bad as Welsh, is something I do not
understand: but . . . often have I seen the tears come into her
eyes over the sermon on the Passion of Our Lord.[59]

The Church, for its part, seems to have followed the practice of
sending Irish priests to many of the newly-founded missions, and
one reads of Irish-speaking priests ministering in their own native
tongue in places as removed from the principal centres of Irish
settlement as Bilston, where Father Sherlock, who had been taught
Irish in his infancy, 'was able to hear the confessions of his countrymen who could speak in no other tongue', York, where the Irish
Vincentian Fathers from Sheffield were sent to organise the Irish
part of the Catholic population into a separate parish, and Merthyr
Tydfil, where Father Caroll contracted the Irish fever, and died in
1847.[60]

Sunday mass provided a natural meeting point in the life of
the community. Indeed Mayhew said that it was their 'consistent
association' at chapel which kept the street Irish of London so
distinct:

In the going to and returning from the Roman Catholic chapels,
there is among these people – I was told by one of the most
intelligent of them – a talk of family and secular matters, - of
the present too high price of oranges to leave full 6d. a day
at two a penny, and the probable time when cherries would
be 'in' and cheap, 'plaze God to prosper them'. In these
colloquies there is an absence of any interference by English
street-sellers, and an unity of conversation and interest
peculiarly Irish. It is thus that the tie of religion, working with
other causes, keeps the Irish in the London streets knitted to
their own ways, and is likely to keep them so, and, perhaps,
to add to their number.[61]

For those who during the week suffered the servitude of the workhouse – or of an English lady's household[62] – the privilege of
attending mass offered a solitary occasion of escape; indeed, it was
so highly regarded by the inmates of the Birmingham workhouse
that Protestant paupers were accused of passing themselves off as
Catholic 'in order to get five days' holiday in the month instead
of one'.[63] In country missions – remote from the ordinary track of
Irish settlement – squads of harvesters, during the season, or
contract labourers, when a railway was building or a canal being
cut, arrived to swell the numbers attending weekly mass,[64] as at

Bollington, Cheshire, for example, where the navvies at work on the Macclesfield and Stockport line walked over in a body from Prestbury, 'and as they always knelt on one side of the church this... was known... as the "Prestbury" side'.[65] At distant points, Sunday brought together isolated groups of labourers to form the nucleus of a congregation, and provided at the same time, as for the street Irish described by Mayhew, a focal point for social gathering. At Abertillery, where mass was celebrated in the room of a public house – as in other parts of Wales the only kind of room which could be hired – and where the congregation was recruited from the Irish mineworkers employed about the pits at Coomtillery, higher up the valley, a priest complained that it was 'with the greatest difficulty' that the congregation could be prevented from 'hovering about', though the service had ended, and 'evincing their gratitude to the landlord' when the public-house opened 'by an unlimited consumption of beer'.[66]

There are thus indications (which it would take a lengthier discussion to vindicate) that the new communities retained strong cultural affinities with the old. There were parishes whose congregations were almost exclusively Irish or of Irish extraction, often served by their own fellow countrymen as priests, and where the national influence was so very strong that it was said to produce a linguistic mutation in the rare 'sprinkling' of English priests who found their way among them: 'by dint of living almost wholly with Irish co-religionists they nearly always have a noticeable brogue'.[67] The presence of large and increasing numbers of Irish priests during the second half of the century, 'in sentiment... even more Irish than they are Catholic', preserved a line of communication with their native land[68]; so too did the continuing arrival of fresh immigrants. The chapel, a 'moral property' in Thomas and Znaniecki's excellent phrase, was a very emblem of the community's collective existence. Its building was in some cases the joint activity of parishioners and priests[69]; its maintenance called forth a loyalty and devotion, in singular contrast to the 'eleemosynary' character so often complained of in evangelical missionary activity among the poor ('some of them would live a week on bread and water rather than be behindhand with their monthly contributions, or their subscription to the Altar Society'[70]); its defence, when menaced by No Popery attacks, brought the impetuous violence of the Irish countryside into the heart of the English town. The church thus served as a nexus of communal solidarity, the very means by which, amidst the deprived conditions of their exile, a national identity among the Irish was preserved.

Moreover, these conditions tended to perpetuate themselves, for the Irish poor, as a community, were conspicuously lacking in those athletic abilities which Professor Tawney, in his work, so memorably described. They scaled no social heights, embarked upon no upward social climb, but remained rather in their own secluded colonies,[71] marrying among themselves, and continuing to inhabit the original quarters of their settlement, a fact which of itself did much to preserve the integrity of the faith: 'Catholics always know each other', Booth remarked, 'and in this way the priest may hear of newcomers.'[72] Whatever the improvement in material circumstances – and the evidence suggests that it was modest – the moral condition of their communities remained strikingly unchanged, and it was in this milieu, tumultuous and plebeian, that for Booth, writing at the end of the century, as for Mayhew, fifty years before, popular Catholicity was to be found in a natural and, it seems, a congenial home:

> Its people are some of the poorest [wrote Booth of the Catholic missions in Bermondsey]: the men and lads getting casual employment at the wharves or elsewhere, whilst the women and girls obtain work at the jam factories or in other similar trades, or are engaged in sack-making. Both the men and women drink heavily; and as to food, all live pretty well, spending little on either their homes or their clothes. Many of the children go barefoot and ill-clad, yet look sturdy and well-fed. These people account for a considerable part of the dark blue on this part of our map, but it is nevertheless their pennies that help to support the church.[73]

Sectarianism

The Irish congregations of the second half of the nineteenth century may be said to have existed, to some degree, in the original condition of a sect. Their churches were characteristically plain and unadorned, and 'externals', for all the attention they received from Protestant controversialists, counted for very little. St Patrick's, Liverpool, appears in an early account as 'very large, but very ugly, quite methodistick in its architecture' though 'nobly crowded with people'[74]; the patronless church in Garstang is described in a visitation return as 'a very plain square building . . . No tower or bells . . . the sanctuary . . . plain'.[75] The smaller chapels seem to have borne a resemblance to those which George Eliot recorded as being thought characteristic of latter-day Methodism – 'low-pitched gables up dingy streets'.[76] Some in fact were Methodist chapels, or independent meeting-houses, converted to Catholic use. St Mary's, Ashton-under-Lyne, was Joseph Rayner Stephens' old chapel in Charlestown[77]; St Bridget's, Liverpool, opened 'in a part of town ... where there was a large Irish Catholic population', was a chapel formerly used by the Methodists[78]; so too was the chapel at Westhoughton, which had also enjoyed a secular period of existence as a weaving shed.[79] Others were commercial buildings, adapted for religious use. At Eldon Street, Liverpool, 'the centre of a most congested district', a warehouse capable of holding 1,000 people was opened as a church, 'and in its gloomy and unattractive rooms began the mission of Our Lady of Reconciliation de la Salette'.[80] St Michael's, Stockport, sacked by the rioters in 1852 ('little else remaining than the four bare walls of the building, and the four bare steps to the altar'), had previously been a theatre, and then a Mechanics' Institute, before it was opened as a Catholic mission in 1851;[81] at Whitworth, near Rochdale, the Catholic mission was opened in a room above the premises of the Cooperative stores; at Kensal New Town in an uninhabited corner building which had been intended for use as a baker's shop ('the inner room served as a sanctuary, the door being removed and the opening widened').

The new missions reflected the line and cluster of Irish settlement, following isolated groups of labourers at distant points, like the Franciscan mission in the Monmouthshire hills,[82] or planting themselves in the midst of the densely-crowded pent-up rookeries of the towns, as at Holy Cross, Liverpool, where 'not a house in the district'[83] was more than seven minutes' walk from the church.

The 'churches' in the newly-founded missions were sometimes no more than temporary chapels, improvised in wood and iron; sometimes merely a hired shop or 'rooms'. The Church of the Sacred Heart, Camberwell, founded as a temporary chapel in 1863, and built upon a site of tumbledown premises, 'comprising a rag-shop with a pig-sty in the rear',[84] may serve to illustrate the characteristically plebeian setting. The mission was deliberately established among the poorest inhabitants, 'so that shabby clothes shall not hinder them from coming to Mass'. It stood on the edge of the Sultan Street area, whose moral and social condition was some years later to invite the anxious investigations of Charles Booth,[85] and it served an Irish colony whose densely-crowded conditions – 'seven or eight different surnames and up to twenty inhabitants ... under one roof' – a recent historian of Camberwell has described.

The adults were all young, mostly employed as labourers and

washerwomen, and, to judge by the ages of the native-born children, most of them had arrived within the previous decade. This tendency towards overcrowding, the intermixture of cowsheds and piggeries with dwelling-houses, and the opening of glue and linoleum factories, and the establishment of haddock-smoking and tallow-melting yards soon combined to give the whole area both the odours and the society of the authentic slum. The sickly smell of coster-mongers' refuse combined with these to make an atmosphere which seemed in the nostrils of one regular visitor to the district to be a concoction of haddocks and oranges, of mortar and soot, of hearthstones and winkles, and of rotten rags and herrings.[86]

The establishment of a new mission was liable to provoke in the local community an outburst of Protestant indignation. Mission rooms were difficult to hire (above all in Wales),[87] obstacles were placed in the way of a purchase of land, and the chapels, as they were building, had sometimes to face a threat of malicious damage; at Carmarthen, for instance, 'it was necessary to enlist the help of voluntary watchmen, for otherwise what was being built in the day would have been pulled down in the night by the hands of unfriendly Protestants'.[88] The arrival of a Catholic priest was in some places an historical event. At Pontypool, for example, where a Franciscan mission was established in 1860, the appearance of Father Elzear in their midst ('a real live monk') provoked among the native Welsh inhabitants an animated curiosity which they were not at pains to hide. 'Every time Father Elzear went out . . . he was surrounded by crowds of eager faces, and his progress through the street caused as much excitement as though he had been the Pope in person.'[89] At distant points, where Protestant feeling was strong, the early congregations met under conditions of menace or even siege. At Colne, for example, where a missioner from Burnley attempted to gather a congregation in 1851, the Catholic worshippers, meeting above a stable in the Angel Inn Yard, were surrounded by a No Popery crowd 'sometimes five times as numerous', a factory manager leading his people to demonstrate against the services, and a Protestant agitator haranguing the priest from below.[90] At Wallasey, where a priest from Liverpool crossed the river to celebrate mass, the congregation had to fill their pockets with stones before setting out for the service, 'it being almost certain that the local Orangemen would assail them either coming or going'.[91] At Cwmbran, in Monmouthshire, where the Irish were employed about the furnaces and ironworks, 'it was for some time no unusual occurrence for stones to be hurled against the windows during Mass or Benediction'; the Catholic chapel, 'an iron building capable of accommodating 250 people,' was surrounded by five hostile chapels, in which, 'Sunday after Sunday', dissenting ministers hurled their anathemas at the stranger in their midst – 'our meek-looking chapel', a Franciscan chronicler wrote, 'standing as a little Goshen amidst the Egyptian darkness'.[92]

The Catholic 'poor schools', to which the church devoted so remarkable an effort in the third quarter of the century, were planted in the very midst of the poor, quite without regard to the reputation of the 'low' Irish neighbourhoods. London Prentice Street, for example, where in 1849 St Chad's Cathedral set up its poor schools in the seven back rooms of a court,[93] was reputedly the most dangerous street in Birmingham; it carried the stigma of a particularly brutal murder in 1835,[94] and was the centre of a rookery 'notoriously infested with bad characters of every description'.[95] Park Street nearby, where in 1846 the Sisters of Mercy established their Sunday School in a loft,[96] was another very poor street; it had received an early influx of Irish,[97] and in 1867, when 'the ragged Catholic children who squat among the dust-heaps and gutter' were recited as a commonplace feature of the street, they had grown so numerous that it provided a natural focus, as the most Irish street in town, for racial and religious riot. The early schools were in no way cloistered. One at Liverpool was 'a large room or loft above a cow-house, in a dirty, back, ill-ventilated lane'[98]; another – rented by Father Parker of St Patrick's when Protestant bigotry turned the Catholic children out of the council schools – was a converted Penny Gaff.[99] At Cardiff, the Catholic school in 1847 was a loft above a cooper's workshop; at Barnsley, 'only a cellar'.[100] In the second half of the century, despite the intense efforts of the Catholic Poor Schools Committee, many of the children continued to be taught in very primitive conditions. The Catholic school in Lincoln, as Joseph O'Connor remembered it in the early 1880s – 'a long walk down the hill . . . through a maze of back streets' – was 'a makeshift of corrugated iron attached to a makeshift chapel of the same depressing material . . . almost hidden on a waste spot in the poorest slum'.[101]

At Kilburn, in 1871,

> The chief school room where the elder children are taught is the upper room of a shopkeeper's house, ill-suited for a school room . . . The infants are taught in a dark kitchen used after the children are dismissed for culinary purposes.[102]

In a crowded part of Westminster, where the Catholic school was housed in a converted theatre, 'formerly . . . very popular among the poor', the children had to make their way at the beginning of the day through a milling crowd of costers.

> There was a very long covered passage leading from the street to the school; to this all the costermongers of the neighbourhood laid claim as having a prescriptive right to deposit there their barrows for the night; so that, what with the children in the morning fighting to get in, and the costers struggling to get out, we may leave the reader to imagine the confusion.[103]

'Child hunting', as Father Vere described it in a memoir of his early days at Soho,[104] was a frequent addition to the ordinary duties of the priest, for the children of the Irish poor were apt to be irregular in their attendance at school, more especially in the great cities,[105] and a great deal depended on the pressure which could be brought to bear upon 'negligent' parents. Even those – they seem in general to have been a small minority – whom the priest found it otherwise 'difficult to touch', might nevertheless be persuaded upon this single point to yield.[106]

At Tarry Town, Hackney Wick, 'a poor and woebegone spot at the junction of Hackney Cut and Duckett's Canal', the Servants of the Sacred Heart went out to hunt up the children of a little colony of lapsed Irish Catholics, and bring them to the Catholic school.[107] At a private 'adventure' school in Periwinkle Street, Tower Hamlets, where upwards of one hundred boys and girls, 'the children of very poor parents', were accommodated in the space of a 'wretched hovel', the local Catholic priest was said to treat the children as though they were his own: 'the school being almost wholly composed of the children of Irish Rom. Catholics, the priest periodically, *but unasked*, visits it in order to take the pupils to their religious duties'.[108] At St Francis Xavier's, Liverpool, the Jesuit Fathers gathered together a host of street urchins on Sunday mornings, provided them with breakfast, and marched them off to mass, some 'almost "sansculotte" ' in appearance, 'most of them shoeless'.[109] Moreover, Protestant aggression – 'the obvious danger of proselytism' – represented in places as potent a danger as apathy or negligence, and the poor schools themselves served in places less as educational establishments than as an improved arm of confessional war. The Oratorian Fathers' 'Ragged School' in Dunne's Passage, for example, was set down in a very cockpit of sectarian strife, with no fewer than seven Protestant schools in the immediate vicinity, 'one within a stone's throw'.[110] St Joseph's infant school in Princes Row, Soho – 'that little school with its close atmosphere and dirty children', as Father Vere affectionately recalled it – housed above the parlours of an itinerant Irish shellfish dealer, who cooked his whelks and winkles in the yard, and sent his own little girls to the school,[111] was set up to counter the rival persuasions of the Puseyite mission which had its headquarters nearby in Crown Street. A scribbled entry in the 'log book' for 1868 (the few tattered pages which are all of the school's existence to survive) records an early triumph,

> May 11th until this date 36 children have left the Puseyite schools to come to St Joseph's, only 6 of them have gone back again
> 3 Griffins Newport Market
> 2 Connolly's Princes Court
> M. A. Morgan Princes Court
> 10 June Anna Griffin again returned having previously been at the Puseyite school[112]

A mile away to the north, at the far end of Charlotte Street, off Fitzroy Square, the Catholic children of another infant school named St Joseph's – crammed into the space of a single ground-floor room – faced the Protestant children of a rival school on opposite sides of the same narrow court. The hectic situation may be imagined. 'Some panes of glass have been removed to ensure ventilation', an Inspector commented, 'but the noise from outside makes satisfactory teaching impossible'.[113]

The priest, in the Irish mission, lived in close vicinity with his flock, having no society other than that of his parishioners – 'no rich to interfere . . . no invitations to ruin the clergy'[114] – nor any round save that of the close quarters and the narrow streets. His daily transactions were conducted as those of a familiar, and yet one who at the same time enjoyed a peculiar and esoteric power, a figure at once accessible and remote. His entire life was devoted to his ministry. He might be called out at any hour to visit the sick, to bring the sacraments to the dying or to act as arbiter in a family quarrel. His life was intimately associated with that of the community, even though he was assigned in an exalted role. As the 'man of God' his blessing was eagerly sought; as the leader of the flock he was looked to for the kindness of a friendly recognition or a brief exchange of words.

The priest's house – no more than a humble workman's cottage in some of the poorest missions[115] – was barely separated from the work of his ministry, but served rather as a second focal point. In earlier years, before the placing of the confessional in church had been made obligatory, it was sometimes used for the reception of penitents; at St Patrick's, Soho, for example, when the clergy lived in Dean Street, 'a long line of penitents knelt all up the stairs' on confessional nights, 'and took their turns for admission to the priest's room'.[116] It was a recipient for 'American' and 'foreign' letters which arrived for members of the congregation ('for James Hogan . . . from Australia', 'from John Dolan, Royal Marine, for his sister', 'Mr. David Magee for Mr. P. O'Brien').[117] It was a natural point of call when trouble broke out in any part of the community. Above all, the priest was perpetually on call for visits to the sick. Each day there was a lengthy list of the sick to be visited; calls continued to come in through the day ('We generally had to look in at the presbytery about midday, to see if any new . . . calls had been sent in'), and the sick bell might be rung even in the dark hours of night.[118] At St Peter's, Birmingham, ministering to a very poor community of Irish, the notices suggest that the parishioners were not reticent in calling upon the services of the priest.

> 23 November 1862 – At the approach of winter when sick calls are more numerous, we beg to give notice that such calls must be left at the Chapel house before 10 in the morning.
> January 1863 – *Once more* we beg to remind the congregation that sick calls must be sent to the Chapel house *before* ten o'clock in the morning, except in very urgent cases which seldom happen as those which are *called* urgent are nearly always nothing of the kind.[119]

The Catholic church of the second half of the nineteenth century thus occupied a singular position. In districts 'too poor for Dissent', and where the Anglican church preached its message as to the heathen, amidst a people whom rival denominations found it difficult, and even dangerous to touch – 'that sadly formidable part of the English people' whose 'spiritual destitution' and 'habitual neglect of . . . religion' the churchman and the philanthropist combined with the statistical enquirer to lament – Irish congregations flourished. They supported the 'round' of the Church's house-to-house collectors; they crowded the chapels at Sunday mass; and they gave to the church, in the neighbourhoods of their settlement, an unmistakably proletarian complexion.

Afterword

When I was travelling the parishes and record offices of northern England, preparing this paper in the summer of 1966, the old Irish districts had not yet succumbed to the bulldozer and the depradations of comprehensive clearance and redevelopment. The churches I visited often seemed to stand in half-deserted urban wastelands, but their original hinterland had not yet been effaced from the map. At St Patrick's, Wigan, in the heart of the old Irish district of the Schooles, the priest was distinctively an Irishman, deeply 'reactionary' in his views (he was uncomfortable about Vatican II, and hostile to 'progressive' innovations within the church), utterly devoted to his parishioners, and in his simple manner of life (we shared the dinner-table with his Irish-born housekeeper) – even in his tobacco-stained waistcoat – recalled pictures one might have had of the old-time soggarth, racy of the soil. Next door to the Catholic church in Bradford, in the old Irish district around Silsbridge Lane, there was a fading notice which read 'J. Walsh, undertaker', and a document in the lumber-room of the town hall (they have now been safely deposited in the public library) disclosed that in the late nineteenth century the church was faced by a pub called 'The Harp of Erin'; a suggestive cluster for the complex of sociability and communal service which helped to bond together the Irish Catholic communities of later Victorian times. At the time I was looking for continuity, and conceptualising it in terms of a timeless tradition, and the traces of this will be evident in the foregoing pages. Subsequent research is more likely to be interested – quite legitimately – in the mutations which took place, even within an apparently unchanging framework, and more alert than I was to the 'Victorian' transformation of both Irish and English Catholicity. I no longer believe, as I believed in 1966, that the Irish Catholics of the end of the nineteenth century were the same as those of the 1840s and 1850s. But the tenacity of both parish organisation and settlement, not only over the second half of the nineteenth century, but at least in the northern towns, right down to the 1960s (at St Andrew's, Newcastle, one of the unofficial pastoral duties was still that of giving help to the wandering Irish beggars who came to the door) suggests that there is indeed here a confessional and social reality which historians – locally as well as nationally – should study, a study which could throw new light on one of the more substantial - and one of the more beleaguered – of those minority cultures of which (it could be argued) the 'majority' culture of modern Britain is composed.

Notes

1 On the agitation to protect the religious status of Catholic pauper children, see PRO HO 45/7646, HO 45/6840; Ed. 9/31. T. Burke, *Catholic History of Liverpool*, Liverpool, 1910, pp. 120–1, 130–4,

141–2, 165. Canon E. St John, *Manning's Work for Children*, London, 1929,
2 The one important question for this subject of soldiers is one I have not explored. In 1861, out of an army of 205,829 men, 58,630 were Roman Catholics. W. G. Lumley, 'The statistics of the Roman Catholics in England and Wales', *Journal of the Statistical Society*, XXVII, 1864, p. 322
3 At Millbank, where the letters RC were appended to the name of the Catholic inmate on his cell door, there was a small room reserved for the Catholic clergyman, 'where the prisoners of that faith confess': H. Mayhew and J. Binney, *The Criminal Prisons of London and Scenes of Prison Life*, London, 1862, p. 257; see also pp. 525–7, 230, 564, 568, 569, 617 for the treatment of Catholics in London prisons.
4 Newman to Bowden, 21 Sept. 1849, in C. S. Dessain (ed.) *The Letters and Diaries of John Henry Newman* London 1963, xiii, pp. 260–1.
5 See also R. Chapman, *Father Faber*, London 1961, p. 234 and the printed and MS. volume in the Brompton Oratory archives, *The Oratory in London*, pp. 94–5. Forty-six patients were anointed, of whom thirty-four died.
6 D. Attwater, *The Catholic Church in Modern Wales*, London, 1935, p. 70.
7 'A London Rambler', *The Romance of the Streets*, London, 1872, p. 298.
8 J. E. Handley, *The Irish in Modern Scotland*, Cook 1947, p. 116.
9 H. Mayhew, *London Labour and the London Poor*, London, 1861, ii, p. 251.
10 Even Pagan O'Leary, the Fenian, a 'fiery truculent man', who 'delighted' in the religious implication of his soubriquet, was ready to respect the association. Questioned by prison officials after his arrest, and ordered to classify himself under the heading of 'Religion', he attempted at first to claim he was a pagan. No, they said, they could not accept that – they had headings in their books 'Roman Catholics', 'Protestant', and 'Presbyterian', but not 'Pagans'. 'Well', he said, 'You have two kinds, the 'Robbers' (meaning Protestants) and the 'Beggars' (Catholics), and if I must choose, put me down as 'Beggar'. John Denver, *Old Rebel*, p. 87.
11 Rylands Library, R62533, Manchester Newspaper Cuttings, 'The census in the slums', no.2.
12 S. Bamford, *Passages in the Life of a Radical*, London, 1905, ii, p. 153.
13 H. Mayhew, *London Labour and the London Poor*, London, 1861, i, p. 110.
14 Mayhew, *op. cit.*, p. 111. Some of the English stood in fear of them. A street-patterer who had not hesitated, in quest of newsworthy sensation, to kill off the Duke of Wellington on two separate occasions – 'once by a fall from his horse, and the other time by a "sudden and myst-erious death" ' – felt it prudent to abstain from exercising his talents upon a comparably prominent Catholic subject. 'He once

thought of poisoning the Pope, but was afraid of the street Irish': Mayhew, *op. cit.*, pp. 240, 244.
15 Charles Booth, *Life and Labour of the People of London*, London, 1902, 3rd ser., iv, p. 202, vii, p. 255; L. G. Vere, *Random Recollections of Old Soho*, Barnet, 1912, p. 27.
16 Wolverhampton Reference Library, Wolverhampton Scrapbook, 'An appeal to the Protestants of Wolverhampton by a True Protestant', *Protestant Record*, March, 1866.
17 LRO, CPR/7.
18 J. Mayhall, *The Annals of Yorkshire*, Leeds, 1865 (?), ii, pp. 50–1.
19 PRO Ed. 9/14, Sandford to Sandford. Mathew Arnold referring to them as 'trying material', PRO Ed, 9/14, Arnold to Sandford, 29 April 1875.
20 Rev. T. Livius, *Father Furnis and His Work for Children*, London and Leamington, 1896, pp. 65, 150. St Chad's Catholic Register, Birmingham, iii, 22 November 1881. St Peter's Register, Birmingham, 29 March 1863; Holy Week, 1864.
21 *Wigan Observer*, 1 July 1859.
22 *Preston Guardian*, 30 May 1868.
23 J. Denvir, *The Irish in Britain*, London, 1894, pp. 306–7,
24 Cf. e.g. Rev. P. Rogers, *Father Theobald Mathew, Apostle of Temperance*, Dublin, 1943, p. 86, for the Irishwomen at Deptford 'with shillelaghs inside their umbrellas', who formed part of a self-appointed bodyguard for Father Mathew; *Aris's Birmingham Gazette*, 28 September 1867, for Mary Ann Gilmour, a rag sorter of 'Little Ireland', Dudley, who disturbed the service at the Wesleyan Free Chapel as the officiating preacher was praying for the conversion of Papists; *Ashton Reporter*, 23 May 1868, for the poor washerwoman of Flag Alley, Bridget Cullen; PRO HO 45/36331/2 for the Regents Park disturbances of 1884, some of the Irishwomen 'having their sleeves tucked up and declaring they were going to "walk in heretics' blood" '.
25 C. Aspin, *Haslingden*, Haslingden, 1962, p. 153, for an Irishwoman taken in charge with a rolling pin.
26 'A stick with a cog-wheel at the end', 'short sticks loaded with lead and iron' and 'portions of scythe blades' were among the weapons recovered from the Ashton-under-Lyne Irish during the Murphy riots: Lancashire County Record Office CPR/1.
27 T. M. Healy, *Letters and Leaders of My Day*, London 1928, i. p. 24. During the Ashton rioting William Ibbetson was shot in the bowels from St Mary's Roman Catholic church, while at St Peter's, Staleybridge, the parish priest himself, the Rev. Joseph Daley, was charged with wounding a man with a gun: LRO CPR/1
28 Birmingham, Carr's Lane MSS, Mr Jackson's Journal, 20 July 1842, 11 August 1843.
29 Carr's Lane MSS, Joseph Frye's Journal, 19 March, 15 May, 4 October 1850.
30 'We were once Catholics and carried Saint Colman of Cloyne about

wid us in a box; but after hearing a sermon at a church about images, we went home, took the saint out of the box, and cast him into a river': G. Borrow, *Wild Wales*, World Classics edn, London, 1927, pp. 609–10.
31 G. Borrow, *op. cit.*, p. 610.
32 Carr's Lane MSS, Mr Sibree's Journal, 28 February 1839.
33 A. Burton, *Rushbearing*, Manchester, 1891, p. 64.
34 PRO HO 45/6794/7; *The Times*, 6 October 1862.
35 *The Times*, 8, 10, 14 and 21 October 1862. On the Garibaldi riots at Birkenhead, see PRO HO 45/7326/10; *The Times*, 10, 17, 18, 25 and 30 October 1862; T. Burke, *Catholic History of Liverpool*, Liverpool, 1910, pp. 154–5. On the Garibaldian disturbances about the Irish quarter of Chester, see *The Times* 30 October 1862. At Cardiff a party of Irishmen, 'armed with bludgeons', attacked and 'severely injured' a rival party of Italian sailors; 'The Irishmen asked ... if they were for Garibaldi or the Pope, and on replying for the former they set upon them': *Preston Guardian*, 1 November 1862.
36 H. Mayhew, *London Labour and the London Poor*, London, 1861, ii, pp. 503–4.
37 J. Toole, *Fighting Through Life*, London, 1935.
38 J. Denvir, *Old Rebel*, p. 244.
39 Charles Booth, *Life and Labour of the People of London*, London, 1902, 3rd Ser., iv, p. 197.
40 Sir James Sexton, *Agitator ... An Autobiography*, London, 1936, pp. 18–19.
41 T. Barclay, *Memoirs and Medleys, the Autobiography of a Bottle-washer*, Leicester 1934, pp. 5–8, 19.
42 George Lansbury, *My Life*, London, 1928, pp. 26–7.
43 T. A. Jackson, *Solo Trumpet*, London, 1953, p. 54, referring to the time of his father's childhood.
44 Rev. T. Livius, *Father Furnis and His Work for Children*, London and Leamington, 1896, p. 90; St Peter's Register, Birmingham, 5 June 1864; Pat O'Mara, *The Autobiography of a Liverpool Irish Slummie*, London, 1934, pp. 143, 153, 218. Sneering at the scapular and *Agnus Dei* which they wore, and in one case destroying them, was one of the humiliations alleged to have been imposed upon the Fenian prisoners in Portland prison: PRO HO 45/19461.
45 When the Manchester martyrs Larkin, Gould and Allen were executed, 'each of the men bore a cross upon his breast': *Preston Guardian*, 237 November 1867.
46 Carr's Lane MSS, Mr Jackson's Journal, 11 August 1843.
47 R. Mayhew, *London Labour and the London Poor*, London, 1861, i, p. 111.
48 Rev. E. Price, *Sick Calls from the Diary of a Missionary Priest*, London, 1850, p. 82.
49 H. Mayhew, *London Labour and the London Poor*, London, 1861, ii, p. 504.
50 Mayhew, *op. cit.*, i, p. 116. Cf. also Mayhew, *op. cit.*, pp. 111, 114.

E. Waugh, *Home-Life of the Lancashire Factory Folk During the Cotton Famine*, London, 1867, pp. 76, 77, 85. J. Denvir, *The Irish in Britain*, London, 1894, pp. 442–3.
51 T. Barclay, *Memoirs and Medleys, op. cit.* p. 7.
52 H. Mayhew, *London Labour and the London Poor*, London, 1861, i, p. 114.
53 *Franciscan Missions Among the Colliers and Ironworkers of Monmouthshire*, London, 1876, p. 69. 'His parents, who died when he was quite young, were Irish and Catholic, and he had, of course, been baptised . . . but he knew nothing himself'; occasionally he attended mass on Sundays 'because he saw that other Catholics did so', but 'he had not the faintest notion what it meant'.
54 'The Irish in England', *Dublin Review*, 1856, p. 504.
55 Rev. E. Price, *Sick Calls from the Diary of a Missionary Priest*, London, 1850, pp. 241–5; J. Denvir, *Old Rebel*, p. 15.
56 *The Nation*, 7 June 1856.
57 Rev. F. J. Kirk, *Reminiscences of an Oblate of St Charles*, London 1905.
58 A Working Man, *Reminiscences of a Stonemason*, London, 1908, pp. 16–17. Cf. also LRO QJD 1/197 for the use of Irish during a riot against the police. *Preston Guardian*, 25 March 1868 for the use of Irish during a neighbourhood row. George Borrow, *Wild Wales*, World Classics Edn, London, 1927, pp. 609–11 for the use of Irish in moments of embarrassment. *The Nation*, 7 June 1856 for the prevalence of Irish among the colony at Wednesbury. Birmingham Reference Library, Journal of T. A. Finigan, Birmingham Town Mission, 1837–1838, and F. W. Hackwood, *Religious Wednesbury*, Wednesbury, 1907, p. 117 for the use of Irish-speaking Scripture readers
59 T. Barclay, *Memoirs and Medleys, op. cit.*, pp. 3, 10, 23.
60 J. Denvir, *The Irish in Britain*, London, 1894, pp. 259–60; St Vincent's, Sheffield, *Centenary*, p. 19; D. Attwater, *The Catholic Church in Modern Wales*, London, 1935, pp. 70–1. Father Sherlock, 'one of the finest specimens of the good old "soggarth aroon",' presided over the first Home Rule Convention in 1873: J. Denvir, *Old Rebel*, pp. 176, 177.
61 H Mayhew, *London Labour and the London Poor*, London, 1861, i, p. 514; cf. also i, pp. 123, 151, 515.
62 Sunday evenings appear to have been the only time of the week when Irish servant girls were allowed by their mistresses to attend their chapels: Vincent Smith MSS, 'Catholic Tyneside', pp. 27–8.
63 *Birmingham Daily Gazette*, 22 May 1879. For a similar situation at the Brownlow Hill workhouse, Liverpool, see T. Burke, *Catholic History of Liverpool*, Liverpool, 1910, p. 133. Cf. also Birmingham Diocese MSS, 'Catholic chapel in the Birmingham Union Workhouse', 24 February 1858. *Birmingham Daily Post*, 8 and 21 May 1879; *Birmingham Daily Gazette*, 18 November 1880. At St Patrick's, Soho, the fourth confessional in the church, 'a temporary arrangement erected by the side of the Altar of the Seven Dolours', was occasionally used 'for

An Irish religion 117

the deaf old people of the workhouse during Sunday Mass': L. G. Vere, *Random Recollections of Old Soho*, Barnet, 1912, pp. 86–7.
64 J. Denvir, *The Irish in Britain*, London, 1894, pp. 408, 410–12. Birmingham Diocese MSS, Lempfried to Ullathorne, 20 December 1848. Foley MSS, iv, p. 345.
65 Rev. B. Kelly, 'Bollington Catholicism', MS history, 1930–40.
66 *Franciscan Missions Among the Colliers and Ironworkers of Monmouthshire*, London, 1876, p. 61. For the same complaint about the congregation at Abersychan, *op. cit.*, p. 26. For a memoir of the congregation at Abertillery, M. F. Ryan, *Fenian Memories*, Dublin, 1945, p. 49.
67 E. M. Sneyd-Kinnersley, *H.M.I. Some Passages in this Life of one of H.M. Inspectorate of Schools*, London 1908, p. 231.
68 The Meaneys, for example, 'a family which . . . sent out many priests from Ireland to labour among the Irish poor abroad', Provided two missionary priests at Blackburn and one at St Mary's, Levenshulme. A nephew of the Blackburn Meaneys, Fr Patrick O'Connor, also worked for a time at Blackburn, Fr Denis Byrne, the first rector at St Patrick's, Bolton, was a brother of Fr Michael Byrne of St Marie's, Bury, and Fr Thomas Byrne of St Michael's, Manchester: Bolton, *op. cit.* pp. 80, 107, 109, 120–1, 143, 145, 174, 190, 212. Father Tracy of Heaton Norris, Stockport, who seems himself to have been a nationalist sympathiser, had a brother Mat, a reporter on the *Cork Examiner*, who was arrested for carrying a musket during the Fenian rising of 1867, but was able to extract compensation from the British government for wrongful arrest. 'Friends gathered round him night after night, to enjoy his compensation and hospitality. At the end of his . . . evenings he would raise his glass in pathetic self-pity, crying "Ah, boys! the British Government has been the ruin of me" ' (T. M. Healy, *Letters and Leaders of My Day*, London 1928 i, p. 25).
69 *Franciscan Missions Among the Colliers and Ironworkers of Monmouthshire*, London, 1876, p. 27. Bolton, *op. cit.* pp. 184, 192. When the foundation stone was laid at St Vincent's, Liverpool (a ceremony observed on St Patrick's day, 1856), 'the Irish ship carpenters of the parish passed in single file, each laying one day's wages on the newly blessed stone. Then followed the dock labourers with their offerings, the total amounting to one hundred pounds, nine shillings', Burke p. 126.
70 *Franciscan Missions Among the Colliers and Ironworkers of Monmouthshire*, London, 1876, pp. 39–40, 59. Foley MSS, iii, series 1, 2, p. 579. P. Alden, 'The problem of East London', in R. Mudie-Smith (ed.), *The Religious Life of London*, London, 1904, J. Denvir, *The Irish in Britain*, London, 1894, p. 303. Charles Booth, *Life and Labour of the People of London*, London, 1902, 3rd series, i, pp. 83, 88, 233, ii, pp. 38–9, iv, p. 127, v, p. 68, vii, pp. 243, 265.
71 At Barrack Yard, Wigan, 'a narrow court . . . off the main street . . . inhabited exclusively by the lowest class of Irish', the mob of colliers and workmen in 1859 wrote the word 'English' 'in white chalk' on the door of one of the very few houses spared from their attack: Lancashire County Record Office, CPR/7.

Religion

72 Booth, *op. cit.*
73 *Ibid.*
74 Birmingham Diocese MSS, Phillips to Walsh, 12 September 1836.
75 Lancs County Record Office, Archdiocese of Liverpool MSS, Visitation Returns, 1855–8.
76 George Eliot, *Adam Bede*, London, 1906, i, p. 52.
77 W. Bowman, *England in Ashton-under-Lyne*, Ashton-under-Lyne, 1963, p. 23.
78 Lancs County Record Office, Archdiocese of Liverpool MSS, 'Notes on Diocesan History'.
79 Bolton, *op. cit.*, p. 150.
80 Burke, *Catholic History of Liverpool*.
81 *Stockport News*, reference mislaid.
82 *Franciscan Missions Among the Colliers and Ironworkers of Monmouthshire*, London, 1876, is an admirable memoir, whose writing takes on something of the dramatic charater of the countryside it describes.
83 Lancs County Record Office, Archdiocese of Liverpool MSS, Visitation Returns, 1865, Holy Cross.
84 Charles Burke, *History of Camberwell Catholic Mission, 1860–1910*, London, nd, p. 7.
85 Charles Booth, *Life and Labour of the People of London*, London, 1902, 3rd series, vi, pp. 18–19.
86 H. J. Dyos, *Victorian Suburb, A Study of the Growth of Camberwell*, Leicester, 1961, p. 111.
87 D. Attwater, *The Catholic Church in Modern Wales*, London, 1935, pp. 72, 137. *Franciscan Missions Among the Colliers and Ironworkers of Monmouthshire*, London, 1876, pp. 22, 35. On Welsh hostility to Roman Catholics generally, see Attwater, *op. cit.*, pp. 33, 38–9, 68–9, 71–2, 91, 101, 115–19, 122, 126, 129–30, 135, 207, 223–4, 275.
88 Attwater, *op. cit.*, p. 91. On the opposition at Wednesbury, where, to undermine the foundations, a Protestant party threatened to purchase the mines and minerals beneath the chapel, see J. F. Ede, *The History of Wednesbury*, Wednesbury, 1950, p. 318, and J. F. Bromfield, *St Mary's Parish Centenary*, Wednesbury, 1950.
89 *Franciscan Missions Among the Colliers and Ironworkers of Monmouthshire*, London, 1876, pp. 16–17.
90 R. Smith, *Ye Chronicles 306–1910 of Blackburnshire*, Nelson, 1910, p. 195. At Burnley itself the opening of St Mary's in 1849 provoked an outburst of Protestant hostility: 'the walls of the town were flooded with "no popery" placards, the exterior carvings round the church were gravely damaged and the statue of Our Lady within the church . . . shot at': Odo Blundell, *Old Catholic Lancashire*, London, 1925, i, p. 30.
91 T. Burke, *Catholic History of Liverpool*, Liverpool, 1910, p. 45.
92 *Franciscan Missions Among the Colliers and Ironworkers of Monmouthshire*, London, 1876, pp. 38–9.
93 Birmingham St Chad's Cathedral MSS, 'Catholic Poor Schools', 21 August, 11 September, 30 November 1849.

94 William Dollman, 'a very powerful, ill-looking man', lodging in London Prentice Street, was alleged to have struck the fatal blow in the Painter murder: Joseph Allday, *Full and Correct Reports of the Trials . . . for the Murder of Mr. Painter, etc.*, Birmingham, 1835, p. 30..

95 *Rep . . . St Peter's District Visiting Society for 1844*, Birmingham, 1845, p. 3. Twenty years later the street was described as containing 'a mixture of the worst class of Irish and of regular thieves': 'The night side of Birmingham', Osborne Newspaper Cuttings, ii, p. 184, Birmingham Reference Library. London Prentice Street was the scene of a famous Protestant scandal in 1848 when Father Malloy, a local Catholic priest, was accused of having seized a New Testament from one of his parishioners and publicly burning it on the ground. For the indignant sermons see Rev. J. C. Miller, *Bible Burning, the Substance of a Sermon*, Birmingham, 1848; Rev. I. C. Barrett, *The Protestant Bible Burnt, a sermon . . .* , London, 1848. 'My scripture reader was actually kicked by an Irishman as he went out of the court, who used the strongest language and exclaimed "Break his neck!" "IT WOULD LEAD TO THE BIBLE!" ': Miller, *op. cit.*, pp. 7–8.

96 R. H. Kiernan, *The Story of the Archdiocese of Birmingham*, Birmingham, nd, p. 33.

97 Birmingham Carr's Lane MSS, 'Mr Clay's Journal', esp. 20 February 1839 on the difficulties among them of a town missionary.

98 Letter signed by 'an English Catholic' in *Birmingham Daily Gazette*, 1 July 1867.

99 James Murphy, *The Religious Problem in English Education: The Crucial Experiment*, Liverpool, 1959, p. 17. T. Burke, *Catholic History of Liverpool*, Liverpool, 1910, p. 73.

100 *Report . . . Catholic Poor School Committee*, London, 1847, pp. 65, 69.

101 Joseph O'Connor, *Hostage to Fortune*, Dublin, 1951, p. 11.

102 PRO Ed 3/19.

103 Kirk, *op. cit.*, p. 90.

104 L. G. Vere, *Random Recollections of Old Soho*, Barnet, 19, p. 28.

105 Rev. T. Livius, *Father Furnis and His Work for Children*, London and Leamington, 1896, pp. 45, 49–50, 143. PRO Ed 3/26, St Leonard's Bromley; Ed 3/6, St Francis Xavier's, Seven Dials. St Peters Register, Birmingham, 19, 26 July 1863; 27 March, 3 April, 7 August 1864. Lancs County Record Office, Archdiocese of Liverpool MSS, School Exam. & Insp. Returns, 1858, St Patrick's Wigan; Visitation Returns, 1858, The Willows. PRO Ed 9/14, Alderson to Sandford, 28 April 1875.

106 Charles Booth, *Life and Labour of the People of London*, London, 1902, 3rd series, vi, p105. L. G. Vere, *Random Recollections of Old Soho*, Barnet, 1912, pp. 24–8.

107 L. G. Vere, *Random Recollections of Homerton Circuit*, Barnet, 1912, p. 199. Father Vere returned to St Patrick's, Soho, after a period of service at Homerton.

108 PRO Ed 3/13.

109 Society of Jesus, London, Foley MSS, iii, Series 1 and 2, p. 728. T. Burke, *Catholic History of Liverpool*, Liverpool, 1910, p. 151.
110 London Oratorian Library, Faber to Lady Arundel, 11 March 1852; Hutchison to Lady Arundel, 5 January 1853; 'The Oratory in London', i, pp. 162–3, 188, ii, p. 78. For some of the rival missions in this part of London see Rev. S. Garratt, *Irish in London*, London, 1852; Maud Stanley, *Work About the Five Dials*, London, 1878; Katherine Warburton, *Memories of a Sister of St Saviour's Priory*, Oxford and London, 1903, pp. 41–75.
111 L. G. Vere, *Old Soho Days*, pp. 31–2.
112 St Patrick's, Soho, MSS, 'St Josephs School'. In all seventy-one of the 135 children whose addresses are recorded came from Princes Row itself, and the remainder were drawn almost entirely from the immediately surrounding neighbourhood. In 1875 the Puseyites left, and their school in Princes Row was taken over on behalf of St Patrick's by the Poor Servants of the Mother of God: L. G. Vere, *Old Soho Days*, pp. 21–2, 31.
113 PRO Ed 3/19, St Joseph's, Fitzroy Court.
114 The words are those of Father Barge, missionary rector of St Patrick's, Soho: L. G. Vere, *Old Soho Days*, p. 72.
115 Father Caroll at Merthyr, an Irish priest who covered the district of Merthyr, Dowlais, Rhymney and Tredegar in the 1830s and 1840s (he died of the fever in 1847), lived in a poor workman's cottage in Dowlais, the entrance to which 'was almost blocked up by two or three sacks of meal or potatoes, which he retailed under market price for the benefit of the poor, yet eking out thereby his own maintenance': D. Attwater, *The Catholic Church in Modern Wales*, London, 1935, p. 74.
116 L. G. Vere, *Old Soho Days, Random Recollections*, p. 87.
117 St Peter's Register, Birmingham, 18 January, 26 April 1863; 13 January 1864. In December 1862 Fr Patrick McLaughlin, Catholic priest at Eastmuir, a village on the outskirts of Glasgow, was committed to prison for contempt of court. He had addressed an envelope for a member of his flock who was making restitution to a fellow-worker in Ireland, the letter containing money he had embezzled. Fr McLaughlin refused to disclose the name of the addressee, and served fourteen days of a thirty-day sentence to prison: J. E. Handley, *The Irish in Modern Scotland*, Cork, 1947, pp. 66–7.
118 L. G. Vere, *Old Soho Days*, pp. 54, 113. Rev. E. Price, *Sick Calls, from the Diary of a Missionary Priest*, London, 1850, pp. 42–3, 318–19; Price was minister at the Sardinian Chapel, Lincoln's Inn Fields.
119 St Peter's Register, Birmingham, 23 November 1862, 11 January 1863. At St Oswald's, Ashton-in-Makerfield, Wigan, it was requested that sick calls 'Should be sent by some responsible person – not by children': St Oswald's Register, Ashton-in-Makerfield, 25 February 1879.

Women

9
The first feminism

BRIDGET HILL

Historians – the vast majority of them male – in looking for a justification for the study of history make grand claims. History, we are told, is concerned with 'the totality of man's past experience'. That totality apparently does not extend to women. History gives a society 'a sense of its own identity'. Yet women are only now beginning to discover theirs. History 'tells us about man in his various activities and environments'.[1] Women are seen as unchanging in history, their activities much the same whatever the environment. They play no part in that grand advance of history. Of course, if one substitutes 'men and women' for 'man', the claims are right. This is what history should be, but it is not the history that so far has been written.

Women have been left outside most written history. It's a role women are long accustomed to. In education and politics, in the economic and indeed the religious spheres, women have had to fight to be allowed entry. The struggles for the vote, for admission to universities, for entry to the professions, for the right to be ordained ministers, have occupied the women's movement since the middle of the nineteenth century – and the struggle is still going on. Denied any part in our historical tradition, women (with the exception of Queens Elizabeth and Victoria and a few others) have often felt virtually shorn of a national identity. So the task of putting women back in history is a formidable one. How best can it be tackled and what should be the concern of feminist historians today?

After the emergence of the women's movement in the 1960s, the initial drive for the discovery of women's history was made into the most recent past. This was not surprising. Interest was focused on the period in which the women's suffrage movement emerged, developed, and, in the period following World War I, largely went to ground. It's been called the 'first wave' of feminism. Since the 1960s there has been produced, and there continues to be produced, a vast amount of immensely rich and varied work covering the period roughly speaking from 1850 to the present day. One of the things which is particularly exciting is the way in which women – individually and in groups - with no academic training and quite outside the institutions in which most historians work, have been motivated by the women's movement to attempt their own contribution to the reconstruction of women's past.

Nevertheless one cannot but be aware that there seems less enthusiasm by feminist historians for entering earlier centuries than the nineteenth. There might seem to be a certain holding back, even wariness, about probing earlier women's history. This is not to underestimate the work that has been done and is in process of being done, on the sixteenth, seventeenth and eighteenth centuries, by individuals and groups of women at universities and polytechnics throughout the country. But in comparison with the work completed on, for example, the period after 1850, it represents a very, very small fraction of the whole.

In her recent work, Deirdre Beddoes claims that 'when the new generation of feminists turned to the study of their history, they found it had not been written'.[2] However, the first wave of feminism also had its historians. As Olwen Hufton has suggested:

> the study of women in the past, while given impetus by the women's movement, is part of a venerable tradition stretching back into the 19th century and much of the work of earlier scholars remains immensely valuable, not merely for its content but for the approaches adopted and the assumptions made.[3]

There has yet to be a study of that remarkable body of women historians writing about women, whose work dates from before the First World War to the late 1920s: Edith Morley, B. L. Hutchins, Barbara Drake, Dorothy Gardiner, Ada Wallas, Margaret McMillan, Eileen Power, Alice Clark, Ivy Pinchbeck and many others.[4] How much of their work was due to the activities of the Fabian Society Women's Group and how much was financed by the Mrs George Bernard Shaw Scholarship at the London School of Economics – a scholarship held by a number of outstanding women historians – has yet to be assessed. But the last two names of that list – Alice Clark whose *Working Life of Women in the 17th Century* was published in 1919, and Ivy Pinchbeck's *Women Workers and the Industrial Revolution 1750–1850* published in 1930 – represent work in women's history which, although after more than half a century a little out of date and overtaken by more recent research, has yet to be replaced by any work, whether by women or men, as scholarly or as all-embracing on either the seventeenth century or the period from the mid-eighteenth to the mid-nineteenth century. It might prove interesting to show the reasons for that relatively short-lived burst of women's history coming to an end. Was it related to Professor Clapham's attack on the work of the Hammonds in his *An Economic History of Modern Britain*?[5] In the debate between the optimists and pessimists over whether or not the standard of living from about 1770–1830 rose, fell or remained static, the Hammonds exemplified the cause of the pessimists. Following Clapham's attack, the debate raged but it was the optimists who were to emerge, at least temporarily, victorious. It was not just the Hammonds or the pessimists who seemed to be discredited but social history in general – and with it women's history. Surely in the debate between pessimists and optimists, the particular experience of labouring women was not unimportant. Or again, was the disappearance of women's history a reflection of the disillusionment that was felt by women when, after years of struggle for the vote, its achievement changed so little – and, as the Depression set in, all the gains that women had won earlier were rapidly eroded.

The process of moving backwards in time – a process that the great majority of feminist historians have followed – is very natural, but is at the same time full of dangers. It is so easy to assume that what characterises the developing women's movement – the nature of marriage within a particular group in society, the relationship between different classes of women and work – in any one period is what is new and distinctive in that period and what distinguishes it from the past. Some feminist historians, for example, have attached supreme importance to the changes that accompanied the Industrial Revolution, defined as 'that process of transformation that occurred in England roughly between the late 18th and early 19th century'.[6] As they see it, these contributed to a sudden and rapid change in the sexual division of labour, the separation of home and work, of public and private spheres, and the emergence of what they have called the 'ideology of domesticity'. Alice Clark in 1919 had seen many of those changes occurring over a century earlier. Recent historians of women like Louise Tilly and Joan Scott[7] have stressed the persistence of traditional values and attitudes during the period of industrialisation – traditional attitudes, indeed, often persisting well into the nineteenth and even into the early years of this century. It is all very well to argue, as Catherine Hall has done, that women's work in pre-industrial society was fundamentally different from that in industrial society. The contrast she makes between spinning and factory work is perhaps hardly a valid one. It is at least debatable whether spinning – admittedly the traditional occupation of the female poor – is representative of women's work in pre-industrial society; but factory work surely was *not* representative of women's work in the Industrial Revolution as defined. Indeed even the 1841 census shows factory employment accounting for only 1 per cent of the female workforce. Much more important, and representative of women's employment in the period, was domestic service, which exhibits some remarkably similar characteristics to pre-industrial service.

Agriculture, curiously neglected by historians of women's work, despite the fact that by far the majority of women continued to live in the countryside and often to work in agriculture well into the nineteenth century, also demonstrates the point of much greater continuity than has been suggested, of just how uneven was the incidence of change in different areas of the country. The work of Ann Kussmaul and K. D. M. Snell[8] has shown, for example, how while in the south-east and the Midlands the quantity and nature of women's work available profoundly changed, in other areas and notably the north and west, women continued to do much the same work they had done for centuries – work exhibiting little sexual division – well into the last half of the nineteenth century.

Hall sees the decline of household production as the result of industrial changes, but what primarily undermined such production was change in agriculture. It is interesting that one reason given for female service in husbandry persisting in the north was the relative shortage of labour due to the growth of mines, textile and iron mills.[9]

In the emergence of this 'ideology of domesticity' great significance has been attached to late eighteenth-century evangelicalism. 'The whole notion of duty', writes Catherine Hall, 'was . . . central to Evangelicalism . . . The first set of duties . . . looking after the home and family was in St Paul's terms "guiding the house" . . . Home should be seen as the wife's centre. There she could influence to the good her children, her servants, and her neighbours.'[10] The same point was made by another writer in advising his daughter of the responsibilities of marriage:

> In many things, though the doing them well may raise your credit and esteem, yet the omission of them would draw no immediate reproach upon you; in others, where your duty is

more particularly applied, the neglect of them is amongst those faults which are not forgiven, and will bring you under a censure . . . Of this kind is the government of your house, family and children, which since it is the province allotted to your sex, and that discharging it well will for that reason be expected from you, if you either desert it out of laziness or manage it ill for want of skill, instead of a help you will be an encumbrance to the family where you are placed.[11]

The writer was George Savile, Marquess of Halifax, writing in 1688. One could find the same point being made in Puritan guides to godliness in the late sixteenth and early seventeenth century, and in courtesy books right through the eighteenth century, long before evangelicalism came on the scene in the late eighteenth century. Miranda Chaytor, from her work on English village records of the late sixteenth and seventeenth century, found 'a society in which . . . household tasks limited and defined women's lives . . . their influence was confined to the "private sphere" '.[12] The 'ideology of domesticity' would seem to have more to do with protestantism in general than with any late-eighteenth-century evangelical manifestation of it, although, having said that, it is a far from clear and simple interrelationship.

The attempt to reduce the past to a flat and boring plain, undisturbed by even a suggestion of a hill, must be rejected; but to suggest that changes associated with a very narrow period from the late eighteenth to early nineteenth century began earlier, and were continuing much later, is not to deny the importance of the changes. The Agricultural Revolution has been substantially redefined over recent years. Changes associated with it are now generally recognised to extend from the seventeenth (or even earlier) to the late nineteenth century. Yet no-one has denied the significance of those changes. The barrier recently erected between 'pre-industrial' and 'industrial' England lends itself to this idea of sudden and dramatic change associated with a limited period of industrialisation and seems to me to obscure important similarities and continuities.

Inevitably feminist historians start with certain assumptions about what they are looking for, what areas of the past are worth probing, assumptions largely dictated by the particular preoccupations of the present-day feminist movement, and by what it sees as the main reason for studying the past. But such preoccupations and such reasons are not always the same. Feminist historians disagree among themselves. This you might think is not a bad thing. It should lead to much greater diversity and range in the kind of women's history studied and the approaches used. As Olwen Hufton has emphasised, 'there is no single history to be told of the history of women in any period but rather many stories'.[13] Equally, different motives for studying women's history might be seen as enriching in their consequences. By all means let 'a hundred thousand flowers bloom'.

Among the main motives with which feminist historians have approached the history of women is that of discovering the roots of modern feminism: 'We need', writes Anna Davin, 'to know our past . . . we must know where we came from to understand what we are and where we are going'.[14] Deirdre Beddoes takes the point further: 'not only can the past explain the present, but a knowledge of the past can also prove a source of strength, encouragement and admonition to women engaged in current initiatives for change'.[15] So perhaps the aim of feminist history was first and foremost one of consciousness-raising. There is nothing wrong with such an aim. We commemorate the struggle of the Tolpuddle Martyrs. Annually we celebrate the stand made by the Levellers at Burford in 1649 in that final crushing of the movement. Of course, it's good to be reminded of those parts of our history in which we can have a pride. The feminist movement is rightly proud of its present-day movement. It is natural that it should seek the same pride in its history and more particularly in its forebears. But for a real understanding of women's past we need to go deeper and further than such an approach involves.

A recent review of a book on eight distinguished nineteenth-century women criticised the author for, as the reviewer said, she 'believes that feminism needs a personal identification with heroines'.[16] It was a valid point of criticism. Is it a valid criticism of other feminist history?

What such an attitude tends to ignore is how many women in the past were not heroines, did not resist or revolt, but wholly accepted the role assigned to them by men, and were often the first to criticise any woman who refused to conform. And these women, unheroic and unrevolutionary as they were, have as great an interest for the understanding of women's past as the heroines. They pose important questions with which we need to get to grips. What made the great majority of women so acquiescent in their role of subordination? What provoked them to attack any of their own sex who even slightly deviated from the norm?

To offer a quick answer to the stereotyping of women that male history has presented – of women being an unchanging feature of history concerned, as they have been seen, solely with home, husband and children – 'it is tempting', writes one feminist historian, 'to start with the material which most obviously challenges the stereotypes – with the suffragettes . . . or with other episodes of women's resistance and revolt'.[17] That was written in 1972 but nearly ten years later the same historian, Anna Davin, wrote: 'Early on in the feminist movement the temptation was very much to look particularly for women who could provide an example and an inspiration, who'd been militant in whatever way; or (the other face of it) to see women as victims. Both of these tendencies continue to recur.'[18]

Recently two books were reviewed by Raphael Samuel in *The Guardian*.[19] 'Ancestor worship', the reviewer wrote, 'is the most conservative of all religions. It invites us to take a sentimental view of our weaknesses and a heroic view of our strengths . . . Ancestor worship is premised on a necessary falsification of the past'. The reviewer went on to suggest that inevitably such a search 'for our noble forebears' is a highly selective approach to history – that it ignores what is convenient to ignore and that it forgets 'the black sheep' of the family. Is this perhaps true of some feminist history? The past has an inconvenient habit sometimes of letting us down.

So in approaching women's past we seek explanations of women's present position. Questions are posed about the nature of women's oppression in the past, about the origins of patriarchy and its changing nature, about the sources of women's economic and social inequality. The 'chief danger' of this approach, writes Rosemary O'Day:

> is that we will find what we seek. The historian who wants to trace the oppression of women in the past will discover that oppression by mining the sources only for such evidence as supports the theme. This danger faces all who study the past – we all have preconceptions, ideas, questions which we want to answer and which to some extent dictate our findings. But it is a particularly acute danger for those who are politically or ideologically committed in an active way to a particular cause.[20]

Clearly she was not just thinking of feminist historians, although it's a salutary warning. Another very real danger Sheila Rowbotham has underlined when she writes:

> we need to be cautious about the assumptions we bring to the past. For instance women have seen the defining features of oppression very differently at different times . . . Feminine anthropologists are particularly aware of the dangers of imposing the values of Western Capitalism on women of other

cultures. But we can colonise women in the past too, by imposing modern values.[21]

Feminist historians have expressed themselves anxious to explode the male-created myth of historical progress. But is there a hint of exactly the same sorts of assumptions in some present-day feminist's criticism of women of the past for failing to behave or think like themselves? Does it go with an implicit assumption that the present-day feminist movement represents the peak of feminist achievement, the zenith of our history? And, just occasionally, is it accompanied by a tendency to a slightly condescending attitude to many of those earlier women and women historians who were the real pioneers in women's history?

Some of the general points I have made can be illustrated by looking at one woman of the late seventeenth and early eighteenth centuries – Mary Astell (1666–1731). Better known in the US than here, nevertheless most feminist historians covering her period make reference to her. She has been described as 'the first major English feminist', 'the founder of the feminist movement', 'undoubtedly a Blue-stocking and a feminist', 'the first systematic feminist in England'.[22] Of course much depends on what is meant by 'feminist'. There may well be many modern feminists who will find it difficult to recognise Mary Astell as a forebear; with Joan Kinnaird, some will see her feminism as 'tame'.

Her claim to being considered a 'feminist' is based on two works: *A Serious Proposal to the Ladies* of 1694 and *Reflections upon Marriage* of 1700. Indeed these are often referred to as her 'feminist' writings. Selected passages are frequently quoted in support of the claim that she was a 'feminist'.

At her best she is highly quotable. In *A Serious Proposal to the Ladies* she challenges women to reject the role custom has dictated for them: 'For shame lets abandon the Old, and therefore one would think unfashionable employment of pursuing Butterflies and Trifles. No longer drudge on in the beaten road of Vanity and Folly, which so many have gone before us, but dare to break the enchanted Circle that Custom has plac'd us in.'[23] In the Preface to her *Reflections upon Marriage* she seems to be challenging the arbitrary power of men in marriage: 'if Absolute Sovereignty be not necessary in a State,' she wrote, not long after James II had been ejected,

> how comes it to be so in a Family? or if in a Family, why not in a State, since no Reason can be alledg'd for the one that will not hold more strongly for the other . . . For if Arbitrary Power is evil in itself, and an improper Method of Governing

Rational and Free Agents, it ought not to be Practis'd anywhere; Nor is it less, but rather more mischievous in Families than in Kingdoms by how much 100,000 Tyrants are worse than one . . . If all Men are born free, how is it that all Women are born Slaves?[24]

Stirring words! Good consciousness-raising stuff! Are the labels attached to her really wrong? My objection is that they grossly oversimplify the woman and her ideas. It would, admittedly, simplify the problem she poses for feminist historians if she was seen as the author of only these two works. It would be very easy then to go along with the view that neatly labels her as an early feminist with enlightened ideas on the education of women, and a bitingly satirical analysis of just what marriage meant for women – or at least for women of the upper class. But such a view of her is inadequate. It distorts the real Mary Astell by ignoring her complexity, by failing to see her contradictions and the paradoxes in her thinking. Whether or not she was a 'feminist', she was so many other things besides. Today we have a feminist movement hotly debating whether it is possible to be a good feminist without being a socialist. And here, at the end of the seventeenth century is Mary Astell – a sincerely devout woman of high Anglican and Tory sympathies – a passionate believer in the divine right of kings at a time when few were still prepared to expound so old-fashioned a doctrine. She was a woman with sufficient familiarity with the scriptures and the then current theological debate to be equal to taking on some of the leading religious thinkers of her time. She was to engage in an angry exchange with Daniel Defoe in the early years of the eighteenth century by savagely attacking dissenters at the time of the debate on occasional conformity.[25] She was to attack Dr White Kennett's sermon on the fast for the martyrdom of Charles I because of its failure to analyse correctly the causes of the Civil War and totally to absolve the King from all blame.

It is this very combination of beliefs which to us today seems incompatible, if not bizarre, that makes Mary Astell worthy of deeper study. It is the conflicting and contradictory nature of her ideas which to my mind poses a real challenge to feminist historians. Few have so far probed that complexity. Of those that have, one American feminist historian, Joan Kinnaird, has not only seen the problem Mary Astell poses but attempted to resolve it. It is a fascinating article.[26] She has recognised that Mary Astell was not alone in her ideas. They were shared to a greater or lesser extent by an interesting group of women who emerged in the last decade of the seventeenth century: Damaris Masham, Lady Mary

Chudleigh, the anonymous Eugenia, and the anonymous author of *An Essay in Defence of the Female Sex*,[27] to mention only a few. So the problem is not one confined to Mary Astell.

Joan Kinnaird argues that, under the leadership of historians like Keith Thomas and Patricia Higgins, we have attached too much importance to the influence of the sects in the 1640s and 1650s in upsetting traditional ideas of women's role both inside and out of marriage. For how is it, she asks, that Mary Astell, acknowledged as 'the first major English Feminist', not only was not a Puritan but was passionately opposed to dissent in any form and looked back with horror on the events of the 1640s. Her conclusion is that we have been wrong in our assumptions that feminism in this period is exclusively linked with political and religious radicalism. She writes: 'fully as much as Puritanism . . . conservative Anglican thought . . . promoted the dignity of women, education, reform, and the idea of companionate marriage'.[28] Yet surely this is to see Mary Astell as totally divorced from the historical context and to attempt to fit her into some preconceived idea of what late-seventeenth and early-eighteenth-century feminism ought to have been. We need to remember that a feminist movement at that stage would have been inconceivable.[29]

In passing it also reveals a misunderstanding, I believe, of Keith Thomas and others who have charted the development of more radical ideas about women, marriage and the relations between the sexes, that coincide with the collapse of censorship and the emergence of the sects in the 1640s. I do not think such authors would want to link such new ideas on women solely to the political and religious radicalism of those years. Rather they might point out how, not until censorship collapses, can such ideas emerge, ideas which may well have been in existence long before. In the same way historians attempting to account for the sudden flowering of a literature on and by women in the late 1690s have pointed to a lapsing of the Licensing Act in 1695 and the new freedom to publish which resulted.

In fact Joan Kinnaird is not entirely happy with her own theory. Perhaps after all, she argues, Mary Astell was not quite the 'feminist' she has been held to have been. She looks again at her *A Serious Proposal*. What was she proposing? It outlines an idea for a 'religious retirement' for women where they could temporarily withdraw from the world. In this retreat their employment would be not only 'to magnify God, to love one another', but also 'to communicate that useful knowledge, which by due improvement of their time in Study and Contemplation'[30] they would obtain. 'The student of feminism', Joan Kinnaird writes, 'must admit to considerable consternation on discovering what her actual programme was'. 'How', she asks, 'could such radical fervour, such feminist zeal end in so tame a proposition . . . nothing more than a revival of Anglican nunneries.'[31] Tut tut! Mary Astell's feminism has been found wanting. Maybe after all she should have been labelled 'proto-feminist, second class'. But on closer study her 'Protestant nunnery' is of much more interest than this suggests. Firstly because here again Mary Astell was not unique in holding such ideas about a 'religious retirement' where women could get on with their education. Such a notion can be traced right from the Reformation down to the end of the eighteenth century – but every now and then it emerges particularly strongly. This is true of the post-Restoration period. It suggests at just what a low ebb the state of girls' education was. The fact that the idea continues to emerge might suggest that very little real improvement in women's and girls' education was seen until the end of the eighteenth century, and perhaps not even then. It also tells us something of the predatory nature of most upper-class men in a society where mercenary marriages were the rule, and how threatened women felt in such a society. For the only method of escaping from the 'bold importunate and rapacious vultures',[32] as Mary Astell called them, was by physically separating themselves from the rest of society to places where, Daniel Defoe wanted to insist, an Act of Parliament made it a felony for any man to enter 'by force or fraud'.[33] His was a sinister comment on the nature of life for upper-class women at that time. It relates to the large number of cases of abduction of heiresses and girls with a sizeable fortune from boarding schools throughout the eighteenth century.

In her attitude to women and marriage, Mary Astell again might be regarded as a somewhat 'tame' feminist. There is no question but that she accepted the subordinate position of women in marriage – for 'order's sake',[34] and because, just as the king was divinely ordained to rule over his subjects, so was the husband to rule over his wife and children. Mary Astell fully recognised that this did not necessarily mean any superiority of the male sex – indeed, often the reverse, wives had to endure marriages with sots and fools that they must treat as gods. Marriage she saw as women's trial. She had no other answer to the misery that most marriages involved among her social equals except more education for women. Perhaps, she argued, if they were better educated they might take more time accepting a man as a husband – and choose better. That it was no real answer she would have been the first to admit. It was making the best of a bad job.

No woman of Mary Astell's time rejected the subordinate role of women in marriage. But what I think makes Mary Astell different is that there is a suggestion – and it was a revolutionary one at the time – that marriage was not the only option open to women, in a society where 'all women are understood either married or to be married',[35] and where, as Mary Astell put it, a woman 'was taught to think marriage her only Preferment'[36] who 'never considered that she should have a higher design than to get her a Husband'. What is remarkable in her suggestion is that not only was spinsterhood not abject failure for a woman, but, on the contrary, it could be a way to maintain women's independence, and even to realise self-fulfilment. Given more education, women might conclude that it 'was not good for a woman to marry'.

Another of the things that distinguishes Mary Astell's writings is her scorn for men and the savagery of her irony in expressing her total contempt for them. Men, she wrote, were 'a cunning, designing enemy from without', 'serpents' and 'deceivers'.[37] 'Have not all the great Actions that have been perform'd', she asks ironically,

> been done by men? Have they not founded Empires and overturn'd them? Do not they make Laws and continually repeal and amend them? Their vast Minds lay kingdoms waste, no bounds or measures can be prescrib'd to their Desires . . . What is it they cannot do? They make Worlds and ruin them . . . All that the wise Man pronounces is an Oracle and every word the Witty speaks a jest.[38]

Such powerful anti-male language had led one historian (male) to write of her, and of many of the women of letters of her time, as sharing 'a common strain of abnormality . . . Orinda, Mary Astell and Mary Manley were, for instance, all sexually odd; the first had lesbian leanings, the second was a man-hating recluse, and the third one of the most notorious demi-mondaines of her day'.[39] Recently a feminist historian in the US has insisted that in Mary Astell's 'feminism' there was 'a rejection of physiological womanhood'.[40] Another has found her expressions of scorn for men 'an unattractive feature of Mary Astell's personality'.[41] But the battle she was fighting, that of rejecting the view of women as intellectually inferior to men, led her to conclude that if and when women were found inferior to men, it was the result of their exclusion from the educational opportunities enjoyed by men and owed nothing to nature. Who was to blame for that exclusion? Men. So the expression of anti-male feeling should not surprise us. In a way it's one of the most modern aspects of Mary Astell and one with which many radical feminists will sympathise in their location of the origins of women's oppression in Men –'the oldest and most basic form of domination' as the *Redstocking Manifesto* put it in 1979. 'All other forms of exploitation and oppression . . . are extensions of male supremacy.'[42]

The nature of these accusations levelled at Mary Astell and other women writers of her time, of their being sexually abnormal, or rejecting 'physiological womanhood', are reminiscent of those contemporary accusations levelled against women of learning, the suggestion for instance that learning was 'masculine' and learned women unsexed. So Dr James Fordyce in his *Sermons to Young Women* of 1766 wrote that 'A masculine woman must be naturally an unamiable creature. I confess myself shocked, whenever I see the sexes confounded . . . any young woman of better rank, that throws off all the lovely softness of her nature, and emulates the daring intrepid temper of a man – how terrible!'[43] And you will recall that it was a woman, Lady Bradshaigh, who in the 1740s wrote to Samuel Richardson 'I own I do not approve of great Learning in Women. I hate to hear Latin out of a Woman's mouth. There is something in it to me masculine. I would fancy such a one weary of the petticoat, talking over a bottle'.[44]

But it is Mary Astell who has the last word. 'On the recommendation from men that women might divert themselves with the study of a little history, she writes:

> with Submission History can only serve us for Amusement and a Subject of Discourse. For tho' it may be of use to the men who govern affairs, to know how their Forefathers acted, yet what is this to us, who have nothing to do with such Business? Some good examples indeed are to be found in History, tho' generally the bad are ten for one; but how will this help our conduct, or excite in us a generous emulation since the men being the Historians, they seldom condescend to record the great and good Actions of Women; and when they take notice of them, 'tis with this Wise remark, that such Women *acted above their Sex* by which one must suppose they wou'd have their Readers understand, that they were not Women who did these great Actions but that they were Men in petticoats![45]

The part played by the careful delineation of the differences between the sexes in justifying women's subordinate role makes one a little nervous of the tendency among some, particularly American, radical feminists, to move from a position of minimising differences between the sexes to a positive emphasis on such differences, and the reassertion of a 'woman-centred perspective'[46] with a claim to their moral superiority over men.

When first I became interested in Mary Astell it was because of her so-called 'feminist writings'. But when I started to look more closely at those writings I was constantly forced to investigate the social, religious and political ideas which she held. It is, for example, quite impossible to understand her views on marriage, with all the ambiguity of much of her writing on the subject, without understanding how deep went the notion of an analogy between relations between king and subjects, and relations between husband and wife. Of course it is an analogy that was made long before Mary Astell, but with the execution of Charles I and, eleven years later, the Restoration, it takes on a new life and more radical purpose.

As relations between king and subject were called into question, so were domestic relations. If, like James II, a king could be 'abdicated' then perhaps so could a husband. 'Supreme Power in any Person, or Assembly,' wrote Locke, 'is forfeited by the miscarriage of those in Authority.'[47] Just as absolute authority of the king was questioned, so was that of fathers and husbands. With the decline of kingly power went a weakening of patriarchal authority. But when Mary Astell asks 'If Absolute Sovereignty be not necessary in a State how comes it to be so in a Family'[48] she is speaking as one still totally wedded to the idea of divine right. She did not believe with Locke that there were circumstances under which subjects had the right to resist and to replace their governor. So in a sense her question is directed at her political opponents, the Whigs; it's an attempt to reveal their inconsistencies as between ideas on the state and ideas of the family. But in another sense she is deliberately probing an analogy which makes her own combination of ideas an uncomfortable one to hold, if not actually an illogical one. If, like the power of the king, that of a husband was divinely ordained, how was it that happy marriages were so few? If the king's subjects had no right of resistance, she was not so sure of wives – slaves to their masters. What results is a tension in her writing. She protests a little too often that it is not her intention 'to stir up sedition' or 'to resist or to abdicate the Perjur'd Spouse'.[49] But if she does not actually confirm the right of women to resist tyrannical power, she goes out of her way to emphasise that 'in fact Tyranny provokes the Opress'd to throw off even a lawful Yoke that sits too heavy'.[50] Women, she emphasises, are 'for the most part wise enough to Love their Chains', but if now they were 'not so well united as to form an Insurrection',[51] if now they were 'too weak to dispute men's authority',[52] is she envisaging a time when, grown stronger, they not only could dispute men's authority but overturn it? We cannot be sure.

So Mary Astell is complex, ambiguous and sometimes downright contradictory. It is unlikely there will be agreement on what were the major influences on her work, or on what exactly she thought, or on how her religious and political views fit with her views on women, marriage and the relations between the sexes. But what makes her more than an individual challenging present-day feminist historians is that she was not alone in her period in holding what to us is a strange combination of ideas. If more remarkable, and certainly more articulate, she was representative of a group of women who combined enlightened ideas on women and women's education with high Tory politics, high church religion, and often both. So that a study of Mary Astell involves us in a study of the social history of a period, 1689–1714, where so far relatively few social historians have ventured, and even fewer historians of women. Of course this group of women was a minority, representing on the whole upper-class women. But it was only these women who had the leisure, the education and the necessary financial independence to write. Trying to come to grips with the problems they pose, trying to make sense of their 'feminism' within this religious and political background, is also to contribute to a greater understanding of the period as a whole.

Notes

1. The source of these quotations is Professor Arthur Marwick in the Open University Arts Foundation Course, A 101. His failing, it must be stressed, is linguistic rather than sexist.
2. Deirdre Beddoes, *Discovering Women's History*, London 1983, p. 3.
3. Olwen Hufton, 'Women in history. I: Early modern Europe', *Past and Present*, 101, November, 1983, p. 125.
4. The list could be extended to include women social historians of that generation: Lilian Knowles, Barbara Hammond, Dorothy George, Dorothy Marshall and Margaret Llewellyn Davis.
5. J. H. Clapham, *An Economic History of Modern Britain*, 1950, second preface; originally published 1926.
6. Catherine Hall and Susan Himmelweit, 'Development of family and work in capitalist society', in Francis Aprahamian and Perry Morley (eds.), *The Changing Experience of Women*, Open University Course, Units 7 & 8, Milton Keynes 1983.
7. Louise Tilly and Joan Scott, *Women, Work and Family*, New York, 1978.
8. See K. D. M. Snell, 'Agricultural seasonal unemployment, the standard of living and women's work in the south and east, 1690–1860', *Economic History Review*, XXXIV, 1981, and his more recent *Annals of*

the Labouring Poor, Cambridge, 1985, and Ann Kussmaul, *Servants in Husbandry in Early Modern England*, Cambridge, 1981.
9 Ann Kussmaul, *op. cit.*, p. 133.
10 Catherine Hall, 'The early formation of Victorian domestic ideology', in Sandra Burman (ed.), *Fit Work for Women*, London, 1979, pp. 27-8.
11 Lord Halifax, *Complete Works*, edited by J. P. Kenyon, Penguin, Harmondsworth, 1969, p. 288.
12 Miranda Chaytor, 'Household and kinship: Ryton in the late sixteenth and early seventeenth centuries', *History Workshop Journal*, 10, Autumn, 1980.
13 Olwen Hufton, 'Women in history. I: Early modern Europe', *Past and Present*, 101, November, 1983, p. 126.
14 Anna Davin, 'Women and history', in Michelene Wandor (ed.), *The Body Politic*, London, 1972, pp. 215-24.
15 Deirdre Beddoes, *Discovering Women's History*, London, 1983, p. 6.
16 Sheila Rowbotham, 'Heroines for the cause', *Times Literary Supplement*, 28 September 1984.
17 Anna Davin, 'Women and history', in Wandor *op. cit.*, pp. 215-24.
18 Anna Davin, 'Feminism and labour history', in Raphael Samuel (ed.), *People's History and Socialist Theory*, London, 1981, p. 179.
19 Raphael Samuel, 'Mr Benn consults some household gods', *Guardian*, 4 October 1984.
20 Aprahamian and Morley *op. cit*, p. 5.
21 Sheila Rowbotham, 'The trouble with patriarchy', in Raphael Samuel (ed.), *People's History and Socialist Theory*, Routledge & Kegan Paul, 1981, p. 367.
22 Joan Kinnaird, 'Mary Astell and the Conservative contribution to English feminism', *Journal of British Studies*, XIX, 1979, p. 55; Robert Halsband, *The Life of Lady Mary Wortley Montagu*, London, 1956, p. 117; Beatrice Scott, 'Lady Elizabeth Hastings', *Yorkshire Archaeological Journal*, vol. 55, 1983, p. 99; Katharine M. Rogers, *Feminism in Eighteenth Century England*, Brighton, 1982, p. 71.
23 Mary Astell, *A Serious Proposal to the Ladies*, Part I, 1696 (1694), pp. 10-11.
24 Mary Astell, *Reflections upon Marriage*, 1706 (1700), preface.
25 Occasional conformity being the practice by means of which nonconformists could qualify for public office, despite the Test and Corporations Act, by putting in an annual attendance at an Anglican church service and thereby receiving a certificate of attendance from the vicar.
26 Joan Kinnaird, 'Mary Astell and the Conservative contribution to English feminism', *Journal of British Studies*, XIX, 1979, p. 55.
27 Anon., *An Essay in Defence of the Female Sex*, 1696; once ascribed to Mary Astell but now more often ascribed to Judith Drake.
28 Joan Kinnaird, 'Mary Astell and the Conservative contribution to English feminism', *Journal of British Studies*, XIX, 1979, p. 75.
29 Sheila Rowbotham, *Women, Resistance and Revolution*, Harmondsworth, 1972, p. 31.
30 Mary Astell, *A Serious Proposal to the Ladies*, Part I, 1696 (1694), p. 47.

31 Joan Kinnaird, 'Mary Astell and the Conservative contribution to English feminism', *Journal of British Studies*, XIX, pp. 64–5.
32 Mary Astell, *A Serious Proposal to the Ladies*, Part I, 1696 (1694), p. 99.
33 Daniel Defoe, *An Essay on Projects*, 1697, in Henry Morley (ed.), *The Earlier Life and Chief Earlier Works of Daniel Defoe*, 1889, pp. 143–6.
34 Mary Astell, *Reflections upon Marriage*, 1706 (1700), p. 33.
35 *The Lawes Resolutions of Women's Rights*, 1632, p. 6.
36 Mary Astell, *Reflections upon Marriage*, 1706 (1700), p. 53.
37 Mary Astell, *A Serious Proposal to the Ladies*, Part I, 1696 (1694), pp. 24, 12.
38 Mary Astell, *Reflections upon Marriage*, 1706 (1700), pp. 55–6.
39 Roger Thompson, *Women in Stuart England and America*, London, 1974, p. 12.
40 Ruth Perry, 'The veil of chastity: Mary Astell's feminism', *Studies in 18th Century Culture*, vol. 9, 1979, p. 25.
41 Joan Kinnaird, 'Mary Astell and the Conservative contribution to English feminism', *Journal of British Studies*, XIX, p. 64.
42 Quoted in David Bouchier, *The Feminist Challenge*, London, 1983, p. 2.
43 Dr James Fordyce, *Sermons to Young Women*, 1766, pp. 104–5.
44 A. L. Barbauld (ed.), *Correspondence of Samuel Richardson*, 1804, vol. 6, p. 52.
45 Mary Astell, *The Christian Religion as Profess'd by a Daughter of the Church of England*, 1705, p. 293.
46 Hester Eisenstein, *Contemporary Feminist Thought*, London, 1984, p. 140.
47 John Locke, *Two Treatises of Government*, edited by Peter Laslett, 1967, Second Treatise, p. 243.
48 Mary Astell, *Reflections upon Marriage*, 1706 (1700), preface.
49 *Ibid.*
50 Mary Astell, *op. cit.*, p. 91.
51 Mary Astell, *op. cit.*, preface.
52 Mary Astell, *op. cit.*, p. 91.

10
Women and history

OLWEN HUFTON

> What one wants, I thought – and why does not some brilliant student at Newham or Girton supply it? – is a mass of information; at what age did she marry; how many children had she as a rule; what was her house like; had she a room to herself; did she do the cooking; would she be likely to have a servant? . . . It would be ambitious beyond my daring I thought . . . to suggest to the students of those famous colleges that they should *rewrite* history; though I own that it often seems a little queer as it is, unreal, lopsided; but why should they not add a supplement to history? Calling it, of course, by some inconspicuous name so that women might figure there without impropriety. (Virginia Woolf, *A Room of One's Own*, 1929)

Virginia Woolf's plea for a history of women evokes a number of immediate responses. First, though Jane Austen had made the point before her, she appreciated that existing history was lopsided; second, her appeal was so modest, requesting no more than 'a supplement to history'; third, she believed that the enterprise must appear discreet so as not to offend and that the end product could be slipped into the mainstream of history unnoticed perhaps by any except those who wanted it to be there. Further, Virginia Woolf's questions related entirely to social matters on marriage and housekeeping and were of an innocuous variety which might spare even the most pronounced anti-feminist offence. No question here of probing why women were for so long denied entry to the professions or refused the suffrage. She was obviously a little disappointed that the early *alumnae* of the women's colleges had not done more in the way of the historic reconstruction of their past.

Yet, most striking of all and however muted she might try to make the enterprise, she knew she was presenting a challenge, throwing down a gauntlet to the young scholar to get to work on the process of retrieval, a process in itself revolutionary. She assumed women themselves would do the job. No call was made to the opposite sex for help in the enterprise. The discreet endeavour of adding balance to the past was woman's work.

The *alumnae* of the women's colleges seeking to hold down jobs in the hostile men's world of the 1930s were not totally unresponsive to the call – Eileen Power or Doris Stenton for example are counted amongst some of the most distinguished historians of the period. For the gauntlet to be picked up by more than a handful of historians, however, one had to wait for the late 1960s. By then, the business of finding out about women in the past was made neither modestly nor discreetly. It was seen as a right and their absence from history as a part of a package of injustices, a veil of ignorance which had helped to perpetuate social inequality. The notion of women's history, however, was still seen, and increasingly so, as a challenge to many of the existing concepts on which historical writing had been based; that there might be a separate woman's experience which could perhaps cut across class, or that there might be *lacunae* in works laying claim to Nietzsche-type totality.

In the mid 1960s the historical world was still dazzled by Goubert's *Beauvais et le Beauvaisis* and Emmanuel Le Roy Ladurie's *Les Paysans de Languedoc*, works proclaiming an in-depth study of society in whose pages women never (or very rarely) appear. Equally disconcerting was the realisation that lurking in some of the great political episodes of the past, such as the English Civil War or the French Revolution, there might be a gender debate in which the claims of women came into headlong conflict with male claims to political and social pre-eminence. Another disturbing factor which soon emerged was that some 'big events', particularly intellectual movements, might have little or no relevance to the history of women. Joan Gadol Kelly revealed a Renaissance whose main intellectual achievements left women's theoretical, legal and social roles unchanged. Paul Hoffman showed that the Enlightenment might have rejected God, the Roman Catholic church, divine right, patriarchy and privilege, but it retained notions of an inferior female locked by 'natural' law (as opposed to divine law) into the rôle of wife and mother. Neither Renaissance nor Enlightenment could then figure as turning points in women's history.

Looking back over the 1970s and 1980s it is clear that much initial time had to be spent in seeking out the relevant questions.

The labour force committed to retrieval fell into a number of categories: there were instant popularisers making the broad sweep and seeking to depict 300 years of our oppression which were important as serving as a consciousness-raising exercise; some who sought to embody a greater awareness of gender differences in works not specifically devoted to women; and young scholars, able to choose a field of study, embarked on specialised work, the detailed monographs needful to establish a historical area within a university syllabus. Much of this work tragically reached fruition when the period of university retrenchment began.

One bonus was that for the early modern period especially, social history was in the ascendant in the 1960s and early 1970s and women's history could nestle within it. The recent *Hutchinson's Social History of England* series bears witness to the concern that women should be given parity of treatment. One mixed blessing was that the history of women was made to develop a special relationship with the history of the family, which became a heavy industry in the 1970s. Setting aside the very professional work done by the demographers in answering all Virginia Woolf's questions about age of marriage and family size, much of the history of the family has been wildly speculative and has created myths which cautious historians must now modify or demolish. Linda Pollock recently pointed out that the history of childhood has, in the hands of the historians of the family, become a history of child-abuse and that, in fact, the hard evidence to support the wild theories of the battered historical child is simply not there. Neither then is the zombie-like, emotionless, baby-machine-cum-basher created by the historians of the family as an image of the women of the past.

Furthermore, the emphasis on the family and women's reproductive capacities has led to a conflation of family history and women's history with unsatisfactory results. It is an extraordinary fact that the woman of the past we know most about is the unmarried mother, who at any one time formed a minute percentage of the population, whilst spinsters and widows who constituted substantial sectors remain in obscurity.

That said, the work of retrieval has thrown light on some of the mechanics of family life, on women in the workforce (though a great deal more needs to be done here, particularly with reference to the period before 1800), their religiosity, rôles in religious protest movements and dissenting sects, in philanthropic work, as nurses, midwives, mystics, witches, patrons of the arts, financial supporters of writers like Jean Jacques Rousseau, as authors and subjects of creative literature. A great deal remains to be done for the period before 1800, but the groundwork for further studies and a recognition of relevant areas now exists.

Historiographical emphasis as far as women's history is concerned has focused on the nineteenth and twentieth centuries, and much of the really creative thinking and writing about the nature of women's history has been based here for a number of sound reasons. One is the richness and variety of the evidence: women could write for themselves; there were discernible critics of the system; issues were often framed in gender terms. There are census data, blue books, the works of Utopian socialists, of Marxian socialists, who were contributing to or conspicuously sidestepping gender issues. There were precocious sociologists like Mayhew, Booth and Rowntree asking pertinent questions about women in the sweated trades, prostitutes and so on. Industrial performance as far as textiles were concerned was based on a largely female workforce.

Political debate and struggles surrounding issues such as the Contagious Diseases Act, the Married Women's Property Act, early socialist formulation and discourse between the male and female workforce on differential wage rates, etc., make it possible to raise women's history to another level far transcending the mere retrieval of social realities. Barbara Taylor's *Eve and the New Jerusalem* (Virago, London, 1981) or Judith Walkowitz's *Prostitution and Victorian Society: Women, Class and the State* (Cambridge University Press, 1980) are examples of work which locates a gender debate throwing light on both men and women, on a whole society and its notions of power distribution.

The recent emphasis on oral history, the appearance on bookstalls of memoirs and the work of women writers, and the concern of the media with women's experience over the past century, bear witness to the fact that women's past is of deep interest to a wide public. Yet the recent discussion of what should be taught as history to the schoolchild has made no reference to this important area. Pleas have been made for a curriculum in which every English child should hear of the Bill of Rights. But whose rights were these? Alternatively, Christopher Hill has spoken cogently of the need to concentrate on the liberties of the 'true-born Englishman'. Until, however, the true-born Englishman is seated amongst his mother, his wife, his sister and his daughter, we transmit a lopsided past. We women have a history and we must demand a place for it in the curriculum.

11
Tommy's Sister: Women at Woolwich in World War I

DEBORAH THOM

In 1915 women were asked to 'Do Your Bit. Replace a Man for the Front'. Thousands did work on munitions. In Woolwich Arsenal itself there were 27,000 women at most, in 1917; in the Woolwich area 60,000 women in war work where women had not been working before. The Health of Munitions Workers Committee reported that some of them had accepted 'conditions of work which, if indefinitely prolonged, would ultimately prove injurious to health'. They ascribed this to patriotic exertions which overcame the factor (or expressed it) that 'woman is the life-giver, not the life destroyer'. Trade unionists feared the patriotism of women because they saw it as a major factor in the risk war posed to established conditions of work. But, as Edith Cavell said in explaining her activities in wartime, which endangered her life while saving others, 'Patriotism is not enough.' It does not explain why women chose the work they did, why some stuck to it throughout and why their comments on it are in the main, enthusiastic. As an issue it demonstrates the need to look at war-work bifocally – as work and as war service – and to recognise the particularity of both in these women's lives at this time. Women created their own allegiances at work in a work-related community, while appropriating or exploiting other evocations of group experience as in class, race or gender and accepting the formulations of patriotism or nationalism when expressed in personal terms.

I shall look at Woolwich, which was a community dominated by war. The Royal Artillery Barracks up on the hill, the Royal Arsenal and the Old Dockyard by the river dominated the town. It was a prosperous town and had a low proportion of working women, married or unmarried.[1] Women worked locally in a shirt factory, three hospitals, the cable works at Siemens or Henley's

Telegraph Company over the river in North Woolwich; or did homework, particularly tennis-ball making in the summer; or commuted by ferry or train across or along the river. Women's work was little affected by war: men's was greatly and Woolwich's male unemployment was high before the war, since the Arsenal had laid off many workers. The Labour movement was strong, well-organised and supported a paper, the *Woolwich Pioneer*, a Labour MP, Will Crooks, and one of the biggest cooperatives, the RACS (Royal Arsenal Cooperative Society). Women's organisations in Woolwich were numerous; some quite large, especially the Women's Co-operative Guild and the Primrose League, but feminist organisations tended to come in from outside – the WSPU and the East London Federation of Suffragettes.[2] Local issues predominated in the press and in the reported proceedings of local organisations; war was, essentially, seen as a local issue. Pacifism was never absent from local labour, but no leading figures were pacifists – even the local Independent Labour Party had dissolved into the British Socialist Party in 1912 and swung behind the war effort.[3] Feminist pacifism, which was a very strong current elsewhere, did not really exist in Woolwich.[4]

When war began women were made unemployed in many parts of the country and in Woolwich the same groups were affected as elsewhere – domestic servants, milliners and dressmakers.[5] But it was not unemployment among women that opened up the Arsenal to women, it was government's need for labour. Other local munitions factories had employed women before government insisted that women go into the Arsenal, and that experience was used to convince employers of women's usefulness on monotonous processes, their docility and tractability, their lack of knowledge of industrial life.[6] These descriptions aroused the fears of organised trade unionists about women's 'innate' power to upset 'time honoured' negotiating procedures in the factory, doubly so because they were women and because they were dilutees.[7] In the Arsenal, though, organised workers in trade unions controlled the dilution process to a greater extent than elsewhere; they even had desks in the main factories for individual members of the shop-stewards' committee who could monitor the replacement of skilled men by the unskilled or semi-skilled.[8] In the Woolwich Arsenal they did this mainly for boys – both management and men remained resistant to the idea of women in the factory.[9] As late as May 1916 there were as many boys as women in the Arsenal (at 8,000). By the winter of 1917, when there were most women workers, there were 27,000 of them. Women hardly entered the Royal Gun Factory or the Gun Carriage Factory, and they comprised only just over 25 per cent of the workers in small arms ammunition factories.[10] Most women in Woolwich and elsewhere were doing new tasks which had been designated as women's work (therefore not subject to equal pay regulation) and they predominated in the mass production, repetition factories. Women particularly made and filled shells, a task that was increasingly done elsewhere in private works or in temporary government-run filling factories. (The Arsenal gradually resumed its function as adjuster for everyone else's production.)

Why did women do munitions' work in the Woolwich Arsenal? Were they driven by patriotic motivation, self-assertion (feminist or otherwise)? Is there anything to distinguish their behaviour in war from peacetime or from that of young men of the same age? Government propaganda like the *Women at Work* pamphlets (with excellent photographs by, among others, Horace Nicholls), was directed mainly at employers.[11] The Ministry of Munitions recorded one factory manager's judgment: 'Girls are more diligent on work within their capacity than boys – they are keen to do as much as possible, are more easily trained.'[12] Feminists argued that women should be allowed to do men's work. Mrs Pankhurst organised a Right to Work march, later renamed the Right to Serve march, in London.[13] Women's trade unions deplored the capacity of such feminists to ignore the need for maintaining wage-levels. Mary Macarthur of the National Federation of Women Workers said, 'There were too many sister Susies sewing shirts for soldiers' – and they were prepared to do it for little or no wages.[14] Women's introduction to newly-opened war employment was shaped by the fact that it took place when women were unemployed in large numbers, and the fact that it posited women's deficiency as workers. Government action added to this emphasis. After the Right to Serve march, Lloyd George in 1915 announced the Women's War Register by which all women would register their availability for war service.[15] Historically, women had not been allowed to do engineering jobs which were needed,[16] so the impression of inexperience was enhanced and actual histories of work ignored. All women became a reserve army of labour, a stage army, to be wheeled on and off as the decision demanded, as if many of them had not been on stage before.

Women describe their own motives in going to the Arsenal in a variety of ways. Many were unemployed – domestic servants in particular. The wives of serving men got very low dependants' allowances. They had to wait for them and go through humiliating processes – even the production of marriage lines.[17] In Woolwich the Army's married quarters had been reallocated to soldiers *en route* for Dover and the Western Front, so a large group of women had been rendered suddenly homeless.[18] In interviews most women recollect economic need as a main motive – but for most of my interviewees not a new motive. Why did they go to the Arsenal? It was the best known munitions factory, wages were supposed to be high and it was central to munitions production. It had both local and national drawing power. I estimate (and there is no extant information to check this, although memories tend to support it) that about one-third of all women workers there came through local contacts. They often entered their jobs by way of a personal introduction to a factory foreman, often by a family member. In this way women followed the procedure current in the Arsenal for years. Girls who entered in this way had not usually worked in the factory before, and often, but not always, had to argue against father or brothers who were reluctant to help. One woman only went in on the understanding not to speak to anyone else at all and only threw off family tutelage after a month of being escorted to the factory by an uncle.[19] Another third of the women came from the local labour exchange, which drew on a large area of south and east London. These women were processed collectively, enrolling for factories rather than as individuals. They often found the process frightening, partly because of the fear of explosions, or of danger work, partly because of the alienating effect of being dealt with by numbers. One woman kept going, even though she did not want to work in the danger sheds (using TNT to fill shells), because she didn't want to admit cowardice to her neighbour.[20] The last third of the women went through the factory's own admission procedure – interview by welfare superintendent and assessment for suitable work medically. Helen Bentwich was vetted by a doctor: 'Hearts, nerves, veins in the legs and eyes were what she looked at, and head [for lice]. The Doctor said, "You shouldn't be here. Aren't you a public school girl?".'[21] The physical assessment was decisive, social considerations were in some repects incidental, and education was important. Women only predominated in one main process, filling shells – 11,692 women and girls to 9,103 men and boys.[22] Women were reduced by this process to units of labour power, slotted in by condition, not by their own wishes. Any attempt to challenge this placing met short shrift. One woman with seven children wanted to leave danger work to earn more money and to do a different shift system, so she went to see Lilian Barker, chief welfare superintendent, and was told either to keep her job or leave altogether.[23] Self-assertion in these circumstances was difficult – but what about joint assertion?

The *Woolwich Pioneer* editorialised 'Both men and women must recognise their interests as workers are identical'[24] but for women in the Arsenal in 1915 this was paricularly difficult at work. Some conflict between the sexes was explicit. Some women met with physical violence, many met with verbal abuse in 1915 when women first entered the various existing factories of the Arsenal.[25] Most women I've spoken to in these first groups accepted this as an expression of *class* prejudice – they were the daughters or wives of skilled men and the men abusing them were labourers. It was what they'd expected of factory life and they saw it as an expression of their difference from the rest. A few were domestic servants and they saw it as factory life as they'd expected it to be, but their indignation at the grossness of language and behaviour was still evident even after all these years. Women who directly replaced men who had gone to the Front, as these substitutes did, tend to say of this hostility 'Well, what would you expect?' and felt little individual antagonism to the men who behaved in this way, and some sympathy for those who, as it were, they'd 'sent' away. Indirect division of interest was very little recognised by women themselves. Most knew that their pay was not the same as the men they replaced, but they did know it was much larger than their own prewar pay and than prewar unskilled men's rates of pay. Women did not get equal *earnings* at all, because war bonuses were different. Women who should technically have got equal pay usually had to fight for it through a tribunal - in the Arsenal, clerks, crane-drivers and inspectors eventually got this.[26] Women on engineering were paid at equal rates (piece rates) but had to pay for the toolsetter who assisted the setting up and maintaining the machines, at 10 per cent of their own earnings.[27] This was not recognised clearly as *not* being equal pay until late 1917, when women had begun to be discharged from the Arsenal after the closure of the Russian Front and therefore had little power because of labour shortage with which to fight back.

At work women were further reduced to units of labour. They wore uniforms with caps. In filling work or in the bullet factories all personal belongings were handed over as women passed from the 'dirty' side (the outside world) to the 'clean' side – matches, cigarettes, purses, hairslides, flowers and jewellery.[28] Outdoor workers had a much freer factory life and often wore trousers,[29] they were less subject to stringent safety rules and did not have to be searched every time they went back to work.[30] Discipline in the Arsenal was very strict indeed. One girl got six months' hard labour for taking a match inadvertently into an explosives site; however, since there were 172 buildings each with 1 ton or more of explosive in an area 3 square miles, such care was needed.[31]

Workers were aware of the danger. Women, however, to whom such discipline was most applied, tended to see the social consequences: men viewed it more benignly. One woman described the poisoning of workshop relations by an incident when her friend was summoned before the factory manager and a policewoman because a lighter had been found in her pocket. She denied it. Her friend supported her claim that someone else had foisted her with it, acting, it seems, both in self-defence and malice. But the woman was dismissed without a character reference and therefore could never resume her old service job.[32] Most did not resent the discipline. One woman chose to work at the much more dangerous Vickers' works at Erith, where she saw one scalping, one mangled hand and one severed arm, because she preferred the more relaxed atmosphere – but this was unusual.[33]

The apparent effects of labour organisation, work enrolment and official discipline on women workers was to reduce the differences between them, and emphasise their common gender. They reacted to this by creating their own collective allegiances, many of which did base themselves on identity as women but always with substantial qualification.[34] Class was one important locus for differentiation or identity – though usually acting negatively. A special hostel, Queen Mary's hostel, was built for 'lady' munition workers and the Arsenal probably had the most of these.[35] There was a large group working with Lady Londonderry running canteens for men at the beginning of the war. The first welfare supervisors were initially of a similar sort. Lilian Barker, chief women's welfare superintendent, excluded them, as she told the canteen committee:

Q. Have you any workers?[36]
A. None.
Q. We ought to commiserate with you.
A. I beg to differ. You ought to congratulate me. I do not think women like voluntary workers, they are such busybodies. They always sum up the girls into the nice girls and the rude girls and the nice girls get attention and the rude girls get nothing. It makes some girls who are not rude, rude.[37]

There were some 'lady' volunteers who managed to stay on as welfare workers, but most of the supervisory staff had become 'women with experience of controlling other women' by 1916. There were some ladies who worked on the shopfloor. One witness said of the ex-suffragettes, 'You'd never have known it. They were so nice, such ladies'.[38] The factory environment did not overcome the difference between the employer of servants and the servant, since the difference was visible. And there was a further difference among women of respectability – the nice girls and the rude girls. Helen Bentwich, Elizabeth Gore (Lilian Barker's niece and biographer) and Gabrielle West who worked as a policewoman, all commented on the roughness of some of the women.[39] Some of my interviewees drew the same distinction – they distanced themselves from swearing, sexual immorality and dirt (though the moral and physical components of that word are not clear). Several witnesses talked of geographical origin as the explanation for this – girls from over the water were East-Enders who differed from respectable Woolwich. Other geographical and ethnic distinctions were made. Irish and Scottish girls were identified as speaking differently and being clannish. Jewish girls were also mentioned as those who were noticeably different.[40]

The qualities of niceness and rudeness that separated women from one another were inherent in the person, not the worker. The Arsenal itself was not at all nice. Even clean, sitting-down work such as that in the wages office took place in a filthy environment.[41] The Arsenal was infested with rats. It was badly ventilated. Lighting was anyway inadequate and frequent Zeppelin raids meant total blackout; three people died in blackout accidents, six in road accidents.[42] The medical system was one doctor and a shed, at the start of war; by the end of the war there were twelve doctors but they worked on vetting applicants and had no therapeutic role.[43]

There was a further division by age. Very young girls did not do filling work; they worked with the invalids in the paper shop. Girls of sixteen to twenty tended to be put to mass-production work, on cartridges for example. The optimum age for filling was twenty-four and many of the fillers were older than this – the placing of women by responsibility was a factor in this.[44] Oddly enough marital status, which is normally a crucial division between women, was relatively unimportant – partly because it impinged so little on factory life, partly because most married working women had absent husbands and were socially single. Having children was a major division, simply because of the time needed to deal with children, added on to a twelve-hour shift; it left hardly any time for friendship or group activity at all.

The main unit of identity in the factory was the workplace – not the work task or the age group. This seems to be because people met in the canteen and then had a chance to share experience in a work-related context. It was also the only place where most women had a chance for voluntary activity of all sorts. Each shift organised concerts for themselves (often performed by themselves) or for wounded soldiers. They competed in sports competitions or, more popularly, in hair-length or hat-making contests.[45] Each workshop had its own song, usually loaded with *double entendres*. One, which was for print and is therefore rather bland, shows a strong sense of identity of purpose with soldiers, wounded and serving.

1 Way down in Shell Shop Two
  You'll never find us blue
  We're working night and day
  To keep the Huns away.

2 All we can think of tonight
  Are the shells all turning bright
  Hammers ringing, girls all singing
  And the shop seems bright.

3 To our worthy foremen here
  Give three good hearty cheers
  Our wounded heroes too
  We're mighty proud of you.

4 And the boys who're still out there
  Good luck be always their share
  And bring them all back
  Everyman Jack
  To their dear old folks at home.[46]

That was intended for public consumption. The one that began 'Old man sitting on the Arsenal wall/ Just like his dad doing sod all' was not.[47] The songwriter, Rubens, who wrote 'Your King and Country' sold 7,000 copies of a song in Woolwich, called 'She works at the Woolwich Arsenal now'.[48]

Women workers took this identification of themselves with their workplace very seriously. They differentiated themselves with coloured shoe-laces, hair-ribbons or flowers. Friends from the group would make shift-changes together so that every fortnight when days changed to nights there was a thirty-six-hour gap in which a little rest could be obtained and they could, if childless, go out to the music-hall, the cinema (which ran frequent programmes between 1915 and 1918, mostly of the 'Perils of Pauline' type of film and newsreels[49]) or even to the theatre in the West End. Shoe-clubs or clothing societies were less important than prewar, since women did not need to save for their clothes, but some did exist and again they were based on the shift-workplace-canteen group.

This grouping was the basis of collective action too. If a

workshop was unionised, the union concerned depended on which had got there first, and that depended in turn on the men in the factory or on individual women's history. Engineering shops tended to be National Federation of Women Workers (NFWW); filling-shops were less unionised but also Federation; bullet, paper and tailoring shops tended to be Workers' Union (WU). The women's branches did not meet inside the factory, and the NFWW and the WU women's branches were only occasionally represented on the Shop Stewards' Committee. Most women unionists were older than the average, most stewards in fact being married women, although the two union organisers were, at twenty and twenty-one, respectively very young by comparison with their male counterparts.[50] The unions battled for the representation of war-workers. Both unions claimed to have had most members in the Arsenal – such figures as do exist would indicate that the WU probably had most by the end of the war, the NFWW the most in 1915–16. The WU certainly put itself forward as the union for the young worker, though their propaganda met with little response among any of my interviewees.

Women's collective protest tended to take different forms from that of men. There were frequent canteen protests about a variety of issues, ranging from unjust supervision and poor canteen service, to speed up and equal pay. It was the former sort of issue – working conditions – that tended to cause most fervour and be most effectively resolved. There are several descriptions of Lilian Barker, chief welfare superintendent, solving the problem and organising the return to work single-handed.

> She was away recruiting and summoned back to hear that three shops were ready to go. She turned up and found 500 girls waiting in the canteen in grim silence. Standing on a chair her hands clenching and unclenching in her pockets she told them in a speech of mounting emphasis, 'to strike in war time was like giving guns to the enemy'. The meeting ended with a ragged cheer for the Lady Superintendent and a 10 minute break before returning to work.

She is reported speaking on output, 'Anyone who limits that is a traitor to sweethearts, husbands and brothers fighting. If a worker does not like her job she should give it up.'[51]

In another incident women covered two supervisors with pudding and pelted them with orange peel because they did not observe a canteen boycott the workers had set up. This was solved by a joint appeal from the male shop stewards' committee and Lilian Barker – using the same rhetoric she had used to such effect at other times and meeting with the same response. A personalised appeal did effect a return to work in the way that a general appeal to the nation or against the Hun never did. Women tried to personalise the war by putting messages in the cases of shells – though they don't appear to have wanted to think then or now what the shells were for at the other end. Comments on the war itself reflect an attempt to distance themselves from it, or to say in terms of great vagueness, 'I just wanted to end it quickly.' Here there is a difference – male Arsenal workers construct their history of the Arsenal in wartime by the chronology of the Front or of national politics, women do not. Both their chronology and their rhetoric are to do with the personal, the domestic, the issues over which their behaviour and attitudes make a difference.

There were several major issues on which women workers could have been evidently patriotic for their locality or sex. On two subjects women were among the protesters, though not leaders of it – on food and rent – but these were women as consumers, as maintainers of the household. On the food question there was nearly an Arsenal-wide strike because of shortages and lengthy queues. Rents were rarely generalised beyond the people who faced the issue.[52] Air raids were a grievance to workers and featured in trade union negotiations and, in retrospect, are often mentioned in interviews.[53] All these were examples of what people now describe as their being badly treated in wartime, but acceptably so, because their conditions were not as bad as those at the Front and because they could act against them. They do not appear to have felt hopelessly victimised, even by the worst excesses of landlords, food traders or factory management. On one issue women might justifiably have felt interested in discussion but were (and I can't find out if consciously so) excluded – that is the discussion of VD, which was one of the rare issues on which the Arsenal management and the shop stewards' committee agreed and acted in concert.[54] Women were often excluded from sheer lack of thought that they might be interested.

Dame Mabel Crout, then Labour Party agent in Woolwich, said that they didn't think it was their job to organise or in any way make connections with the women munition workers who came to live and work in Woolwich in this way. Women who were politically active in the town were not women workers and the gap between women at work and at home was particularly wide – although it was overcome within the family context in which political organisation took place. People would say 'Oh, but we were always Labour you see' and that unexplained 'we' was usually elaborated as 'our family' or 'my father'. If 'my mother' was mentioned it was usually in the context of the Women's Co-operative Guild which was not an organisation to which women themselves had belonged until they married. Labour patriotism, if expressed at all, was usually with reference to a later period, when interviewees had themselves had a limited purchase on political power through Labour's long dominance of the Woolwich Borough Council.

People do and did have a strong sense of loyalty. It is not something volunteered as an explanation for behaviour then or now (except negatively, in that people would use arguments of the 'Now, don't think I'm not patriotic' sort). The loyalty, though, is to groups over which women can have some control, in which the way they exercise power can matter. For women of this time and in this place, adherence to abstractions had little part in the complex of loyalties that kept them going through a hard, dangerous and unhealthy war at work. One of the reasons that women refer to Queen Mary's visits so often in their recollections is that this personal contact did translate the notion of the head of state into a real person, and was thereby sustaining. The war itself was unpopular, although the chance to work with friends and be both decently paid and publicly approved for it was not. Although women did work long hours they did not ever lose the sense that this was only for a while, that it was special and that it was helping some people whom they loved. Each woman, though, had her own views about the factory environment, about the benevolence of management, and the way in which work was organised, which prevented any ready acquiescence on work that was beyond capacity. A woman acted collectively or individually against exploitation, depending on her situation, history and workplace – she was not a victim of man or of the state but an active and often conscious historical agent. The factory did not detach women from domesticity: it helped to reproduce a domestic ideology and extend it to the state. To talk of emancipation in this context is to blur the issues of class, race and gender by reducing them to too simple an abstraction.

Notes

I would like to thank the staff at the Greenwich Local History Library for all their help with the work I have done on Woolwich between 1974 and 1983, and Ian Patterson for his support.

1 Gilbert Stone (ed.), *Women War Workers*, London 1917; Lady Randolph Churchill (ed.), *Women's War Work*, London 1916; Hall Caine, *Our*

Girls, 1916; A. Marwick, *Women and the First World War*, London 1977; G. Braybon, *Women workers and the First World War*, London 1980.

2 D. Thom, 'Women Workers in the Woolwich Arsenal in the First World War', MA thesis, Warwick University, 1975, for the general information. On this particular point the evidence is negative. The women's organisations had no local speakers after 1910, and local activity, like interrupting the Minister for War in 1912, was carried out by women from outside the area. Local activists were involved with the Adult Suffrage Association and large groups attended their rallies and demonstrations. On occupations, PP1913 Cd 7018, *General Report of the Returns of the Census of England and Wales*, p. 404, shows what women were doing at the time of the 1911 census, as, slightly earlier, do some articles in the local Labour paper, the *Woolwich Pioneer*, Jan.-Feb. 1908.

3 British Socialist Party collection at the London School of Economics. Annual conference reports 1912–1914 and miscellaneous paper fols. 10–11. W. Kendall, *The Revolutionary Movement in Britain*, London 1969, pp. 49, 88.

4 S. Pankhurst had open access to the *Woolwich Pioneer* as long as she wrote on maternal welfare or working women or suffrage, but not when she wrote on pacifism, particularly when, after 1917, she moved closer to communism. There were no counterparts to the socialist pacifists Jill Liddington and Jill Norris have described in *One Hand Tied Behind Us*.

5 PP1914–1916, xxvii, Cd 7848, *Interim Report of the Standing Committee on Women's Employment*.

6 G. Braybon *Women Workers*. Also D. Thom, 'The Ideology of Women's Work, 1914–1924, with special reference to the NFWW and other trade unions', PhD thesis for the CNAA at Thames Polytechnic, 1982.

7 G. D. H. Cole, *Trade Unionism in Munitions*, Oxford, 1923; B. Drake, *Women in the Engineering Trades*, 1917.

8 J. Hinton, *The First Shop Stewards Movement*, 1973.

9 Records of the Ministry of Munitions at the PRO, MUN 5.55, secret labour reports, comment on the particularly low figure for the Arsenal. SUPPLY (Records of the Ministry of Supply, also at the PRO)6, records the number entering the Arsenal by Departments. O. F. G. Hogg, *The Royal Arsenal*, vol. 2, Oxford 1963, p. 977.

10 *Official History of the Ministry of Munitions*, vol. 8, pt 2, pp. 16–17.

11 War Office *Women at Work on Munitions* and *Women at Work in non-Munitions Industries*, War Office, Dec. 1916.

12 Records of the Ministry of Munitions at the PRO, MUN 2.27, 16 Oct. 1916, p. 40.

13 *Times*, 17 July 1915. Records of the Ministry of Munitions at the PRO, MUN5.90.17, negotiations over costs, 11.8.1915–28.8.1915. *Woman Worker*, April 1918, p. 8.

14 Cited several times in the Gertrude Tuckwell collection at the TUC, file Mary Macarthur, 1915 (the collection consists mainly of press

cuttings). The quote is *Daily Sketch*, 8 Nov. 1915 and Imperial War Museum 47.
15 E. S. Pankhurst, *The Home Front*, 1932. C. Addison, *Politics from-Within*, London 1924, pp. 121–7. H. Wolfe, *Labour Supply and Regulation*, Oxford p. 18. M. B. Hammond. *British Labor Conditions and Legislation*, New York, 1923, p. 18.
16 B. Drake, *Women in the Engineering Trades*, London 1917 (she also wrote the historical introduction to the *Report of the War Cabinet Committee on Women in Industry*, PP1919, Cd 136). B. L. Hutchins, *Women's Work in Modern Industry*, 1915. All these accounts of the traditional determinants of women's exclusion from certain trades reflect the Fabian Women's Group view, as expressed by Drake in her evidence to the Atkins' committee, that 'if anyone should be excluded from industry it had better be the women.'
17 E. S. Pankhurst cites several examples in *The Home Front*, pp. 77–82.
18 *Woolwich Pioneer*, August 1914.
19 Interview with Mrs Mackenzie, 1977, by the author.
20 Interview with Mrs Robinson, 1977, by the author.
21 H. Bentwich, *If I Forget Thee*, London 1973, p. 80.
22 O. F. G. Hogg, *The Royal Arsenal*, vol. 2, p. 977.
23 Interview with Mrs Hewes, 1977, by the author.
24 *Woolwich Pioneer*, 7 July 1916.
25 Interviews with Mrs Mackenzie and Mrs Fleming, 1977, by the author. BBC, 'Yesterday's Witness' on the Arsenal (1977), directed by Chris Cook and produced by Stephen Peet, had some examples of the same thing.
26 D. Thom, 'Women workers in the Woolwich Arsenal in the First World War', MA thesis, Warwick University, 1975, Chapter 5.
27 B. Drake, *Women in the Engineering Trades*, London, 1917, pp. 51–7.
28 Health of Munitions Workers Committee pamphlet 11, *Handbook for Overseers*, 1916.
29 Not that this made the difference in consciousness attributed by one male historian. Unfettered legs don't necessarily make unfettered minds, or, put another way, to wear men's clothing is not necessarily to become free. A. Marwick, *Women at War*, London 1977.
30 Health of Munitions Workers Committee, *The Employment of Women*, PP1916, xxiii, Cd 8185.
31 O. F. G. Hogg, *The Royal Arsenal*, Oxford, vol. 2, 1963, p. 959.
32 Interview with Mrs Ayres, 1977, by the author.
33 Interview with Mrs Hansen, 1977, by the author.
34 I do not want to labour this point, but I do feel it important to make it clear that, although no-one would expect men to react in the same way to a situation, they do expect this of women.
35 *Official History of the Ministry of Munitions*, vol. 5, pt 5, p. 25.
36 The word 'workers' here means 'voluntary workers' – an interesting semantic shift, where, for women, work or worker meant voluntary social work. This meaning had gone by 1918, and the National Union of Women Workers had become the National Council for Women.

37 Imperial War Museum, Women's Work Collection. Records of the Ministry of Munitions at the PRO, MUN 18², 24.11.1916, p. 25, evidence to the Atkins committee.
38 Interview with Mrs Hansen, 1977, by the author.
39 Imperial War Museum documents, unpublished diaries of Gabrielle West.
40 The women who were most emphatic about this were those who had been domestic servants before the war, in rural areas, and who were new to both the city and the factory.
41 Interview with Mrs McCaffery, 1975, by the author.
42 Statistics collected from newspapers of the war period. There may have been other such accidents for which the inquests were held elsewhere.
43 See A. Ineson and D. Thom, 'Women workers and TNT poisoning in the First World War in Britain', in P. Weindling (ed.), *A Social History of Occupational Health*, Croom Helm, London, 1986.
44 Imperial War Museum, MUN has several reports for individual factories which list workers by age, task and pay.
45 In Woolwich, said the *Official History of the Ministry of Munitions*, girls were not very fond of educational classes and preferred to go dancing.
46 *Woolwich Pioneer*, 16 February 1917.
47 Interview with Tom and Mabel Biggs, 1977, by the author.
48 *Woolwich Pioneer*, 11 April 1917.
49 Programme adverts in the local press, and interviews by the author.
50 I am grateful to Richard Hyman, who let me look at his file on Florence Pilbrow who, as Lunnon, was Workers' Union organiser. Interview with Dorothy Jones, 1975, by the author; as Dorothy Ellitt, she was National Federation of Women Workers organiser at the start of her long career in unionism as the practical component of the social work diploma at the London School of Economics.
51 E. Gore, *The Better Fight*, London 1975, p. 90.
52 See D. Thom, 'Women workers in the Woolwich Arsenal in the First World War', MA thesis, Warwick University, 1975, Chapter 4.
53 Records of the Ministry of Supply at the PRO, SUPPLY 6.
54 Records of the Ministry of Munitions at the PRO, MUN 2.15, 13.4.1918, p. 8; 2.28, 23.6.1917. *Woolwich Pioneer*, 22 March 1918.

12
Women in the armed services, 1940–5

DI PARKIN

Accounts of Britain in the Second World War present the myth of total war, a 'people's war', in which pride and prejudice were dispensed with for the sake of the common good. Brass-hats lost their dignity, mansion-houses their railings. The Home Front and the army were at one. The 'Dunkirk spirit' entered the language as a synonym for sacrifice – the British at their best when their backs were to the wall, the supreme example of national oneness. If national unity was unquestioned, then nothing should have stood in its way.

But other sources of identity were important. There was a contest about the place of the working class within the nation and, thereby, around the meaning of nation. Factory workers went on seeing themselves as workers, organising in trade unions – and mounting unofficial strikes – to prove it. There was also a contest around the place of women in the nation; the nature of masculinity and femininity, and the lines to be drawn between them. Patriarchy and patriotism were at war. According to the first, women's place was that of servicing the men – the 'them' to whom the women were mere auxiliaries. An early recruiting appeal in the War Ministry archives expressively makes the point[1] (see Figure 12.1).

Women's own perception was different, yet even in the more affirmative she still remained, as in World War I, Tommy's sister. Here is how the magazine *Woman's Own* saw it in June 1941:

> You should have heard the fellows laff
> When sister Sue became a WAAF,
> and seen the pained grimaces when
> Matilda Jane became a WREN.
> We can't abide,
> They said

Women in the armed services, 1940–5 159

Auxiliary Territorial Service

**New Platoons must be formed.
Join the "A.T.S." NOW and serve with your friends
Help as only YOU can**

THE MEN WILL DO THE FIGHTING
YOU MUST DO THE REST

COOK FOR THEM	They need good meals.
WAIT ON THEM	Have you ever Waited in a Tea Shop? Do the same in the Army.
CLERK FOR THEM	Can you use a Typewriter? If not, we will teach you.
STOREKEEP FOR THEM	Have you ever been responsible for Stores?
HOW ABOUT DRIVING?	Ah!——but have you a <u>clean</u> licence?
CAN YOU OPERATE A TELEPHONE SWITCHBOARD?	Were you good at school? If so, we will teach you.
EVER HEARD OF TELEPRINTING?	Are you quick at learning? If so, we will teach you that too.

THE MEN WILL DO THE FIGHTING
YOU MUST DO THE REST

[8557] 18437/8256 350m 7/10 4358 G & S 704

FIGURE 12.1 Recruiting poster

> The ATS!
> Give us,
> They cried,
> Tho-se crazy hats!
> But now when boom and zoom resound
> You hear the whisper going round:
> Defence balloons are manned by Sue
> and naval guns, Matilda's crew
> and strange to say
> That pre-war Pearl was jilted for a Khaki girl.[2]

That was one attempt to claim that traditional notions of a woman's place were compatible with her taking the role of soldier. Yet in the recruitment of women into soldier roles, the tensions and contradictions between the needs of winning the war and the needs of maintaining the traditional gender order are revealed. There was a line to be held and that line was that women should not play combat roles, not become warriors.

In times of war women have frequently moved from roles in the realm of reproduction to roles in the realm of providing subsistence as men 'went for a soldier'. What they have not done (mythic Amazons, Pallas Athene, Joan of Arc, transvestite girl-soldiers apart) is gone for soldiers themselves – taken the role of warrior. Indeed, the resistance to their doing so is so strong it can be called nothing less than a taboo. The exceptions to it are, cross culturally and historically, minuscule. Women have borne arms exceedingly rarely and almost always only in revolutionary armies rather than in the armies of established nation states. Indeed, the cases where women have borne arms on behalf of the army of a nation state have been nation states in an early establishing phase rather than in firmly established states. Only in the Soviet Union and China in World War II did women bear arms other than in a defensive way, guarding hearth and home. Women do not invade. Women no longer prepare for combat in the Israeli army, now the army of an established nation state. Women rarely kill in war. The ideological construction of soldiering, as Cynthia Enloe argues in *Does Khaki Become You?*, 'is tightly bound to masculinity and combat'.[3]

It has been possible in the twentieth century to accept women in uniform, women in the armed forces, but only within a very tight sexual division of labour within the armed forces, which renders women auxiliary. Women can be in the armed forces but they have to retain, in the main, a feminine identity. If they do not do so they are very threatening to the gender order. Or, to put it more directly, women bearing guns are very threatening to men. Dixon in *The Psychology of Military Incompetence* discusses the importance of maintaining male sanctuaries; women in the army makes being a soldier something even sissies could do and implicitly questions the male monopoly of fighting competence. Thus, in the main, women must play the traditional servicing roles (in the army) of cook, clerk and storekeeper.[4] Enloe argues that the sexual division of labour in the army is rooted in two rather tenuous notions: 'Firstly that there is a clear line between combat and non combat and secondly that there is a geographically real place called "The rear".'[5] The century of total war renders both these distinctions absurd, but they have not lost their force as symbolic masters. Army nurses, for example, have worked very near the front line, under the direct range of enemy fire, in spartan living conditions, subject to psychological strain and exhaustion whilst nursing the appallingly wounded. What was different about allowing these women into the arena of combat at the front was that they remained in a feminine role – servicing, nurturing – and did not threaten the masculine sanctuary. Their toughness and resilience under gunfire took second place to their feminine and nurturing role.

Just as the concept of female economic dependency and the family wage helps force men out to work, so female defenceless-ness forces men to go out to fight, assists the militarisation of men. It is, after all, an extraordinary puzzle why men should continue to face the gunshot, march into the arms of death – rational self-interest would suggest flight as a more sensible course than to fight. Discipline in armies has to depend on more than the fear of punishment, on the shooting of deserters and the threat of the glasshouse. Commitment to being a soldier has to be internalised and is well reinforced by armies' drill. Yet men do not go through all this for mere abstract ideas like love of nation. Love of nation has to be expressed in a way that is more psychologically real and the motivation to fight grounded in a crucial sense of self. The notion of manhood, virility and vigour are better motivators. The notion of aggressive fighting manhood is enormously helped by having its 'opposite' (let us remember to blench at that notion) – female defencelessness. This has been actively used to motivate men going to war; 'Women of Britain say Go' implored the posters as ex-suffragettes handed out white feathers.

Along with the image of men as necessarily aggresssive goes, of course, that of women as necessarily peaceful, nurturing and antagonistic to war. Woman the bringer of life? How can she be the carrier of death? The deep-seated belief in women as bringers of life[6] makes women as carriers of death a horrific notion, overturning the supposedly natural order, touching at men's awe and dread of women's supposed life-giving properties. (In reality men and woman are both necessary to create new life.)

But the image of women, biologically mothers, naturally nurturing, has a deep hold. It is not merely used by right-wing ideologues seeking to justify women's passivity and helplessness. From the Women's International League for Peace and Freedom: 'Not the heroism connected with warfare and destruction but that which pertains to labour and the nourishment of life'.[7] And from a Greenham woman: 'I have been accused of being cruel and hard hearted for leaving my children behind, but it is exactly for my children that I am doing this. In the past men have left home to go to war. Now women are leaving home for peace.'[8] This view has recently been challenged by some radical feminists who point out that the Greenham appeal to the earth – mother and nurturer is an acceptance of traditional images.[9] We do not need to look further than the war-mongers Margaret Thatcher, Golda Meir and Indira Gandhi, to see that arguments about women's biological natures rendering them incapable of war are hogwash.

Enloe demonstrates the ideological character of the objections to women's combat roles. Pregnancy and menstruation, the difficulties of making mixed-sex arrangements when troops are advancing, are now superseded by the view that it is women's upper bodily strength (UBS) which is inadequate.[10] That differentials of average UBS may well exist between men and women (but never prevented women hauling coal tubs underground in the nineteenth century or women carrying heavy loads of fuel, water, children, food) does not of course mean that some women may not have or could not develop the requisite UBS. These arguments are evidently smokescreens for those based on essential deeply-held concepts of masculinity and femininity. These concepts are not merely to do with the ascription of a bland social gender but with the sexual itself. I believe that the tenacity with which men were opposed to women bearing arms, as well as the awesome dread of the life giver turning death dealer, had to do with notions of masculine valour, vigour and virility of a sexual kind. Reich points to the sexual symbolism and significance of the phallic gun barrel, of firing the shot;[11] and it is certainly true that in the Second World War it was the women of the ATS who came nearest, in the ack-ack battalions, to firing shots and it was the ATS who were regarded as more sexually loose and promiscuous than other service women.

One of the many myths of the Second World War is that the

drawing of women into the war economy involved a fairly unproblematic loosening of the traditional gender order. Penny Summerfield, in her study of women's war work, shows that despite the provision of nursery places, the responsibilities for child care remained essentially those of the mother.[12] The resistance to women taking the role of warrior is illustrated in the refusal to allow women to join the Home Guard. It would have been easier to allow women to join this body than to arm them in the full services, as it had a wholly defensive function; there was no question of being sent overseas, women could have remained at home defending the hearth. Yet resistance there was. The justification offered was that the Home Guard were obliged to be trained in the use of arms. Brownrigg, of the Home Guard directorate, wrote:

> We have made this rule I think from earliest days partly in order to prevent conscientious objectors and others being able to slide into the Home Guard to get the protection of the uniform and yet decline to prepare themselves to fight the King's battles. We should not be able to apply the same conditions to women.[13]

Margesson, Minister of State for War, in a speech to the House of Commons on 18 Dec 1941 said:

> The Home Guard has been based thoroughly upon the military model. Its operational command and many of its admin. services are based upon military arrangements affecting the Field Army and I am not yet convinced that there is an adequate place for women in this part-time army whose role is armed with the most modern death-dealing weapons we can find to fight the enemy to the end.[14]

There was an additional worry, that women in the Home Guard would have to be given equal compensation to men for loss of wages and injuries. This equality was not acceptable. (A long battle was waged by the Women's Freedom League during the war to get equal compensation for civil defence workers and the like. This was finally won, one of the few legal gains for women in the war.)

Anxiety about women using weapons reached agitated levels. When an article appeared in the *Daily Mail* (29 October 1945) showing women at a Tolworth factory who had bought their own uniforms, used rifles and trained with the Home Guard, the Regional Director of the Home Guard wrote to the officer in charge at Tolworth: 'You should issue orders *at once* to the effect that no person who is not enrolled in the Home Guard should carry out training with them.' The works director of the firm replied: 'They are entirely separate from our Home Guard Unit and the idea is purely domestic and nothing to do with any outside organisation whatsoever. What little firing they have done is with a .22 on the works own miniature range. The only time they mix with the men is when they provide food for them.'[15]

Dr Edith Summerskill MP, who campaigned for women's rights in the war, cited the large numbers of women who 'are asking to join the Home Guard – but not only as auxiliaries to cook, scrub and do clerical work'. A petition signed by a number of dignitaries, including Home Guard commanders, asked for women to be enrolled in the Home Guard. This was not to be granted and Dr Summerskill set up an informal body – the Women's Home Defence – in March 1942, which trained women in the mechanism of loading, cleaning and firing rifles and tommy guns, unarmed combat and the use of grenades. By the end of the year it had 150 units with 10,000 members in London alone. A letter from the War Office to the Women's Home Defence organiser expressed the official horrified attitude: 'A woman's duty is to give life and not to take it, and the training which your unit gives in unarmed combat, signalling, fieldcraft and musketry is abhorrent to me.' For Sir James Grigg, the War Minister, *not* arming women was a matter of principle, so seemingly self-evident it did not need elaborating. He wrote to Morrison, on 22 December 1942, 'Most of what you have read in the papers on the subject of women in the Home Guard is untrue, particularly that part (nearly the whole in fact) which derives from our amazonian colleague, Summerskill.'[16]

Yet women were needed in the armed services, just as they were in war munitions work. Registration of women for war work began in 1941 and continued until October 1942, by which time all women under forty-five could be directed into jobs and single women between twenty and thirty were conscripted into industry or the services.

TABLE 12.1 Wartime employment of women (000s)[17]

Year	Auxiliary services	Civil defence	Muni- tions	Other work	Rest of female pop.	Total 14–59
1939	—	—	506	302	10,901	16,040
1941	103	59	1,106	146	9,874	16,030
1942	307	80	1,705	59	9,082	16,030
1943	461	70	1,928	36	8,747	16,020
1944	467	56	1,851	31	8,869	16,020

One of the obstacles to recruitment for the ATS was the belief that it was unfeminine. The initial propaganda stressed that being in the army was a *womanly* activity, one involving serving the fighting men. Articles in women's magazines – those 'High Priestesses of the Feminine'[18] – encouraged women to participate in the armed services in a womanly way. *Women and Beauty* had an article recommending the ATS: 'If you are Houseproud, if you love the detail, the timing, the insistence that everything should be just so, you will be in your element when you come to work like this. Needlewoman you are cut out for work like this. The fingers that are used to a fine needle and a fine stitch will help you here.' Notions of the feminine could be stretched to include the wearing of military uniform and cleaning up the officers' mess. Thus *Woman*, in an article on searchlight battalions (July 1944), assured readers that 'while auxiliaries and officers rough it during their training, they make every effort to make their battery quarters as comfortable and feminine as possible'. Helen Temple, *Woman*'s beauty editor, reassured her readers: 'The authorities are most keen that you should look attractive and smart in your uniform – a walking recruiting poster. Of course they allow make up. Remember rose shaded tints of lipstick are best, for khaki can make the complexion rather sallow.'[19]

However members of the ATS did not seem so convinced of its femininity. War-Time Social Survey asked members of the ATS what their dislikes of it were, and 21 per cent of the dislikes mentioned related to uniform, hair-style regulations and loss of femininity. The next highest number of complaints (10 per cent) concerned drill. One woman commented: 'Like the stockings (khaki) the underwear hardly encouraged a feeling of femininity – khaki bloomers down to the knees.'[20] The notion that the ATS were unfeminine was held even more strongly by men. Recruitment problems were put down to the anxiety and hostility of men to their wives and girlfriends joining. Mass Observation (MO) reported 'There can be no doubt that the general propaganda of men is against the services in general but overwhelmingly against the ATS in particular.' When MO asked soldiers their opinions of the ATS, WAAF, etc. they received the following replies[21]:

Would you like your wife to join?

Would stop her	36%
Certainly not	32%
Wouldn't like it	16%
Wouldn't mind	4%
Other	12%

Similarly the War-Time Social Survey found, when it asked women what the attitudes of their relatives and friends were to women joining the services, that although 50 per cent of the total surveyed felt their relatives and friends would advise them to join, 14 per cent of them thought their women-friends and relatives would advise against their joining the WAAF and 8 per cent of them thought their men-friends would advise against their joining the WAAF (11-16 per cent for the WRNS), and 16 per cent of them thought their women-friends and relatives would advise against joining the ATS, as compared to a staggering 28 per cent of them thinking their men-friends would advise against their joining the ATS. The War-Time Social Survey concluded: 'It can be said that the civilian man is rather more biased against the ATS than the civilian woman.'[22] It was thus men who were more concerned that the definition of the feminine should not be contested to include women soldiers. A woman wrote sadly to *Woman*: 'What hurt me most was meeting a boy whom I used to like very much who is now in the Navy. He said "O are you in the ATS – what a pity." '[23]

What was the basis of their hostility? Again, it seems to involve some conflict over the notion of the feminine, how women should be. The fear of groups of women together (particularly working-class women) took the form of sexual panic. This was not new. In the First World War 'Whenever women were travelling or wherever they were being congregated together in groups there was always among the authorities women as well as men a great preoccupation with the topic of "morality".'[24] Despite the contradictory notion that women were sexually passive, here is clearly contained the fear of women as sexually rapacious. Unless women are directly controlled by individual men – husbands/fathers – then they will become sexually promiscuous. It is not of course men who are to blame for this, but women. The denials and protestations from official quarters and from women's magazines, of course, seemed like the smoke without which there was no fire. The Director of Northern Command of the ATS protested: 'Immorality is a far less serious problem in the ATS than in civilian life.'[25] However the reminiscences of one ATS put the matter in the best perspective:

> We were probably the least popular of the women's services and among civilians we seem to have had the reputation for immorality, drunkenness and bad language. We were of course a cross section of the female population and inevitably there were bad girls and there were good girls. I suppose that our

behaviour as a body was no worse and no better than that of civilian women although that may be a reflection on us and in any case we probably had less opportunity to misbehave than others not subject to military discipline and restrictions. Not that all ATS were angels by any means, least of all one of our number who used to lipstick her nipples before going out of camp at night. I can only conjecture her reason for this, but at the time it seemed to me to be an awful waste of a scarce commodity.

One of the accusations levelled against us was that we were 'officers' groundsheets'. If we were, I was unaware of it. I knew of only one girl who claimed to have had sexual relations with one of our lieutenants. She said that he had seduced her while she was under the influence of drink. (Her story was convincing in its details and she maintained its truth, but I still don't know whether or not she was fantasising.)

At about the time I joined the ATS a male officer was court martialled for having sexual intercourse with an ATS private in his unit. It was well publicised in the national newspapers which not unnaturally make the most of every detail.[26]

The appeal of the ATS to some women was not in its traditional femininity but in the equal challenge of it. In a recruiting leaflet of 1941 the stress was no longer on the traditional servicing role. Indeed the leaflet denied this:

> First of all, if you have any foolish ideas that the ATS are just the servants of the army, put it out of your head at once, because it is not true. The army invites you into its ranks because it has been proved that women and girls can do some of the most important activities as well as men.[27]

A woman wrote to *Woman's Own* describing it thus: 'I've driven three ton army lorries in convoys of 300 in the worst weather day and night, through gun fire and bombs in Kent and over bleak Kent hills and Scottish highlands. Not once have we been hit: it's been great fun.'[28] In August 1941 the advert became even more egalitarian:

> Did you ever think you would see women soldiers drilling side by side with men in the ranks – a co-ed army? ATS girls in the Royal Army camps now line up with the gunners, serve on an equal footing, feed in the same dining halls, officers' messes. Said former London student oculist, now lance bombardier: 'You really feel part of the army now, women and men are partners in this job.'[29]

The kinds of women who did join the ATS, as the War-Time Social Survey established, were those who were interested, at a practical level, in *not* being differentiated from men. And nowhere was the lack of differentiation more apparent than in the mixed ack-ack batallions. But the lack of differentiation only held up to a point. *Woman's Own* described them: 'The first girls to go into action against the enemy, the ATS are training to serve in AA gun pits in army battle dress. They will handle predictors and other complicated instruments and direct gun fire.'[30] But it was in the mixed batteries that the distinction between combat/non-combat, front and rear, was most clearly seen as absurd. Women directed the searchlights and radio-located the enemy planes, yet were not allowed to fire the guns. The reminiscences of a woman in the ack-ack are to the point:

> Work on the searchlight sites was unenviable at the best of times, but it was doubly so for the women because unlike the men, they had no means of retaliation if, as sometimes happened, an illuminated enemy aircraft gunned down the searchlight beam. It seemed illogical that women could direct the searchlight, or in our case the guns, and yet had to stop short of actually pulling the trigger. We have proved ourselves steady in action so presumably someone must have considered that it would be unfeminine for us to take the final step.[31]

Indeed the Commander-in-Chief of the ack-ack, Sir Frederick Pile, agreed that women should be allowed to fire the guns. And the chief controller of the ATS agreed, as *Woman's Own* reported: 'Is there anything in woman's makeup to exclude her from using lethal weapons in war? Mrs Jean Knox, chief controller of ATS has said there is not, provided medical opinion approves.'[32] These military persons expressed one interest – that of militarily winning the war. That, after all, was the interest of the nation. But patriotism had its limits. Women firing weapons – as, later, women serving overseas – was perceived as too radical a challenge to the traditional definition of the feminine *and* masculine. But it was a challenge that some women, like Dr Edith Summerskill and the woman in the ack-ack batallion, wanted to make.[33]

Notes

1 PRO War Office Papers, WO32/9423.
2 *Woman's Own*, 8 June 1941.
3 Cynthia Enloe, *Does Khaki Become You?*, London, Pluto, 1983.

4 Norman F. Dixon, *The Psychology of Military Incompetence*, London, Jonathan Cape, 1967.
5 Cynthia Enloe, *Does Khaki Become You?*, London, Pluto, 1983.
6 Karen Horney, 'The dread of women', in *Feminine Psychology*, New York, Norton, 1967.
7 Gertrude Bussey and Margaret Tims, *Pioneers for Peace: Women's International League for Peace and Freedom 1915–1965*, London, Allen & Unwin, 1980.
8 *The Greenham Factor*, 1983.
9 *Breaching the Peace*, London, 1982.
10 Cynthia Enloe, *Does Khaki Become You?*, London, Pluto, 1983.
11 Wilhelm Reich.
12 Penny Summerfield, *Women Workers in the Second World War*, London, Croom Helm, 1984.
13 PRO WO32/9423.
14 *Ibid.*
15 *Ibid.*
16 *Ibid.*
17 Vera Douie, *Daughters of Britain*, London, Women's Publishing Association, 1949, p. 19.
18 Marjorie Ferguson, *Forever Feminine*, London, Heinemann, 1982.
19 *Woman*, July 1944.
20 Central Office of Information, 'An investigation of attitudes to the ATS'. *War-Time Social Survey*, October, 1941.
21 Sussex University MSS, Mass Observation, File report no. 952, 'The ATS' 8, November 1941.
22 Central Office of Information, 'An investigation of the attitudes to the ATS', *War-Time Social Survey*, October, 1941.
23 *Woman*, 4 June 1942.
24 Arthur Marwick, *Women at War*, London, Macmillan, 1977.
25 *Woman's Own*, 3 February 1942.
26 Imperial War Museum MSS, Second World War memoirs compiled by Ronald Hadley, Miss G. Morgan, 1972.
27 PRO WO32/9423.
28 *Woman's Own*, 3 May 1941.
29 PRO WO32/9423.
30 *Woman's Own*, 9 June 1943.
31 Imperial War Museum MSS, Second World War memoirs compiled by Ronald Hadley, Miss G. Morgan, 1972.
32 *Woman's Own*, 6 March 1942.
33 PRO WO32/9423.

Nations within nations

13
Scott and the image of Scotland[1]

CHRISTOPHER HARVIE

I

The father of the great German novelist Theodor Fontane (1819–98) lived through the heroic age of German literature, the age of Schiller, Goethe and Hegel. Yet his library consisted of only one author's works, which he re-read incessantly. The writer was Walter Scott, and the apothecary of Swinemunde, though an extreme case, was not alone in his enthusiasm. Goethe, re-reading *Waverley* towards the end of his life, reportedly said that it must be placed 'alongside the best things that have ever been written in the world'.[2] In the great age of literary nationalism, Scott's direct European influence was to extend from Balzac to Manzoni, from Strindberg to Mickiewicz in Poland, Gogol and Pushkin in Russia.

Fontane himself was deeply influenced by Scott, and when he came to Britain as a press correspondent, between 1855 and 1859, the Waverley novels drew him north. He was not disappointed: he found a distinct sense of community 'on the other side of the Tweed' and attributed its effectiveness to Scott: 'What would we know of Scotland without Scott! He collected the songs of his country and preserved its history through his own poetry.'[3] Fontane recognised that in the greatest works of his literary canon Scott was not a British but a Scottish writer, whose perceptions only made sense when placed in the context of a specific national experience – within British history, true, but in many respects quite distinct from it.

Many of Scott's most influential interpreters have been less circumspect. Georg Lukács, in *The Historical Novel* (1937), a work which helped re-establish European interest in Scott and did much to bring the sequence of Scottish novels forward as his supreme achievement, refers throughout to Scott's treatment of 'the history of England'. The 'classic' Marxist preoccupation with the formation of the economic base recognised Scott's skill in delineating the transition from militant to industrial society, but, since mature industrial capitalism was a British (and to most Europeans *ipso facto* an *English*) phenomenon, Scott was seen through those lenses and defined as an English author. That contemporary Marxist writers have restated Scott's Scottish identity is only partly due to the twentieth-century Scottish cultural renaissance; post-Gramscian revaluations of the superstructure's influence on the economic base have counted for as much.

Such factors have not, however, inhibited the 'English-men-of-letters' school, who lump together Scott's enormous range of historical novel-writing, his own life and his politics, and produce from the resulting lucky-bag a patriotic Briton, a gentlemanly Tory, and an intriguing provincial who can interest and absorb without in the least subverting their ideal of British nationalism. For Lord Dacre (Professor Hugh Trevor-Roper) Scott is 'one of those intelligent Scotchmen [who] rejoiced in the removal of their national politics to London'.[4] This is, of course, calculated to bring the Scots to the surface, snapping unconvincingly, irritated more by being called 'Scotchmen' than by the political gibe.

With which, anyway, they may well agree. Carlyle in 1837 assaulted Scott as a deracinating and commercialising force; MacDiarmid a century later wrote of his books as 'the great source of the paralysing ideology of defeatism in Scotland, the spread of which is responsible at once for the acceptance of the Union and the low standard of nineteenth-century Scots literature'.[5] In contrast to the Burns cult, *as a writer* Scott has been all but forgotten in modern Scotland. It's doubtful whether more than a handful of the Edinburgh councillors who stopped British Railways getting rid of the name of the city's main station – Waverley – had read the novel. Compared with Dickens and Hardy, reprints have been few and far between, and only a couple of television adaptations of the Scottish novels – *Redgauntlet* and *Rob Roy* – have been made. Even if he excites more academic interest than he used to, the Great Unknown has become the Great Unread.

If Scott is Scottish, he is a very unsatisfactory sort of literary patriot to have. He may have created the genre of the nationalist novel, but in Scotland he is still regarded as deferential, commercially-minded, and reactionary, the celebrant of the eccentric and archaic in the national life. Few of his compatriots seem, at any rate until recently, to have thought it worthwhile to attempt to frame him in his Scottish historical context. The problem is not helped by Scott's own transparent, level-headed, sociable personality: the *saeva indignatio* seems to be absent that made Swift, another Tory from the British periphery, a tragic visionary of the Irish predicament.

Following in Swift's tradition, Yeats enjoined the importance in national consciousness of the 'overreach' which characterises formal tragedy: 'Nations, races and individual men are unified by an image, or bundle of related images, symbolic or evocative of the state of mind, which is of all states of mind not impossible, the most difficult to that man, race or nation.'[6] The traditional interpretation of Scott, and Scott's own statements, apparently deny this possibility. Scott provides for the tranquil perusal of 'old unhappy far-off things, and battles long ago', for a rich cast of character-actors, but not for the moments of prophecy and insight which both accompany and negate the central actors in tragic drama. If, as in Herder's view, the nation is like an individual seeking – always unsuccessfully but inspiritingly – to realise the potential of its life, then this view is little reflected in Scott. If his national 'characters' are part of a retreating past, the ultimate successes of Scott's flat heroes and heroines seem to signify a non-Scottish future.

And yet, it is into the mouths of his Scottish characters that Scott puts passages which penetrate to levels of prophetic insight that his anglified characters are never capable of. Once admit that Scott could attain this, and you have a much more complex, formidable character than Lockhart's genial if rather snobbish antiquary – someone much closer to the embittered patriot who broke down as he accused Francis Jeffrey: 'Little by little, whatever your wishes may be, you will destroy and undermine until nothing of what makes Scotland Scotland shall remain.'[7] *Saeva indignatio*, indeed, but it leaves us with the problem, why did it not take concrete political form?

There is a more effective 'North British' approach than Lord Dacre's. This argues that, until about 1832, the year of Scott's death, Scotland remained politically 'semi-dependent'. Its landed, legal and clerical establishment and its institutions received, as the *quid pro quo* for their acquiescence in a placeman-dominated parliamentary representation, a degree of effective devolution greater, say, than anything on offer in the 1970s. Their problem was not one of combating the incursion of English government, but of preventing Scots distinctiveness from choking off the avenues to patronage and promotion in the south.

Scott, had, in this wise, little enough to be indignant about. He and his class, the beneficiaries of improvement and enlightenment, were concerned to sell out to the South for as good a deal as they could get – in a process in which his apolitical cultural nationalism could be mobilised when the process of assimilation threatened to get out of control. Dr Nicholas Phillipson, in his essay 'Nationalism and ideology', has seen Scott's nationalism, expressed for example in the *Malachi Malagrowther* letters of 1826, as, at least objectively, part of a strategy of 'noisy inaction' whereby inessential points such as Scottish banknotes were fought over, even won, while the main positions were amicably conceded.[8]

Phillipson's is a well-argued case, and one which I find in most respects explains adequately the motivation of the Scottish landed and professional establishment in the half-century of accelerating assimilation between 1793 and 1843. But I don't think it fair to Scott and his achievement to count him in as an accessory to this process – at least, not all the time. It is difficult for a start to impose consistency on Scott's career and attitudes. The lives of few law-abiding literary men have been so tumultuous. The rise to government favour and an enormous salary by the age of twenty-eight; the runaway success of the narrative poems; the injudicious involvement in business and landowning, and then the engendering of the 'Author of Waverley' doppelgänger, with his production of five of the greatest novels in the language in fewer than four years. All this would have been exceptional enough, before the collapse of 1825, and the tragedy – in the full dramatic sense – of the last six years. So there must be limits to Scott's 'representative' quality.

It is no easier to ascribe normative characteristics to the society in which Scott lived. He was born in the year in which Richard Arkwright began the factory production of cotton yarn. By the time he reached university, cotton had become the most advanced industrial sector, in Scotland as well as in England. He was eighteen when the French Revolution broke out, and forty-four when Britain and France stopped fighting one another, in 1815. In his last years the mechanisation of cotton production became complete, but at the cost of immense hardship to hand-workers and a declining rate of profit to the industrialists. To many commentators the risks of British industrialisation began to seem vertiginous. Each trade depression was worse than the last, with mounting indications of working-class organisation and industrial violence. When Scott died in 1832 the solution of this problem through the exploitation of new technological options – principally the railway – was still only dimly visible.

II

Scott was always the man to stress the importance of environment in conditioning behaviour, and the transactions which governed his own career were deeply influenced by political and economic factors. In fact the only years when these did not grip him too tightly were the 1810s, when he produced the great sequence of Scots historical novels on which his enduring reputation depends. From the 1790s to about 1815 the context of his art and life was law, patronage and British patriotism, all-subsumed under an organising metaphor of modernisation and legalism which he derived from Border society. *The Antiquary* of 1816, the most 'contemporary' of the great sequence with its picture of a rural *Gemeinschaft* – Scottish but also British – uniting against French invasion, is the point of balance. Thereafter a more conservative, bitter and pessimistic note emerges – with a promise that, perhaps, the manic productivity of the 1820s denied us: that Scott had in fact passed through Jonathan Swift's 'dark grove'. At any rate, I would argue that, in the relatively few occasions in his last years where he allowed rein to his subconscious, a vision of Scotland emerges which is vivid, nationalistic and sombre, and exemplified not by the Borders but by the betrayed and repressed society of the Highlands.

Law was, for Scott, not only the antipode of the 'romantic' violence of earlier times; it was also a symbol of Scottish national identity. Its influence had expanded enormously since Stair wrote his *Institutes* in 1681, and in particular after the 'heritable jurisdictions' – the 'justice' meted out by the territorial magnates – were abolished in 1746. By Scott's day it had almost acquired a fetish quality, as he recorded tartly in his *Journal* in 1825:

> There is a maxim almost universal in Scotland, which I should like much to see contrould. Every youth of every temper and almost every description of character is sent either to study as a lawyer, or to a Writer's office as an apprentice. The Scottish seem to conceive Themis the most powerful of goddesses.[9]

But it was also an economic implement whereby customary and status relationships were transformed into commercial ones. This was principally achieved through its application to landholding. Eric Hobsbawm is not alone, in 'Capitalisme et agricolture', in demonstrating how law was an essential element of the 'improvement' mechanism which transformed feudal tenures into absolute property rights.[10]

It was, however, a transformation achieved on a painfully

narrow social base. The systematic removal of traditional land rights from rural cottars, which converted them into a landless (and increasingly an urban) proletariat, miserable even by English standards, was *prima facie* at risk from radical agitation. Indeed, Scotland's response to the French Revolution was, proportionate to population, even more enthusiastic than that of England. For a couple of years, 1792–4, the hothouse growth of Scots agrarian and industrial capitalism felt a keen wind – just at the time that the young advocate Scott first started to pace the floor of Parliament House. The response to the challenge from France and from Scotland's own radicals was an enhanced sense of Britishness among the menaced classes, analagous to that which drove the Anglo-Irish ascendancy into the union of 1800.

Scott was ambitious; he wanted to exchange the hodden grey of his father's writer's office for the aristocratic ambience of the Scottish bar; and he lost no time ingratiating himself with the repressive Tory government of 1790s Scotland. His advocate's thesis, 'On the disposal of the bodies of executed criminals', was dedicated, aptly enough, to Lord Braxfield, in 1792, the year before that old monster became the scourge of Scottish radicalism. 'God help the people who have such judges' – Charles James Fox's comment – was not one that Scott was likely to echo.

Allied to the 'British' theme of law was Scott's experience of the Border, in which much of his childhood had been spent and where, in the 1790s, he started on the work of ballad-collecting. Everyone familiar with the area knows the ambiguous cultural identity of the Border, where national characteristics break up into local family and occupational loyalties, and cultural traditions – particularly those of the ballads – are equally strong on the English and Scottish sides. Later in the nineteenth century the philologist James Murray (1837–1915), a Denholm man, found that the dialect of Northumberland was almost the same as his own.[11] The 'heroic' period of the Border reivers, and the later imposition of law, were thus both shared processes. The latter was, in fact, the direct result of the Union of the Crowns of 1603. So it is not surprising that the assumptions underlying the folkloristic efforts – *The Minstrelsy of the Scottish Border* (1801) – which first gained Scott fame were essentially ones which confirmed the beneficence of the Union. Two of the 'good things' in that grossly uneven novella, *The Black Dwarf* (1816), which he set around 1707, are the description, taken straight from the ballads, of the cattle raid on Hobbie Elliot's peel tower, and the assembly in Ellieslaw Castle of an absurd collection of Jacobites and non-jurors from both sides of the border:

'Our commerce is destroyed,' hallooed old John Rewcastle, a Jedburgh smuggler, from the lower end of the table.

'Our agriculture is ruined,' said the Laird of Brokengirthflow, a territory which, since the days of Adam, had borne nothing but ling and whortle-berries.

'Our religion is cut up, root and branch,' said the pimple-nosed pastor of the Episcopal meeting-house at Kirkwhistle.

'We shall shortly neither dare shoot a deer nor kiss a wench without a certificate from the presbytery and kirk-treasurer,' said Mareschal Wells.

'Or make a brandy jeroboam in a frosty morning without license from a commissioner of excise,' said the smuggler.

'Or ride over the fell in a moonless night,' said Westburnflat, 'without asking leave of young Earnscliff or some Englified justice of the peace. Thae were gude days on the Border when there was neither peace nor justice heard of.'

'Let us remember our wrongs at Darien and Glencoe,' continued Ellieslaw, 'and take arms for the protection of our rights, our fortunes, our lives, and our families.'

'Think upon genuine Episcopal ordination, without which there can be no lawful clergy,' said the divine.

'Think of the piracies committed on our East-Indian trade by Green and the English thieves,' said William Willieson, half-owner and sole skipper of a brig that made four voyages annually between Cockpool and Whitehaven.

'Remember your liberties,' rejoined Mareschal, who seemed to take a mischievous delight in precipitating the movements of the enthusiasm which he had excited, like a roguish boy who, having lifted the sluice of a mill-dam, enjoys the clatter of the wheels which he has put in motion, without thinking of the mischief he may have occasioned – 'remember your liberties,' he exclaimed; 'confound cess, press, and presbytery, and the memory of old Willie that first brought them upon us!'

'Damn the gauger!' echoed old John Rewcastle; 'I'll cleave him wi' my ain hand.'

'And confound the country keeper and the constable!' re-echoed Westburnflat; 'I'll weize a brace of balls through them before morning.'

'We are agreed then,' said Ellieslaw, when the shouts had somewhat subsided, 'to bear this state of things no longer?'

'We are agreed to a man,' answered his guests.[12]

III

Scott's legal career in the 1790s was one of steady integration into the Tory establishment: Curator of the Advocate's Library in 1795 and, through Dundas and Buccleuch influence, Sheriff-depute of Selkirkshire in 1799. Instead of earning £150 a year as a somewhat lowly advocate – or £240 a year by being brilliant but politically unacceptabled like the Whig Francis Jeffrey – he had at the age of twenty-eight over £1,000 a year, most of which was his official salary. Scott's Toryism had solid material foundations; when he turned in his novels to the social evolution of post-reformation Scotland the underlying assumptions are those of Braxfield:

> The British Constitution is the best that ever was since the creation of the world, and it is not possible to make it better. For is not every man secure? . . . Does not every man reap the fruit of his own industry and sit safely under his own fig tree?[13]

In the early 1800s, as Scott cast about the Borders for an estate, he could have no serious quarrel with Braxfield's amplification of his outlook as a great Scottish 'feudal' (i.e. land) lawyer. Scott was never so exclusive. But his conviction – common enough among the Scottish gentry – remained that only land implied real citizenship, and he demonstrated this in his obsessive extensions of the Abbotsford estate.

Thus, providing a mental substructure to the *Waverley Novels* there is, not Lukács' idea of an accelerating social progress, but an image of stability achieved by a fruitful combination of enterprise, authority, good sense and paternalist responsibility, the locus of which is landed property. Lukács' famous howler, putting *Rob Roy after* the '45, is compounded by a further misconception: Bailie Nicoll Jarvie is not so much a stage of evolution away from his cousin Rob Roy MacGregor but the traditional 'Sancho Panza' foil to the wayward heroic figure, versions of which can be found in several Scott novels dealing with earlier historical periods. The goal of Jarvie, just as of Dugald Dalgetty in *A Legend of Montrose*, is one of solid worth and permissible eccentricity, with a connection to stable landed society. Such stability and consistency *were* innovations in eighteenth-century Scotland and rejoicing in them didn't imply allegiance to a dogma of continuous social change. The sort of example that intrigued Scott was the transformation of the 'bauld Buccleuch' of the ballads into his own landowner neighbour and patron, the Duke.

Landed society fascinated Scott with its continuities, contrasts and peculiarities; as a Tory he regarded it as a sort of microcosm of the Burkeian, anti-revolutionary ideal of the body politic, with its valuation of the unusual, the curious, the 'unjustifiable in any rational sense', and its linkages to the past. The Border ballads fitted into this image, and so too did his own narrative poetry. His first attempt, *The Lay of the Last Minstrel*, was commissioned in traditional bardic style by the Countess of Dalkeith, wife of the heir to the chief of Scott's own clan, but it also coincided with a favourable political climate and shifts in the publishing business which were to redound, at least initially, to Scott's advantage.

The Lay was a runaway success with a middle-class readership. It was partly an adaptation of the demotic ballad-style to the material of Burkeian conservatism, a sort of literary analogue to the language of the evangelical revival, where, as Victor Kiernan has put it, 'if high and low were to join in worship', it must be 'the worship of the poor' (but firmly under the direction of the rich).[14] It was also a 'healthy' amalgamation of gothic sensations and a patriotic view of history at a time when the newly United Kingdom was sending armies into Europe for the first time in many years. Nearly half of the population lived, after all, in the non-English parts, and a literary form which gave significance to these distinct national experiences within the Kingdom, written by a figure of proven conservatism and loyalty, was timely.

The Lay also appeared at a time when the leisure interests of the well-off English were being reorientated. Not only was the Grand Tour of the continent out, thanks to Napoleon, but the number of middling-rich people who wanted to travel but had neither the wish nor the money to venture far abroad had steadily increased, and the means of road transport had been radically improved. Edinburgh was scarcely two days away from London, a journey which not long before Scott's birth had taken two weeks. Scotland would have got on to the tourist map anyway, but the fact that Scott's poetry featured romantic and above all accessible parts such as the Border abbeys and the Trossachs dramatised its attractions at the right moment.

The Lay made Scott a wealthy man. It put him in the way of achieving his landed ambitions. But it also embroiled him even deeper in the chaotic financial world of his publishers Ballantyne and Constable which was ultimately to bring about his financial ruin. High though his financial liabilities were, we can't identify in the motives which led him into them the classic rationality of the capitalist. The badly secured loans of his friends, the reckless land-purchases, the endowment of his children, the building of Abbotsford after 1812, were much more part of a desire to recreate himself not only as a landed gentleman, but one who would restore the sense of obligation and family authority which was, for him, the justification of the type. It was this impulse, already becoming one of some urgency, and the foreclosing of the narrative verse option by the meteoric rise of Byron after the publication of the first two cantos of *Childe Harold* in 1812, that led him to the novel.

IV

If there was, on the whole, something decorative and conformist about the narrative poems, with their tourist Scotland and blameless patriotism, the gestation and production of the Waverley novels was more complex and ambiguous. Scott's 'bardic' success and the favour shown him by government had masked a range of less orthodox options and relationships. He was still, emotionally at least, a Jacobite; he had earlier thrilled to the lyricism and demotic Scottishness of Burns; and he had connections, through his wife's friends the Doumergues, with the radical illuminati of the Birmingham Lunar Society; more, his wife's benefactor, the Marquis of Downshire, had been denounced as a traitor and expelled from the Privy Council for his fervour in the lost cause of Irish autonomy. It was probably not surprising that it was Maria Edgeworth, who combined these 'enlightened' and Irish strands, whose novel *Castle Rackrent* (1800) seemed to prod him towards a genre which combined narrative action with a rich sense of the social reality provided by the scenery, buildings and people of Scotland.

Scott's purpose in writing the greatest of the Waverley novels was inevitably obscured by the rapidity with which these were composed. The 'somnambulistic' quality of this headlong production plainly enhanced qualities which were otherwise latent in his subconscious. The most deliberate parts of Scott's novels – the prefaces – are also the most unreadable, while his greatest creations all but took him over. As he wrote in the 'Introduction' to *The Fortunes of Nigel* (1822):

> I have repeatedly laid down my future work to scale, divided it into volumes and chapters, and endeavoured to construct a story which I meant should evolve itself gradually and strikingly, maintain suspense, and stimulate curiosity. But I think there is a demon who seats himself on the feather of my pen when I begin to write, and lead it astray from my purpose. Characters expand under my hand; incidents are multiplied; my regular mansion turns out a Gothic anomaly,

and the work is closed long before I have attained the point I proposed.[15]

The endemic weakness in plotting, the penchant for 'bringing in good things', result however in a greater fidelity to the spirit of historical reconstruction, and help fulfil the major intention of the sequence, to show the transition of Scotland from what his fellow-Borderer Sir Henry Maine was to call a society based on status to one based on contract. In part the novels drew on, and perpetuated, the qualities of Scotland which the narrative poems had opened up. Its landscape and weather were dramatic enough to figure as actors in their own right; its history was complex and eventful but never – unlike Ireland – utterly tragic. But the novels added more: the language of the ballads was now delivered in the prose of ordinary speech. A gallery of Scotsmen and Scotswomen was created whose vividness, Scott himself recognised, overshadowed the stock heroes and heroines whom his plots demanded. Some were grotesques – Scots legalism, pietism or self-serving driven into the extremes of Puir Peter Peebles, Gifted Gilfillan and Andrew Fairservice. Some were tragic, such as Evan Dhu Maccombich and Ephraim Macbriar. But most were the sort of figures of civic worth – Bailie Nicol Jarvie, Mr Pleydell, Dandie Dinmont, Hobbie Elliot – whose consent had been necessary to achieve Scotland's modernisation. In the instance of possibly his greatest novel – *The Heart of Midlothian* – the leading and truly heroic role falls to a girl, Jeanie Deans, from the lower classes, speaking in the vernacular but making painful moral decisions which would have tested anyone in George Eliot.

The political position behind the great novels is – one cannot deny it – one of satisfaction with the Union, improvement and legality. In Bailie Nichol Jarvie's words in *Rob Roy*

> Whisht, sir! – whisht! It's ill-scraped tongues like yours that makes mischief between neighbourhoods and nations. There's naething sae gude on this side o' time but it might have been better, and that may be said o' the Union. Nane were keener against it than the Glasgow folk, wi' their rabblings and their risings, and their mobs, as the ca' them nowadays. But it's an ill wind that blaws naebody gude – let ilka ane roose the ford as they find it. – I say, let Glasgow flourish! whilk is judiciously and elegantly putten round the town's arms by way of byword. Now since St Mungo catched herrings in the Clyde, what was ever like to gar us flourish like the sugar and tobacco trade? Will anybody tell me that, and grumble at a treaty that opened us a road west-awa' yonder?[16]

This is the Border settlement writ large; the supersession of feudal loyalty and the rule of force by sensible modernisation and economic progress. But not too much progress.

The Antiquary, set in 1793 or thereabouts, brings on a comic villain, Dousterswivel, who is half alchemist, half speculator: pure cardboard, but there is probably a hint here about the insubstantiality of experimentation in general, while, in the novel's most vivid character, the Gaberlunzie man, or licensed beggar, Edie Ochiltree, we have celebration of the Tory ideal of the dependence that does not dishonour.

The spirit of the greatest novels certainly celebrated former Scottish distinctiveness within the generally beneficent process of assimilation. But, I would date it as early as 1819, there is a shift either away from the novel of Scotland, or into a darker tone. Crises of social development are more difficult to resolve, the results messier. *The Bride of Lammermoor* (1819), a melodrama in which revenge and madness drag down Whig and Tory alike, may indicate the effects of Scott's serious illness in 1817–18, but it also shows him admitting that such crises do not always resolve themselves painlessly; that their outcomes can be tragically destructive.

V

Scott was seemingly at the peak of his career in 1820–2. His most popular novel, *Ivanhoe*, was published early in 1820, and in the summer of 1822 George IV paid the first state visit of a reigning monarch to Scotland since Stuart days. It was the political apotheosis of Scott's combination of unionism and cultural nationalism, the symbolic confirmation of the Hanoverian line, the transference of remaining Jacobite and nationalist sentiments to wider British imperial loyalties, but it had also specifically nationalist implications, reminding the political metropolis and its élite that Scots loyalty, though full-hearted, was not wholly unconditional.

Beneath this, however, was a darker political theme. Scotland's Tory rulers were made uncomfortably aware, by the events of 1819 and 1820, of their vulnerability. The unrest caused by the ending of the high-wage war economy in 1815 was swollen by the first of a new type of cyclical trade depression. This climaxed in 1820 in riots, allegations of conspiracy, and the brief 'radical war', when a small group of Glasgow radicals attempted to march on the Carron Ironworks at Falkirk, were rounded up by troops, and suffered exemplary punishment.

Scott was deeply concerned by this, not simply because of his financial problems but because of his mounting suspicion of urban, industrial society. 'Improvement' no longer automatically tended towards the 'rule of law'; the assumption which underlay the 'conjectural history' of the Waverley sequence no longer seemed tenable. His response was not, however, straightforward: on one side his attachment to the older society – not simply nostalgic but increasingly pessimistic – increased; on the other, so too did his dependence, and that of his class, on coercion provided by the English connection. Escape from such pressures into the world of medieval chivalry, which also proved remarkably rewarding financially, was one way out; the sheer volume of work that Scott undertook in the early 1820s was also, to some extent, a means of avoiding difficult political decisions. Yet I would submit that, out of his 'somnambulistic' writing, emerged not only some of the best things he ever wrote, but a new and dark vision of the modern Scots predicament.

Two difficulties, however, stand in the way of this interpretation. After 1825 Scott kept a *Journal*, published partly in Lockhart and wholly in the 1890s, which gave his political reactions in some detail. Apart from the Malagrowther episode, which Phillipson counts as hyperbolic, these seem to be those of an English Tory country squire, increasingly apprehensive at the approach of parliamentary reform. His *History of Scotland*, prepared for Johnie Lockhart in 1827, manages to sweep from 1745 to the present in ten pages, whose message is one of straightforward assimilation. Yet these sources are themselves ambiguous. The *Journal*, written with publication in mind, is almost wholly social and domestic in character; few writers have been so uninformative, not simply about their method of working but about any personal engagement with their material. Secondly, Scott's history was, literally, the *Tales of a Grandfather*, a series of good stories to absorb an ailing little boy – who, notoriously, couldn't stand the chapter on 'civilisation' and begged Scott to stop reading it. Neither source aids our understanding of the creative demon which possessed Scott in his best work – the sense of understanding a national community so that it appeared to speak directly from its conscious and subconscious memory.

Huge obstacles fell across Scott's ability to do this in the 1820s. He was tied to the treadmill of profitable romanticism, before and even more after his bankruptcy in 1825. He was politically constrained by a Toryism which was increasingly unpopular, even if his own version of it was qualified. And his view of society as a whole was much less optimistic, deeply alarmed by industrial developments and wholly uninterested in the recrudescence of religious politics – centred on the issue of patronage – which passed for Scottish identity at this time.

The Scots novels of the early 1820s – *St Ronan's Well* and *Redgauntlet* – are both elegiac in tone, and were badly received by Scott's public. In both, the contrast of old and new Scotland does not come out to the advantage of the new. Mag Dods of the Cleikum Inn, and Redgauntlet himself, are fully realised figures against whom the representatives of the new age seem not simply insubstantial but inferior.

Scott's conservative nationalism appeared to reach a climacteric with the *Letters of Malachi Malagrowther* of 1826, written in protest against the intention of the government to stop the issue of Scottish banknotes. Phillipson is over-sceptical about this (monetarist thinking was not in full flood in 1968); the power to control the supply and circulation of money was important in a developing provincial economy – a similar agitation, led by Thomas Attwood, was at the centre of Birmingham radicalism – and such an attack on the Scots banks would have had very serious effects. Scott's visit to Ireland in 1825 had disclosed the costs of an unequal partnership with England and an unpatriotic gentry – in Lockhart's words, 'the wanton and reckless profligacy of human mismanagement, the withering curse of feuds and factions, and the tyrannous selfishness of absenteeism.'[17] This threat must have been in mind when he wrote the *Malagrowther* letters, and in the aggressive *Journal* entries which accompanied them:

> Then down fall – as national objects of respect and veneration – the Scottish Bench, the Scottish Bar, the Scottish Law herself, and – and – 'there is an end of an auld sang'. Were I as I have been, I would fight knee-deep in blood ere it came to that. But it is a catastrophe which the great course of events brings daily nearer–
>
> 'And who can help it, Dick?'
>
> I shall always be proud of *Malachi* as having headed back the Southron, or helpd to do so, in one instance at least.[18]

In terms of imaginative fiction, Scott produced in the last eight years of his life scarely anything comparable with the novels of 1814–18. The only time he returned to the theme of recent Scots history was in the *Chronicles of the Canongate* (1828), the first of his fiction to be published under his own name. Unpopular at the time, rarely reprinted (only five entries in the British Library Catalogue), these show that the opinions and perceptions of Malagrowther went deeper than decorative patriotism.

VI

The Chronicles of the Canongate include three short stories, 'The highland widow', 'The two drovers' and 'The surgeon's daughter', of which the first two are generally acknowledged to be among Scott's best work.[19] There is also a long prologue of sixty-four pages in which their ostensible writer, Chrystal Croftangry, introduces himself.

Now Croftangry, despite the quaintness of his name, is not a pawky, prolix old bore like Jedediah Cleishbotham, to be avoided *en route* to Chapter I of *Old Mortality*. Nor is he an autobiographical construct – at least not wholly. His account of his life and acquaintance is sparely written, and sober in content. It is also one of the few occasions in which Scott employs first-hand narration, and sets the narrative at the actual time of writing.

Croftangry is a landed gentleman and lawyer forced by loose living and financial reverses to become an Abbey Laird, a tenant of the area around Holyroodhouse, where he could exist free from distraint for debt. When a lawyer friend sorts his affairs out, Croftangry goes abroad, makes a modest fortune, and thirty years later returns to Scotland. He finds his benefactor senile, his friends decayed or dispersed, the family mansion in Clydesdale demolished and replaced by the raw, but already empty and decaying, 'castle' of a cotton-spinner. Meeting up again with the Highland landlady of his Canongate 'imprisonment', he returns to the Abbey precincts – from which his own name derives – to write.

John Buchan praised the *Chronicles* for their 'cold autumnal light . . . an economy and a certainty which recall some of the best work of Turgenev'.[20] With the *Tales of a Grandfather* they stand out from the treadmill work of Scott's last years, both in quality and in subject matter. The subject matter is Scotland, and the tone one of vehement although pessimistic nationalism, linked perhaps to a broader pessimism about the future of civil society.

The scar of the banknote controversy and the *Malagrowther* letters went deep. Croftangry writes about his *Chronicles*:

> I am ambitious . . . that they should cross the Forth, astonish the long town of Kirkcaldy, enchant the skippers and colliers of the east of Fife, venture even into the classic arcades of St. Andrews, and travel as much farther to the north as the breath of applause will carry their sails. As for a southward direction, it is not to be hoped for in my fondest dreams. I am informed that Scottish literature will be presently laid under a prohibitory duty.[21]

There is irony here, of course, but also an underlying seriousness. All the metaphor and language of the *Chronicles* suggest that Scott was taking up an explicitly national position. 'Croftangry', from 'Croft-an-ri' – 'the King's croft' by Holyroodhouse – could pass for 'the Kingdom', and the 'author' goes on to praise this vantage point between Edinburgh and Arthur's Seat with its 'two extremities of the moral world' which are also simulacra of modern Scotland:

> A nobler contrast there can hardly exist than that of the huge city, dark with the smoke of ages, and groaning with the various sounds of active industry or idle revel, and the lofty and craggy hill, silent and solitary as the grave . . . The city resembles the busy temple, where the modern Comus and Mammon hold their court, and thousands sacrifice ease, independence and virtue at their shrine; the misty and lonely mountain seems as a throne to the majestic but terrible genius of feudal times, when the same divinities dispensed coronets and domains to those who had heads to devise and arms to execute bold enterprises.[22]

Croftangry both surveys and represents an emblematic Scotland, on which both his own experiences and his tales comment, ironically and pessimistically.

Scott turns to the Highlands for 'The highland widow' and 'The two drovers', but neither tale has any of the reassurance of the earlier novels. Both concern 'men in the middle' attempting to make the transition from the dying society to the developing one. Hamish Bean MacTavish, son of a 'cateran' or 'gentleman drover' of the Rob Roy type, killed in action, is bred to the trade by his mother, but realises that the old Highland life is dead, and joins the army at Dumbarton. Returning on embarkation leave, he tells his mother, who is horrified by the news, and contrives to make him miss the deadline for his return to depot. She calculates that he will turn outlaw rather than face a whipping for desertion, but he realises that the time for taking to the hills has long gone. He waits for the search party from the depot, but when they turn up, and their leader, his friend Allan Breack Cameron, offers Hamish the chance of a mitigated sentence, he fires on him, fatally. Hamish gives himself up, and is taken back to Dumbarton and there executed. His mother loses her reason.

Robin Oig McCombich in 'The two drovers' has made the transition from 'gentleman drover' to successful commerce, and, sometime in the 1790s, is taking his cattle south via Carlisle, along with an English companion, Harry Wakefield, and his drove.

Wakefield, an insensitive but good-natured sort, is deceived by an English bailiff into grazing his cattle on land whose owner has separately agreed to let it to Robin Oig. He makes way for the Highlander with a bad grace and later, in an alehouse, is provoked by the locals, and the dishonest bailiff, into challenging him to a wrestling match. Robin Oig refuses, Wakefield leaps on him, and he is thrown to the ground and humiliated. Robin Oig leaves, goes to another drover to obtain a knife which he has left with him, returns and stabs Wakefield to death. He then gives himself up, without resistance, to trial and inevitable execution.

These two late stories are, to me, testaments to the failure of integration. The 'man in the middle' in the classic novels ultimately comes down on the side of 'progress' and wins his secure niche in landed society, though this repeated 'dilemma of divided loyalties' is surely of more use as a device for 'bringing on good things'. Scott's two young Highlanders are not, however, in the passive position of most Scott heroes. They are the central actors in the stories, and their only hope of survival in a hostile world is by submission, to the discipline of the British army or the social hegemony of the English. Both are literally, landless men, suffering – in the Braxfield view – all the deprivation of right that this involves. And for both the only honourable response when their situation becomes critical is a form of suicide.

The Highland predicament was a particularly painful one for Scott. His aristocratic friends, the Countess of Sutherland and Alexander MacDonell of Glengarry, were so deeply implicated in some of the most drastic evictions (which reached a climax between 1810 and 1820) that he could never directly speak out against them. The passage in *Tales of a Grandfather* describing the clearances is haltingly diplomatic in tone. On the other hand, the attempt to celebrate and restore a familial society of 'Duinnewassals', which Abbotsford had exemplified, could only be completely destroyed by such developments. The attitude expressed in the 'Introduction' to *A Legend of Montrose* is more indicative of Scott's actual views than his otherwise guarded statements of fact. The old Highland sergeant More MacAlpin returns from the wars to his native glen:

> The fires had been quenched upon thirty hearths; of the cottage of his fathers he could but distinguish a few rude stones; the language was almost extinguished; the ancient race from which he boasted his descent had found a refuge beyond the Atlantic.

MacAlpin's rejection of the chief who evicted his kinsfolk is as bitter a comment as Scott allows: 'I cannot curse him . . . I will not curse him; he is the descendant and representative of my fathers. But never shall mortal man hear me name his name again.'²³

My argument is not simply that the two stories show the clash of two cultures, and the destruction of the weaker, but that, both in the stories and in their frame, Scott makes the Highland predicament a metaphor for Scotland as a whole. There is no longer the expectation, fundamental to the classic novels, that the British future is secure and inevitable. Instead a collapsing Scottish culture is being replaced by an even more imperilled industrial 'civilisation'.

The *Chronicles of the Canongate* stories are instances of what Scott might have achieved had he not decided to martyr himself. As a project, however, it was foredoomed. James Cadell, Scott's taskmaster in the last years, found that it was less popular than the medieval romances, and prodded Scott back to eminently forgettable projects such as *Count Robert of Paris* and *Castle Dangerous*. Enough, however, remains to suggest that, had his freedom of action and intellectual powers remained, Scott might have made a powerful addition to conservative nationalism.

This Conservatism is important. The Whig in Scott was parliamentary and assimilationist; the Conservative placed greater emphasis on the structure of society, and wished to strengthen it partly through coercion – 'terror under law' – and partly through paternalist measures of social welfare. Scott saw the drive to reform and assimilation being paralleled by mounting economic dislocation, and realised that he was powerless to prevent either. As he wrote in his *Journal* in 1826:

> They are gradually destroying what remains of nationality, and making the country *tabula rasa* for doctrines of bold innovation. Their lowering and grounding down all those peculiarities which distinguished us as Scotsmen will throw the country into a state in which it will be universally turned to democracy, and instead of canny Saunders, they will have a very dangerous North British neighbourhood.²⁴

Whatever this is, it is not enthusiastic about assimilation.

VII

Scott's Jacobitism was sentimental; his attachment to the Union deep and sincere. But he regarded the Union as a type of fundamental law within an Anglo-Scottish constitutional arrangement which was essentially federalist. Like the supremacy of the landed interest, this constitutional stability was the basis of the conservative, hierarchical, paternalist society which he favoured and celebrated. His great novel sequence was a testament to this balance, transforming the uneasy coexistence of improvement and an historic Scottishness (which was, momentarily at least, more vivid and penetrating) into a fascinating dialogue. In the arrangements of his own life Scott believed that he, and others of his politics, could preserve such a balance within the Scottish cultural dimension of the Union.

But after about 1819 things changed. Industrialisation began to carry 'improvement' away on its own stronger current and towards the rapids of social upheaval. To defend themselves, Scott and his class became ever more reliant on the coercive power of English government. At the same time, Scott's own commercial ventures trapped him deeper and deeper in a morass of debts, from which the only way out seemed to be by increasingly commercial exploitation of his own talents. From being in the position of a detached commentator, Scott became a living example of the fate he feared for Scotland as a whole. When his own crisis came, in 1825, he had two options. He could stay true to his art, accept the humiliations that Croftangry suffered, and view his country – and himself – through new and disillusioned eyes. He tried this with *Malagrowther* and with *Chronicles*. The result was alienation from his political allies and his largest readership. Coupled with a dying wife and family problems, this was too much. Out of much the same state of cultural and personal irresolution that he had described in Hamish Bean and Robin Oig he chose, like them, self-destruction.

Notes

1 This chapter originally appeared in Alan Bold (ed.), *Sir Walter Scott. The Long-Forgotten Melody*, Vision and Barnes & Noble, 1983, pp. 17–42.
2 John Buchan, *Sir Walter Scott*, Cassell, London, 1932, p. 137.
3 Theodor Fontane, *Jenseits des Tweed* in *Ges. Werke*, Bd. 17, pp. 407ff.
4 Lord Dacre, 'Scotching the myths of devolution', in *The Times*, 28 April 1976.
5 Hugh MacDiarmid, *Lucky Poet*, 1942, p. 220.
6 W.B. Yeats, quoted in Christopher Harvie, *Scotland and Nationalism*, Allen & Unwin, London, 1977, p. 272.
7 J. G. Lockhart, *Life of Sir Walter Scott*, Blackwood, 1836–38, vol II, p. 299.
8 Nicholas Phillipson, 'Nationalism and ideology', in J. N. Wolfe (ed.), *Government and Nationalism in Scotland*, Edinburgh University Press, 1969, pp. 167–88.

9 Sir Walter Scott, *Journal*, 6 December 1825, Oliver and Boyd, Edinburgh, 1950, p. 31.
10 Eric Hobsbawn, 'Capitalisme et agriculture', *Annales*, 1978 pp. 580–600.
11 Elisabeth Murray, *Caught in the Web of Words*, Yale University Press, 1977, pp. 11–12.
12 Sir Walter Scott, *The Waverley Novels*, Adam & Charles Black, standard edition, 1879, vol. V. p. 94.
13 Summing up at the trial of Thomas Muir, 1793, quoted in Thomas Johnston, *The History of the Working Classes in Scotland*, 1920, Unity Press edition, 1946, p. 221.
14 Victor Kiernan, 'Evangelicalism and the French revolution', *Past and Present*, vol. I, 1952, pp. 49–50.
15 Sir Walter Scott, *The Waverley Novels*, Adam & Charles Black, standard edition, 1879, vol. XIV, pp. xxi-xxii.
16 Quoted in John Buchan, *Sir Walter Scott*, Cassell, London, 1932, pp. 182–3.
17 Quoted in H.J.C.Grierson, *Sir Walter Scott, Bart*, pp. 243–4.
18 Sir Walter Scott, journal entry for 9 June 1826, in *The Journal of Sir Walter Scott*, Oliver & Boyd, Edinburgh, 1950, pp. 183–4.
19 A.O.J.Cockshut, *The Achievement of Sir Walter Scott*, Collins, London, 1969, pp. 56–62.
20 John Buchan, *Sir Walter Scott*, Cassell, London, 1932, p. 315.
21 Sir Walter Scott, *The Waverley Novels*, Adam & Charles Black, standard edition, 1879, vol. XIX, pp. 374–5.
22 Sir Walter Scott, op. cit., pp. 373–4.
23 Sir Walter Scott, op. cit., vol. V, p. 146.
24 Sir Walter Scott, journal entry for 14 March 1826, in *The Journal of Sir Walter Scott*, Oliver & Boyd, Edinburgh, 1950, p. 133.

I would like to thank my wife, Virginia, for reading through Scott's Scottish novels and discussing them with me, my parents for their hospitality in Scott's countryside, and Birte Gräper for typing the text.

14
The anglicisation of South Wales

TIM WILLIAMS

> When a language dies, it is not because a community has forgotten how to speak but because another language has gradually ousted the old one.[1]

At the beginning of the nineteenth century almost all of the Welsh spoke Welsh. However, as early as 1891, the first year in which the census of population supplied information on the Welsh language, only 54 per cent of the people of Wales could speak their native tongue. In 1901 this figure fell to 50 per cent, and the proportion of monoglot Welsh speakers was estimated at a mere 15 per cent. Since then there has been a steady decline in the proportion of Welsh speakers, from 37 per cent in 1931 to less than 20 per cent in 1981. Moreover, the monoglot Welsh speaker has virtually disappeared – though the most recent census did identify a number of adult Welsh monoglots in the centre of Cardiff, but as I know one of them has a degree in English from Cambridge, I'm a little suspicious of the validity of such statistics.

The conclusion is inescapable. English has not been a foreign language to the Welsh for some considerable time. Indeed, it has in the twentieth century been the only language, the mother tongue, of the majority of the Welsh. To understand how this was achieved it is necessary to dispel two illusions. The first, the most pernicious because most widely held, is that the Welsh language was destroyed by the administrative decree of an alien government. The second is that Wales is an internal colony of England. In challenging these notions I hope to make a contribution to the evolving debate on language and democracy, and also to establish the centrality of the hitherto marginalised Welsh Question to an understanding of the nature of Britain.

By the 1960s, Welsh nationalist intellectuals had elaborated a

TABLE 14.1 Welsh-speaking population: percentage of population aged three and over at censuses of 1901, 1931, 1951 and 1961

	Welsh Monoglots (%)				All Welsh speakers			
	1901	1931	1951	1961	1901	1931	1951	1961
Anglesey	48	24	10	6	92	87	80	76
Brecknock	9	2	1	1	46	37	30	28
Caernarfon	48	21	9	5	90	79	72	68
Cardigan	50	20	7	5	93	87	80	75
Carmarthen	36	9	4	3	90	82	77	75
Denbigh	18	5	2	1	62	49	39	35
Flint	8	1	—	—	49	32	21	29
Glamorgan	7	1	—	—	44	32	20	17
Merioneth	51	22	9	6	94	86	75	76
Monmouth	1	—	—	—	13	6	4	3
Montgomery	16	7	3	1	48	41	35	32
Pembroke	12	4	2	1	34	31	27	24
Radnor	—	—	—	—	6	5	5	5
All Wales	15	4	2	1	50	37	29	26

Sources: Censuses of England and Wales 1951 and 1961.

highly successful, if extremely meretricious, form of psycho-history to account for the anglicisation of Wales. The Welsh, it was claimed, had suffered from an inferiority complex induced by the brainwashing habitually indulged in by the schools of the British state, which supplemented their symbolic violence towards the Welsh language by meting out physical punishment to its speakers. This conception, sired by Hegel out of Freud, of the history of the Welsh is both condescending and wrong. This is because it exaggerates the influence of schools in the process of linguistic transition, ignores the capacities of majorities to resist oppression when they feel their interests to be at stake, and – crucially – misrepresents the character of the state and the form of Wales's insertion into it.

Languages can be neither killed nor resuscitated by means of the schools alone. This is as true of Wales as it is of Ireland. It's not difficult to find evidence for this proposition. There is, for example, the simple matter of the linguistic contrasts to be found within Wales. Thus in Anglesey in 1901, fully 92 per cent of the population could speak Welsh, whilst in Glamorgan it was only 44 per cent – and yet they were both subject to the same education system. In addition, how, if this apparatus – inaugurated in 1870, made compulsory in 1880 and free in 1891 – was the linguistic murder machine it's made out to be, was it that a large majority of those too old to have come under the influence of the new education system could speak English? A full 80 per cent, in 1901, of those in the forty-five to sixty-four years age-bracket spoke English. Anglicisation therefore preceded state schooling and was not dependent upon it. What it depended upon was the central development in modern Welsh history – coal industrialisation and the civil society it nurtured.

Population growth, consequent upon the explosive growth of the coal industry, was traumatic by any standards. Between 1861 and 1911 the population of Glamorgan grew by 253 per cent. It grew by 33 per cent in the period 1901–11 alone. And individual areas grew at even more prodigious rates. The Rhondda in 1851 had under 1,000 people; by 1911 it had over 150,000 and was still growing. Barry in 1881 had eighty-five inhabitants; by 1891 it had over 13,000. Crucially, between 1801 and 1901 the population of Glamorgan and Monmouthshire in relation to all other Welsh counties changed from a ratio of 1 to 4 to 3 to 1 as the insatiable demands for workers in the labour-intensive coalfield of South Wales emptied first rural Wales and then the West of England of their surplus and footloose people.

Whilst the demographic consequences of coal industrialisation are beyond dispute, the linguistic consequences have been a matter of controversy. This – essentially a Welsh version of the Hartwell–Hobsbawm standard of living debate – concerns whether industrialisation was a Good Thing for the Welsh language or not. It seems to me that, just as in the Hartwell–Hobsbawm debate, the answer depends on chronology. That is, up until the 1870s the coalfield's demands for labour were being met by migrants from other parts of Wales. Fleetingly, this massive movement of people formed a Welsh-speaking industrial labour force, with the resources to support sophisticated and costly vernacular publishing ventures of a sort unrealisable in rural societies. In other words, the Welsh, through industrialisation, were colonising their own country, thereby avoiding the fate of rural minorities in the nineteenth century – emigration and the marginalisation of their language.

The moment passed. The coalfield's needs could not be satisfied by internal or Welsh reserves of labour, and so we find, already in the 1870s, almost 40 per cent of migrants came from the agricultural districts of the West of England. By the time of the climax of the immigration, in the Edwardian period, when Wales was absorbing population at a rate second only to that of the USA, most of the migrants were English. According to the census of 1911, over half the population of Glamorgan was either born outside Wales or born to at least one non-Welsh parent.

TABLE 14.2 United States: Number of immigrants (with and without occupation) from Wales, England, Scotland and Ireland, decennially, 1881–1930[2]

Period and country of origin	Mean population of country of origin (000)	Immigrants to USA (with occupation)	Annual rate per 10,000 mean population	Total immigrants to USA (with and without occupation)	Annual rate per 10,000 mean population
Wales					
1881–90	1,677	5,682	3	12,640	8
1891–1900	1,895	5,005	3	11,219	6
1901–10	2,238	11,708	5	18,631	8
1911–20	2,538	9,988	4	15,379	6
1921–30	2,629	8,402	3	16,267	6
England					
1881–90	25,812	391,118	12	644,680	25
1891–1900	28,861	128,107	4	224,350	8
1901–10	32,061	237,227	7	387,005	12
1911–20	34,440	271,181	8	419,526	12
1921–30	36,290	258,523	7	472,873	13
Scotland					
1881–90	3,881	79,342	20	149,869	39
1891–1900	4,249	28,006	7	60,046	14
1901–10	4,617	83,976	19	133,333	29
1911–20	4,822	100,824	21	164,131	34
1921–30	4,862	177,476	36	293,764	60
Ireland					
1881–90	4,540	382,368	77	655,182	133
1891–1900	4,582	280,054	61	404,045	88
1901–10	4,429	316,340	71	371,772	84
1911–20	4,372	187,902	43	240,041	55
1921–30	4,265	278,794	65	362,921	84

The consequences for the Welsh language were serious. Immigration clearly added to the difficulties of transmitting the language from one generation to the next in a context in which one's neighbours, schoolfriends, drinking partners, team-mates, colleagues, comrades and lovers – in a phrase, civil society – might speak only English. This was obvious to participants in the process, such as the writer Jack Jones, describing Merthyr in the 1880s:

The Welsh were in a minority in Tai-Harry-Blawd, where they

FIGURE 14.1 Wales, Scotland and England: Decennial net gain or loss by migration, 1851–1957 (annual rate per 10,000 mean population).[3]

mixed with English, Irish and Scottish people . . . At first I knew only Welsh from my parents and grandparents, but as I went on playing with the Scott, Hartley, Ward and McGill children, I became more fluent than in my native language. Dad was annoyed when I started replying in English to what he had said in Welsh, but our mam said in Welsh: 'Oh, let him alone. What odds anyway?'[4]

However, minority languages have survived in the face of great difficulties, even tyranny, where the collective will has been exhibited to sustain them. The fact that the Welsh had no such collective will, and indeed seemed to view the crisis facing the language with a certain amount of equanimity, has led some to argue that their choices were made under physical or psychological duress. I would argue, on the contrary, that the Welsh language has shrivelled in the air of freedom.

Those who stress the use of violence against Welsh speakers in the schools of the British state base their entire argument on the existence of something called the Welsh Not. This was a small piece of wood hung around the neck of a pupil caught speaking Welsh; at the end of the school day the wearer would be punished by a teacher. Undoubtedly a cruel teaching aid, the Welsh Not was sometimes used in private or denominational schools paid for out of the pennies of the parents in the era prior to the advent of state education. There's no evidence that its use was ever sanctioned in the schools of the Imperial British Government. The state did not persecute the language: the threat to its survival came not from Whitehall but from Wales.

If coercion is discounted, what of deference? Perhaps the Welsh lacked confidence in themselves and their language or suffered from a defective national consciousness fostered by the 'ideological apparatus' of the British state, which peddled an unscrupulous myth of 'Britishness' subversive of the indigenous nationalism? I think not.

The problem with such assumptions is that they are normative – a defective consciousness presupposes a proper one – and also that they reproduce in a Welsh form the errors of the social control ideology in which the study of the people gets collapsed into the study of the forces operating on them, so that successful domination from above is assumed and resistance from below is forgotten. This is not an adequate approach; in a complex capitalist society people are not open spaces which institutions can enclose at will. And so we find in Wales, in the era of compulsory state education, that school log-books, newspapers, government inquiries, police files and nonconformist reports, all bear witness to the difficulties of controlling the inhabitants of the new industrialising Wales, exploding around them. The phrase, 'the problem of South Wales' coined at this time conveys the awareness of failure in this endeavour, as does the following newspaper report:

> We understand that the Independents of Rhydfelen visited Mr Hamlen Williams at Fairfield. While the participants were indulging in various games in the field they were rudely assailed by a banded squad of Pontypridd 'uncontrollables' who marched about interrupting the past-times, much to the annoyance of all . . . They would not enjoy themselves neither would they allow others to do so. When civilly reprimanded by a ministerial gentleman their harsh retorts were most degrading. One of the 'squad' especially replied most rudely to his civil injunctions, and out of sheer disrespect and ignorance, sarcastically commenced to sing a Welsh hymn in which the whole 'squad' participated. The ministerial gentleman turned away in disgust. It is to be regretted that such scandalous behaviour is permitted.[5]

Moreover, such things as opposition to the Boer War, the growth of the Labour movement and of syndicalism, and the coalfield stoppage of 1915, would seem to indicate the limited capacity of the state to inculcate passivity and loyalty in reluctant citizens. Hence the need for a proper social history of education to dovetail a history 'from above' with a history 'from below', and consider not merely the intentions of elites but also the desires and resistances displayed by those other, much ignored, participants in the educational process – the working class majority in the schools.

The irony of anglicisation is that the Welsh were reluctant to remain Welsh monoglots, whilst the educational elites in London were eager to promote the Welsh language.

The Welsh people themselves were eager anglicisers:

> it is the Welsh themselves who are letting English in, and making an effort to turn Welsh out of their families, chapels and trade . . . It is up to the Welsh themselves as to whether Welsh dies or lives, and if it dies the blame will be theirs. Let every Welshman keep his language on the hearth, in chapel and in business and it will live.[6]

This is because, to paraphrase Brecht, the Welsh peoople had no wish to be a Folk. Disadvantaged by social class, they had no desire to compound this evil by being deprived of the language of the state. That is, a utilitarian people, believers in free trade after all, showed a sensible awareness of necessary change, and sought to exchange the language of the museum for the language of modernity and power. And this without much sentiment – an item invented in the twentieth century, with the spread of idealist notions of culture and the fetishisation of language and literature as the essence of a people.

If they had wished to be a Folk, nobody could have stopped them. The democratic revolution of the 1880s and 1890s placed power in local government and above all education in the hands of directly-elected Welsh radicals; the first public secondary schools anywhere in Britain were a product of this. This democratic irruption, expressed in Liberalism, combined with the burgeoning significance of Wales within Britain's export economy to provide the launching pad for the propulsion of people like Lloyd George to the centres of power, and to allow, also, the reciprocal granting of separate institutions to the Welsh. The most significant of these was the Welsh Department of the Board of Education, established in December 1906.

When we examine the activities of this devolved government agency it becomes clear that it attempted to propagate not some ideology of Britishness, but a linguistically-based Welshness. That is, it was indefatigable in its attempts to give the Welsh language a prominent position in school life. It failed. And it failed because of the nature of the Welsh democracy. It seems to me that this failure tells us more about the reality of Wales' insertion into Britain than the theoretically threadbare notion of internal colonialism; a failure which highlights the inadequacy in seeing Britishness negatively and abstractly, as mere ideology, as opposed to seeing it as a positive set of practices and possibilities.

In 1931 J. E. Lloyd, the Welsh historian, and, in his own way, language activist, emphasised that 'None were better friends to the [language] movement than the Capital's education officials and their inspectors in Wales', and that this had been true since the end of the nineteenth century. After 1907, this sympathy was embodied in a policy which, 'as enunciated by the Welsh Department . . . would have permitted almost any use of the Welsh language in education that the local authorities might have decided'.[7] Indeed, so committed was the Department and its inspectorate (and under the leadership of that doyen of Welsh nationalists, Owen M. Edwards, Chief Inspector, how could it fail to be?) that it often found itself isolated from Welsh opinion on the question of the language.

The frustrations arising out of dealing with a sceptical and utilitarian Welsh democracy find eloquent expression in the Department's files: 'There is far too much apathy in Wales on this subject . . . It is the time now for the people and Authorities and Denominations in Wales to rouse themselves and do their part on behalf of the mother tongue.'[8] This position is restated in the Secretary's reply to a request from a Baptist Association that Welsh be made compulsory in training colleges. Pointing out how much the Department already does for the language in education, Alfred Davies suggests:

> that the proper quarter to which the efforts of the membership of your Association as well as of others who share their views in favour of the teaching of the home language, should be mainly addressed, is the Local Authorities to whom Parliament has entrusted the responsibility for providing education . . . If local public opinion throughout Wales is fully aroused to the importance of Welsh, the resulting demand for its teaching will undoubtedly make itself felt by the Local Authorities and the Governors of secondary schools . . . The necessary driving force to enable full advantage to be taken of the facilities . . . offered by the Welsh Department . . . must . . . be supplied by people on the spot who are in a position to influence public opinion by the usual methods of the written and spoken word and the vote.[9]

This is not an isolated example. The Department was constantly exhorting 'people on the spot' to be as sympathetic to Welsh as the Department itself. Consider the following unequivocal counsel given to the children of Wales in a St David's Day pamphlet issued by the Department in 1915:

> Question – How can Welsh children uphold the Welsh language?
> Answer – By speaking, by reading and by writing it whenever they can, at home and abroad, at work or at play. A good knowledge of Welsh is a thing to be proud of and all Welsh children should praise their Mother Tongue.

Davies' gloss on this advice is devastating, and indicative of the Department's increasing impatience with those who sought to shift responsibility for maintaining the language from Wales to Whitehall:

> It is fairly certain that no Government Department within the British Empire, or indeed any Central Government has ever given such warm encouragement to the use of the Mother Tongue as is to be found in the foregoing and other like advice which has issued during the last sixteen years from the Welsh Department. Possibly what is now needed in the way of a stimulant is a little hostility and less benevolence towards the native language on the part of the Central Authority.[10]

The Secretary's indignation was fuelled by the acute awareness that in spite of the endeavours of his Department, the language had not assumed as central a position in the curriculum as it might because of the lack of enthusiasm on the part of local education authorities and school governors, and the indifference of the Welsh people, 'through whose earnest efforts . . . will Welsh be kept alive as the language of hearth and home'.[11]

Such efforts were never forthcoming. Faced with the evidence that the fate of the language cannot be entrusted to the Welsh people, partisans of the language have resorted to strategies aimed at either persuading or compelling state agencies to save it for them, 'behind their backs'. This has proved both futile and undemocratic: futile because legislation and official benevolence cannot substitute for the will of the people in this domain; and undemocratic in that the active participation of the majority is explicitly spurned, attention being concentrated on the 'commanding heights' of the linguistic economy, from the Welsh Department to the Welsh Office. In this way, cultural decentralists have shown themselves to be political centralists where policies favoured by them are supported by central and not by local government.

The very democracy which was a barrier to the advance of the Welsh language within the schools is one of the reasons why the conception of Wales as anybody's colony is a non-starter. Wales was an integral part of the British state. It's a strange colony which possesses the same civil rights as any other part of the country, and in which total control over education, and much else besides, is vested in elected representatives of the community; just as it is a strange colony which is more prosperous in the period of coal industrialisation than most parts of the 'colonising power'. It could be argued that if anywhere was underdeveloped by anybody else, it was the West of England by Wales, as the latter became (via the market and not the state) by 1914 not so much a peripheral region of Britain but one of its industrial heartlands, with its own world empire of coal.

That internal comparison takes us to the heart of the conceptual weakness of internal colonialism. If Wales is a colony, how do we theorise the other regions of the United Kingdom? The external comparison is even more important; it reminds us of the international context in which the Welsh were acutely aware of operating, and from which they drew, it seems to me, the appropriate conclusions:

> I consider myself a very patriotic Welshman; but at the same time I have nothing but cause to respect the nations in the same empire as us. Whatever the Englishman was in the past, I consider the Briton to be the most honest friend of freedom today. Germany exiles even serving girls from the Danish parts for speaking the language of their fathers; and oppressive Russia has just announced that every official in Finland must be able to speak Russian. But Welsh can be spoken in all the councils in Wales. It would be best to forego declaiming patriotism on St David's Day whilst Welsh people refuse to speak Welsh in their own local councils . . . The government is not to blame now; we are.[12]

This is still the case.

Notes

My thinking on the organisation of Wales has been greatly influenced by discussion with Sue Dermont and Dr David Smith. I thank them for their guidance and inspiration.

1. Jean Aitchison, *Language Change*,
2. Brinley Thomas, 'Wales and the Atlantic economy', in B. Thomas (ed.), *The Welsh Economy: Studies in Expansion*, University of Wales Press, Cardiff, 1962.
3. *Ibid.*
4. Jack Jones, *Unfinished Journey*, London, 1938, p. 22.
5. *Glamorgan Free Press*, 1 July 1893.

6 Michael D. Jones, *Y Geninen*, October, 1984, p.
7 D. Reynolds and A. Packer, *The Attempted Reconstruction of the Welsh Language: Theory, Myth, Evidence*, University of Wales Press, Cardiff, 1982, p. 6.
8 PRO Ed. 91/57, A. Davies, Secretary to the Welsh Department, minute of 6 July 1916.
9 PRO Ed. 91/57, A. Davies, Secretary to the Welsh Department, letter of 1 July 1916.
10 PRO Ed. 91/57, A. Davies, Secretary to the Welsh Department, memo dated 17 January 1923.
11 *Ibid*.
12 Owen M. Edwards, *Cymru*, vol. 16, 1898, p. 118.

Minorities

15
Jews in London, 1880–1914

DAVID FELDMAN

I

In what sense and to what extent was it possible for Jews and Jewish immigrants to become English in the late Victorian and Edwardian years? In this essay I examine the problem of anglicisation in its most obviously ideological aspect: the ways in which immigrants adjusted and were enjoined to adjust politically and culturally to English conditions. There was a profusion of articles, pamphlets and speeches prescribing different alignments of Jewish and English, immigrant and native identities in this period. It is these diverse projections of the Jewish future in England, their expression and partial realisation in conflicting institutions that will be at the centre of my discussion.

Over the last two decades the history of the Jewish minority in England, and particularly the history of Jewish immigration from eastern Europe, has received an increasing amount of attention from historians. One stimulus to this minor renaissance has been the increased number and diversity of immigrants and ethnic minorities in postwar Britain. As these groups have been perceived in relation to problems of social policy and political practice it is not surprising that some have turned to the study of historical precedents.[1]

In consequence the history of Jewish immigrants has sometimes been presented as a model which other, more recent, newcomers might follow profitably. This view draws upon the celebratory and modernisationist perspectives dominating mainstream Anglo-Jewish historiography. The celebration is twofold. British society is applauded as having been tolerant and accommodating of its Jewish minority. At the same time, the established Jewish community is congratulated for having aided east European immigrants in adjusting to the exigencies of life in Britain.[2] It is in Gartner's *The Jewish Immigrant in England* that the immigrants' history is most clearly presented as one of their entry to the modern world. In this interpretation, their origins in the small towns and villages of Lithuania, Poland and the Ukraine were bounded by a 'traditional way of life' and their 'enlightenment' in England was 'simply . . . an inevitable consequence of migration to a western country'. The immigrants' own efforts, in contrast, are seen to have been aimed largely at preserving the habits of life in eastern Europe.[3]

In this interpretation, relations of power are not considered to have been central to the processes of cultural transformation; rather, the experience of Jewish immigrants is rendered as a history of socialisation and adaptation. As in other areas of social history, in the historiography of Jewish immigration models of 'socialisation' have been challenged by historians who see instead the action of 'social control'.[4] This re-interpretation has been allied to a marxian analysis that places class interest and class conflict as the central organising principles of the Jewish past in England. Accordingly, the immigrants' anglicisation is seen to have been an expression of a successful programme of bourgeois social control; one in which the Anglo-Jewish elite played a central role. Writing about Manchester, for example, Bill Williams has argued that the immigrants' anglicisation 'served most of all the class ambitions of the Jewish bourgeoisie'.[5]

Following their emergence in other areas of enquiry, concepts such as 'modernisation' and 'social control' have been brought to bear upon the history of Jews in England. In this essay the emphasis will be upon their shortcomings in explaining the process of anglicisation among Jewish immigrants. It may be that the attempt to provide an alternative perspective has implications for our understanding of cultural change more widely. In another respect too, this is a history whose interest extends beyong the study of the Jewish minority. Jews and immigrants were two groups against which the nature and limits of national identity were tested and contested between 1865 and 1914, and as such they can illumine its history from a perspective which is both pertinent and unfamiliar.

II

Colonies of Jewish immigrants from Russia, Poland, Galicia and Roumania gathered in several English cities between 1870 and 1914. Above all they congregated in the East End of London. Between 1871 and 1911 the Russian and Russian Polish population in London, a modest indicator of the Jewish immigrant presence, grew from 5,000 to 63,000. Throughout this period about 80 per cent of these immigrants were concentrated in an expanding Jewish East End. In fact, the Jewish population of the district was much larger than the number of immigrants alone. In part this was due to an earlier Jewish settlement, but it was also a reflection of the rapid rate of natural increase among the immigrants. In 1903 it was estimated that between 45–50 per cent of the population of St George's in the East and Whitechapel was Jewish.[6] To many English observers the immigrants' English-born children dramatised the need for an effective programme of anglicisation.

Jewish immigrants to London entered a city containing an established Jewish population. In 1880 this numbered over 40,000 and comprised two-thirds of all Jews in England. The leaders of Anglo-Jewry sought to exercise the predominant influence over the immigrants' anglicisation. As others have noted, this elite was abidingly anxious to present a favourable image of Jews to gentile society.[7] In consequence the nature of their interaction with the state and society was central to their responses to Jewish immigration.

The institutions of London Jewry were reformed in the mid-nineteenth century in ways that highlight the pattern of the communal elite's social and political integration within the majority society. In 1859 the distribution of poor relief was reorganised, along lines later adopted by the Charity Organisation Society, by the newly-established Jewish Board of Guardians (JBG). Of equal significance was the consolidation of the Jewish Board of Deputies' (JBD) role as mediator between the state and organised Jewry. In this respect the Marriage Registration Act of 1836 was a landmark. The Act recognised the JBD as the power competent to record marriages and to ensure they were correctly performed 'according to the usages of the Jews'.[8] These institutions and others were dominated by a 'cousinhood' of leading families.[9] At the summit, prominence in Jewish affairs was accompanied by recognition in the majority society – in business, philanthropy and, increasingly, politics. In short, Jewish immigrants entered a city in which there was an established structure of communal authority and a leadership that sought to mediate Jewish integration with the state and to shape their image within public discourse.

English Jews did not welcome immigration from eastern Europe. Indeed some of the greatest efforts of Anglo-Jewish institutions were spent in preventing migrants from settling in Britain. This policy reflected the fears of the capital's propertied classes in general for the effects of immigration upon the labour and housing markets of the East End.[10] Yet there were also particular problems confronting English Jews as a result of the influx. These stemmed from the uncertain integration of English Jewry within the polity and the nation.

The Parliamentary Oaths Act of 1866 allowed Jews to sit in Parliament upon terms of equality with other Englishmen. However, the acquisition of virtual political equality by Jews failed to kill the Jewish Question; their place within the nation remained problematic and subject to debate. As with other groups, the admission of Jews to the political nation was conditional upon them conforming to ideals of citizenship and respectability. It depended upon the abandonment of those signs of Jewish particularism which might offend these ideals; signs of national separateness above all.[11] Religious toleration thus developed alongside demands for other sorts of conformity.

Jewish emancipation was an expression of a view of the political nation that was in one obvious sense more inclusive. In this, Jewish emancipation contributed to the forces undermining its own stability. The demands for conformity with the nation now reached beyond the former inability of professing Jews to take a Christian oath, on which ground they had been excluded from being members of parliament and from other offices, and touched more widely upon their capacity to identify with the texture and traditions of national life. It was this which George Eliot noted in 1879. Reflecting upon the rise of anti-Jewish attitudes, she sympathised with those who were apprehensive at 'what must follow from the predominance of wealth acquiring immigrants, whose appreciation of our political and social life must often be as approximate or fatally erroneous as their delivery of our language'.[12] Eliot wrote in the early part of a period during which ceremonial practices multiplied, the cult of the monarchy being only the most promiscuous.[13] One effect of these formal affirmations of national identity was a growing pressure upon groups – such as Jews – whose feeling for the nation was held in question to demonstrate their loyalty. It followed that Jewish approval of Disraeli's belligerent support for Turkey against Russia between 1876–8, if it was given or imputed from particularly Jewish motives (on account of financial investments and the better treatment of their co-religionists under Turkish rule), could be seen to be incompatible with their obligations as citizens. Indeed, Gladstone believed the Prime Minister's 'Jewish feeling' was the key to his policy, and T. P. O'Connor accused Disraeli of subverting national policy to Jewish ends.[14]

The emergence of ideological anti-semitism in the late 1870s in a form that presented Jews as unassimilable to the nation, fundamentally upon grounds of race, can thus be seen as one edge of a more general tendency. It was not merely a new formulation of an 'ancient hatred', as historians and some contemporaries perceived; it was also an attempt to define the nation in terms so exclusive that Jews were not seen as merely unpatriotic Englishmen but not as Englishmen at all.[15] It was in the writings of Goldwin Smith that criticism of the Jews' conduct over the Eastern Question was most clearly developed into a critique of Jewish emancipation. 'Judaism, like the whole circle of primitive religion of which it is a survival, is a religion of race', Smith argued.[16] This backwardness was predicated upon the emergence of a higher, more rational, more universal religion – Christianity. 'The affinity of Judaism is not to non-conformity but to caste', he concluded; an inexorable barrier to the development of patriotism.[17]

These arguments did not go unanswered by leading Jews, but their response to the stresses of emancipation was to insist ever more firmly upon the correctness of its premises. Articles written by them yielded a stark reassertion of the religious definition of the Jewish community and the firm relegation of any national aspects of Jewish tradition to an antique past. Far from yearning for their ancient homeland, English Jews were presented as second to none in patriotic feeling for the empire.[18] At the same time, Jewish writers sought to refute the suggestion that 'the essential doctrines of the Jewish religion are tribal and stand consequently in direct opposition to the religious and political tendencies of modern civilization'.[19] The departure from tribalism was the achievement of Judaism, it was claimed. In recognising the existence of one 'God' for all humanity, Judaism had been the great dynamic agent of modern civilisation and foundation of both Christianity and Islam.[20]

Yet it was also recognised there were other tendencies in the Jewish past and that Jewish life had emerged from insularity in recent times only. Claude Montefiore indicated as much when he explained that for the purpose of his essay, 'Is Judaism a tribal religion?', Judaism was to be defined as 'the religion of educated Jews in the civilized countries at the present time'.[21] The conception of modern Judaism constructed at the same time another traditional Judaism from which Anglo-Jewry was said to have long since evolved. However, the immigrants, as Russian Jews, came from an empire seen not to have moved towards either liberalism or rational religion, and inevitably they inhabited this 'other' Judaism. The point was made clear each time the Jewish East End was referred to as 'the ghetto', for whether the term was intended as a pejorative or sentimental one, the ghetto represented a form of social life that was assuredly pre-modern.[22]

The vigorous and partly defensive identification of English Jews with patriotism and progress left them vulnerable to the effects of Jewish immigration from empires seen to be underdeveloped politically and intellectually. In this light it becomes apparent that the apprehension of Anglo-Jewry in the face of Jewish immigration was not simply a matter of class interest. It not only reflected the niche occupied by the leaders of London Jewry among the propertied classes of the capital but also the difficulties and pressures they experienced after emancipation in aligning patriotism and Jewishness.

III

To Jewish and non-Jewish observers alike the streets of Whitechapel appeared as a piece of eastern Europe thrown down in the capital of the world's largest empire. 'The feeling is of being in a foreign town', wrote Charles Booth's co-worker George Duckworth.[23] Leonty Soloweitschik richly described the impression of difference which suffused the Jewish East End; the streets decorated with advertisements in Yiddish announcing the arrival of a theatre troupe from New York, the services for coming religious festivals and for a Yiddish newspaper soon to be published. Even the Post Office printed its instructions in Yiddish.[24] The impression of separateness was intensified by the competition between immigrants and natives in the housing market of the district and in the workshop trades – tailoring, boot and shoe making, and cabinet making – in which Jewish workers were concentrated.[25] The issue of immigration thus became bound up with debates over sweated labour and the housing shortage in London.

However, the problems accredited to Jewish immigrants were not limited to the field of social policy. They possessed a political dimension which cut to the heart of Jewish emancipation. This was made clear, for example, in an 1887 article in the *St James Gazette*.

> Take the colony as it stands. Eliminate the idea that it represents an invasion and treat its members neither as foreigners nor as paupers. Look at them as citizens, ratepayers, heads of families and trades people. Inquire how far they fulfill the ordinary duties of civilised life as members of a free and independent community. The answer to that question might be given in a single sentence: they never forget they are Jews and that other

people are Gentiles. They are a people apart. Long as they may live among us they will never become merged in the mass of the English population.[26]

But the problematic interaction of the immigration question with the legacy of Jewish emancipation occurred at the level of social policy too, and was revealed in the language of public debate. The leading restrictionists insisted that the religion of the aliens was a matter of indifference to them; what was important was that they were destitute.[27] But the Jewish Question could not be prevented from intruding by this device for contrary to theoretical prescription, men and women continued to perceive Jews as something more than a dissenting religious minority. The manner in which the everyday perception of the immigrants as Jews did emerge despite the intention to repress it is illustrated in a characteristic remark, made by an East End insurance agent, who complained that 'Christians' in the East End were being swamped by 'aliens' – an observation which is intelligible only once it is acknowledged that the aliens in question were not Christian which, in this case, plainly meant they were Jews.[28] Criticism of aliens thus overspilled into commentary upon Jews. It is no wonder that the *Jewish Chronicle*, the principal Anglo-Jewish newspaper, despaired at the 'difficulty which the popular mind has in maintaining a distinction' between 'Jews' and 'aliens'.[29]

The political dynamic of the anti-immigration agitation further aggravated the contradictions of Jewish emancipation. As the expanding collectivism of the state added to the consequences of popular suffrage, so the ideals and needs of the nation to which Jews had to conform became increasingly wide. It is no coincidence that the proponents of statutory restriction aligned their cause with that of *national* efficiency.[30] In 1905, speaking in favour of an Aliens Bill which became law, Balfour, then prime minister, asserted his belief that 'we have a right to keep out everybody who does not add to the strength of the community – the industrial, social and intellectual strength of the community'.[31] By opposing the Bill, the behaviour of many English Jews raised the question of whether their loyalties were with the national or the Jewish community. Balfour himself expressed these doubts, and others outside Parliament made the same point less politely.[32]

These were the conditions of public debate which gave urgency to Anglo-Jewish efforts to reduce the gap between the immigrants' behaviour and the image of the modern and patriotic Jew. Especially was this so from the early 1890s, as immigration appeared to be a problem of some permanence and as calls for statutory immigration restriction gained a more prominent place in Parliament, on the hustings, and in trade unions.[33] Whereas public discourse resisted the efforts to establish criteria for the legitimate identification of Jews and the sanitisation of their image, there remained another strategy to follow; this was to guide and discipline the immigrants so that the most unacceptable aspects of their difference might be erased. Underlying attempts to reform the immigrants' manners and mores was a growing unease at the political consequence of their presence.

From 1893–4 the anglicisation of East European Jews was a part of the programme of the two Anglo-Jewish institutions that most came into contact with them – the JBG and the Russo-Jewish Committee. The individual most closely associated with the changes of these years was N. S. Joseph. In 1893 he warned that 'in ten or fifteen years, the children of the refugees to-day will be men and women constituting in point of numbers the great bulk of the Jews of England. They will drag down, submerge or disgrace our community if we leave them in their present state of neglect.'[34] The answer, in part, was to develop a more personal, less bureaucratic system of philanthropy in which a central part was played by teams of visitors. Their 'great aim' was 'by direct influence to improve and anglicize them [their cases] and to render them self-supporting'.[35] Significantly, it was only at this stage that optimistic attempts were made to disperse the ghetto and that the Russo-Jewish Committee began to hold English classes; in 1894 it published a Yiddish-English phrase book.

Interconnected with the task of anglicisation was the work of civilising the immigrants. In this respect their origins as Russians impinged heavily upon their reception in England. As early as 1881 the *Jewish Chronicle* had presented the question of how English Jews were 'to aid these bretheren of ours towards that higher standard of culture offered by English life'.[36] The minister of a North London synagogue expressed a similar evolutionist and modernising view, observing that 'Russia today is like Spain of the sixteenth century'.[37] The fanatical and ritualistic temper of the immigrants' religion was seen to reflect this, as did their 'jargon' – Yiddish – and their customary standard of life. 'The Russian Jew – when he first comes here – is often abominably filthy; because he is a Russian, of course, not because he is a Jew', argued David Schloss.[38]

Increasingly the hopes of communal leaders were placed in the immigrants' children. The proponents of an Aliens Act were answered with reports claiming that Jewish children in East End schools were 'the most desirable citizens, physically, intellectually and in their love for the country in which they dwell'.[39] It was not only compulsory schooling which was intended to effect this transformation. In the 1890s a number of youth clubs and a Jewish Lads Brigade were established with the aim of developing English virtues among the young. Moral rectitude would follow upon physical well-being. The Brigade's commander explained that his aim was to 'instil into the rising generation all that is best in the English character, manly independence, honour, truth, cleanliness, love of active health giving pursuits'.[40]

In this light the great barriers to the children's thorough anglicisation were those institutions whose aim it was to reproduce East European Jewish culture. Above all, this threat was posed by the religious schools of the East End. The *chedarim* – small classes taught in a single room – and the *talmud torah* schools – large institutions, charitably funded, in part, containing up to 1,000 children and like the *chedarim* engaged almost exclusively in the education of boys – were attended after day school and at weekends. They were the focus of much discussion at a conference on Jewish elementary education in June 1898. The main paper on the subject described *chedarim* as the peculiar products of Russian conditions. Presented thus, they were ripe for modernisation and reform. The *melammdim* who taught in the schools were said to be unsuitable 'both in their manners and in their method of teaching'. Physical conditions in the schools were seen to reflect the immigrants' low standard of life and primitive values. By 1898 the *chedarim* had become scapegoats for the failure to achieve a more far-reaching improvement among the rising generation.[41] The assumptions underpinning this attack were made explicit by the Chief Rabbi. 'It was not correct to speak of a *chedar* in Booth Street Buildings as only two hundred yards from the nearest Board school', he stated, 'the fact was two hundred years lay between them'.[42]

IV

For the leaders of Anglo-Jewry, the immigrants' anglicisation and their ascent to a higher level of social development were closely connected. These same goals were yoked together from a radically different political perspective by anarchist and social democrat revolutionaries in the Jewish East End. Central to Jewish history in these decades, in eastern Europe, the United States and England, was the conjuncture which brought together educated Russian Jewish revolutionaries with the emergent Jewish working class. In the 1880s London was at the centre of this development.[43]

The pioneers of the radical press perceived themselves in an educative as well as a political role. *Di poylishe yidel* was the earliest of these newspapers, first appearing in July 1884. Its readership was encouraged to learn English; a step, it was anticipated, that would lead to improved relations with English workers and enable east European Jews to read books unavailable in Hebrew or Yiddish. The commitment to Yiddish was thus pragmatic and the editors looked forward to a time when the newspaper could be published in English.[44]

The educational intent of *Di poylishe yidel* was not exceptional, and a similar purpose was central to the Jewish revolutionary press throughout this period. Likewise, the stock-in-trade of socialist and anarchist clubs were lessons in English, libraries and reading rooms, and lectures on scientific and literary, as well as political, themes.[45] The organisation of the workers and the revolution itself were conceived of as projects of enlightenment which, at the same time as they liberated the proletariat, would signify progress for humanity as a whole.[46] It was an idea that drew upon a social evolutionist current widespread within the revolutionary movement as well as within the liberal tradition. In the Jewish case it also drew upon the self-image of the *maskilim* – the enlighteners – as harbingers of westernisation amidst the stagnating and inward-looking Jewish masses.[47] Although located within the ghetto, participation in the revolutionary movement was also a means of transcending it. Trade unionism, cultural progress and the solution to the Jewish question were brought together in this version of anglicisation, with the first of these elements presented as the key.

> Don't stand off from your English comrades. Throw away the asiatic customs you have brought from Russia. Unite in unions and join English unions wherever possible. Don't allow yourselves to be sweated by the bloodsuckers. Live like human beings and demand human wages. In a word become men (at present you are half wild) and citizens . . . Here are your means; only in this way can the Jewish Question be resolved.[48]

It is in the context of their belief in the existence of humanly discernible laws of development in nature and society that the fierce atheism of so many of the revolutionaries must be placed. Free thought and the revolution were connected since, it was argued, the ties and beliefs of Judaism misled the workers, leading them to put their faith in 'God' and their hopes in philanthropists rather than in their collective strength.[49] 'Before becoming a progressive, a socialist, even a nationalist, simply a civilised person, a European equal with other men, he [a Jew] must first become anti-religious', was a characteristic belief, expressed in this instance by Karl Liberman.[50]

In both the free-thinking propaganda of immigrant revolutionaries and in the responses of Anglo-Jewish philanthropists to institutions such as the *chedarim*, there was a striking agreement upon the backward origins of the Jewish immigrants and the expression of these in forms of religious orthodoxy. In fact, these views tell us more about the contours of discourse than they do about the responses of the immigrant orthodox to the technological, cultural and political opportunities of their new environment.

The *Machzike Hadath* was the institution which focused the opinion of the militantly orthodox in the Jewish East End. During 1891–2 the society was engaged in a dispute with the communal authorities over the ritual cleanliness of meat slaughtered under the supervision of the latter. An *impasse* was reached and the militants responded by building their own slaughterhouse and by repudiating the religious authority of the Chief Rabbi. At a cost of £4,500 a chapel was bought and converted to accommodate the expanding needs of the synagogue and the *talmud torah* attached to it.[51]

The fundamentalist beliefs motivating the controversy over ritual slaughter were expressed succinctly by one supporter when he asserted simply that 'Jews who do not obey Jewish laws have no religious principles'.[52] But alongside the principle of unbending religious integrity lay a conflict over anglicisation. *Der yidisher ekspres* described the support gathered around the *Machzike Hadath* as expressing a protest against the treatment of Russian Jews as 'ignorant beggars, as barbarians who must be civilised through Sabbath sermons, soup kitchens and such like'.[53] Against this, the leaders of the *Machzike Hadath* did embrace a project of anglicisation. At one of the earliest meetings the chairman assured the audience that the defenders of Jewish law also intended to be patriotic citizens. He pointed out, the Jew who keeps the dietary laws, 'that very Jew knows the tradition "thou shalt pray for the welfare of the Kingdom" '.[54] This opinion was confirmed by the synagogue's religious leader, Rabbi Aba Werner, who also expressed his belief that 'there is no reason why secular education should alienate Jews from their own literature'.[55]

Even upon the issue of religious education the opposition to Anglo-Jewish prescription was not atavistic. A meeting held at the Jewish Working Men's Club in response to the Anglo-Jewish educational conference was described by the *Jewish Chronicle* as very large by the standards of the Jewish East End and notably aggressive.[56] The speakers denounced the religious education

English Jews wished to introduce to the Jewish East End and which was said to leave its pupils in a state of substantial ignorance. Yiddish was required in the East End, it was said, partly because immigrant teachers were most comfortable in that language. But, further, the defence of Yiddish was a vivid refusal to accept the condescension of English Jews and was an assertion of the desire to achieve a different accommodation with English society.[57] The speakers did not reject educational reform, however. Eliazer Laizerovich, a journalist for *Der yidisher ekspres* called for better accommodation and shorter hours in the *chedarim* and Joseph Cohn-Lask, the leader of the Union of *melammdim*, claimed that critics underestimated the degree to which changes had taken place.[58] Thus even upon the side of the militantly orthodox there was a willing patriotism and an engagement with new forms of learning.

Both Werner and Laizerovich were political zionists and *Der yidisher ekspres* was a consistent supporter of Herzl's movement. It was through political zionism that a view was most clearly articulated of Jewish integration within the political system, different from the one promoted by the leaders of Anglo-Jewry. Inevitably the movement was anathematised by the communal leaders. At root, political zionism was an embarrassment because it appeared to discard the demands of emancipation by claiming for Jews a political identity alongside one of loyalty to the states in which they were subjects.[59] For zionists, however, this indicated an understanding of Jewish emancipation which did not require the effacement of Jewish interests. At the time of the Boer War, *Der yidisher ekspres*, a consistently zionist newpaper, combined its support for the British in the war with a Jewish populist viewpoint. The anti-alien Conservatives met with a strong response: 'the question is not whether Jews think of England as their home now but how England will later regard the Jews; as its own people or as foreigners'.[60] It was a bold statement rejecting those relations of power, inherent to the conditional acceptance of Jews within the nation, which bore so heavily upon English Jews.

V

The forms of anglicisation urged upon Jewish immigrants by Anglo-Jewish philanthropists, revolutionaries, the religious orthodox and zionists, shared elements of analysis and prescription, each welcoming political emancipation and engaging with new forms of knowledge. But despite this confluence, the meaning of anglicisation, the shape of the modern world and the position of

Jews within it were subject to contestation between widely different programmes. Having indicated the diversity of passages to anglicisation, however, there still remains the problem of accounting for the relative success and failure of each. Something which leads back to the arguments and interpretations – divided between models of modernisation and social control – indicated at the beginning of this essay.

At the very least, a contextualised understanding of anglicisation must take account of the range of possible transformations that were imagined to lead to this goal and which sought to define it. It is a step with interpretive as well as descriptive consequences, for, in contrast to the view that immigrant life was motivated by traditional concerns, attention has been drawn to the widespread eruption of modernising ideologies and practices in the Jewish East End. In this light an opposition between immigrant traditionalism and western modernity appears as an abstraction. The immigrant colony was the site of a conflict, not between traditionalism and modernity, East European culture and anglicisation, but between diverse conceptions of westernisation and 'anglicism'. Our understanding of anglicisation will depend upon our view of these conflicts.

A requirement of any plausible explanation must be that at the same time as accounting for the decline of religious practice and belief and the general weakness of socialism and anarchism, it does not preclude an understanding of the persistence of fundamentalist Judaism or revolutionary dissent. In this respect it is notable that fundamentalist Judaism was a presence among English as well as foreign Jews in these years. Although the religious temper of Judaism in late Victorian England was generally similar to that of a lackadaisical Anglicanism, there was a pious minority which sustained an uncompromising faith in traditional Jewish belief.[61] Since fundamentalist beliefs and practices constituted a significant presence within Anglo-Jewry, there is reason to doubt whether the westernisation of Jewish immigrants necessarily implied secularisation as well. Indeed, a sociological account of an orthodox Jewish community in New York City in the mid-1950s has concluded that 'the urban setting does not necessarily limit or arrest the *Hasidic* way of life; it may even contribute positively to its growth and development'.[62]

Without doubt, confrontation with new scientific knowledge, technological innovation and the dynamics of capitalism have presented traditional Jewish beliefs and practices with new challenges. But in view of the persistence of fundamentalist beliefs among a significant minority, an interpretation of secularisation among Jewish immigrants as an inevitable consequence of modernity and migration westwards is unpersuasive.[63] Nevertheless tenets of Jewish religious practice, such as sabbath observance, did fall away in London. By the 1920s, the anxieties of Anglo-Jewish ministers were caused no longer by the undecorous and ritualistic character of the immigrants' Judaism but by the need to rescue the English-born generation from indifference.[64]

The decline in religious observance can be explained more readily in terms of the attenuated opportunities, following emigration, to sustain and reproduce traditional beliefs and practices. For in the movement away from Russia and Poland the institutional foundations of Judaism were removed from a context in which they enjoyed close integration with the sources of political and economic power. They were transplanted to a society in which they were forced to compete for the allegiance of their constituency, not only with the *maskilim* and Jewish revolutionaries, as in eastern Europe, but with the conflicting messages of institutions supported by the state and Anglo-Jewry. In comparison to the legal powers and financial resources available to day schools, for example – which aimed to turn pupils into what they conceived to be 'good English subjects' – the resources of immigrant synagogues were puny.[65] In the Russian Empire, the synagogue had enjoyed a compulsory financial subvention from the Jewish community, something it did not enjoy in London. Furthermore, the role of the rabbinate in managing the legal integration of Jews with the state also disappeared. Despite encroachments made by the centralising administration in St Petersburg, Jewish communities in Russia retained measures of legal autonomy, including a large degree of rabbinical control over marriage and divorce.[66] In Britain, in contrast, one of the principal gains on the way to political and legal equality had been the integration of Jews within the general framework of marriage law – an arrangement mediated by the laity, the JBD, not the rabbinate.[67]

Alongside the disposition of political-legal power, religious orthodoxy in London was hobbled by the economic life of the immigrant quarter, for in the East End, pious Jews were neither sufficiently numerous nor wealthy to protect themselves from the rhythms of trades which induced Sabbath desecration. Poll's study of the *hasidim* of New York illustrates the significance of these factors in enabling orthodoxy to insulate itself from the disintegrating currents of city life.[68] In east London, by contrast, Sabbath desecration was widespread. In the tailoring trade much of the blame was placed upon contractors who required work returned complete on Saturdays before noon. But even where Saturday was a rest day, the frenetic pace and long hours of the latter half of the week, characteristic of the workshop trades, left many workers wanting only to rest.[69] Yet it would be mistaken to overestimate the extent of secularisation. Synagogue attendance was not displaced as the common currency of public Jewish expression. In the East End, on high holydays, theatres, school halls and meeting places such as the Great Assembly Rooms, were used to accommodate the additional thousands attending services.[70]

It was not only in respect of Sabbath observance that the orthodox were handicapped by the local economy. The uncertain and fragmented conditions of small-scale production and exchange which typified the Jewish East End, generated a milieu in which it was impossible for the immigrant orthodox, revolutionaries, or zionists to achieve the stability from which a sustained challenge to communal authority could be built. The financial resources upon which to found such an effort did not exist. Moreover, in comparison to the situation in some cities in eastern Europe and the United States, the Jewish population was not sufficiently large to be able to overcome the debilitating effects of poverty by weight of numbers.[71] Among the orthodox, the *Machzike Hadath* were compelled to return to the communal fold in 1905 when Lord Rothschild and Lord Swaythling cleared its debts of £5,000. The most radical implications of immigrant orthodoxy had been contained as a consequence of financial necessity. This outcome is the more telling since among the leaders of the *Machzike Hadath* were individuals drawn from the wealthiest stratum of the immigrant population – traders and merchants who had risen above the milieu of the workshop trades.[72] In other respects, too, poverty took its toll upon other independent initiatives. The Great Garden Street *Talmud Torah*, for example, helped secure its survival by pledging to conduct lessons in the English language.[73]

A concept such as secularisation is too large to convey the complexity of these developments. The term does, indeed, describe a general tendency but it is in the contested and specific relations between religious institutions, society and the state that the dynamic leading to the decline of traditional Jewish observance and belief has been located. The persistence of orthodox religious belief is thus comprehensible, not as a quirk contrary to the tendency of social development but as a reflection of the capacity of minorities to erect structures of social and cultural independence.

Away from religious orthodoxy immigrant institutions were similarly weak. The newspapers and clubs established by revolutionary groups, for example, endured a hand-to-mouth existence in most of these years. They attained heights of influence in the

Jewish East End in 1889–90 and again between 1911 and 1914. In the first instance, however, the defeats of new unionism in the Jewish East End led to a powerful reversal. In the latter instance, the growth was oriented towards the anarchist movement and was largely destroyed as a result of repression and internal division during the First World War.

While the challenges emanating from the East End were necessarily ephemeral, the political and economic resources of the Anglo-Jewish elite provided powerful weapons with which to stifle disruptive influences and foster more desirable ones. Yet to explain this effort as an exercise in bourgeois social control and to account for the process of anglicisation in similar terms will not do, first, because it takes too narrow a view of what propelled Anglo-Jewish social policy. In the early sections of this essay it was seen that for English Jews the demands of citizenship and patriotism were continuing sources of ambiguity and, at times, discomfort. Their responses to Jewish immigration were shot through with perturbation in the face of these imperatives. At one with the capital's properties classes, as Englishmen they were vulnerable and forever in danger of being challenged. More than one relation of power structured the interaction of Englishmen, Jews and immigrants.

Responses to immigration from within the communal elite were not uniform. One effect of these divisions was to create opportunities for dissident forms of political, cultural and religious expression. Thus a further problem with the social control model of anglicisation is that it overestimates the coherence of elite interventions within the immigrant colony. Political zionism, for example, benefited from the support of one member of the cousinhood – Sir Francis Montefiore.[74] But the most significant phenomenon in this respect was the patronage received by the Federation of Synagogues from Samuel Montagu. The Federation was established in 1887 as a combination of sixteen synagogues in the East End. By 1911, it encompassed fifty-one synagogues and 6,000 seatholders. It was the largest and most long-lived institution in the Jewish East End. The self-governing synagogues of the Federation appealed to Montagu's Liberal politics, their religious principles aligned well with his own, and the organisation itself improved his prestige and power-base within Jewry. From 1887 until his death in 1912, he supported the organisation with loans and donations and was its dominant figure.[75]

In many cases, the synagogue officers were drawn from among the workshop masters of the district and the Federation allowed them to advance their status.[76] To a degree, the Federation may be seen to have allowed the co-option of a section of East End opinion and its leaders. When the *Machzike Hadath* schism occurred, Montagu prevented discussion of the issue by the Federation's committee. Moreover, the Federation was an agent of modernisation along particular lines; Yiddish was banned from its councils and, more constructively, Montagu encouraged and provided loans for the replacement of insanitary places of worship with purpose-built synagogues.[77] But within the East End there was ample support for precisely this combination of orthodoxy, anglicisation and communal loyalty. Above all, under Montagu's leadership, East Enders could secure the existence of their synagogues and find a voice within the communal organisation, urging it to become more strict in its observance and more democratic in its government.[78]

It was not only through the Federation that concessions were gained. The leaders of Anglo-Jewry pursued goals which at times contradicted a policy of vigorous anglicisation. One such was the need for communal unity; something felt with special keenness as the campaign for an Aliens Act neared fruition. This was the background to the financial and political concessions which persuaded the *Machzike Hadath* to rejoin the official community.[79] Further compromises were made as a result of the desire to combat the influence of Jewish revolutionaries. Forms of religious expression which were otherwise regarded as backward, such as the performances of *maggidim* (preachers), gained patronage through a desire to divert Jewish workers from the agitators' influence.[80] External factors, among which the actions of the state could have the greatest impact, could also affect the balance of forces in the contest over anglicisation. The Balfour Declaration of 1917, to take the most outstanding example, by declaring the government's support for a Jewish homeland in Palestine, appeared to contradict official Anglo-Jewish policy and adjusted the terms of Jewish debate in favour of political zionism.[81] Approval for Yiddish culture from prestigious sources likewise produced a confusing message over how best to achieve acceptance within gentile society.[82] The abundant concessions, compromises and contradictions that are to be found within Anglo-Jewish responses to immigration never transformed relations between Anglo-Jewry and the immigrants, nor did they render British society and politics any more welcoming of a self-conscious and public Jewish presence. But they did provide resources, create niches, and occasionally supply opportunities for expansion, to a plurality of immigrant adjustments to their transformed circumstances.

Finally, we should take into account the resistance of East End Jews to cultural forms and messages that were not to their liking.

From the English working class, reformers met with a response that was selective at best.[83] Jewish immigrants were not different from the native population in this regard. Efforts to disperse the 'ghetto' foundered upon the need of Jewish immigrants to live in easy distance of their workplaces, the street labour markets through which opportunities could be found, and the support networks they had established.[84] When the political responses of Jewish immigrants were strongly touched, whether in response to the Kishiniev pogrom in 1903 or the tailors' strike in 1906, the calls for Jews not to demonstrate publicly were hugely ignored.[85] Indeed, during the First World War, Lucien Wolf, a leading figure within Anglo-Jewry, wearily conceded that the majority of immigrants remained in sentiment a part of their countries of origin.[86] Even among the 'rising generation', whose thorough anglicisation was loudly advertised by Anglo-Jewish propagandists, the process was only partial and its results not always those intended. In the inter-war period, when this generation reached positions of influence in the Jewish East End, the visible, occasionally violent, response to the campaign of the British Union of Fascists, in contrast to the policy of quietness advocated by the JBD, illustrates the continuing force of radical forms of Jewish self-expression in the East End.[87] The same point is apparent from the course of the zionist movement in the period. In the mid-1920s the Federation of Synagogues was captured for political zionism by a new generation who, in the process, ejected Samuel Montagu's son from the presidency of the organisation. Significantly, a central drama in the revolt was the decison taken to allow Yiddish to be spoken at meetings of the Federation's committee.[88] In fact, the greater assertiveness of East End Jews in the inter-war period – the claims made for Yiddish, the declaration of independence from West End patrons, and the vigorous response to anti-Jewish political movements – were all unparalleled between 1880 and 1914. As well as tendencies towards anglicisation, plainly, there were others towards a more forceful assertion of Jewish identity in England.

Neither 'westernisation' nor 'social control' adequately conveys the contested and fractured process of anglicisation in the Jewish East End. It was framed by the interaction of political, legal, economic and ideological forces which determined the opportunities available to immigrants as they adjusted to a new environment. But within these limits the process of cultural and political change was shaped by the participants' own perspectives upon becoming English. Their actions followed from choices made as they sought to reconcile the obvious necessity of change with their formation as East European Jews. The conflicts arising from this concerned the boundaries and content of British as well as Jewish identity. At issue were the terms upon which Jews and immigrants might be contained within the national community, just how inclusive was that community to be? In this light, if ethnic minorities in contemporary Britain, and the factions among them, can draw any lesson from the Jewish immigrant past it may be encapsulated within a maxim from the Jewish scholar Hillel – one which appeared often in the immigrant press, 'If I am not for myself, who will be? If not now, when?'

Notes

For commenting on earlier versions of this paper, I am grateful to George Behlmer, Jennifer Davis and Linda Pollock.

1 J. A. Garrard, *The English and Immigration: A Comparative Study of the Jewish Influx, 1880–1910*, 1971, pp. 3–10 and K. Lunn (ed.) *Hosts, Immigrants and Minorities: The Historical Responses to Newcomers in British Society, 1870–1914*, Folkestone, 1980, pp. 1–8 are two examples of studies which explicitly place historical enquiry within the contemporary context.
2 C. Holmes, *Anti-semitism in British Society, 1876–1939*, London 1979, pp. 108–9, 220–34; H. Pollins, *Economic History of the Jews in England*, New Brunswick, N.J. 1982, p. 141; see also the comments of the Chief Rabbi on 'problems of the inner cities' published in the *Jewish Chronicle*, January 1986, pp. 27–9.
3 L. Gartner, *The Jewish Immigrant in England, 1870–1914*, 2nd edition, London 1973, pp. 166, 241–2, 268.
4 For a discussion of 'socialisation' and 'social control' see F. M. L. Thompson, 'Social control in Victorian Britain', *Economic History Review*, second series, vol. XXXIV, 1981 no. 2, pp. 190–2.
5 Bill Williams, 'The anti-semitism of tolerance: middle class Manchester and the Jews, 1870–1900', in Alan J. Kidd and K. W. Roberts (eds), *City, Class and Culture: Studies in Social Policy and Cultural Production in Victorian Manchester*, Manchester, 1985, p. 92. See also Jerry White, *Rothschild Buildings: Life in an East End Tenement Block, 1887–1920*, 1980, pp. 174, 257–8.
6 For a more detailed exposition of the demographic impact of Jewish immigration upon the East End see D. M. Feldman 'Immigrants and workers, Englishmen and Jews: Jewish immigrants in the East End of London, 1881–1906', Cambridge University doctoral thesis, 1986, pp. 23–36.
7 T. Endelman, 'Native Jews and foreign Jews in London, 1870–1914' in D. Berger (ed.), *The Legacy of Jewish Migration: 1881 and Its Impact*, New York, 1981 pp. 109–29. Bill Williams, 'The anti-semitism of tolerance: middle class Manchester and the Jews, 1870–1900', in Alan J. Kidd and K. W. Roberts (eds), *City, Class and Culture: Studies in Social Policy and Cultural Production in Victorian Manchester*, Manchester,

1985, gives a different view of why Anglo-Jewry were concerned about English opinion.
8 M. C. N. Salbstein, *The Emancipation of the Jews in Britain: The Question of the Admission of Jews to Parliament*, New Brunswick, N.J. 1982, pp. 47, 90.
9 The term is Chaim Bermant's. See C. Bermant, *The Cousinhood*, London 1971.
10 D. M. Feldman, 'Immigrants and workers, Englishmen and Jews: Jewish immigrants in the East End of London, 1881–1906', Cambridge University doctoral thesis, 1986, pp. 127–52.
11 Bill Williams, 'The anti-semitism of tolerance: middle class Manchester and the Jews, 1870–1900', in Alan J. Kidd and K. W. Roberts (eds), *City, Class and Culture: Studies in Social Policy and Cultural Production in Victorian Manchester*, Manchester, 1985 pp. 75–6. As Gladstone put it, when speaking in favour of Jewish emancipation for the first time, 'they [Jews] had discarded many of their extravagant and anti-social doctrines and had become much more fit to become incorporated within the framework of general society' (*Parliamentary Debates*, third series, XCV, cols. 1285–6).
12 G. Eliot, *Impressions of Theophrastus Such*, Edinburgh 1879, p. 346.
13 D. Cannadine, 'The context, performance and meaning of ritual: The British monarchy and the invention of tradition, c.1820–1977', in E. Hobsbawm and T. Ranger (eds), *The Invention of Tradition*, Cambridge, 1983, pp. 120–38; E. Hobsbawm, 'Mass-producing traditions in Europe, 1870–1914', in E. Hobsbawm and T. Ranger (eds), *op. cit.*, pp. 263–307.
14 R. T. Shannon, *Gladstone and the Bulgarian Agitation, 1876*, London 1963, p. 199; *The Times*, 20 December 1879, p. 11; T. P. O'Connor, *Lord Beaconsfield: A Biography*, 1879, London, p. 672. A. Ramm (ed.), *The Political Correspondence of Mr Gladstone and Lord Grenville, 1876–86*, Oxford, 1962, pp. 24, 28.
15 Lucien Wolf portrayed the Jews' enemies as irrational spokesmen of a medieval hatred that would fall before the civilising movement of 'modern liberalism': L. Wolf, 'A Jewish view of the anti-Jewish agitation', *Nineteenth Century*, February, 1881, p. 335.
16 G. Smith, 'England's abandonment of the protectorate of Turkey', *Contemporary Review*, February, 1878, p. 618.
17 G. Smith, 'Can Jews be patriots?', *Nineteenth Century*, May, 1878, p. 879; G. Smith, 'The Jewish question', *Nineteenth Century*, October, 1881, p. 499.
18 H. Adler, 'Can Jews be patriots?', *Nineteenth Century*, April, 1878, p. 643.
19 C. Montefiore, 'Is Judaism a tribal religion?', *Contemporary Review*, September, 1882, p. 362.
20 C. Montefiore, *op. cit.*, pp. 364–70; H. Adler, 'Can Jews be patriots?', *Nineteenth Century*, April, 1878, pp. 638–40; H. Adler, 'Jews and Judaism: a rejoinder', *Nineteenth Century*, July, 1878, pp. 135–40; L.

Wolf, 'What is Judaism? a question of today', *Fortnightly Review*, August, 1884, p. 243.
21 C. Montefiore, 'Is Judaism a tribal religion?', *Contemporary Review*, September, 1982, p. 361.
22 Dept. of English, Univ. of Leeds, B. Cheyette, 'The Jewish stereotype and Anglo-Jewish fiction', unpublished paper, 1985; S. Ashheim, 'The East European Jew and German Jewish identity', *Studies in Contemporary Jewry*, Vol. I 1984, pp. 3–25.
23 London School of Economics and Political Science, Booth collection, B; 351, p. 49.
24 L. Soloweitschik, *Un proletariat méconnu*, Brussels, 1898, p. 30.
25 This pessimistic view of the immediate economic effects of immigrants is argued in D. M. Feldman, 'Immigrants and workers, Englishmen and Jews: Jewish immigrants in the East End of London 1881–1906', Cambridge University doctoral thesis, 1986, pp. 75–80, 83–90.
26 *St James Gazette*, 4 April 1887, p. 4.
27 See for example *Parliamentary Debates*, fourth series, CXLV, col. 721.
28 Parliamentary Papers, 1903, IX, *Royal Commission on Alien Immigration*, qq. 5,433–6, 5,829
29 *Jewish Chronicle*, 8 August 1902, p. 14.
30 G. R. Searle, *The Quest for National Efficiency: A Study in British Politics and Thought*, Oxford, 1981.
31 *Parliamentary Debates*, fourth series, CXLV, col. 821.
32 *Parliamentary Debates*, fourth series, CIL, cols 1,282–3; *Jewish Chronicle*, 15 November 1901, p. 91, 28 February 1902, p. 19.
33 B. Gainer, *The Alien Invasion: The Origins of the Aliens Act of 1905*, London, 1972, pp. 170–80.
34 *Jewish Chronicle*, 3 February 1893, p. 16.
35 Jewish Board of Guardians, *Annual report for 1893*, p. 67.
36 *Jewish Chronicle*, 12 August 1881, p. 9.
37 London School of Economics and Political Science, Booth Collection, 197, p. 45.
38 D. F. Schloss, 'The Jew as workman', *Nineteenth Century*, June, 1891, p. 99.
39 *Jewish Chronicle*, 28 April 1902, pp. 20–1.
40 Ibid., 23 August 1901, p. 6.
41 Ibid., 17 September 1898, pp. v–vi.
42 Ibid.
43 On this subject see W. J. Fishman, *East End Jewish Radicals, 1875–1914*, 1975; E. Mendelsohn, *Class Struggles in the Pale: the Formative Years of the Jewish Workers Movement in Tsarist Russia*, Cambridge, 1970; E. Tcherikover, *Di geshikhte fun der yidisher arbayter bavegung in di faraynikte shtaten*, 2 volumes, New York, 1943–5.
44 *Di poylishe yidel*, 8 August 1884, p. 9.
45 E. Tcherikover, *Di geshikhte fun der yidisher arbayter bavegung in di faraynikte shtaten*, New York, 1945, vol. 2, pp. 110–11; W. J. Fishman, *East End Jewish Radicals, 1875–1914*, London, 1975, Chapter 2; R. Rocker, *In shturm*, Buenos Aires, 1951, pp. 310–12.

46 *Der veker*, 6 January 1893, p. 1.
47 *Di fraye velt*, July 1892, pp. 71–2, presents the self-image of the enlightened socialist intelligentisia labouring among the ignorant Jewish masses.
48 *Der veker*, 23 December 1892, p. 1.
49 *Der arbayter fraynd*, 22–9 March 1889, p. 2.
50 *Di fraye velt*, July 1892, p. 72.
51 B. Homa, *A Fortress in Anglo-Jewry*, London, 1953 pp. 1–54.
52 *Jewish World*, 18 August 1892, p. 4. For an exploration of the World of Jewish fundamentalism see J. Jung, *Champions of Orthodoxy*, London 1974. For a statement of its tenets see the letter from Rabbi Mayer Lerner to Samuel Montagu in the Federation of Synagogues minute book, 12 July 1892.
53 *Der yidisher ekspres*, 24 July 1901, p. 4.
54 University College London, Anglo-Jewish archives, Minute book of the *Machzike Hadath*, 7 *Adar* 5651.
55 *Jewish Chronicle*, 9 February 1911, p. 20.
56 *Ibid.*, 22 July 1898, p. 25.
57 *Der yidisher ekspres*, 22 July 1898, p. 4; on the inadequacies of the religious education provided by Anglo-Jewry see, Federation of Synagogues, minute book, 7 April 1891.
58 *Der yidisher ekspres*, 22 July 1898, p. 4, 29 July 1898, p. 3.
59 S. Cohen, *English Zionists and British Jews: The Communal Politics of Anglo-Jewry, 1895–1920*, Princeton University Press, 1982, pp. 47–9.
60 *Der yidisher ekspres*, 2 February 1900, p. 4.
61 On Montagu's Judaism see Lily H. Montagu, *Samuel Montagu First Baron Swaythling: A Character Sketch*, nd, pp. 18–31; The *Machzike Hadath* also found allies among the Jews of North London, B. Homa, *A Fortress in Anglo-Jewry*, London, 1953, p. 7. Moreover, even the majority of the elite observed major Jewish holidays, the sabbath and dietary laws, on which see T. Endelman, 'Communal solidarity among the Jewish elite', *Victorian Studies*, Spring 1985, pp. 491–526.
62 S. Poll, *The Hasidic Community of Williamsburg: A Study in the Sociology of Religion*, New York, 1969, p. 254.
63 For an account of English Christianity which is critical of the theory of secularisation see J. Cox, *The English Churches in a Secular Society: Lambeth 1870–1930*, Oxford, 1982. A different view can be found in A. Gilbert, *The Making of Post-Christian Britain*, London 1980.
64 See for example, J. Hertz, 'Jewish religious education', *Fourth annual Conference of the Central Committee on Jewish Education*, 1924, p. 9.
65 Jerry White, *Rothschild Buildings: Life in an East End Tenement Block, 1887–1920*, London, 1980, p. 167.
66 On the incomplete erosion of Jewish authority and autonomy within the Russian Empire see S. Dubnow, *History of the Jews in Russia and Poland from the Earliest Times Until the Present Day*, vol. II, Philadelphia, 1918, pp. 59–61, 195.
67 M. C. N. Salbstein, *The Emancipation of the Jews in Britain: The Question of the Admission of Jews to Parliament*, London, 1982, p. 47. Parliamen-

tary Papers 1912/13 XXI, *Royal Commission on Divorce and Matrimonial Causes*, qq. 41,384, 41,467, 41,500, 41,482. For a view asserting the primacy of 'God's Law' see University College London, Anglo-Jewish archives, Gaster papers, bound vol. 18, M. Gaster to C. H. L. Emmanuel, 17 January 1911.
68 S. Poll, *The Hasidic Community of Williamsburg: A Study in the Sociology of Religion*, New York, 1969, p. 254.
69 Parliamentary Papers 1895 XIX, *Report of the Chief Inspector of Factories and Workshops*, 1894, p. 48; Parliamentary Papers 1906 XV, *Report of the Chief Inspector of Factories and Workshops*, 1905, pp. 50–1.
70 Woburn House, London, Minute book of the United Synagogue, 6 November 1894; C. Russell and H. Lewis, *The Jew in London*, London 1900, p. 123.
71 This is a point which may help explain differences between London and other, lesser, centres of immigrant settlement, such as Manchester and Leeds.
72 Greater London Record Office, records of the Spitalfields Great Synagogue, A/S95 35/36.
73 P.L.S. Quinn, 'The Jewish schooling system of London, 1656–1956', University of London doctoral thesis, 1958, vol. II, p. 611.
74 S. Cohen, *English Zionists and British Jews: The Communal Politics of Anglo-Jewry, 1895–1920*, Princeton University Press, 1982, p. 49.
75 J. Blank, *The Minutes of The Federation of Synagogues*, 1912, *passim*.
76 *Jewish World* 1 January 1892, p. 3; *Der yidisher ekspres*, 14 January 1903, p. 4.
77 Federation of Synagogues minute book, 10 November 1891, 8 December 1891, 19 November 1899.
78 *Ibid.*, 16 January 1888.
79 *Jewish Chronicle*, 17 February 1905, p. 28.
80 *Jewish World*, 18 February 1894, p. 6. J. Jung, *Champions of Orthodoxy*, London, Chapter 2.
81 S. Cohen, *English Zionists and British Jews: The Communal Politics of Anglo-Jewry, 1895–1920*, Princeton University Press, 1982, pp. 291–7.
82 *Jewish Chronicle*, 29 June 1900, p. 181, 13 July 1900, p. 7.
83 F. M. L. Thompson, 'Social control in Victorian Britain', *Economic History Review*, second series, vol. XXXIV, no. 2, *passim*.
84 In 1911 83 per cent of Russians and Russian Poles in London remained in the East End, that is in the boroughs of Stepney and Bethnal Green. Parliamentary Papers, *Census of 1911*, IX, p. XIX.
85 *Jewish Chronicle*, 29 May 1903, p. 14, 26 July 1903, pp. 10–11, 27 June 1906, p. 9.
86 YIVO, New York, David Mowshowitch collection, papers of Lucien Wolf, folder 47, memorandum by Lucien Wolf, 31 January, 1917.
87 G. Lebzelter, *Political Anti-Semitism in England, 1918–39*, New York, 1978, Ch. 2.
88 Federation of Synagogues, minute book, 3 November 1925, 2 December 1925.

16
The making of black identities

WINSTON JAMES

Introduction

Although much has been written on the forces behind Caribbean migration to Britain and the social and economic conditions of black people in this country, precious little work has been done on the nature of the national and ethnic identity of the people from the Caribbean and their descendants here. The following remarks are therefore concerned with a provisional exploration of this issue of black identity in Britain with particular reference to people of Afro-Caribbean descent, most of whom arrived in this country after the Second World War. As I shall endeavour to show, the exploration of aspects of black identity is by no means an academic exercise in the pejorative sense of the term: the way in which black people identify themselves within British society has a direct bearing upon their political capacities and practices. Consciousness and action are inextricably intertwined.

The Caribbean

British racism has helped to create an identity – which perhaps under different circumstances would not have developed – among Afro-Caribbeans living in Britain. The crude bipolar (black/white) allocation of ethnic groups within Britain has helped severely to undermine the colour hierarchy which vitiated the Caribbean psyche. As elsewhere, colonisation in the Caribbean did not only entail economic, political and military domination of the indigenous and colonised population; it also involved the sometimes overt, but often surreptitious, process of cultural oppression. One of the major facets of this cultural domination was the undermining of any positive self-image which the colonised might have had. In the Americas, as a consequence of the trade in Africans and the enslavement of millions more, the image of Africa and Africans was continuously and systematically tarnished.[1] In the eyes of the slave owners, humanity in Caribbean slave society was not only conceived to be congenitally hierarchical (with the European in the superordinate position), but the African barely reached the lowest rung of the human species.

Not surprisingly, a complex hierarchy of human shades, what one prominent Caribbeanist has aptly termed a 'multilayered pigmentocracy',[2] evolved wherein those who approximated most closely to the European type (in terms of hair texture, skin colour, facial characteristics, etc.) were attributed with high status (which almost invariably corresponded with their location within the class structure of the society), and those without, or with few such characteristics were likewise attributed with low status. Thus the 'coloureds' (the so-called 'mulattoes') – offsprings of the union of Europeans (almost invariably men) and African (almost invariably women)[3] – were regarded to be congenitally superior to 'pure Africans' and moreover, *were treated as such*.[4]

The coloureds were quite often manumitted and, moreover, were bequeathed substantial property by their slave-owning fathers. Of such significance was this practice of granting property to 'mulatto' offspring that in Jamaica, for instance, in 1761 after an enquiry of the House of Assembly of the island had discovered that property already bequeathed to 'freedmen' (people who were born into slavery but later manumitted, the vast majority of whom were 'coloured'),[5] was valued between £200,000 and £300,000, legislation was promptly put into place that 'prohibited whites from leaving real or personal property worth more than £1,200 (sterling) to any coloured or black . . . The whites had decided that it was more important to keep the land in European hands than to follow parental instincts.'[6] This Act in Jamaica, like similar attempts elsewhere in the Americas, did not, however, in any way undermine the material privilege of the coloured over the Africans in the Caribbean pigmentocracy. Indeed, even when they were kept as slaves, the coloureds were given preferential treatment and occupied 'superior' positions in the slave hierarchy; they were given greater opportunity to learn skills, to become artisans, and many worked as house or domestic slaves – positions much sought after by the slaves, male as well as female, who had to work more arduously under a harsher regimen in the fields.[7] It is also instructive to note that in the early years of the slave system, in correspondence with the slave hierarchy, many of the enslaved Africans who were put to work as house slaves in Jamaica at least, were the relatively 'light-skinned' 'Madagass' (so-called because they were imported from the island of Madagascar) slaves.[8]

The point being made is important and deserves emphasis. Not only did the pigmentocracy operate at the level of ideology *per se*, it also operated at the level of a *material force* linking colour with class position and privilege, thus generating the *forced coincidence* of colour and class in Caribbean societies.

Slave societies in the Americas were profoundly race/colour conscious. A whole plethora of social types based upon 'race' were designated and hierarchically structured in such a thoroughly and consciously organised manner that by comparison the obnoxious triad (white, coloured, black) of contemporary apartheid seems singularly crude. In the British colonies for instance, the following categories obtained:[9]

Negro	Child of negro and negro
Sambo	Child of mulatto and negro
Mulatto	Child of white man and negress
Quadroon	Child of mulatto woman and white man
Mustee	Child of quadroon (or pure Amerindian) and white man
Mustiphini	Child of mustee and white man
Quintroon	Child of mustiphini and white man
Octoroon	Child of quintroon and white man

The Spanish and the Dutch colonies had even more multitudinous categories. The former, for instance, had *saltatras* (mulatto/quadroon), *givero* (sambo Indian/sambo mulatto) and the almost incredible *tente-enel-ayre* (translated literally as 'suspended') which designated the offsprings of the union of quadroon and mustee. Indeed, in Spanish America no less than 128 gradations were possible.[10] In the British Caribbean (with apparently the sole exception of Barbados) one was designated legally white after the category of mustee and became automatically free.[11] One way therefore of becoming legally free in Caribbean slave society was literally to breed the African blood out of one's system over a series of generations, thus underlining the concatenation of blackness and servitude (and the absence of human attributes) and whiteness and freedom (and the epitomisation or attainment of human status). But even then, one was not completely 'safe' in white society. Heuman cites the case of a white patroness of a ball in the Eastern Caribbean who

> strongly criticized a British captain for having danced with a 'costie', a term describing a person who was *one-sixteenth*

colored. The woman sponsoring the event then provided the captain with a list of the various castes between mulattoes and 'costies' and presumably the rules of behaviour for an English officer.[12]

This almost incredible exhibition of astonishingly sharp social demarcation occurred as late as the middle of the nineteenth century, two decades after the abolition of the enslavement of African people in the British Caribbean.

Whilst the coloureds were demeaned and humiliated by whites even after death,[13] they, in turn, bloated with what the eighteenth century planter-historian Edward Long aptly called the 'pride of amended blood',[14] had few qualms about pouring scorn upon Africans, including those who were legally free like themselves.[15] Excluded by the whites, the coloureds had their spectacular balls from which the Africans, but not whites, were excluded. The coloureds also expressed their social insecurity by ruthlessly oppressing the African slaves in their possession. They were notorious, even amongst the white plantocracy, for exceptional cruelty against slaves.[16] A common Jamaican saying among the African slaves reflected this state of affairs: 'If me fe have massa or misses, give me Buckra one – no give me mulatto, dem no use neega well.'[17]

Understandably, the African slaves and their descendants were affected by the values attributed to different human 'types', indeed, so much so that even in Jamaica, an island renowned for its relatively high retention of African culture, eighteenth-century accounts testify to the contempt with which the newly-arrived African slaves were often met by other 'creole' (or local born) slaves. Newly-arrived Africans, traumatised successively by capture, the march to the coast, the horrendous middle passage across the Atlantic, the humiliation of 'inspection' by prospective buyers, the branding of their bodies as if they were cattle, were derogatively referred to by creole slaves as 'salt-water negroes' and 'Guiney birds'.[18] Such were some of the ironies of Caribbean slave society.

The post-slavery period was marked more by continuity than by change in the colour-class complex which was firmly laid in place over a period of more than three centuries of African chattel slavery in the Americas. An element of self-doubt, if not self-contempt, afflicted the African section of the population during and after slavery. It could hardly have been otherwise: 'The traditions of the dead generations weigh like a nightmare on the minds of the living.'[19] Various symptoms reflected this state of affairs; the straightening of the hair, which was described to a Jamaican sociologist by one hairdresser as, significantly, the 'cultivating' of the hair,[20] the bleaching of the skin and the obsession with skin colour are some of the most well-known expressions of the colonial legacy in the Americas.[21]

The first generation

It was from such a cultural milieu – albeit one persistently punctuated by African resistance[22] to the European value system foisted upon them during the colonial era – that the post-war Caribbean migrants to Britain emerged.[23] In the 'mother country' no regard was paid to the complex hierarchy of shades; the pattern of racism which the Caribbean migrants experienced here did not correspond to the complexion hierarchy which they had left behind in the Caribbean. They were regarded monolithically as 'coloureds', 'West Indians', 'blacks', 'immigrants', and even 'wogs', with no reference to differential shades. As an Indo-Trinidadian writing about his experience in Britain as a student in the early 1960s accurately observed:

> Leaving the West Indies and coming to Britain is like entering a land where the natives suffer from a curious kind of colour blindness in the contemplation of human groups. This special form of blindness manifests itself in an insensitivity to racial discriminations and variant shades within the category 'black'. It registers two crude categories, black and white.
>
> The West Indian consciousness is outraged by the crudity of the categorisation. In the rarefied atmosphere of the mother country, the delicate instrument ceases to function. All West Indians are black.[24]

A compatriot of the author of the above, a man of Portuguese–Madeiran extraction, was outraged by the shade blindness of the British. 'I was accepted as a white person in Trinidad. For all practical purposes,' he complained, 'I am coloured in England.'[25] Over the years this dichotomy of black/white in British 'race relations' has helped to undermine, if not totally destroy, this hierarchy of shades of black which the Caribbean working class had itself, by and large, adhered to. The erosion of this hierarchy of shades, not the means by which it has been undermined in Britain, is without doubt, a positive political development. In a moving and courageous autobiographical essay by a 'light skinned' (her expression) Trinidadian woman studying in Britain during the early 1960s, the following conclusion was reached:

The whole experience of living in England, though at first almost traumatic, is of extreme value for the West Indian student, particularly the light coloured student. I have no knowledge of what the experience does for the African or Indian, but I cannot help feeling that the consequences for the light coloured West Indian student are more wide ranging. He [sic] has removed an incipient white-type colour prejudice; he has his position as a member of one of the coloured races clearly outlined for the first time; he has a whole series of class prejudices overturned; he has the colonial myth of his almost British personality completely destroyed. In the end realization of this makes it impossible for him to be bitter about his stay in England. The English have at last rendered him a service.[26]

The second way in which the experience of migrating to Britain has entailed political demystification for Caribbean migrants is to be found in the undermining of island chauvinism. Divided by the expanse of the sea – the distance between Port of Spain (Trinidad) and Kingston (Jamaica) is equivalent to that from London to Moscow – and mutual suspicion in the Caribbean, the passage to Britain has brought Jamaicans, Barbadians, Grenadians, Kittians, Guyanese, Trinidadians, etc., in close proximity to each other for the first time. Although island loyalties still remain, the people of the Caribbean have been brought together by London Transport, the National Health Service and most of all, by the centripetal forces of British racism, to recognise their common class position and common Caribbean identity. No doubt the remnants of island chauvinism still linger on in the metropolis,[27] but it is equally true that this phenomenon has waned over time.[28]

The somewhat innocent journey to Britain has also served as an unparalleled eye-opening experience to the 'West Indian pioneers'. In the Caribbean few have ever seen the European in the class location of the working class,[29] they had never associated Europeans with subordination and poverty. As a Guyanese female migrant related:

I learnt very early to associate being white with being wealthy. A man who left my village long before I was born returned when I was about ten. He brought back a red-skinned woman with him. Probably she was no more than a whore he picked up in Georgetown, but she was very fair with long hair down her back. She must have been a half-caste, or something. But this man, I think his name was Adam, could not afford to give her a car and servants. You know, every day I expected the police to come and arrest Adam for making this white or near white woman walk around the village barefoot, carrying tin cans of water on her head? Yet all the time we were walking barefoot. That was the point, black was something you associated with poverty. Now and again I would be taken to Georgetown and I would see the girls in offices working away at typewriters. I wanted to be able to be a typist too, but never dared to tell anyone, for working in an office meant a pale skin. I had an aunt who used to work for some white people in New Amsterdam. I went there once and saw the little fair-haired children skipping about the place. My aunty warned me that if they spoke to me, I should be very polite and should never forget to call them 'master' and 'miss'. My aunty would never work for a black man even if he was made of gold. She would never call a little black boy master, or a little black girl miss. It was all so very confusing.[30]

An Indo-Trinidadian male confessed: 'I had not the slightest idea of the existence of a working class in Britain.'[31] The shock of discovering the existence of a working class in Britain is by no means confined to those who lack a formal education. As George Lamming informs us the *petit bourgeoisie* also experience a sense of bewilderment at discovering that Britain has *white* workers. To him the shock of this discovery has not so much to do with lack of knowledge about England, *per se*, but more with the strength and persistence of what he calls 'the *idea* of England'.[32] Like whites in the Caribbean, the white Britons *as a whole* are conceived to be above manual labour.

On arriving in Britain the scales fell abruptly from the Caribbean migrants' eyes.

As Mrs. Stewart put it 'In Jamaica we used to take white people as gods. We always look up to them; they put on such a way you can't understand. People I know work for whites and would make their bath and bring them coffee, like slaves. The whites put themselves on such a pedestal, you really thought they were something.' Thinking back to her previous attitude, she gave a bitter laugh. For in England whiteness is no longer synonymous with high status occupations, large incomes, and authority; many whites are members of the working class performing menial tasks and living in relative poverty. 'What makes things strange,' one man told me, 'is that when I came over here, I was surprised to see the state of a lot of the English. I expected something else, not a lot of drunks some even begging. That's what I don't rightly understand. A lot of white folks see us as worse than them. Some of the time it's not even true.'[33]

There are two particularly noteworthy consequences of such experiences. Firstly, they help to destroy the erroneous association of white people *qua* whites with superordination; the mystique of whiteness dissolves in the air of a class-stratified English society. And secondly, coupled with their experiences of racism in Britain, they generate a corresponding valorisation of blackness on the part of Caribbean people.[34] Indeed, the whole experience of living in a white racist society has helped to forge a black identity where in many cases such an identity did not previously exist, or not consciously thought about. 'The colour of your skin matters here. In Jamaica it is class not colour,' stated, albeit far too categorically, one of Foner's respondents. Another told her 'I think most of my friends *feel* Jamaican. The English helped us to do it.'[35] Needless to say the English also helped Afro-Caribbean people in Britain to *feel* 'West Indian' and *feel* 'black',[36] in fact so much so that in one study as many as 70 per cent of the interviewees felt that all Jamaicans were in the same social class.[37] Overwhelmed by the pervasiveness of the class-blind racism in Britain, the Afro-Caribbeans have themselves, understandably, become somewhat blinded by the class differentiation and class formation taking place amongst people of their own colour and cultural background. The *Labour Force Survey* has shown that although Caribbean people in Britain are overwhelmingly concentrated within the ranks of the working class, they are nevertheless by no means all located within this category.[38]

It would be a mistake to believe that the first generation of Afro-Caribbeans regard their experience of living in Britain as an unmitigated disaster. They experience racism and they occupy in their vast proportion the lowest rung of the social hierarchy of Britain. Nevertheless, in material terms, the overwhelming majority enjoy a standard of living in Britain which many could only have dreamt of back in the Caribbean.[39] It is therefore not unexpected that their conception of Britain is an ambivalent one. As one migrant explains:

> These have been the hardest years of my life. I think about them, and I ask myself, Sonny, tell the truth, coming here, was it a good decision or not? Think before you answer, like your dead mother used to say. So I think. And I answer, 'Yes,' it was good that we came, and that we stayed. I found work, my wife is happy, happy enough. My children are happy and healthy. I thank the good Lord for all of that. I

thank Him everyday, just as my dead mother told me I should. I pray to Him and I ask Him. I wish too. I wish this could be like this and that could be like that. I wish I were with my family, my father, my brother, my cousins. I wish I lived in a newer home, and made more money. I wish I would have come here and be treated like I was equal by all these people. But I came as someone they thought was a dope smuggler, and that's about the way they treat me.[40]

Another expressed the same sentiments but more concisely: 'It's all right here basically but we are kind of treated inferior.'[41]

In recent years, with the rise in unemployment, many more than hitherto are returning home.[42] But even more feel 'trapped' within Britain because they are incapable of mobilising the financial wherewithal to resettle in the Caribbean. There is also a considerable number who have returned home to the Caribbean and discovered to their great cost that the meagre financial resources which they have scrimped and saved over the years in Britain were not enough to facilitate resettlement – in the land they have loved and romanticised during their painful sojourn in Britain – in circumstances of high unemployment and rampant inflation.[43] These, woefully dejected, have had to return to the Britain they had fought and worked hard to escape from, savings depleted, virtually to start all over again. There are also others who have returned home and realised that they had stayed 'too long' in Britain and cannot re-adapt to a relatively parochial Caribbean lifestyle.[44] These too have trekked back to Britain or have moved on to North America. One man informed the writer that on his return 'home' to Jamaica for a visit he discovered that he was regarded to be a 'foreigner in [his] own country'. Resentful of his being dubbed, albeit jovially, as 'the Englishman' and with the growing realisation that all his friends and relatives were either in Britain or North America, he decided to remain in Britain – a decision which radically overturned his twenty-seven-year-old dream of the return.[45]

The second generation and after

Most second-generation Caribbeans in Britain have either lived in this country since early childhood or were actually born and brought up in Britain. In other words, they have either spent the greater proportion of their lives in the 'Mother Country' or have resided here for all their lives. This important characteristic of 'the second generation' has profound implications for their view of themselves and the world in which they live.

Unlike their parents, they compare their position and life-chance within British society, not with the conditions of pre-independent Caribbean society, but with their white British counterparts. Consequently their experience of racism in Britain is more immediate and their perception of the phenomenon is more uncluttered. It is therefore no surprise that their opposition to British racism is more instantaneous and more forthright. Not for them the consolation 'It's all right here, basically, *but* we are kind of treated inferior': for them it is 'It is not all right here, *because* we are treated as if we are inferior.' Their consciousness of themselves as a black enclave within British society is therefore even greater than that of their parents. It is true, as one commentator has written,[46] that their commitment to a sense of blackness is by no means even but, nevertheless as an aggregate, it is no doubt true that the vast majority consider themselves to be black and belonging to an oppressed minority within British society.

The power of island chauvinism has waned among the first generation, but for the second and indeed third generations of Afro-Caribbeans in Britain we can declare with almost complete certitude that this politically debilitating disease has hardly infected them. Even in the cases where these prejudices have been transmitted by parents to the young child, racism in the school ensures that it never takes root. As one member of this generation eloquently declared: 'As you grow older you just see them [small islanders] as black. When you're in school you all get harassed together, and see yourself as one – *all a we is one.*'[47]

Separated from any immediate and far-reaching experience of the society of their parents, surrounded by a sea of white hostility, many have been attracted to ideas of the Rastafarian 'movement' in an attempt to make sense of and survive their travail in Babylon. In essence, a plebeian form of *négritude*, the signal contribution of the Rastafarian 'movement' is the affirmation of pride of race and the celebration of the African provenance. Despite its well-recognised, but poorly understood, weaknesses and silences, the 'ideology'[48] of Rastafarianism has made a tremendous contribution to the black counter-culture against the spell of white supremacy.

Unlike their parents, who have less attachment to Britain, the second generation of 'Caribbeans' are, willy-nilly, black Britons. They might speak a form of the Jamaican language and sport Rastafarian locks, but in Kingston many would not be understood and many more would not be able fully to understand the language of their Jamaican counterparts. The second generation are therefore, by default, creating new cultural forms based largely, but by no means exclusively, upon the legacy of their parents and foreparents. They are also forging new forms of resistance, like their North American counterparts, aimed at the specific problems which they face within British society.

A note on the generations

As the above analysis indicates, there are noteworthy differences in the experiences of the first and second generations of people of Afro-Caribbean descent in Britain. It would be a mistake, however, to assume that the two generations have little or nothing in common, as some writers seem to do. The fact of the matter is that, over time, both generations have converged in their perspectives, a convergence which largely arises from the simultaneity of their experiences in Britain. Many apparently do not know this, but parents, as well as their children, grow and learn from new experiences. Contrary to the stereotype of a passive first generation and a wild second generation, the evidence of the black experience in Britain clearly suggests that, despite the psychological constraints placed upon political activity by the desire to return home within a limited time frame (usually five years), the first generation of Afro-Caribbean people in Britain have put up some tremendous and astonishingly courageous struggles in defence of their dignity and their personal well-being in this country. It took tremendous audacity to pull Oswald Mosley off his podium in Notting Hill in the 1950s, yet a Jamaican did just that and single-handedly. When the racists attacked in Nottingham and Notting Hill in 1958, black people organised and effectively repulsed their challenges.[49] Day-to-day resistance at the workplace was also an important element of black people's life in Britain during the early years. Poor documentation of such resistance does not mean that it did not take place. Even the so-called *bête noire* of Caribbean literature, Vidia Naipaul, had to admire the fortitude of the early Caribbean migrants to Britain.[50] The video *Motherland*, based upon the experiences of twenty-three women who migrated from the Caribbean to Britain in the 1950s and 1960s and dramatised by their teenage daughters, is a striking expression of the growing awareness and celebration by young black people of their parents' struggles.[51]

Needless to say, youths of Afro-Caribbean descent in Britain are by no means homogeneous in their political perspectives and activity; some are far more militant than others, and others are downright conservative. Thankfully, this latter category, it is fair to say, are in the minority, thanks to the radicalising effect of British racism. The black youths have been learning from their parents and the parents have been learning from their children. Some years ago some parents would not believe the barbarities which occurred in British schools against their children. One black woman, whose English teacher in Britain consistently referred to her as 'the savage' in classrooms, did not even tell her parents because she knew they would not have believed her. The Caribbean background had not accustomed her parents to teachers behaving in such a manner. In the 1970s, due to the overwhelming evidence of racism within British schools and the emergence of extremely vocal black pressure groups, parents on the whole became aware that schools in Brixton are quite different to those in rural Barbados. Some years ago many parents found incredible the stories told to them by their children about police harassment; many now have a healthy suspicion of the police.

In short there has been a high degree of convergence in the experiences and political perspectives of black parents and their offspring in Britain which many commentators, blinded by their stereotype of the 'generational conflict' among Afro-Caribbean people, have hardly recognised.

The limits of black fraternity

Like all nationalities or ethnic groups, Afro-Caribbean people in Britain have erected boundaries in relation to those with whom they identify. In this case boundaries have been established which exclude the people whom many would regard as 'natural allies' of Afro-Caribbean people in Britain. Although the situation is quite dynamic, it is fair to say that at present Afro-Caribbeans do not on the whole identify with people of Asian descent in Britain.[52] Nor, it should be said, do Asian people identify with Afro-Caribbean people in Britain. This state of affairs is of course a major obstacle to the maximisation of concerted action against British racism. There is a tendency among black radicals of both Asian and African descent to sweep this problem under the carpet. But to make a subject taboo, to repress it, is one thing; to make it disappear is quite another.

Anyone who moves among Afro-Caribbean and Asian people in Britain with eyes to see and ears to hear would readily recognise that there does exist some antagonism, or, more typically perhaps, a tacit agreement of a peaceful, but cold co-existence, between the two groups. A number of commentators have registered the phenomenon,[53] but Daniel Lawrence is the only one (to my knowledge) to have attempted to gather data on the problem. In his study of race relations in Nottingham he found that

> As many as 83 per cent of the West Indians and 43 per cent of the Indians and Pakistanis said that they had most in common with the English. However, a further 31 per cent of the Indians and Pakistanis said that as far as they were concerned they had nothing in common with either. No more than 8 per cent of the West Indian and 20 per cent of the Indians and Pakistanis felt that they had more in common with each other than with the English.

Lawrence also found that as many as 42 per cent of West Indian respondents commented upon the extent to which the Asians were 'different and kept themselves to themselves': 'They're clannish. Their way of thinking and behaving is entirely different from ours. I have known a few but it's hard to get through to them.' Twenty-two per cent of Afro-Caribbeans expressed explicitly critical remarks about Asians: 'A people who grab money!' 'Well you see most of the Indians they, for some reason or another, they don't call themselves coloured – you know they think they are better than we are.' Only 11 per cent made 'friendly or not unfavourable' comments about Asians: 'They're very genuine people – they are nice.'[54]

For their part, Indians and Pakistanis expressed more 'critical than friendly' remarks about Caribbean people. Lawrence discovered that 'By far the most common complaint was that West Indians were rough, aggressive and generally uncultivated':

> Well they're not like us – take crime for instance – there isn't a day when one of them isn't in the paper for doing something. They are a bit more aggressive and crude – but that's just because they are ignorant. From the day we are born we are taught that you must respect your elders – even if they are not any relation to you – and I think even among English people you don't find this sort of thing. But the West Indians don't seem to know how to behave – they are rude and rowdy you know not like Indians or the English.[55]

Lawrence found that 30 per cent of Asians who gave their opinion about Afro-Caribbeans made favourable, 'or at least not unfavourable', comments, but from the three examples which he gave, two expressed a far from disinterested admiration of Caribbean people: 'West Indians are good for *us*. If any English man fights *us* West Indians help *us*. Our own people run away.' 'West Indians are good. If *they* were not here *we* would not have been able to live here.' And: 'West Indians are OK – they are friendly when they speak to me.'⁵⁶

Although Lawrence does not indicate specifically when his fieldwork was carried out, from the internal evidence and the date of publication of the book (1974) it is almost certain that the fieldwork on which the book is based was carried out in the early 1970s (perhaps in the late 1960s but obviously not later than 1974). Since that time there have been a number of positive developments in Afro-Caribbean/Asian relationships. The 'Bradford twelve' defence campaign was to receive significant and active support from Afro-Caribbean as well as Asian people in defence of twelve Asian youths in Bradford who were charged with 'making an explosive substance with intent to endanger life and property' and 'conspiring to make explosive substances' during the uprisings of 1981. And more recently in east London Asians and Afro-Caribbeans united in the defence of the 'Newham seven', a group of Asian youths who were charged with affray in the aftermath of an attempted defence of their community from fascist attacks. These are just two of the more well-known cases of Afro-Asian unity in action. The list could be extended. But to assume that the contradictions between the Afro-Caribbeans and Asians is a thing of the past is to commit a gross error. They still remain.⁵⁷ On balance it is fair to say that a relative state of indifference, if not antagonism, prevails over the more positive developments, mentioned above, between Afro-Caribbeans and Asians.

So, what are the bases of this problem?

Firstly, as the comments cited above indicate, there do exist major cultural differences between people of Asian descent and those of Afro-Caribbean origin. The mutual ignorance of, if not downright disrespect for, each other's culture and the internalisation by each of the British stereotype of the other help to explain this state of affairs.⁵⁸

Secondly, aspects of Afro-Caribbean antipathy towards Asians are rooted in the Caribbean background. To augment labour supply and to increase their control over the labour forces, the plantocracy, throughout the Caribbean, as well as others elsewhere, turned to the Indian subcontinent after the enslavement of Africans had come to an end.⁵⁹ This system, known as 'Indian indentureship', lasted from the 1830s to 1917, at which time, thanks largely to Indian nationalist opposition in the subcontinent, this barbaric practice, very much akin to slavery, came to an abrupt end. The motives, organisation, practices and consequences of induced Indian immigration to the Americas are well documented.⁶⁰ The important point here is this: the process was specifically and expressly geared at breaking the increased power of the formerly enslaved Africans within the newly-created labour market. Elaborate strategies were conscientiously devised by the plantocratic bourgeoisie and its state to create the maximum division between Africans and the newly arrived and cruelly deceived Asians in the Caribbean. These, unfortunately, were extremely effective; the African and Indian exploited and oppressed were thoroughly divided;[61] mutual strike-breaking, for instance, was virtually a commonplace in late-nineteenth century Guyana. The animosities between the groups, though less intense than hitherto, exist to the present day.

Thirdly, the differences in the distribution, spatial as well as industrial, and location of Asians and Afro-Caribbeans in Britain - differences which do exist and which are often overlooked – also militate against the cohesion of these two groups in their fight against racism.[62]

Fourthly, racism in its concrete operation does not affect both groups in an identical manner. The specificities of the rhythm of Asian migration to Britain, for instance, have meant that people from the Indian subcontinent, not those from the Caribbean, have felt the brunt of racist immigration controls in Britain. Afro-Caribbeans for their part, undergo an exceptionally high degree of state harassment on a day-to-day level. The perceived differences in the problems which each group come up against, *vis-à-vis* the state, have hampered united action based upon common priorities.[63]

Finally, clearly identifiable differences in the *distribution* of Asians and Afro-Caribbeans within the class structure of Britain, and the lack of coincidence and unevenness of the respective dynamic of their class formation work against the development of unity of perspective on British racism and, even more, against combined political action.

There are thus a whole series of factors which inhibit the boundaries of the Afro-Caribbean fraternity *vis-à-vis* people of Asian descent in Britain, and vice versa. These need to be urgently and seriously addressed if the struggle against racism, being carried out – almost by default – on a daily basis by each group, is to be more effectively waged. There are no easy nor instant solutions to this problem, and in any case space here does not permit serious elaboration on the possible means of overcoming this obstacle to unity.[64]

By way of conclusion

Our experiences in Britain have sharpened our perspectives of our place within the world: we have been forced, where some of us were hitherto reluctant, to recognise and validate our blackness; the 'shade'-blind and 'island'-innocent racism within British society have helped us to shed some of the most absurd and deluding idiocies of Caribbean life. 'The English have at last,' as Patricia Madoo rejoiced, 'rendered [us] a service.' The centripetal effects of British racism, thus far at least however, have not been sufficiently uniform and strong to breach the partially antagonistic ethnic boundaries established between people of Asian and African descent in Britain. But in partial 'compensation', the struggle of living within the metropolis has entailed the unintended 'privilege' of us seeing the world from the perspective of the persecuted 'outsider': our vision of the world has been broadened and as a consequence we are in a better position to identify with the oppressed within and outside of Britain. It is therefore no accident that whilst the white working class engages in its periodical flirtation with Toryism, Caribbean people in Britain in their vast majority entertain no illusion about the Conservative Party, as their persistently high *anti*-Tory (not to be confused with *pro*-Labour) vote in successive elections testifies.

As the dream of 'the return' of the first generation becomes more pulverised with every passing day, and as the second generation becomes more aware of the need to transform the Britain in which they live into a home, the slogan 'Here to Stay, Here to Fight' rings more true. But because of the pervasive non-class-specific and non-gender-bound racism of British society, we have and will continue to have, alas, for some time yet, few allies. It is a hard road to travel. Fortunately, however, black people in Britain have, for some time now, recognised this fact and the necessary precondition for the solution of any problem is the prior acknowledgment of its existence.

Notes

A longer version of this paper has been published in *Immigrants and Minorities*, vol. 5, no. 3, November, 1986.

1 Frank Snowden has shown that in previous epochs of European history the image of Africa had been quite different. See his *Blacks in Antiquity: Ethiopians in the Greco-Roman Experience*, Cambridge, Mass., 1970. Cf. C. A. Diop, *The African Origin of Civilisation*, Westport, 1970.
2 G. Lewis, 'Race relations in Britain: a view from the Caribbean', *Race Today*, vol. 1, no. 3, July, 1969, p. 80; G. Lewis, *Main Currents in Caribbean Thought*, Kingston, 1983, p. 9.
3 For some of the exceptions see E. Brathwaite, 'Caribbean women during the period of slavery', *Caribbean Contact*, vol. 11, no. 12, May, 1984, p. 13. Cf. E. Brathwaite, *The Development of Creole Society in*

Jamaica, Oxford, 1971, pp. 188–91. The historical records of Barbados have so far yielded only one such marriage during the entire period of slavery. This marriage took place in 1685. See J. Handler, *The Unappropriated People: Freedom in the Slave Society of Barbados*, Baltimore, 1974, p. 201.

4 Gad Heuman's, *Between Black and White: Race, Politics and the Free Coloureds in Jamaica, 1792–1865*, Oxford, 1981, is undoubtedly one of the finest case studies of this social category within the New World. For a good overview of the position within the Americas as a whole, see D. Cohen and J. Greene (eds), *Neither Slave Nor Free*, Baltimore, 1972. Cf. Mavis C. Campbell, *The Dynamics of Change in a Slave Society: A Socio-Political History of the Free Coloureds of Jamaica 1800–1865* New Jersey, 1976.

5 It has been estimated that in eighteenth-century Jamaica 80 per cent of 'freedmen' were coloured, whilst 20 per cent were black. G. Heuman, *Between Black and White: Race, Politics and the Free Coloureds in Jamaica, 1792–1865*, 1981, p. 4.

6 Heuman, *op. cit.*, p. 6.

7 This is not to say that domestic slaves did not experience atrocious violations of their humanity. See E. Brathwaite, *The Development of Creole Society in Jamaica 1770–1820*, Oxford, 1971, pp. 156–7 for some gruesome examples of violence against domestic slaves. In spite of the cruelty which they quite often experienced from their so-called masters and mistresses, domestic slaves were nevertheless 'regarded by most slaves and the master as being in a more "honourable" position than the field slaves': Brathwaite, *op. cit.*, p. 155; cf. O. Patterson, *The Sociology of Slavery*, London, 1967, pp. 57–9.

8 F. Henriques, *Family and Colour in Jamaica*, 2nd edition, London, 1968, p. 33.

9 E. Brathwaite, *The Development of Creole Society in Jamaica, 1770–1820*, Oxford, 1971, p. 167; D. Hall, 'Jamaica' in D. Cohen and J. Greene, *Neither Slave Nor Free*, Baltimore, 1972, p. 196; and B. Higman, *Slave Population and Economy in Jamaica 1807–1834*, Cambridge, 1976, p. 139. According to Handler this hierarchy did not obtain in Barbados. Here one was 'coloured', 'black' or 'white'. The permutations did not take the form of the ramified social categories which existed say in Jamaica: J. Handler, *The Unappropriated People: Freedman in the Slave Society Of Barbados*, Baltimore, 1974, p. 6. Cf. H. Beckles, 'On the backs of blacks: the Barbados free-coloureds' pursuit of civil rights and the 1816 slave rebellion', *Immigrants and Minorities*, vol. 3, no. 2, July, 1984, p. 185, note 1.

10 E. Brathwaite, *The Development of Creole Society in Jamaica, 1770–1820*, Oxford, 1971, p. 167. Cf. M. Morner, *Race Mixture in the History of Latin America*, Boston, 1967; L. B. Rout, *The African Experience in Spanish America, 1502 to the Present Day*, Cambridge, 1976, and F. Knight, *Slave Society in Cuba During the Nineteenth Century*, Wisconsin, 1970.

11 'In Barbados . . . no one of known negroid ancestry, no matter how

remote, could be considered *white* with respect to social or legal status':
J. Handler, *The Unappropriated People: Freedmen in the Slave Society of Barbados*, Baltimore, 1974, p. 6 (emphasis in original).
12 Gad Heuman, *Between Black and White: Race, Politics and Free Coloureds in Jamaica, 1792–1865*, Oxford, 1981, 76.
13 'The separation of browns and whites continued after death. Each group had its own burial ground, and church bells rang longer for whites than for people of colour': G. Heuman, op. cit., p. 12.
14 Cited in G. Lewis, *Slavery, Imperialism and Freedom*, New York, 1978, p. 338 and in G. Lewis, *Main Currents in Caribbean Thought*, Kingston, 1983, p. 9.
15 This does not, however, mean that political alliances did not occur between freed Africans and coloureds – they did. But these alliances were extremely fragile, uneasy, and on the whole ephemeral. Gad Heuman, *Between Black and White: Race, Politics and Free Coloureds in Jamaica, 1792–1865*, Oxford, 1981 documents this very well in the case of Jamaica. With perhaps the qualified exceptions of Cuba and Brazil, this state of affairs was typical of the Americas as a whole.
16 Fanon's observation of the behaviour of West Indians who joined the French Army and served in Africa before 1939 serves as an appropriate parallel here:

> the West Indian, not satisfied to be superior to the African, despised him, and while the white man could allow himself certain liberties with the native, the West Indian absolutely could not. This was because, between whites and Africans, there was no need of a reminder; the difference stared one in the face. But what a catastrophe if the West Indian should suddenly be taken for an African! (F. Fanon, 'West Indians; and Africans', in his *Toward the African Revolution*, Penguin, Harmondsworth, 1970, p. 30)

It should be noted that not an insubstantial number of Africans were owned as slaves by mulattoes. In Jamaica in 1826 they were claimed to have owned 50,000 slaves out of a total slave population of 310,368: Mavis C. Campbell, *The Dynamics of Change in a Slave Society: A Socio-political History of the Free Coloureds of Jamaica 1800–1865*, New Jersey, 1976, p. 62.
17 Cited in Gad Heuman, *Between Black and White: Race, Politics and Free Coloureds in Jamaica, 1792–1865*, Oxford, 1981, p. 14. Translated: 'If I must have a master or mistress, give me a white one – don't give me a mulatto, they don't treat black people well.' 'Bukra' or 'backra' are derived from the Efik *mbakara* meaning 'he who surrounds or governs'. In the Caribbean it soon became synonymous with white people. Cf. F. Cassidy, *Jamaica Talk*, 2nd edition, London, 1971, pp. 155–6, and F. Cassidy and R. Le Page, *Dictionary of Jamaican English*, 2nd edition, Cambridge 1980.
18 O. Patterson, *The Sociology of Slavery*, London, 1967, pp. 146–7.
19 K. Marx, 'The Eighteenth Brumaire of Louis Bonaparte', in K. Marx,

Surveys From Exile, ed. by D. Fernbach, Penguin, Harmondsworth, 1973, p. 146.

20 It should be noted that in contemporary Britain, hair straightening among black people has, to a certain extent, developed into an autonomous form of black aesthetics; a form, in other words, that has to a significant extent broken with, or perhaps more accurately, has *forgotten*, its provenance in the class-colour complex of slave society in the Caribbean. The colonial legacy, however, has not by any means, been completely eradicated. Cf. Caribbean Teachers' Association (ed.), *Black Youth Speak Out* (report of the CTA, Youth Conference 1984), London, 1984, pp. 38–9, and 'Are we proud to be black?' *Black Voice*, vol. 15, no. 3. For interesting overviews of the situation in the USA today see 'Is skin color still a problem in black America?', *Ebony*, vol. XL, no. 2, Dec., 1984, pp. 66–70 and two recent brief, but exceptionally courageous films on the subject: Warrington Hudlin's *Color* (1982) and Ayoka Chinzira's *Hairpiece* (1983).

21 The fact that black women are far more involved in these practices than black men is no accident; the phenomenon is directly related to the oppression of women by men and the historical preference on the part of black men for women with phenotypical characteristics which approximate most closely to Europeans. With the exception of the extant Maroon enclaves (communities established by escaped slaves in the Americas in the sixteenth to eighteenth centuries, most notably in Jamaica and Surinam), it is one of the New World as a whole. Cf. M. Herskovits, *The Myth of the Negro Past*, Boston, 1958, pp. 125-6; F. Henriques, *Family and Colour in Jamaica*, 2nd edition, London, 1968, p. 57; and especially Ann Cook, 'Black pride? Some contradictions', in Toni Cade (ed.), *The Black Women: An Anthology* New York, 1970. In an otherwise solid analysis, Errol Lawrence ('In the abundance of water the fool is thirsty: sociology and black "pathology" ', in Centre for Contemporary Cultural Studies, *The Empire Strikes Back: Race and Racism in 70s Britain*, London, 1982) grossly underestimates some of the negative legacies of colonialism in the Caribbean and is far too defensive about their manifestations. The issues, to my mind, are wrongly posed by the author. What ought to be explained are why should hair-straightening be a means of dressing the hair at all and why should lotions for whitening the skin be applied at all? It should be noted that the idea of black 'negative self-image' was not occasioned by white reactionaries but by black nationalists, who were desperately worried about the economic as well as the psychological state of their people. The fact of the matter is that colonialism, not surprisingly, has done us tremendous harm in a whole variety of ways. Our task is to understand the nature of the harm done, how it occurred, how it persists and how we ought to combat it. The process of reflecting upon this can be painful and embarrassing, but the alternatives of silence and misinformation are far more detrimental to the cause of our people. The internalisation of the pigmentocracy, however, did not take place to the same depth and range by Afro-Caribbean people regardless of

class. The evidence suggests that those most affected by what Henriques has termed the 'white bias' in Caribbean society are the coloured and black middle classes (F. Henriques, *Family and Colour in Jamaica*, 2nd edition, London, 1968, p. 171 and *passim*; N. Foner, *Status and Power in Rural Jamaica*, New York, 1973, p. 27; F. Fanon, *Black Skin, White Mask*, London, 1970; E. Williams, *The Negro in the Caribbean*, Connecticut, 1969; G. J. Kruijer, *A Sociological Report on the Christiana Area*, Kingston, 1969, pp. 22-3; C. L. R. James, 'The West Indian middle classes', in his *Spheres of Existence*, London, 1980; E. F. Frazier, *Black Bourgeoisie*, New York, 1957), However, it would be a mistake to assume that the white bias is merely an expression of the Caribbean *petit bourgeois*. The coloured and black middle classes are most affected by it, but the working class and even the peasantry do not go unscathed.

22 It can hardly be over-emphasised the extent to which resistance was mounted by Africans in the Americas to their enslavement. The literature on the subject is a vast and growing one. Eugene Genovese has a detailed bibliographical essay in *From Rebellion to Revolution: Afro-American Slave Revolts in the Making of the New World*, Baton Rouge, 1979. But special mention ought to be made of the following texts: C. L. R. James, *The Black Jacobins*, 2nd edition, New York, 1963; R. Price, (ed.), *Maroon Societies: Rebel Slave Communities in the Americas*, Baltimore, 1979; R. Bastide, *African Civilisations in the New World*, London, 1971, and *The African Religions of Brazil*, Baltimore, 1978; M. Craton, *Testing the Chains: Resistance to Slavery in the British West Indies*, New York, 1982; Hilary Beckles, *Black Rebellion in Barbados: The Struggle Against Slavery 1627-1838*, Bridgetown, 1984; and on women and slave resistance, Lucille Mathurin, 'The arrivals of black women', *Jamaica Journal*, vol. 9, nos. 2 and 3 Feb., 1975, and *The Rebel Woman in the British West Indies During Slavery*, Kingston, 1975; Barbara Rush, 'Defiance or submission? The role of the slave woman in slave resistance in the British Caribbean', *Immigrants and Minorities*, vol. 1, no. 1, March, 1982; and E. Brathwaite, *Wars of Respect: Nanny, Sam Sharpe and the Struggle for People's Liberation*, Kingston, 1977.

23 The distribution of migrants from the various territories during the early years of migration have been estimated to have been as follows. Jamaica, 1953-61: 148,369 Barbados, 1955-61: 18,741. Trinidad and Tobago, 1955-61: 9,610. British Guiana, 1955-61: 7,141. Antigua, 1955-61: 4,687. Montserrat, 1955-61: 3,835. St Kitts-Nevis-Anguilla, 1955-61: 7,503. Dominica, 1955-61: 7,915. Grenada, 1955-61: 7,663. St Lucia, 1955-61: 7,291. St Vincent, 1955-61: 4,285. See C. Peach, *West Indian Migration to Britain*, London, 1968, pp. 106-7.

24 K. Ramchand, 'The colour problem at the university: a West Indian's changing attitudes', in H. Tajfel and J. Dawson (eds), *Disappointed Guests: Essays by African, Asian and West Indian Students*, London, 1965, p. 28.

25 A. M. Gomes, 'I am an Immigrant' in A. Salkey (ed.), *Caribbean*

Essays, London, 1973, p. 53. Cf. P. Madoo, 'The transition from "light skinned" to "coloured" ' in Tajfel and Dawson (eds.), *op. cit.*
26 P. Madoo, op. cit., pp. 61-2.
27 D. Pearson, 'West Indian communal associations in Britain: some observations', *New Community*, vol. V, no. 4, Spring-Summer, 1977, and *Race, Class and Political Activism: A Study of West Indians in Britain*, Farnborough, 1981.
28 It is not without significance that it was a woman in Montserrat – and not one in London – who had never clapped eyes upon a Jamaican but still advised against her daughter marrying a Jamaican and having anything to do with Jamaicans as they are 'the wickedest people on earth': cited in S. Philpott, 'The Montserratians: migration dependency and the maintenance of island ties in England', in J. Watson (ed.), *Between Two Cultures: Migrants and Minorities in Britain*, Oxford, 1977, p. 110. There are some first-generation Caribbeans who still hold frankly idiotic ideas about people from islands apart from their own; a Jamaican in Leicester got on perfectly well with his Kittian neighbour but completely ostracised the latter once he discovered that he was a 'small islander'. But the prize for 'island chauvinism' must go to the Guyanese (Guyana of course is an enclave, not an island strictly speaking) man in Brixton who said in the early 1970s: 'We Guyanese are like the English, the Jamaicans are terrible people, just peasants really. They are not good stock . . . There are too many Jamaicans in Brixton, that's why the area is full of thieves and boys who don't work – you see their island is next to Cuba' (cited in S. Benson, *Ambiguous Ethnicity: Inter-racial Families in London*, Cambridge, 1981, p. 98). Although published in 1981, the fieldwork upon which Benson's study is based was carried out in Brixton between February 1970 and September 1971. It is my contention that the point in time that such sentiments are expressed is of some significance; the closer we move to the present, the more unlikely it is that we will hear such blatant expressions of island chauvinism.
29 For the qualified exceptions of Barbados and Grenada, see F. Henriques and J. Manyoni, 'Ethnic group relations in Barbados and Grenada', in UNESCO, *Race and Class in Post-Colonial Society: A Study of Ethnic Group Relations in the English-Speaking Caribbean, Bolivia, Chile and Mexico*, UNESCO, Paris, 1977.
30 Cited in D. Hinds, *Journey to an Illusion: The West Indian in Britain*, London, 1966, pp. 11-12.
31 Hinds, *op. cit.*, p. 15. Cf. S. Patterson, *Dark Strangers: A Study of West Indians in London*, Penguin, Harmondsworth, 1965, p. 15.
32 G. Lamming, *The Pleasures of Exile*, London, 1984, pp. 25-7.
33 N. Foner, *Jamaica Farewell: Jamaican Migrants in London*, London, 1979, p. 51. Cf. R. Sherwood, *The Psycho-dynamics of Race: Vicious and Benign Spirals*, Brighton, 1980, pp. 318-19 and P. Schweitzer (ed.), *A Place to Stay: Memories of Pensioners from Many Lands*, London, 1984, p. 30.
34 As Fanon recognised: 'It is the white man who creates the Negro. But it is the Negro who creates négritude.' And as the originator of the

concept, Aimé Césaire has explained the adoption of the concept *négritude* was a conscious act of defiance, not a term haphazardly or fortuitously chosen. As for its root-word, *nègre*, Césaire tells us: 'Since there was shame about the word *nègre*, we chose the word *nègre*.' See Fanon's *A Dying Colonialism*, New York, 1965, p. 47, and Césaire's interview with René Depestre in the former's *Discourse on Colonialism*, New York, 1972, pp. 73-4. Césaire's prime work of African celebration of awareness is of course, *Return to My Native Land*, London 1969. Cf. Jean-Paul Sartre, *Black Orpheus*, Paris, 1976: an exceptional analysis of negritude and an authentic expression of Sartre's anti-imperialism and solidarity with the oppressed. This essay was to have a profound influence upon the young Franz Fanon.

35 N. Foner, *Jamaica Farewell: Jamaican Migrants in London*, London, 1979, pp. 117 and 143 (emphasis in original). A St Lucien man concluded: 'I think people lose respect for us when we let them think we want to be black Englishmen. We are going to be reckoned with the black heads of this world, when they are being counted. We must see ourselves in this context' (D. Hinds, *Journey to an Illusion: the West Indian in Britain*, London, 1966, pp. 16-17). Cf. P. Schweitzer (ed.), *A Place to Stay: Memories of Pensioners from Many Lands*, London, 1984, p. 32.

36 Indeed, Foner points out: 'Respondents generally used the term "black", "colored", "West Indian", and "Jamaican" interchangeably (many times in the same sentence) when speaking, both informally and in answer to direct questions, about their position in English society. This was so even though the interview questions always used the category Jamaican': N. Foner, *Jamaica Farewell: Jamaican Migrants in London*, London, 1979, p. 144.

37 Foner, *op. cit.*, pp. 134-5.

38 See Office of Population Censuses and Surveys (OPCS), *Labour Force Survey, 1981*, HMSO, London, 1982, Table 4.25, p. 22. Cf. C. Brown, *Black and White Britain: The Third PSI Survey*, London, 1984, Tables 79 (p. 185), 91 and 92 (pp. 197-8), 95 (p. 201), 120 and 121 (pp. 223-4).

39 It must be said that this state of affairs is less a positive credit to Britain than a major indictment of the nation states of the Commonwealth Caribbean – many of which are unviable as economic entities – which Britain has plundered and disfigured over the centuries, and their mimetic indigenous ruling classes who, though nominally presiding over independent states, have kept intact the fundamental pillars of the social structure erected under colonialism.

40 Cited in T. Cottle, *Black Testimony: The Voices of Britain's West Indians*, London, 1978, p. 16.

41 N. Foner, 'The meaning of education to Jamaicans at home and in London', *New Community*, vol. IV, no. 2, Summer, 1975.

42 For a good index of this new mood among the older generation of Afro-Caribbeans in Britain, see the views expressed *in their own words* in the otherwise astonishing, insensitive and downright mocking

articles by David Selbourne, 'The new black exodus: blacks who have their eyes set on home' and 'I'm getting out before it fall on me', in *New Society*, 19 May 1983 and 23 May 1983. It should be noted that the return migration of Caribbeans to the islands is by no means a new phenomenon. On the experience of the early returnees see Betty Davidson, 'No place back home,' *Race*, vol. IX, no. 4, 1968 and H. Orlando Patterson, 'West Indian migrants returning home', *Race*, vol. X, no. 1, 1968.

43 From personal observation there seems to be a *prima facie* correspondence between the frequency of visits to the Caribbean and conceptions of the Caribbean as home: those who visit their country of origin more frequently are those who have drifted most from the utopian view of the Caribbean as home, whilst those who have not visited the Caribbean at all or visit it less frequently – precisely because their ideas of home have not been interrupted by the concrete spectacle of their native land – keep intact more successfully the romantic ideas of home which, it should be remembered, do help to sustain them in the harsh social environment of Britain. For analyses of recent events in the country from which the vast majority of Caribbean migrants derive, Jamaica, see W. James, 'The decline and fall of Michael Manley: Jamaica 1972-80', *Capital and Class*, no. 19, Spring, 1983 and 'The IMF and "democratic socialism" in Jamaica', in Latin America Bureau (ed.), *The Poverty Brokers: The IMF and Latin America*, London, 1983.

44 Edward Brathwaite, himself an Afro-Caribbean poet and historian of distinction, has not inaccurately summarised the position of the Caribbean writer as being that of an 'eccentric at home and an exile abroad'. But this sense of homelessness is by no means exclusive to the intellectuals of the Caribbean. It equally applies, quite often, to ordinary working-class Caribbean people returning 'home'. (Brathwaite is cited in Gordon Rohler, *Pathfinder: Black Awakening in the Arrivants of Edward Kamau Brathwaite*, Tunapura, Trinidad, 1981, p. 6.)

45 Cf. P. Schweitzer (ed.), *A Place to Stay: Memories of Pensioners from Many Lands*, London, 1984, p. 30. British migration statistics are notoriously inadequate in terms of precise magnitudes, but the fact that a *net overflow* of 2,800 to the Caribbean was recorded for 1982, the highest single figure for over a decade, is not insignificant and implausible. It seems equally plausible that a reversal in the trend had occurred in 1983, when a net figure of 3,000 Caribbean migrants entering Britain was recorded. The first figure seems to reflect the exceptionally strong mood for returning which existed among Caribbean migrants in the early 1980s as the economic crisis in Britain deepened, and the second seems to reflect the crisis in the economies of the Caribbean, when many who could return to Britain took the opportunity to do so. As a Jamaican community worker informed the writer, 'all those who can come back are doing so'. For the figures see Office of Population, Censuses and Surveys (OPCS), *International Migration: Migrants Entering and Leaving the United Kingdom and England*

and Wales, 1982 (Series MN No. 9), HMSO, London, 1984, Table 2.3, p. 6 and OPCS Monitor, *International Migration, 1983*, HMSO, London, 1984, Table 3. For a discussion of the shortcomings of the statistics see Runnymede Trust and the Radical Statistics Race Group, *Britain's Black Population*, London, 1980, pp. 120-9; C. Peach, 'Ins and outs of Home Office and IPS migration data', *New Community*, vol. IX, no. 1, 1981 and the ensuing debate between Peach and Jones: P. Jones, 'Ins and outs of Home Office and IPS migration data: a reply', *New Community*, vol. IX, no. 2, 1981 and C. Peach, 'Straining at gnats and swallowing camels', *New Community*, vol. IX, no. 2, 1981.

46 B. Troyna, 'Differential commitment to ethnic identity by black youths in Britain', *New Community*, vol. VII, no. 3, Winter, 1979.

47 Caribbean Teachers' Association (ed.), *Black Youth Speak Out* (report of the CTA Youth Conference, 1984), London, 1984, p. 42, emphasis in original.

48 The inverted commas are used advisedly here as the Rastafarians are so ramified in their views of the world that it is a gross mistake to speak of *a* Rastafarian ideology in the singular; and it is risky to speak of *a* or *the* Rastafarian movement. By far the best analysis of the early Rastafarians is Ken Post, 'The Bible as ideology: Ethiopianism in Jamaica, 1930-38', in C. H. Allen and R. W. Johnson (eds.), *African Perspectives*, London, 1970, which is also developed at much greater length in his majestic trilogy on Jamaica, *Arise Ye Starvelings: The Jamaican Labour Rebellion of 1938 and its Aftermath*, The Hague, 1978, and *Strike the Iron* (2 vols), New Jersey and The Hague, 1981. Post has amplified and revised some of his earlier ideas in his paper 'Class, race and culture in the Caribbean: some speculations on theory', mimeo, 1984. The fine, but unfortunately little known, essay by Robert Hill, 'Leonard P. Howell and millenarian visions in early Rastafari', *Jamaica Journal* (quarterly of the Institute of Jamaica), vol. 16, no. 1, Feb. 1983, is also essential reading for an understanding of the genesis of Rastafarianism. The seminal work of M. G. Smith *et al.*, *The Report on the Ras Tafari in Kingston*, Kingston, 1960 and Rex Nettleford's, *Mirror, Mirror: Race, Identity and Protest in Jamaica*, Kingston, 1970, are indispensable. Joseph Owen's *Dread: The Rastafarians of Jamaica*, Kingston, 1976, though somewhat overly romantic, is by far the best analysis of the Rastafarians in contemporary Jamaica. See also the special issue of *Caribbean Quarterly*, vol. 26, no. 4, December, 1980, which is entirely devoted to essays on Ras Tafari.

49 See *Riots and Rumours of Riots*, a filmed documentary directed by Imruh Caesar, and *From You Were Black You Were Out*, another directed by Colin Prescod. Also see A. Sivanandan, *A Different Hunger*, London, 1983. Cecil Gutzmore's research into the experience and struggles of black people in Notting Hill in the early years of settlement will fill an important gap in the literature and dispel much of the ignorance: 'Carnival, the state and the black masses in the UK', *Black Liberator*, Dec., 1978.

50 See V. S. Naipaul, *The Middle Passage*, London, 1969, pp. 10f.

51 The video *Motherland* (1983), is directed by Elyse Dodgson and is available from Inner London Education Authority Learning Resources Branch.
52 Some years ago at least, similar, but less intense contradictions existed between Africans and Afro-Caribbeans in Britain (for some examples see S. Benson, *Ambiguous Ethnicity: Inter-racial Families in Britain*, Cambridge University Press, 1981, pp. 40, 97-9). However, the largely identical nature of racism which they faced in their everyday life, the disproportionately large role which continental Africans played in the Black Power movement in Britain in the late 1960s (cf. Obi Egbuna, *Destroy This Temple: The Voice of Black Power in Britain*, London, 1971) and the spectacular rise of pan-Africanist ideas via Ras Tafari in the mid-1970s in Britain, all helped to defuse tension.
53 D. Lowentha, 'West Indian emigrants overseas', in C. Clarke (ed.), *Caribbean Social Relations*, Centre for Latin-American Studies, University of Liverpool, monograph no. 8, 1978, p. 89; G. Lewis, *Slavery, Imperialism and Freedom*, New York, 1978, pp. 336-7; P. Ratcliffe, *Racism and Reaction: A Profile of Handsworth*, London, 1981, pp. 294, 303; R. Sherwood, *The Psycho-dynamics of Race: Vicious and Benign Spirals*, Brighton, 1980, pp. 222-3, 327-8.
54 D. Lawrence, *Black Migrants: White Natives*, Cambridge University Press, 1974, p. 156.
55 *Ibid*.
56 *Ibid*, emphasis added.
57 P. Harrison, *Inside the Inner City*, Penguin, Harmondsworth, 1983, p. 381.
58 In the Caribbean new migrants, Indians and others, quite quickly adopted the stereotype established by the dominant European culture of the African. The Africans in their turn saw the Indians largely through the spectacle of the hegemonic European stereotype. Cf. D. Lowenthal, *West Indian Societies*, London, 1972, pp. 156ff, and L. Braithwaite, *Social Stratification in Trinidad*, Kingston, 1975, pp. 44ff.
59 In the case of the British colonies in the Caribbean this epoch finally ended between 1834 and 1838.
60 H. Tinker, *A New System of Slavery: The Export of Indian Labour Overseas 1830-1920*, London, 1974, K. Laurence, *Immigration into the West Indies in the Nineteenth Century*, Aylesbury, 1971; J. La Guerre (ed.), *Calcutta to Caroni: The East Indians of Trinidad*, Port of Spain, 1974; and W. Rodney, *A History of the Guyanese Working People, 1881-1905*, London, 1981. The numbers of Indian indentured labourers brought into the Caribbean were as follows: British Guiana, 238,909; Trinidad, 143,939; Jamaica, 36,412; Martinique, 25,519; Guadeloupe, 45,000; Surinam, 34,304; Windward Islands, 10,026. Source: K. Laurence, *op. cit.*, p. 57.
61 By far the most thorough case study of these strategies of divide and rule in the Caribbean in relation to Africans and Asians is to be found in W. Rodney's posthumously published *A History of the Guyanese Working People, 1881-1905*, London, 1981, pp. 174ff.

62 This point is dealt with at length in W. James, 'The myth of the "black community" ', in W. James and C. Gutzmore (eds), *Inside Babylon: Caribbean People and Their Descendants in Britain*, Pluto Press, London, forthcoming.
63 For some recent indications of the differences in priorities of these two groups, see the survey results cited in M. Fitzgerald, *Political Parties and Black People*, London, 1984, p. 57. C. Brown, *Black and White Britain: The Third PSI Survey*, London, 1984, brings out a number of these differences on a whole range of issues: see especially tables 116-19 and 135-8.
64 For further elaboration see W. James, 'The myth of the "black community" ', in W. James and C. Gutzmore (eds), *Inside Babylon: Caribbean People and Their Descendants in Britain*, London, forthcoming.

17
The idea of sexual minorities

JEFFREY WEEKS

Social regulation provides the conditions within which those defined can begin to develop their own consciousness and identity. In the nineteenth century, law and science, social *mores* and popular prejudice established the limits, but homosexual people responded. In so doing they created, in a variety of ways, self-concepts, meeting places, a language and style, and complex and varied modes of life. Michel Foucault has described this process in the following way:

> There is no question that the appearance in nineteenth century psychiatry, jurisprudence, and literature of a whole series of discourses on the species and subspecies of homosexuality, inversion, pederasty, and 'psychic hermaphrodism' made possible a strong advance of social controls into this area of 'perversity', but it also made possible the formation of a 'reverse' discourse: homosexuality began to speak on its own behalf, to demand that its legitimacy or 'naturality' be acknowledged, often in the same vocabulary, using the same categories by which it was radically disqualified.[1]

But this 'reverse discourse' was by no means a simple or chronologically even process. It is difficult to fit homosexual behaviour into any preconceived mould; on the contrary, it pervades various aspects of social experience and, as the recent work from the Kinsey Institute of Sex Research has indicated, despite the plethora of definitions and social regulations there is not a single homosexuality but, on the contrary 'homosexualities': 'There is no such thing as *the* homosexual (or *the* heterosexual, for that matter) and [that] statements of any kind which are made about human beings on the basis of their sexual orientation must always be highly qualified.'[2]

It is the social categorisation which attempts to create the notion of uniformity, with always varying effects. The very unevenness of the social categorisation, the variations in legal and other social responses, meant that homosexual experiences could be absorbed into a variety of different lifestyles, with no necessary identity as a 'homosexual' developing. The casual encounter, for instance, perhaps in the context of wider sexual experiences, rarely touches the self-concept. It can easily be dismissed as a drunken aberration or a passing phase or even the deliberate attempt to explore a new experience. A classic example of this is provided by the author of *My Secret Life*, who experimented with homosexuality after years of compulsive sex with all manner of women. There is no suggestion that his own basic self-concept was in any way disturbed. 'Have all men had the same letches which late in life have enraptured me?' he asked.[3] The implication was that homosexuality was not something that was solely the prerogative of any particular type of being.

A second type of homosexual involvement which avoids all the problems of commitment and identity was the highly individualised, deeply emotional and possibly even sexualised relations between two individuals who were otherwise not regarded, or did not regard themselves, as 'homosexual'. It was widely accepted in Victorian society that strong and indeed often emotional relationships between men were normal. W. T. Stead was appalled at the consequences of the Wilde trial, precisely because, he argued, a greater publicity concerning homosexuality would make such relationships more difficult. He wrote to Edward Carpenter: 'A few more cases like Oscar Wilde's and we should find the freedom of comradeship now possible to men seriously impaired to the permanent detriment of the race.'[4] But while male friendship became more suspect with a greater public discussion upon homosexuality, no one questioned the legitimacy of strong emotional relationships between women, and indeed highly personalised relationships, with a negligible development of lesbian self-concepts, probably remained the most common form of female homosexual relationships until very recently.

A third type of homosexual behaviour can best be described as 'situational': activities which were often regarded as legitimate, or at least acceptable, in certain circumstances, without affecting self-concepts. Classic examples of this were provided by the prevalent schoolboy homosexuality in public schools which became a matter of major concern for a number of social-purity advocates from the 1880s onwards. By the mid-nineteenth century, indeed, homosexuality seems to have been institutionalised in some of the major schools. J. A. Symonds described his horror at the situation in

Harrow, where every boy of good looks had a female name and was either a 'prostitute' or a 'boy's bitch'. A little later Goldsworthy Lowes Dickinson described Charterhouse as a 'hothouse of vice'. Other examples of such situational homosexuality occurred then, as now, in the army, the navy and prison, each giving rise to specific rituals and taboos. The Brigade of Guards was notorious for its involvement in male prostitution from the eighteenth century, and as one practitioner put it, 'as soon as (or before) I had learnt the goose step, I had learnt to be goosed'.[5] Such situational homosexuality possibly revealed more clearly than anything else a constant homosexual potential which could be expressed when circumstances and the collapse of social restraints indicated; but for that reason demanded elaborate strategies of evasion to avoid entering into a stigmatised identity.

The absorption of the various types of homosexual experiences into 'a total way of life' was more problematical. The notion that 'a homosexual', whether male or female, could live a life fully organised around his or her sexual orientation is consequently of a very recent origin. Even the most famous homosexual of the nineteenth century, Oscar Wilde, who appears to have participated in a wide range of homosexual subcultural activities, was respectably married with an upper-middle-class family life, and indeed in many ways the only difference between him and many others of his social status was that his casual sexual encounters were with working-class youths rather than young women. The experiences of Sir Roger Casement, the Irish patriot, who was executed for treason in 1916, are perhaps even more typical. His diaries record various homosexual encounters in Africa, South America, as well as in London and Dublin. He records the sexual liaisons, all of which appear to have been casual, with great pleasure, noting the size of the organs of his pick-ups as well as their cost in his financial accountancy. But there is no sense, in his diary, of his seeing the possibility of a full homosexual lifestyle. On the contrary, his lifestyle was that common to his class and public career, on the surface at least. His homosexuality was a matter of secrecy and furtiveness even though in the colonial offshoots as well as in the streets of London, Casement had no difficulty in meeting sexual partners.[6]

Homosexuality has existed in various types of societies, but it is only in some cultures that it becomes organised into distinctive subcultures, and only in contemporary cultures that these became public. Homosexual behaviour in the Middle Ages and after was no doubt recurrent, but only in certain closed communities was it ever probably institutionalised: in some monasteries and nunneries, as many of the medieval penitentiaries suggest; in some of the chivalric orders; in the courts of certain monarchs, such as James I and William III; and in and around the theatrical profession, and such-like fringe cultural activities. Other homosexual contacts are likely to have been casual, fleeting and undefined. The development of wider, more open subcultures was probably of a comparatively recent origin. Though in Italy and France there is evidence for some sort of male homosexual subculture in the towns in the fourteenth and fifteenth centuries, in Britain there was no obvious public subculture, bringing together various social strata, until the late seventeenth century. Certainly by the early 1700s there were signs of a distinctive network of overlapping homosexual subcultures in London associated with open spaces, pederastic brothels, and latrines. From the eighteenth century these were known as 'markets', reflecting in part the current heterosexual usage, as in the term 'marriage market'.[7] But it does underline what seems to have been characteristic of these subcultural formations well into the twentieth century: their organisation around forms of prostitution, the exchange of money and services between unequals, rather than peer partnerships. It seems quite likely that the only frequent or regular participants in these subcultures were the relatively few 'professionals'. The evidence of the trials from the eighteenth century suggests that a wide variety of men from all sorts of social classes participated in the subculture, but very few organised their lives around them. The most distinctive aspects of these small subcultures were the stereotyped 'effeminacy' and transvestism often associated with them, a mode which still characterises the relatively undeveloped subcultures of areas outside the major cities of Western Europe and North America. In the nineteenth century J. A. Symonds described the homosexual stereotype: 'lusts written on his face . . . pale, languid, scented, effeminate, oblique in expression'. This imagery was reinforced by the words used for homosexuals: 'molly', 'marjorie', 'maryanne', characteristic terms of abuse for generations.[8]

The Boulton and Park scandal in 1871 revealed to a startled and agog public a group of people whose transvestism became a way of life for them, socially justified in terms of the participants' involvement in 'theatricals'. In the case of Ernest Boulton, his parents had known and accepted his transvestism from a very early age. The notion that a homosexual lifestyle necessarily involved elements of cross-gender behaviour, of effeminacy, persisted well into the twentieth century and the humour known as 'camp' partook of its ambiguity precisely because of this. Camp was not just a vehicle of communication between peers, but a way of presenting oneself to the 'straight' world. It was deeply ambivalent because it celebrated effeminacy while retaining a sharp awareness of conventional values. It could become a form of 'minstrelisation', an ambiguous playing to the galleries, the homosexual variant of the negro stereotype in the films and plays of the 1930s to 1950s; but in other ways it provided a subcultural language within which the elements of identity could cohere.

The concern with how to behave in public was a characteristic of another form of the homosexual subculture, a specific homosexual slang known as 'palare'. Derived from theatrical circus slang, it was language for evaluating appearances and mannerisms and in which to gossip. It was not so much concerned with sex, what people did in bed, as with how to behave in public. By the end of the nineteenth century there was a widespread and often international homosexual argot suggesting a widely dispersed and organised subculture, at least for men.[9]

But the most common form of homosexual social intercourse was not so much subcultural as 'coterie' orientated. There is abundant evidence for the existence of networks of homosexual friendships, which sometimes acted as mutually supportive picking-up networks. The circle of which Oscar Wilde was part, around Charles Taylor, was a good example of this – and not surprisingly it soon encountered legal attention.[10]

By the latter decades of the nineteenth century we can see the emergence of groups of people with a much more clearly-defined sense of a homosexual identity. From the 1860s the poet and critic John Addington Symonds was attempting to grapple with the new theories on inversion which were appearing in Europe. His essay *A Problem in Greek Ethics*, privately printed in 1883, examined homosexuality as a valid lifestyle in Ancient Greece and this emphasis on the Greek ideal, despite its transparent anachronisms, was a very important one for self-identified homosexuals into the twentieth century. His essay *A Problem in Modern Ethics*, privately published in 1891, was a synthesis of recent views and a plea for law reform. With Havelock Ellis, he began the preparation for the first comprehensive British study of the subject, *Sexual Inversion*, which appeared after his death, and after his family had withdrawn their consent, under Ellis's name alone. Although married, with children, there is no doubt that J. A. Symonds was striving to articulate a way of life quite distinct from those which had gone before. Edward Carpenter and his circle of socialists and libertarians provide another example of the development of a distinctive homosexual identity, in his case associated with politico-social commitment. From the 1890s he lived a relatively open homosexual life with his partner, George Merrill.[11] Oscar Wilde and his circle also constitute an example of a social network where a sense of a homosexual way of life was developing. Individuals from these interlocking circles, such as George Cecil Ives, later became important in the small-scale homosexual reform movements which began to develop in the early years of the twentieth century, and saw themselves very much as fighting for 'the Cause' against legal and moral repression.[12]

Most homosexual encounters were, however, casual, non-defining, less articulate and typically furtive. For many indeed the excitement and danger of this mode was an added incentive; Oscar Wilde's fascination for 'feasting with panthers' was only the most outrageously expressed. But for many others, participation in the homosexual world was accompanied by a deep shame and sense of guilt and anxiety as the moral and medical ideologies penetrated. The rather frenetic life of the better-off homosexual world might establish the norms, but they were by no means universal. The common element, pulling men of different classes together, was simply a desire for sexual contact and often there was little else. The use of the term 'trade' for any sort of sexual transaction, whether or not money was involved, indicates this graphically and it certainly seems to have been used in this sense by the mid-nineteenth century, as a vivid metaphor for the sexual barter. In such a world, particularly given the great disparities of wealth and position of participants, the cash nexus with all its class resonances pervaded all sorts of relationships. It is likely that there was a much more clearly defined homosexual sense of self-identity amongst men of the upper and middle classes and a greater possibility, through mobility and money, of frequent homosexual encounters, as could be seen in the career of Roger Casement, but also of many others. J. R. Ackerley and Tom Driberg in their memoirs during the mid-twentieth century record the type of possibilities that existed.[13] And despite the wide social range of the subculture, from pauper to peer, it was the sexual ideology of the male upper classes which seems to have dominated. One indication of this was a clearly observable and widely recognised upper-middle-class fascination with crossing the class divide, a fascination which indeed shows a direct continuity between male heterosexual *mores* and homosexual. The patterns for instance of the heterosexual narrator of *My Secret Life* are strikingly paralleled by the evidence for the behaviour of homosexual men of the same class.

J. A. Symonds might disapprove of some of his friends' compulsive chasing of working-class contacts, but it was undoubtedly a major component of the subculture, as the major scandals revealed to a delightedly shocked Victorian public. It was a world of promiscuity, particularly if you had the right contacts, and many sections of the working class were drawn in, often very casually, as the Post Office messenger boys in the Cleveland Street scandal of 1889–90 and the stable-lads, newspaper sellers, bookmaker's clerks in the Wilde trials vividly illustrate. One participant in the Cleveland Street brothel described how casually money and sex might overturn youthful scruples. The young Charles Ernest Thickbroom, aged 17, recounted how he was asked 'If I would go to bed with a man. I said "no". He said "you'll get four shillings for a time" and persuaded me.'[14] The moving across the class barrier, on the one hand the search for 'rough trade', and on the other the belief in the reconciling effect of sex across class lines, was an important and recurrent theme in the homosexual world. Lasting partnerships did of course develop, but in a world of relatively easy casual sex, in a society where open homosexuality was tabooed, promiscuity was a constant temptation, and this in turn reflected complex emotional patterns. One homosexual, who had many homosexual friends from the First World War onwards, found it difficult to have sex with his friends. He had a fascination with guardsmen, suffering, as he put it, from 'scarlet fever': 'I have never cared for trading with homosexuals . . . I have always wanted to trade with men . . . I don't say I never went with homosexuals because I did. But I would say that as a rule I wanted men'.[15] As this suggests, two factors closely interacted: the desire for a relationship across the class lines, a product largely of a feeling that sex could not be spontaneous or natural within the framework of one's own moralistic and respectable class; and a desire for a relationship with a 'real' man, a heterosexual. E. M. Forster wanted 'to love a strong young man of the lower classes and be loved by him'. J. R. Ackerley felt that 'the ideal friend . . . should have been an animal man. The perfect human male body always at one's service through the devotion of a faithful and uncritical beast.'[16]

There are very complex patterns recurring here which historians have largely ignored. What they underline again are the class differentiation of identities and attitudes. In writings on homosexuality of the late nineteenth century there was a widespread belief that the working class was relatively indifferent to homosexual behaviour, partly because they were 'closer to nature', and the two great swathes of male prostitution, with working-class youths in their teens, and with guardsmen, notorious from the eighteenth century throughout Europe for their easy prostitution, seemed to justify this belief. Havelock Ellis noted the almost 'primitive indifference' to homosexuality of the guardsmen. Or, as one regular customer observed, 'they were normal, they were working class, they were drilled to obedience'.[17] These class and gender interactions (working class = male = closeness to nature) were to play important roles in the homosexual world affecting, in particular, the rituals of prostitution.

Prostitution was an indispensable part of the male homosexual milieu, though, unlike female prostitution, no distinctive subculture of male prostitution seems to have developed in the nineteenth and early twentieth centuries. Jack Saul, a notorious 'professional Maryanne' in the 1880s and 1890s, observed that he 'did not know of many professional male sodomites',[18] and such evidence as exists confirms the picture of a basically casual prostitution, with participants beginning usually in their mid-teens and generally leaving the trade by their mid-twenties. And the routes out were numerous, from becoming a kept boy, either in a long-term relationship or in successive relationships, to a return to ordinary heterosexual and family life. At least two of the boys involved in the Cleveland Street affair, despite their early traumas, seem to have led successfully heterosexual lives and entirely to have lost contact with the world of homosexuality.[19] In most cases the decisive factors were likely to be the willingness of the participants to accept perilous self-concepts as homosexual and as prostitute.

The keynote of the homosexual world was ambivalence and ambiguity. It *was* possible to lead a successful homosexual life within the interstices of the wider society. Nor was the life entirely shaped by legal repression. Jack Saul in his deposition in 1889 was asked:

'Were you hunted out by the police?'

'No, they have never interfered. They have always been kind to me.'

'Do you mean they have deliberately shut their eyes to your infamous practices?'

'They have to shut their eyes to more than me.'[20]

Probably more important than the legal situation was the social stigma that attached to homosexual behaviour and that seems to have increased in the late nineteenth and early twentieth centuries. It is this which gives social significance to the development of the small-scale and secretive homosexual reform movement. One circle associated with the criminologist George Cecil Ives, the Order of Chaeronea, appears, on the evidence of his three-million-word diary, to have been active from the early 1890s in succouring homosexuals in trouble with the law. It developed an almost Masonic style and ritual, insisting on secrecy and loyalty, and developed international 'chapters'.[21] Many of the participants in this Order, men like Ives and Laurence Housman, were active in the British Society for the Study of Sex Psychology, founded on the eve of the First World War to campaign for general changes in attitudes towards sexuality. One of the major planks of the society was reform of the law relating to homosexuality, and in the 1920s this too became part of an international movement for sex reform.[22] It is characteristic of these movements that although they were generally founded and operated by homosexuals they were not ostensibly homosexual organisations, On the contrary, their ability to remain publicly respectable was an important part of what success they gained.

Despite the ambiguities, it is clear that by the end of the nineteenth century a recognisably 'modern' male homosexual identity was beginning to emerge, but it would be another generation before female homosexuality reached a correspondingly level of articulacy. The lesbian identity was much less clearly defined, and the lesbian subculture was minimal in comparison with the male, and even more overwhelmingly upper class or literary. Berlin and Paris might have had their meeting places by the turn of the century and there is clear evidence of coteries of literary lesbians such as those associated with the Paris salon of Natalie Clifford Barney.[23] A chronicler of homosexual life in the early part of this century mentions various lesbian meeting places, including the London Vapour Bath on ladies' day, and by the 1920s the better-off lesbians could meet in some of the new nightclubs. But it is striking that the best-recorded examples of a lesbian presence referred to the defiantly 'masculine appearance and manner' of the participant. The novelist Radclyffe Hall, for instance, became notorious for her masculine appearance. Only by asserting one's identity so vehemently, as Radclyffe Hall recognised, could you begin to be noticed and taken seriously.[24] But the numbers who could dress this way and could afford to defy conventional opinion were tiny and the lives of the vast majority of women with lesbian feelings were unknown, perhaps unknowable. Even the enthusiastic categorisers of early twentieth-century sexology stopped short of female homosexuality. In 1901 Krafft-Ebing noted that there were only fifty known case histories of lesbianism, and even in the early 1970s, two modern writers on homosexuality could note that 'the scientific literature on the lesbian is exceedingly sparse'.[25] Writers like Magnus Hirschfeld and Havelock Ellis whose scientific and polemical interest in the subject was genuine seem to have found it difficult to discover much information, or many lesbians whose case histories they could record.

No doubt the absence of any legal regulation of lesbian behaviour and a consequent absence of public pillorying and scandal was an influence in shaping the low social profile of female homosexuality, but the basic reason for the indifference towards lesbianism is probably more fundamental. It relates precisely to different social assumptions about the sexuality of men and women and in particular to dominant notions of female sexuality. Havelock Ellis, whose wife was lesbian, felt the need to stress that female homosexuals were often particuarly masculine, and in Radclyffe Hall's *The Well of Loneliness*, a major novel of lesbian love published in 1928, it is the 'masculine' woman in the story who is the true invert. Stephen, masculine in name and behaviour, is forced to endure the agonies of her nature, the biologically given essence, while the feminine Mary in the story is in the end able to opt for a heterosexual married life.

This concern with the masculinity of lesbians can only be explained in terms of the overwhelming weight of assumptions concerning female sexuality. As J. H. Gagnon and William Simon have put it, 'the patterns of overt sexual behaviour on the part of homosexual females tend to resemble those of heterosexual females and to differ radically from the sexual patterns of both heterosexual and homosexual males'.[26] Several intertwined elements determined attitudes to lesbianism, and the consequent possibilities for lesbian identity: the roles that society assigned women; the ideology which articulated, organised and regulated this; the dominant notions of female sexuality in the ideology; and the actual possibilities for the development by women of an autonomous sexuality. The prevailing definitions of female sexuality in terms of the 'maternal instinct', or as necessarily responsive to the stimulation of the male, were overwhelming barriers in attempts to conceptualise the subject. Ideology limited the possibility for even an attempt at a scientific definition of lesbianism. But even more important, the social position of most women militated against the easy emergence of a distinctive lesbian identity. It remained very difficult for respectable young ladies to be 'independent'. So it is likely that most women with lesbian inclinations fitted inconspicuously into the general world of women. There is as we have seen abundant evidence in eighteenth- and nineteenth-century diaries and letters that women as a matter of routine formed long-lived emotional ties with other women. Such relationships ranged from a close supportive love of sisters, through adolescent enthusiasms, to mature avowals of eternal affection. Many of the early writers on lesbianism spoke of the greater emphasis on cuddling, on physical warmth and comforting, of kissing and holding hands between female homosexuals, at the expense of exclusively sexual activity.

This was precisely the line of continuity between all women whatever their sexual orientation. Deep and passionate declarations of love recur without any obvious signs of sexual expression.[27] The conditions for a polarity between 'normal' female sexuality and 'abnormal' were almost non-existent and it is this which makes it presumptuous to attempt to explore female homosexuality in terms of categories derived from male experiences.

It is striking that it is amongst the new professional women of the 1920s that the articulation of any sort of recognisable lesbian identity became possible for the first time, and it was indeed in the 1920s that lesbianism became in any way an issue of public concern, following a series of sensational scandals. Towards the end of the First World War the criminal libel prosecution brought by the dancer Maude Allan against the right-wing member of Parliament, Noel Pemberton Billing, who accused her of being on a German list of sexual perverts, was a *cause celèbre* which brought lesbianism to the headlines. In 1921 there were attempts to bring lesbianism into the scope of the criminal law. During the 1910s and 1920s a series of novels, and even a film, portrayed lesbian experiences; and in 1928 came the most famous event of all, the banning and prosecution of Radclyffe Hall's lesbian novel, *The Well of Loneliness*. As Lord Birkett, who appeared for the publishers, later pointed out, the Chief Metropolitan Magistrate, Sir Chartres Biron, found against the novel largely because Radclyffe Hall 'had not stigmatised this relationship as being in any way blameworthy'.[28] Nevertheless, paradoxically, and in line with the impact of the Oscar Wilde trial, the prosecution gave unprecedented publicity to homosexuality. This perhaps is the outstanding feature of the case; the publicity it aroused did more than anything to negate the hopes of reticence expressed by Lords Desart and Birkenhead in 1921. Thousands of lesbian-inclined women wrote to Radclyffe Hall. She more than anyone else during this period gave lesbianism a name and an image. As a lesbian of a later generation put it, 'When . . . I read *The Well of Loneliness* it fell upon me like a revelation. I identified with every line. I wept floods of tears over it, and it confirmed my belief in my homosexuality.'[29]

In any study of homosexuality the important point to observe is that there is no automatic relationship between social categorisation and individual sense of identity. The meaning given to homosexual activities can vary enormously. They depend on a variety of factors: social class, geographical location, gender differentiation. But it is vital to keep in mind when exploring homosexuality, which has always been defined in our culture as a deviant form, that what matters is not the inherent nature of the act but the social construction of meanings around that activity, and the individual response to that. The striking feature of the 'history of homosexuality' over the past hundred years or so is that the oppressive definition and the defensive identities and structures have marched together. Control of sexual variations has inevitably reinforced and reshaped rather than repressed homosexual behaviour. In terms of individual anxiety, induced guilt and suffering, the cost of moral regulation has often been high. But the result has been a complex and socially significant history of resistance and self-definition which historians have hitherto all too easily ignored.

Notes

This chapter first appeared as part of a longer chapter, 'The construction of homosexuality', in my book *Sex, Politics and Society*, Longman, London, 1981, pp. 121.

1 Michel Foucault, *The History of Sexuality*, Allen Lane, London 1979 vol. 1, p. 101. There is now a growing corpus of work on the history of homosexual resistance and self-definition. For a general discussion see Vern. L. Bullough. 'Challenges to social attitudes towards homosexuality in the late nineteenth and early twentieth centuries', *Social Science Quarterly*, vol. 58, no. 1, June, 1977. On Britain, Jeffrey Weeks, *Coming out: Homosexual Politics in Britain from the Nineteenth Century to the Present*, Quartet, London, 1977 is the only full length book. On America, see Jonathan Katz, *Gay American History: Lesbians and Gay Men in the USA*, Thomas Cromwell Co., New York, 1976. On Germany, see John Lauritsen and David Thorstad, *The Early Homosexual Rights Movement*, Times Change Press, New York, 1974: and James D. Steakley, *The Homosexual Emancipation Movement in Germany*, Arno Press, New York, 1975.
2 Alan P. Bell and Martin S. Weinberg, *Homosexualities: A Study of Diversity among Men and Women*, Mitchell Beazley, London, 1978, p. 23.
3 'Walter', *My Secret Life*, Amsterdam, privately printed 1877, vol. 1, p. 14.
4 Stead to Edward Carpenter, Ms 386–54(1–2), June, 1895, Edward Carpenter collection, Sheffield City Library.
5 J. A. Symonds, *Memoirs*: unpublished manuscript in the London Library; Dennis Proctor (ed.), *The Autobiography of G. Lowes Dickinson*, Duckworth, London, 1973, p. 8; *The Sins of the Cities of the Plain: or the Recollections of a Mary-Ann*, London, privately published 1881, vol. 1, p. 84, (The ostensible memoirs of the male prostitute, Jack Saul).
6 See the Casement Diaries, Public Record Office.
7 Randolph Trumbach, 'London's sodomites: homosexual behaviour

and Western culture in the 18th century', *Journal of Social History*, Fall, 1977.
8 Quoted in Brian Reade, *Sexual Heretics: Male Homosexuality in English Literature from 1850–1900*, Routledge & Kegan Paul, London 1970, p. 251.
9 Mary McIntosh, 'Gayspeak', *Lunch*, no. 16, January, 1973; Joseph J. Hayes, 'Gayspeak', *Quarterly Journal of Speech*, vol. 62, October, 1976.
10 R. Croft-Cooke, *The Unrecorded Life of Oscar Wilde*, W. H. Allen, London, New York, 1972.
11 See Phyllis Grosskurth, *John Addington Symonds*, Longman, London, 1964; Jeffrey Weeks, *Coming Out: Homosexual Politics in Britain from the Nineteenth Century to the Present*, Quartet, London, 1977, Chapter 6.
12 On Ives, see Weeks, *op. cit.*, pp. 118ff.
13 J. R. Ackerley, *My Father and Myself*, The Bodley Head, London, 1968; Tom Driberg, *Ruling Passions*, Jonathan Cape, London, 1977; see also Christopher Isherwood, *Christopher and His Kind*, Eyre Methuen, London, 1977; Michael Davidson, *The World, the Flesh and Myself*, Mayflower-Dell, London, 1966.
14 Public Record Office; HO 144/X24427/1, copies of depositions.
15 In an interview with the author.
16 E. M. Forster, *The Life to Come and Other Stories*, Penguin, Harmondsworth, 1975, p. 16; J. R. Ackerley, *My Father and Myself*, Bodley Head, London, 1968, p. 218.
17 Havelock Ellis, *Studies in the Psychology of Sex* (4 vols), vol. 2, *Sexual Inversion*, Random House, New York, 1936, p. 9; J. R. Ackerley, *My Father and Myself*, Bodley Head, London, 1968, p. 135.
18 *The Sins of the Cities of the Plain: or the Recollections of a Mary-Ann*, London, privately published, 1881, vol. 2, p. 109. For general discussion of this topic see Jeffrey Weeks, 'Inverts, perverts and mary-annes: male prostitution and the regulation of homosexuality in England in the nineteenth and early twentieth centuries', *Journal of Homosexuality*, vol. 6, nos 1 and 2, 1981.
19 L. Chester, D. Leitch and C. Simpson, *The Cleveland Street Affair*, Weidenfeld & Nicolson, London, 1976, p. 225.
20 Public Record Office: DPP 1/95/4, File 2: Saul's deposition.
21 Jeffrey Weeks, *Coming Out: Homosexual Politics in Britain from the Nineteenth Century to the Present*, Quartet, London, 1977, pp. 122ff.
22 *Sex, Politics and Society*, Longman, London, 1981, pp. 184ff.
23 See George Wickes, *The Amazon of Letters; The Life of Natalie Barney*, W. H. Allen, London, 1977; Gayle Rubin, Introduction to Renee Vivian, *A Women Appeared to Me*, New York, 1976; Blanch Wiesen Cook, 'Women alone stir my imagination: lesbianism and the cultural tradition', *Signs: Journal of Women in Culture and Society*, vol. 4, no. 4, 1979; and 'The historical denial of lesbianism', *Radical History Review*, no. 20, Spring/Summer 1979. See also Jeffrey Weeks, *Coming Out: Homosexual Politics in Britain from the Nineteenth Century to the Present*, Quartet, London, 1977, Chapters 7–9.

24 Lovat Dickson, *Radclyffe Hall at the Well of Loneliness*, Collins, London, 1977.
25 J. H. Gagnon and W. Simon, *Sexual Conduct*, Hutchinson, London, 1973, p. 176, note 1.
26 *Ibid*.
27 Carroll Smith-Rosenberg, 'The female world of love and ritual: Relations between women in nineteenth century America', *Signs: Journal of Women in Culture and Society*, vol. 1, Autumn, 1975. See also Blanche Wiesen Cook, 'Female support networks and political activism: Lillian Wald, Crystal Eastman and Emma Goldman', *Chrysalis*, no. 3, Autumn, 1977; reprinted as a pamphlet by Out and Out Books 1979. For similar British references see Jeffrey Weeks, *Coming Out: Homosexual Politics in Britain from the Nineteenth Century to the Present*, Quartet, London, 1977, Chapter 7.
28 See Jeffrey Weeks, *op. cit.*, Chapter 9, and *Sex, Politics and Society*, Longman, London, 1981, pp. 217–18.
29 Quoted in Charlotte Wolff, *Love Between Women*, Duckworth, London, 1971.

18
London and Karachi

HANIF KUREISHI

London

I was born in London of an English mother and Pakistani father. My father, who lives in London, came to England from Bombay in 1947 to be educated by the old colonial power. He married here and never went back to India. The rest of his large family, his brothers, their wives, his sisters, moved from Bombay to Karachi, in Pakistan, after partition.

Frequently during my childhood I met my Pakistani uncles when they came to London on business. They were important, confident people who took me to hotels, restaurants and Test matches, often in taxis. But I had no idea of what the subcontinent was like or how my numerous uncles, aunts and cousins lived there. When I was nine or ten a teacher purposefully placed some pictures of Indian peasants in mud huts in front of me and said to the class: Hanif comes from India. I wondered: did my uncles ride on camels? Surely not in their suits? Did my cousins, so like me in other ways, squat down in the sand like little Mowglis, half-naked and eating with their fingers?

In the mid-1960s, Pakistanis were a risible subject in England, derided on television and exploited by politicians. They had the worst jobs, they were uncomfortable in England, some of them had difficulties with the language. They were despised and out of place.

From the start I tried to deny my Pakistani self. I was ashamed. It was a curse and I wanted to be rid of it. I wanted to be like everyone else. I read with understanding a story in a newspaper about a black boy who, when he noticed that burnt skin turned white, jumped into a bath of boiling water.

At school, one teacher always spoke to me in a 'Peter Sellers'

Indian accent. Another refused to call me by my name, calling me Pakistani Pete instead. So I refused to call the teacher by *his* name and used his nickname instead. This led to trouble; arguments, detentions, escapes from school over hedges, and eventually suspension. This played into my hands; this couldn't have been better.

With a friend I roamed the streets and fields all day; I sat beside streams; I stole yellow lurex trousers from a shop and smuggled them out of the house under my school trousers; I hid in woods reading hard books; and I saw the film *Zulu* several times.

This friend, who became Johnny in my film, *My Beautiful Laundrette*, came one day to the house. It was a shock.

He was dressed in jeans so tough they almost stood up by themselves. These were suspended above his boots by Union Jack braces of 'hangman's strength', revealing a stretch of milk bottle white leg. He seemed to have sprung up several inches because of his Doctor Marten's boots, which had steel caps and soles as thick as cheese sandwiches. His Ben Sherman shirt with a pleat down the back was essential. And his hair, which was only a quarter of an inch long all over, stuck out of his head like little nails. This unmoving creation he concentratedly touched up every hour with a sharpened steel comb that also served as a dagger.

He soon got the name Bog Brush, though this was not a moniker you would use to his face. Where before he was an angel-boy with a blond quiff flattened down by his mother's loving spit, a clean handkerchief always in his pocket, as well as being a keen cornet player for the Air Cadets, he'd now gained a brand-new truculent demeanour. My mother was so terrified by this stormtrooper dancing on her doorstep to the 'Skinhead Moonstomp', which he moaned to himself continuously, that she had to lie down.

I decided to go out roaming with BB before my father got home from work. But it wasn't the same as before. We couldn't have our talks without being interrupted. Bog Brush had become Someone. To his intense pleasure, similarly-dressed strangers greeted Bog Brush in the street as if they were in a war-torn foreign country and in the same army battalion. We were suddenly banned from cinemas. The Wimpy Bar in which we sat for hours with milkshakes wouldn't let us in. As a matter of pride we now had to go round the back and lob a brick at the rear window of the place.

Other strangers would spot us from the other side of the street. BB would yell 'Leg it!' as the enemy dashed through traffic and leapt over the bonnets of cars to get at us, screaming obscenities and chasing us up alleys, across allotments, around reservoirs, and on and on.

And then, in the evening, BB took me to meet with the other lads. We climbed the park railings and strolled across to the football pitch, by the goal posts. This is where the lads congregated to hunt down Pakistanis and beat them. Most of them I was at school with. The others I'd grown up with. I knew their parents. They knew my father.

I withdrew, from the park, from the lads, to a safer place, within myself. I moved into what I call my 'temporary' period. I was only waiting now to get away, to leave the London suburbs, to make another kind of life, somewhere else, with better people. In this isolation, in my bedroom where I listened to Pink Floyd, the Beatles and the John Peel Show, I started to write down the speeches of politicians, the words which helped create the neo-Nazi attitudes I saw around me. This I called 'keeping the accounts'.

In 1965 Enoch Powell said: 'We should not lose sight of the desirability of achieving a steady flow of voluntary repatriation for the elements which are proving unsuccessful or unassimilable.'

In 1967 Duncan Sandys said: 'The breeding of millions of half-caste children would merely produce a generation of misfits and create national tensions.'

Also in 1967, Enoch Powell – who once said he would love to have been Viceroy of India – quoted a constituent of his as saying that because of the Pakistanis 'this country will not be worth living in for our children'.

And Powell said, more famously: 'As I look ahead I am filled with foreboding. Like the Roman, "I seem to see the River Tiber foaming with much blood".'

As Powell's speeches appeared in the papers, graffiti in support of him appeared in the London streets. Racists gained confidence. People insulted me in the street. Someone in a café refused to eat at the same table with me. The parents of a girl I was in love with told her she'd get a bad reputation by going out with darkies. Parents of my friends, both lower-middle-class and working-class, often told me they were Powell supporters. Sometimes I heard them talking, heatedly, violently, about race, about 'the Pakis'. I was desperately embarrassed and afraid of being identified with these loathed aliens. I found it almost impossible to answer questions about where I came from. The word 'Pakistani' had been made into an insult. It was a word I didn't want used about myself. I couldn't tolerate being myself.

The British complained incessantly that the Pakistanis wouldn't assimilate. This meant they wanted the Pakistanis to be exactly like them. But of course even then they would have rejected them.

The British were doing the assimilating: they assimilated Pakistanis to their world view. They saw them as dirty, ignorant and less than human – worthy of abuse and violence.

At this time I found it difficult to get along with anyone. I was frightened and hostile. I suspected that my white friends were capable of racist insults. And many of them did taunt me, innocently. I reckoned that at least once every day since I was five years old I had been racially abused. I became incapable of distinguishing between remarks that were genuinely intended to hurt and those intended as 'humour'.

I became cold and distant. I began to feel I was very violent. But I didn't know how to be violent. If I had known, if that had come naturally to me, or if there'd been others I could follow, I would have made my constant fantasies of revenge into realities, I would have got into trouble, willingly hurt people, or set fire to things.

But I mooched around libraries. There, in an old copy of *Life* magazine, I found pictures of the Black Panthers. It was Eldridge Cleaver, Huey Newton, Bobby Seale and their confederates in black vests and slacks, with Jimi Hendrix haircuts. Some of them were holding guns, the Army .45 and the 12-gauge Magnum shotgun with 18-inch barrel that Huey specified for street fighting.

I tore down my pictures of the Rolling Stones and Cream and replaced them with the Panthers. I found it all exhilarating. These people were proud and they were fighting. To my knowledge, no one in England was fighting.

There was another, more important picture.

On the cover of the Penguin edition of *The Fire Next Time* was James Baldwin holding a child, his nephew. Baldwin, having suffered, having been there, was all anger and understanding. He was intelligence and love combined. As I planned my escape I read Baldwin all the time, I read Richard Wright and I admired Muhammad Ali.

A great moment occurred when I was in a sweet shop. I saw through to a TV in the backroom on which was showing the 1968 Olympic Games in Mexico. Thommie Smith and John Carlos were raising their fists on the victory rostrum, giving the Black Power salute as the 'Star Spangled Banner' played. The white shopkeeper was outraged. He said to me: they shouldn't mix politics and sport.

During this time there was always Muhammad Ali, the former Cassius Clay, a great sportsman become black spokesman. Now a Muslim, millions of fellow Muslims all over the world prayed for his victory when he fought.

And there was the Nation of Islam movement to which Ali belonged, led by the man who called himself the Messenger of Islam and wore a gold-embroidered fez, Elijah Muhammad.

Elijah was saying in the mid-1960s that the rule of the white devils would end in fifteen years. He preached separatism, separate development for black and white. He ran his organisation by charisma and threat, claiming that anyone who challenged him would be chastened by Allah. Apparently Allah also turned the minds of defectors into a turmoil.

Elijah's disciple Malcolm X, admirer of Gandhi and self-confirmed anti-Semite, accepted in prison that 'the key to a Muslim is submission, the attunement of one towards Allah'. That this glorious resistance to the white man, the dismissal of Christian meekness, was followed by submission to Allah and worse, to Elijah Muhammad, was difficult to take.

I saw racism as unreason and prejudice, ignorance and a failure of sense; it was Fanon's 'incomprehension'. That the men I wanted to admire had liberated themselves only to take to unreason, to the abdication of intelligence, was shocking to me. And the separatism, the total loathing of the white man as innately corrupt, the 'All whites are devils' view, was equally unacceptable. I had to live in England, in the suburbs of London, with whites. My mother was white. I wasn't ready for separate development. I'd had too much of that already.

I had no idea what an Islamic society would be like, what the application of the authoritarian theology Elijah preached would mean in practice. I forgot about it, fled the suburbs, went to university, got started as a writer and worked as an usher at the Royal Court Theatre. It was over ten years before I went to an Islamic country.

Karachi

The man had heard that I was interested in talking about his country, Pakistan, and that this was my first visit. He kindly kept trying to take me aside to talk. But I was already being talked to.

I was at another Karachi party, in a huge house, with a glass of whisky in one hand, and a paper plate in the other. Casually I'd mentioned to a woman friend of the family that I wasn't against marriage. Now this friend was earnestly recommending to me a young woman who wanted to move to Britain, with a husband.

To my discomfort this go-between was trying to fix a time for the three of us to meet and negotiate.

I went to three parties a week in Karachi. This time, when I could get away from this woman, I was with landowners, diplomats, businessmen and politicians: powerful people. This pleased me. They were people I wouldn't have been able to get to in England and I wanted to write about them.

They were drinking heavily. Every liberal in England knows you can be lashed for drinking in Pakistan. But as far as I could tell, none of this English-speaking international bourgeoisie would be lashed for anything. They all had their favourite trusted bootleggers who negotiated the potholes of Karachi at high speed on disintegrating motorcycles, with the hooch stashed on the back. Bad bootleggers passed a hot needle through the neck of your bottle and drew your whisky out. Stories were told of guests politely sipping ginger beer with their ice and soda, glancing at other guests to see if they were drunk and wondering if their own alcohol tolerance had miraculously increased.

I once walked into a host's bathroom to see the bath full of floating whisky bottles being soaked to remove the labels, a servant sitting on a stool serenely poking at them with a stick.

So it was all as tricky and expensive as buying cocaine in London, with the advantage that as the hooch market was so competitive, the 'leggers delivered video tapes at the same time, dashing into the room towards the TV with hot copies of *The Jewel in the Crown*, *The Far Pavilions*, and an especially popular programme called *Mind Your Language*, which represented Indians and Pakistanis as ludicrous caricatures.

Everyone, except the mass of the population, had videos. And I could see why, since Pakistan TV was so peculiar. On my first day I turned it on and a cricket match was taking place. I settled in my chair. But the English players, who were on tour in Pakistan, were leaving the pitch. In fact, Bob Willis and Ian Botham were running towards the dressing rooms surrounded by armed police and this wasn't because Botham had made derogatory remarks about Pakistan. (He said it was a country to which he'd like to send his mother-in-law.) In the background a section of the crowd was being tear-gassed. Then the screen went blank.

Stranger still, and more significant, was the fact that the news was now being read in Arabic, a language few people in Pakistan understood. Someone explained to me that this was because the Koran was in Arabic, but everyone else said it was because General Zia wanted to kiss the arses of the Arabs.

The man at the party, who was drunk, wanted to tell me something and kept pulling at me. The man was worried. But wasn't I worried too? I was trapped with this woman and the marriage proposal.

I was having a little identity crisis. I'd been greeted so warmly in Pakistan, I felt so excited by what I saw, and so at home with all my uncles, I wondered if I were not better off here than there. And when I said, with a little unnoticed irony, that I was an Englishman, people laughed. They fell about. Why would anyone with a brown face, Muslim name and large well-known family in Pakistan want to lay claim to that cold little decrepit island off Europe where you always had to spell your name? Strangely, anti-British remarks made me feel patriotic, though I only felt patriotic when I was away from England.

But I couldn't allow myself to feel too Pakistani. I didn't want to give in to that falsity, that sentimentality. As someone said to me at a party, provoked by the fact I was wearing jeans; we are Pakistanis, but you, you will always be a Paki – emphasising the slang derogatory name the English used against Pakistanis, and therefore the fact that I couldn't rightfully lay claim to either place.

In England I was a playwright. In Karachi this meant little. There were no theatres; the arts were discouraged by the state – music and dancing are un-Islamic – and ignored by practically everyone else. So despite everything I felt pretty out of place.

The automatic status I gained through my family obtained for me such acceptance, respect and luxury that for the first time I could understand the privileged and their penchant for marshalling ridiculous arguments to justify their delicious and untenable position as an élite. But as I wasn't a doctor, or businessman or military person, people suspected that this writing business I talked about was a complicated excuse for idleness, uselessness and general bumming around. In fact, as I proclaimed an interest in the entertainment business, and talked much and loudly about how integral the arts were to a society, moves were being made to set me up in the amusement arcade business, in Shepherd's Bush.

Finally the man got me on my own. His name was Rahman. He was a friend of my intellectual uncle. I had many uncles, but Rahman preferred the intellectual one who understood Rahman's particular sorrow and like him considered himself to be a marginal man.

In his fifties, a former Air Force officer, Rahman was liberal, well-travelled and married to an Englishwoman who now had a Pakistani accent.

He said to me: 'I tell you, this country is being sodomised by religion. It is even beginning to interfere with the making of money. And now we are embarked on this dynamic regression, you must know, it is obvious, Pakistan has become a leading country to go away from. Our patriots are abroad. We despise and envy them. For the rest of us, our class, your family, we are in Hobbes's state of nature: insecure, frightened. We cling together out of necessity.' He became optimistic. 'We could be like Japan, a tragic oriental country that is now progressive, industrialised.' He laughed and then said, ambiguously: 'But only God keeps this country together. You must say this around the world: we are taking a great leap backwards.'

The bitterest blow for Rahman was the dancing. He liked to waltz and foxtrot. But now the expression of physical joy, of sensuality and rhythm, was banned. On TV you could see where it had been censored. When couples in Western programmes got up to dance there'd be a jerk in the film, and they'd be sitting down again. For Rahman it was inexplicable, an unnecessary cruelty that was almost more arbitrary than anything else.

Thus the despair of Rahman and my uncles' 'high and dry' generation. Mostly educated in Britain, like Jinnah, the founder of Pakistan – who was a smoking, drinking, non-Urdu speaking lawyer and claimed that Pakistan would never be a theocracy ('that Britisher' he was sometimes called) – their intellectual mentors were Tawney, Shaw, Russell, Laski. For them the new Islamisation was the negation of their lives.

It was a lament I heard often. This was the story they told. Karachi was a goodish place in the 1960s and 1970s. Until about 1977 it was lively and vigorous. You could drink and dance in the Raj-style clubs (providing you were admitted) and the atmosphere was liberal – as long as you didn't meddle in politics, in which case you'd probably be imprisoned. Politically there was Bhutto: urbane, Oxford-educated, considering himself to be a poet and revolutionary, a veritable Chairman Mao of the sub-continent. He said he would fight obscurantism and illiteracy, ensure the equality of men and women, and increase access to education and medical care. The desert would bloom.

Later, in an attempt to save himself, appease the mullahs and rouse the dissatisfied masses behind him, he introduced various Koranic injunctions into the constitution and banned alcohol, gambling, horse-racing. The Islamisation had begun, and was fervently continued after his execution.

Islamisation built no hospitals, no schools, no houses; it cleaned no water and installed no electricity. But it was direction, identity. The country was to be in the hands of the divine, or rather, in the hands of those who elected themselves to interpret the single divine purpose. Under the tyranny of the priesthood, with the cooperation of the army, Pakistan would embody Islam in itself.

There would now be no distinction between ethical and religious obligation; there would now be no areas in which it was possible to be wrong. The only possible incertitude was of interpretation. The theory would be the written eternal and universal principles which Allah created and made obligatory for men; the model would be the first three generations of Muslims; and the practice would be Pakistan.

About twelve people lived permanently in my uncle's house, plus servants who slept in sheds at the back, just behind the chickens and dogs. Relatives sometimes came to stay for months. New bits had to be built on to the house. All day there were visitors; in the evenings crowds of people came over; they were welcome, and they ate and watched videos and talked for hours. People weren't so protective of their privacy as they were in London.

This made me think about the close-bonding within the families and about the intimacy and interference of an extended family and a more public way of life. Was the extended family worse than the little nuclear family because there were more people to dislike? Or better because relationships were less intense?

Strangely, bourgeois-bohemian life in London, in Notting Hill and Islington and Fulham, was far more formal. It was frozen dinner parties and the division of social life into the meeting of couples with other couples, to discuss the lives of other coupling couples. Months would pass, then this would happen again.

In Pakistan there was the continuity of the various families' knowledge of each other. People were easy to place; your grandparents and theirs were friends. When I went to the bank and showed the teller my passport, it turned out he knew several of my uncles, so I didn't receive the usual perfunctory treatment. This was how things worked.

I compared the collective hierarchy of the family and the permanence of my family's circle, with my feckless, rather rootless life in London, in what was called 'the inner city'. There I lived alone, and lacked any long connection with anything. I'd hardly known anyone for more than eight years, and certainly not their parents. People came and went. There was much false intimacy and forced friendship. People didn't take responsibility for each other.

Many of my friends lived alone in London, especially the women. They wanted to be independent and to enter into relationships – as many as they liked, with whom they liked – out of choice. They didn't merely want to reproduce the old patterns of living. The future was to be determined by choice and reason, not by custom. The notions of duty and obligation barely had positive meaning for my friends; they were loaded, Victorian words, redolent of constraint and grandfather clocks, the antithesis of generosity in love, the new hugging, and the transcendence of the family. The ideal of the new relationship was no longer the S and M of the old marriage – it was F and C, freedom plus commitment.

The family scrutiny and criticism were difficult to take, as was all the bitching and gossip. But there was warmth and continuity for a large number of people; there was security and much love. Also there was a sense of duty and community – of people's lives genuinely being lived together, whether they liked each other or not – that you didn't get in London. There, those who'd eschewed the family hadn't succeeded in creating some other form of supportive common life. In Pakistan there was that supportive common life, but at the expense of movement and change.

In a flat high above Karachi, an eighteen-year-old kid strung-out on heroin danced cheerfully around the room in front of me and pointed to an erection in the front of his trousers, which he referred to as his Imran Khan, the name of the handsome Pakistan cricket captain. More and more of the so-called multinational kids were taking heroin now. My friends who owned the flat, journalists on a weekly paper, were embarrassed.

But they always had dope to offer their friends. These laid-back people were mostly professionals: lawyers, an inspector in the police who smoked what he confiscated, a newspaper magnate, and various other journalists. Heaven it was to smoke at midnight on the beach, as local fishermen, squatting respectfully behind you, fixed fat joints; and the 'erotic politicians' themselves, the Doors, played from a portable stereo while the Arabian Sea rolled on to the beach. Oddly, since heroin and dope were both indigenous to the country, it took the West to make them popular in the East.

In so far as colonisers and colonised engage in a relationship, with the latter aspiring to be like the former, you wouldn't catch anyone of my uncle's generation with a joint in their mouth. It was *infra dig* – for the peasants. Shadowing the British, they drank whisky and read *The Times*; they praised others by calling them 'gentlemen'; and their eyes filled with tears at old Vera Lynn records.

But the kids discussed yoga exercises. You'd catch them standing on their heads. They even meditated. Though one boy who worked at the airport said it was too much of a Hindu thing for Muslims to be doing; if his parents caught him chanting a mantra he'd get a backhander across the face. Mostly the kids listened to the Stones, Van Morrison and Bowie as they flew over ruined roads to the beach in bright red and yellow Japanese cars with quadrophonic speakers, past camels and acres of wasteland.

Here, all along the railway track, the poor and diseased and hungry lived in shacks and huts; the filthy poor gathered around rusty stand-pipes to fetch water; or ingeniously they resurrected wrecked cars, usually Morris Minors; and here they slept in huge sewer pipes among buffalo, chickens and wild dogs. Here I met a policeman who I thought was on duty. But the policeman lived here, and hanging on the wall of his falling-down shed was his spare white police uniform, which he'd had to buy himself.

If not to the beach, the kids went to the Happy Hamburger to hang out. Or to each other's houses to watch Clint Eastwood tapes and giggle about sex, of which they were so ignorant and deprived. I watched a group of agitated young men in their mid-twenties gather around a 1950s medical book to look at the female genitalia. For these boys, who watched Western films and mouthed the lyrics of pop songs celebrating desire ('come on, baby, light my fire'), life before marriage could only be like spending years and years in a single-sex public school; for them women were mysterious, unknown, desirable and yet threatening creatures of almost another species, whom you had to respect, marry and impregnate but couldn't be friends with. And in this country where the sexes were usually strictly segregated, the sexual tension could be palpable. The men who could afford to flew to Bangkok for relief. The others squirmed and resented women. The kind of sexual openness that was one of the few real achievements of the 1960s, the discussion of contraception, abortion, female sexuality and prostitution which some women were trying to advance, received incredible hostility. But women felt it was only a matter of time before progress was made; it was much harder to return to ignorance than the mullahs thought.

'England, your England'

In Pakistan, England just wouldn't go away. Relics of the Raj were everywhere: buildings, monuments, Oxford accents, libraries full of English books, and newspapers. Many Pakistanis had relatives in England; thousands of Pakistani families depended on money sent from England. Visiting a village, a man told me through an interpreter, that when his three grandchildren visited from Bradford, he had to hire an interpreter to speak to them. It was happening all the time – the closeness of the two societies, and the distance.

Although Pakistanis still wanted to escape to England, the old men in their clubs and the young eating their hamburgers took great pleasure in England's decline and decay. The great master was fallen. Now it was seen as strikebound, drug-ridden, riot-torn, inefficient, disunited, a society which had moved too suddenly from puritanism to hedonism and now loathed itself. And the Karachi wits liked to ask me when I thought the Americans would decide the British were ready for self-government.

Yet people like Rahman still clung to what they called British ideals, maintaining that it is a society's ideals, its conception of human progress, that define the level of its civilisation. They regretted, under the Islamisation, the repudiation of the values which they said were the only positive aspect of Britain's legacy to the sub-continent. These were: the idea of secular institutions based on reason, not revelation or scripture; the idea that there were no final solutions to human problems; and the idea that the health and vigour of a society was bound up with its ability to tolerate and express a plurality of views on all issues, and that these views would be welcomed.

But England as it is today, the ubiquity of racism and the suffering of Pakistanis because of it, was another, stranger subject. When I talked about it, the response was unexpected. Those who'd been to England often told of being insulted, or beaten up, or harassed at the airport. But even these people had attitudes similar to those who hadn't been there.

It was that the English misunderstood the Pakistanis because they saw only the poor people, those from the villages, the illiterates, the peasants, the Pakistanis who didn't know how to use toilets, how to eat with knives and forks because they were poor. If the British could only see *them*, the rich, the educated, the sophisticated, they wouldn't be so hostile. They'd know what civilised people the Pakistanis really were. And then they'd like them.

The implication was that the poor who'd emigrated to the West to escape the strangulation of the rich in Pakistan deserved the racism they received in Britain because they really were contemptible. The Pakistani middle class shared the disdain of the British for the *émigré* working class and peasantry of Pakistan.

It was interesting to see that the British working class (and not only the working class, of course) used the same vocabulary of contempt about Pakistanis – the charges of ignorance, laziness, fecklessness, uncleanliness – that their own, British middle class used about them. And they weren't able to see the similarity.

Racism goes hand in hand with class inequality. Among other

things, racism is a kind of snobbery, a desire to see oneself as superior culturally and economically, and a desire actively to experience and enjoy that superiority by hostility or violence. And when that superiority of class and culture is unsure or not acknowledged by the Other – as it would be acknowledged by the servant and master in class-stable Pakistan – but is in doubt, as with the British working class and Pakistanis in England, then it has to be demonstrated physically. Everyone knows where they stand then – the class inequality is displayed, just as any other snob demonstrates superiority by exhibiting wealth or learning or ancestry.

So some of the middle class of Pakistan, who also used the familiar vocabulary of contempt about their own poor (and, incidentally, about the British poor) couldn't understand when I explained that British racists weren't discriminating in their racial discrimination: they loathed all Pakistanis and kicked whoever was nearest. To the English all Pakistanis were the same; racists didn't ask whether you had a chauffeur, TV and private education before they set fire to your house. But for some Pakistanis, it was their own poor who had brought this upon them.

Coming back to England was harder than going. I had culture shock in reverse. Images of plenty yelled at me. England seemed to be overflowing with . . . things. Things from all over the world. Things and information. Information, though, which couldn't bite through the profound insularity and indifference.

In Pakistan people were keen to know: not only about Asia and the Middle East, but about Europe and the United States. They sought out information about the whole world. They needed it. They ordered books from Europe, listened to international radio and chewed up visiting academics like pieces of orange.

In Britain today, among the middle class, thinking and argument are almost entirely taboo. The other taboo, replacing death in its unacceptability, is money. As our society has become more divided, the acknowledgment of that division – which is a financial division, a matter of economic power – is out of the question. So money is not discussed. It is taken for granted that you have it: that you have means of obtaining it: that you are reasonably well off and gain status and influence over others because of it.

Accompanying this financial silence, and shoring up both the social division and the taboo, is the prohibition on thought. The discussion of a serious subject to a conclusion using logic, evidence and counter-evidence is an unacceptable social embarrassment. It just isn't done to argue: it is thought to be the same as rowing. One has opinions in England, but they are formed in private and clung to in public despite everything, despite their often being quite wrong.

There is real defensiveness and insecurity, a Victorian fear of revealing so much as a genital of an idea, the nipple of a notion or the sex of a syllogism. Where sexual exhibitionism and the discussion of positions and emissions is fashionable, indeed orthodox, thinking and argument are avoided.

In Pakistan it was essential to have knowledge because political discussion was serious. It mattered what you thought. People put chairs in a circle, sat down and *talked*. What was said to each other was necessary. Intellectual dignity was maintained, earnest anxiety was expressed; you weren't alone; ideas and feelings were shared. These things had to be said, even in low voices, because absolute silence was intolerable, absolute silence was the acceptance of isolation and division. It was a relief to argue, to exercise intelligence in a country where intelligence was in itself a weapon and a threat.

I will never forget the hospitality, warmth and generosity of the people of Pakistan; the flowers on the lawn of the Sind Club, the sprawling open houses, full of air and people and the smell of spices; the unbelievable brightness of the light shining through a dust haze; the woman walking perfectly straight-backed along a street with an iron balanced on her head; the open-air typists outside the law courts; butterflies as big as clock faces; the man who slept with a chicken in his bed; my uncle's library, bought in the 1940s in Cambridge, where he was taught by Russell – though when I opened the books after being given the library, they were rotten with worms, the pitted pages falling apart just as I stood there. And the way the men shake hands. This is worth going into.

First you offer them your hand and they grasp it. The clasped hands are slapped then with their spare hand as an affirmation of initial contact. This is, as it were, the soup. Now they pull you to them for the main course, the full embrace, the steak. As you look over their shoulder, your bodies thrust together, your heat intermingled, they crack you on the back at least three times with their open palm. These are not negligible taps, but good healthy whacks, demonstrating equality and openness. Depending on the nature of the friendship, these whacks could go on a considerable time and may debilitate the sick or weak. But they must be reciprocated. This done, they will let you move away from them, but still holding your right hand. You are considered fully, with affection overbrimming, as they regard all of you, as they seem to take in your entire being from top to toe, from inside to out. At last, after complete contact has been made, all possibility of concealment or inhibition banished, they carefully let go of your hand as if it were a delicate object. *That is a greeting.*

And there was the photograph of my father in my uncle's room, in which he must have been about the same age as me. A picture in a house that contained fragments of my past: a house full of stories, of Bombay, Delhi, China; of feuds, wrestling matches, adulteries, windows broken with hands, card games, impossible loves, and magic spells. Stories to help me see my place in the world and give me a sense of the past which could go into making a life in the present and future. This was surely part of the way I could understand myself. This knowledge, garnered in my mid-twenties, would help me form an image of myself: I'd take it back to England where I needed it to protect myself. And it would be with me in London and the suburbs, making me stronger.

When I considered staying in Pakistan to regain more of my past and complete myself with it, I had to think that that was impossible. Didn't I already miss too much of England? And wasn't I too impatient with the illiberalism and lack of possibility of Pakistan?

So there was always going to be the necessary return to England. I came home . . . to my country.

This is difficult to say. 'My country' isn't a notion that comes easily. It is still difficult to answer the question, where do you come from? I have never wanted to identify with England. When Enoch Powell spoke for England I turned away in final disgust. I would rather walk naked down the street than stand up for the National Anthem. The pain of that period of my life, in the mid-1960s, is with me still. And when I originally wrote this piece I put it in the third person: Hanif saw this, Hanif felt that, because of the difficulty of directly addressing myself to what I felt then, of not wanting to think about it again. And perhaps that is why I took to writing in the first place, to make strong feelings into weak feelings.

But despite all this, some kind of identification with England remains.

It is strange to go away to the land of your ancestors, to find out how much you have in common with people there, yet at the same time to realise how British you are, the extent to which, as Orwell says, 'the suet puddings and the red pillar boxes have entered into your soul'. It isn't *that* you wanted to find out. But it is part of what you do find out. And you find out what little choice you have in the matter of your background and where you belong. You look forward to getting back; you think often of England and what it means to you – and you think often of what it means to be British.

Two days after my return I took my washing to a laundrette and gave it to the attendant, only to be told she didn't touch the clothes of foreigners: she didn't want me anywhere near her blasted laundrette. More seriously, I read in the paper that a Pakistani family in the East End had been fire-bombed. A child was killed. This, of course, happens frequently. It is the pig's head through the window, the spit in the face, the children with the initials of racist organisations tattooed into their skin with razor blades, as well as the more polite forms of hatred.

I was in a rage. I thought: who wants to be British anyway? Or as a black American writer said: who wants to be integrated into a burning house anyway?

And indeed I know Pakistanis and Indians born and brought up here who consider their position to be the result of a diaspora: they are in exile, awaiting return to a better place, where they belong, where they are welcome. And there this 'belonging' will be total. This will be home, and peace.

It is not difficult to see how much illusion and falsity there is in this view. How much disappointment and unhappiness might be involved in going 'home' only to see the extent to which you have been formed by England and the depth of attachment you feel to the place, despite everything.

It isn't surprising that some people believe in this idea of 'home'. The alternative to believing it is more conflict here; it is more self-hatred; it is the continual struggle against racism; it is the continual adjustment to life in Britain. And blacks in Britain know they have made more than enough adjustments.

So what is it to be British?

In his 1941 essay 'England Your England' Orwell says: 'the gentleness of the English civilisation is perhaps its most marked characteristic'. He calls the country 'a family with the wrong members in control' and talks of the 'soundness and homogeneity of England'.

Elsewhere he considers the Indian character. He explains the 'maniacal suspiciousness' which, agreeing, he claims, with E. M. Forster in *A Passage to India*, he calls 'the besetting Indian vice'. But he has the grace to acknowledge in his essay 'Not Counting Niggers' 'that the overwhelming bulk of the British proletariat [lives] ... in Asia and Africa'.

But this is niggardly. The main object of his praise is British 'tolerance' and he writes of 'their gentle manners'. He also says that this aspect of England 'is continuous, it stretches into the future and the past, there is something in it that persists'.

But does it persist? If this version of England was true then, in the 1930s and 1940s, it is under pressure now. From the point of view of thousands of black people it just does not apply. It is completely without bias.

Obviously tolerance in a stable, confident wartime society with a massive Empire is quite different to tolerance in a disintegrating uncertain society during an economic depression. But surely this would be the test; this would be just the time for this much-advertised tolerance in the British soul to manifest itself as more than vanity and self-congratulation. But it has not. Under real continuous strain it has failed.

Tolerant, gentle British whites have no idea how little of this tolerance is experienced by blacks here. No idea of the violence, hostility and contempt directed against black people every day by state and individual alike in this land once described by Orwell as being not one of 'rubber truncheons' or 'Jew-baiters' but of 'flower-lovers' with 'mild knobbly faces'. But in parts of England the flower-lovers are all gone, the rubber truncheons and Jew-baiters are at large, and if any real contemporary content is to be given to Orwell's blind social patriotism, then clichés about 'tolerance' must be seriously examined for depth and weight of substantial content.

In the meantime it must be made clear that blacks don't require 'tolerance' in this particular condescending way. It isn't this particular paternal tyranny that is wanted, since it is major adjustments to British society that have to be made.

I stress that it is the British who have to make these adjustments.

It is the British, the white British, who have to learn that being British isn't what it was. Now it is a more complex thing, involving new elements. So there must be a fresh way of seeing Britain and the choices it faces: and a new way of being British after all this time. Much thought, discussion and self-examination must go into seeing the necessity for this, what this 'new way of being British' involves and how difficult it might be to attain.

The failure to grasp this opportunity for a revitalised and broader self-definition in the face of a real failure to be human, will be more insularity, schism, bitterness and catastrophe.

The two countries, Britain and Pakistan, have been part of each other for years, usually to the advantage of Britain. They cannot now be wrenched apart, even if that were desirable. Their futures will be intermixed. What that intermix means, its moral quality, whether it is violently resisted by ignorant whites and characterised by inequality and injustice, or understood, accepted and humanised, is for all of us to decide.

This decision is not one about a small group of irrelevant people who can be contemptuously described as 'minorities'. It is about the direction of British society. About its values and how humane it can be when experiencing real difficulty and possible breakdown. It is about the respect it accords individuals, the power it gives to groups, and what it really means when it describes itself as 'democratic'. The future is in our hands.

Name index

Abertillery 104
Ackerley, J. R. 261–2
Adorno, Theodore 15
Africa 230
Ali, Muhammad 273–4
Allan, Maude 266
Americas 231–4
Amigo, Peter Emmanuel 24
Anglesey 194
Animal Farm 30
The Antiquary 177, 184
Arkwright, Richard 176
Ashton-under-Lyne 97, 106
Astell, Mary 130–7
Attwood, Thomas 186
Austen, Jane 140

Baggett, Ian 81–2, 85–6
Balaklava 61, 65, 66
Baldwin, James 273
Balfour, Arthur James 213
Balzac, Honoré de 173
Bamford, Samuel 95
Barbados 232
Barclay, Tom 100, 102
Barker, Lilian 147, 150, 152
Barney, Natalie Clifford 264
Barnsley 108
Beauvais et le Beauvaisis 141
Beddoes, Deirdre 124, 128
Berlin 264
Bermondsey 18, 23, 105
Berner, Lilian 149

Bethnal Green 100
Betjeman, John 11, 13
Bexhill 85
Bhutto, Zulfikar Ali 277
Bicester 81–2, 87, 92
Big Chief I-Spy 9–14, 16–17
Billing, Noel Pemberton 266
Bilston 103
Birkenhead, Frederick Edwin Smith, Lord 266
Birkett, William Norman, Lord 266
Birmingham 103, 108
Biron, Sir Charles 265
Black Dwarf 7–8
The Black Dwarf (Sir Walter Scott) 178–9
Blackman, Les 85
Bollington, Cheshire 104
Booth, Charles 96, 105–6, 143, 212
Borders of Scotland, 177–81, 184
Borrow, George 97
Botham, Ian 275
Boulton, Ernest 259
Boyce, Frank 9–17
Bradford 96, 101, 112, 243
Braxfield, Robert MacQueen, Lord 178, 180, 189
Brecht, Bertolt 199
The Bride of Lammermoor 184
Brideshead Revisited 18
Bridgeman, Rev. Mother 65, 66
Brigden, Ray 85–6

Name index

Britain, *see* subject index
Brownrigg, Sir W. Douglas S. 163
Buchan, John 187
Burnley 107
Burns, Robert 174, 182
Byron, George Gordon 182

Cadell, James 190
Camberwell 106
Camin, Baron de 96–7
Canning (Stratford de Redcliffe), Lady 66, 71
Cardiff 108
Caribbean 230–41
Carlos, John 273
Carlyle, Thomas 174
Carmarthen 107
Caroll, Father 103
Carpenter, Edward 257, 260
Casement, Sir Roger 258, 261
Castle, Pablo 85
Castle Dangerous 190
Castle Rackrent 182
Cavell, Edith 144
Chamberlain, Mary 18–36
Charlie Brown 51–3
Chaytor, Miranda 39–42, 127
Childe Harold 182
Chipping Norton 85
Chronicles of the Canongate 186–8, 190–1
Chudleigh, Lady Mary 131–2
Clapham, J. H. 125
Clark, Alice 124–5
Clay, Cassius 273–4
Clerkenwell 101
Clough, Miss 61, 65, 66
Clyde, Sir Colin 61
Cobbett, William 89
Cohn-Lask, Joseph 218
Colne 107
Coming Up for Air 13
Constantinople 66
Count Robert of Paris 190
Crimea 57–78
Crooks, Will 145
Crout, Mabel 153
Cwmbran 107

Dacre, Lord (Hugh Trevor-Roper) 174–5
Daily Mail 9, 163
Davin, Anna 128–9
Davies, Alfred 200–1
Davis, Margaret Llewellyn 137
Defoe, Daniel 131, 133
Desart, Lord 266
Dickens, Charles 174
Dickinson, Goldsworthy Lowes 258
Disraeli, Benjamin 210
Dixon, Norman F. 160
Douglass, Dave 43–56
Dover 3, 147
Downshire, Wills Hill, Marquis of 182
Doyle, Father Thomas 24
Drake, Barbara 124
Driberg, Tom 261
Duckworth, George 212
Durham County 39

East End of London 207–29
Eastbourne 88
An Economic History of Modern Britain 125
Edgeworth, Maria 182
Edwards, Owen M. 200
Eliot, George 105, 183, 210
Ellis, Havelock 260, 262, 264–5
Elzear, Father 107
Encyclopaedia Britannica 30
England 236, 284
England Your England 285
Enloe, Cynthia 160, 161
An Essay in Defence of the Female Sex 132
Eve and the New Jerusalem 143
Everitt, Zacchariah 83

Failsworth 97
Fanon, Frantz 274
The Far Pavilions 275
Father and Son 13
Feldman, David 207–29
Field, John 3–8
The Fire Next Time 273

Folkestone 3–8
Foner, N. 237
Fontane, Theodore 173
Fordyce, James 135
Forster, E. M. 262, 285
The Fortunes of Nigel 182
Foucault, Michel 256
Fox, Charles James 178
France 178, 259
Franco, Francisco 24
Frost in May 23
Fry, Elizabeth 72

Gagnon, J. H. 265
Garibaldi, Giuseppe 98–9, 101
Gardiner, Dorothy 124
Gartner, L. 208
Gavazzi, Father Alessandro 96
George, Dorothy 137
Gillick, Victoria 20
Gladstone, William Ewart 59, 82, 210
Glamorgan 194–5
God Save Ireland 100–1
Goethe, Johann Wolfgang von 173
Gogol, Nikolai Vasilievich 173
Gore, Elizabeth 150
Goretti, St. Maria 34
Gosse, Sir Edmund 13
Goubert, Pierre 141
Grigg, Sir James 164
The Guardian 129
Guyana 244

Hall, Catherine 126
Hall, John 65, 66
Hall, Radclyffe 264–6
Hammond, Barbara 137
Hardy, Thomas 174
Hartwell, Ronald 195
Harvie, Christopher 173–92
Haywards Heath 90
The Heart of Midlothian 183
Hedges, Sid 87
Hegel, Georg Wilhelm Friedrich 173
Herbert, Elizabeth 57, 64
Herbert, Sidney 57, 61, 64, 65, 67

Herzl, Theodor 218
Heuman, Gad 232
Higgins, Patricia 132
The Highland Widow 188
Highlands of Scotland 188–90
Hill, Bridget 123–39
Hill, Christopher 143
Hill, Octavia 74
Hillel 225
Hirschfeld, Magnus 264
The Historical Novel 173
History of Scotland 185
Hobsbawm, Eric 177, 195
Hoffman, Paul 141
Hospitals and Sisterhoods 60, 69
Housman, Lawrence 264
Howkins, Alan 81–93
Hufton, Olwen 124, 128, *140–3*
Hume, Cardinal Basil 20
Hutchins, B. L. 124
Hutchinson's Social History of England 142
Hyde Park 98

Institutions of the Law of Scotland 177
Ireland 21
Italy 259
Ivanhoe 184
Ives, George Cecil 261, 263–4

Jamaica 231, 233–4
James, Henry 3
James, Winston 230–55
Jameson, Anna 74
Jeffrey, Francis 180
Jessop, Augustus 86
The Jewel in the Crown 275
Jewish Chronicle 213–14, 217
The Jewish Immigrants in England 208
Jinnah, Mohammed Ali 277
Jones, Jack 196
Joseph, N. S. 214
Journal (Sir Walter Scott) 177, 185–6, 190

Karachi 270–87
Kellett, E. E. 87

Kelly, Joan Gadol 141
Kennedy, John F. 21
Kennett, Dr. White 131
Kensal (New) Town 102, 106
Kent, Monseigneur Bruce 20
Key, Robert 83
Kiernan, Victor 181
Kilburn 108
Kinnaird, Joan 130–2
Knowles, Lilian 137
Knox, Jean 169
Krafft-Ebing, Richard 264
Kulali 65, 66, 68–70
Kureishi, Hanif 270–87
Kussmaul, Ann 126

Ladurie, Emmanuel Le Roy 141
Laizerovich, Eliazer 218
Lamming, George 236
The Lamp 62
Langston, Emma 65
Lansbury, George 100
Laski, Harold Joseph 277
Lawrence, Daniel 241–2
The Lay of the Last Minstrel 181
A Legend of Montrose 100, 189
Leicester 100, 102
Letters from Malachi Malagrowther 176, 186–7, 191
Liberman, Karl 217
Life 273
Limerick 100
Lincoln 108
Liverpool 10–11, 106, 108–9
Lloyd, J. E. 200
Lloyd George, David 146, 199
Locke, John 136
Lockhart, John Gibson 185–6
London 18, 101, 207–29, 259, 270–87
Londonderry, Lady 149
Long, Edward 233
Long Crendon 85
Lukács, Georg 173, 180

Macarthur, Mary 146
MacDiarmid, Hugh 174
MacDonell, Alexander 189

McMillan, Margaret 124
Machzike Hadath 217
Madagascar 232
Madoo, Patricia 245
Maine, Sir Henry 13
Manchester 95, 98, 208
Manley, Mary 134
Manzoni, Alessandro 173
Margesson, Henry David Reginald 163
Marshall, Dorothy 137
Marylebone 98
Masham, Damaris 131
Mattishal, Norfolk 90
Maurice, Rev. F. D. 59
Mayhew, Henry 95, 99, 101–5, 143
Mellish, Bob 21
Merrill, George 261
Merthyr Tydfil 103, 196
Mickiewicz, Adam 173
Mind Your Language 275
Minstrelsy of the Scottish Border 178
Monmouthshire 195
Montagu, Samuel, Lord Swaythling 221–4
Montefiore, Claude 211
Montefiore, Sir Francis 222
Morley, Edith 124
Morley, John 82
Morrison, Herbert 164
Mosley, Oswald 240
Mosston, Surrey 102
Motherland 240
Muhammad, Elijah 274
Murray, James 178
My Beautiful Laundrette 271
My Secret Life 257, 261

Naipaul, Vidia 240
Newman, Cardinal John Henry 94
News Chronicle 9, 15
Newtown, Manchester 95
Nicholls, Horace 146
Nicol, Martha 67, 70, 73–4
Nightingale, Florence 57–61, 64–6, 70–1, 74
Norman, Matilda 63

Name index

Not Counting Niggers 285

O'Connell, Daniel 101
O'Connor, Joseph 108
O'Connor, T. P. 210
O'Day, Rosemary 129
Old Mortality 187
Orwell, George 13, 285–6

Paine, Tom 92
Paisley, Rev. Ian 21
Pakistan 270–87
Pankhurst, Emmeline 146
Panmure, Fox Maule Ramsay
  Dalhousie, Lord 61
Paris 264
Parkin, Di 158–70
A Passage to India 285
Les Paysans de Languedoc 141
Peterloo 95
Phillipson, Nicholas 176, 185–6
Pile, Sir Frederick 169
Pinchbeck, Ivy 124
Poland 173, 220
Poll, S. 220
Pollock, Linda 142
Pontypool 107
Pontypridd 198
Powell, Enoch 272, 284
Power, Eileen 124, 141
Di Poylishe Yidel 216
A Problem in Greek Ethics 260
A Problem in Modern Ethics 260
Prostitution and Victorian Society 143
*The Psychology of Military
  Incompetence* 160
Pushkin, Alexander 173

Radnor, Lord 3, 5
Raglan, FitzRoy James Henry
  Somerset, Lord 61, 66
Redgauntlet 174, 186
Redstocking Manifesto 135
Reflections upon Marriage 130
Reich, Wilhelm 162
Renkioi 65
Rix, George 83, 85, 88
Rob Roy 174, 180, 183

A Room of One's Own 140
Rothschild, Lord 221
Rousseau, Jean Jacques 142
Rowbotham, Sheila 129
Rowntree, Benjamin Seebohm 143
Rubens, Paul Alfred 151
Russell, Bertrand 277, 283
Russia 57, 173, 210, 220
Russia, the Atom and the West 55

St Helens 99
St James Gazette 212
St Ronan's Well 186
Salford 99
Samuel, Raphael 94–119, 129
Sandys, Duncan 272
Sarsfield, Patrick 100
Saul, Jack 263
Savile, George, Marquess of
  Halifax 126
Schiller, Johann Christoph
  Friedrich von 173
Schloss, David 214
Scotland 173–92
Scott, Joan 125
Scott, Sir Walter 173–92
Scutari 57–8, 64–7, 71
Sellon, Priscilla Lydia 59
A Serious Proposal to the Ladies 130, 132
Sermons to Young Women 135
Sexton, James 99
Sexual Inversion 260
Shaw, George Bernard 274
Sherlock, Father 103
Simon, William 265
Smith, Goldwin 211
Smith, John (of Yarmouth) 82
Smith, Thommie 273
Smyrna 65–8
Snell, K. D. M. 126
Soho 109
Soloweitschik, Leonty 212
South Wales 193–203
Stair, Sir James Dalrymple,
  Viscount 177
Staleybridge 97
Stanley, Mary 57, 60–71

Name index

Stead, W. T. 257
Stenton, Doris 141
Stephens, Joseph Rayner 106
Stewart, Jane Shaw 61, 65, 74
Stockport 106
Stratford de Redcliffe (Canning), Lady 66, 71
Strindberg, Johan August 173
Sullivan, T. D. 100
Summerfield, Penny 163
Summers, Anne 57–78
Summerskill, Edith 164, 169
Sutherland, Countess of 189
Swaythling, Samuel Montagu, Lord 221–4
Swift, Jonathan 175, 177
Symonds, John Addington 257, 259–61

Tales of a Grandfather 185, 187, 189
Tarry Town, Hackney Wick 109
Tawney, Prof. Richard Henry 105, 277
Taylor, Barbara 143
Taylor, Charles 260
Taylor, Frances Margaret (Mother Magdalen) 61–2, 67–8, 70, 73
Temple, Helen 165
Therapia 65, 67–8
Thickbroom, Charles Ernest 262
Thom, Deborah 144–57
Thomas, Keith 132
Thomas, William I. 10
Tilly, Louise 125
The Times 29, 30, 32, 59, 64, 279
Toole, Joe 99
Tower Hamlets 109
Tredegar 97
Trevor-Roper, Hugh (Lord Dacre) 174–5
Turgenev, Ivan Sergeyvich 187
Turkey 64–5, 67, 210
Twining, Louisa 72, 74
The Two Drovers 188
Tyneside 43–56

Upper Heyford 83

Vere, Father L. G. 109

Wales 104, 107, *193–203*
Walkowitz, Judith 143
Wallas, Ada 124
Wallasey 107
Walworth 18, 22–3
Waverley 173, 180, 182, 185
Weeks, Jeffrey 256–69
The Well of Loneliness 265–6
Werner, Aba 217–18
West, Gabrielle 150
Westminster 108
White, Antonia 18, 23
Whitworth, Rochdale 106
Wigan 96–7, 101, 112
Wilde, Oscar 257–8, 260–2, 266
Williams, Bill 208
Williams, Tim 193–203
Willis, Bob 275
Wolf, Lucien 224
Wolverhampton 96
Woman 166
Woman's Own 158, 168–9
Women and Beauty 165
Women at Work 146
Women Workers and the Industrial Revolution 124
Woolf, Virginia 140, 142
Woolwich 61, 144–57
Woolwich Pioneer 145, 147
Working Life of Women in the 17th Century 124
Wright, Richard 273

X, Malcolm 274

Yeats, William Butler 175
Der Yidisher Ekspres 217–18
York 103

Zia-Ul-Haq, Mohammad 275
Znaniecki, Floryan 104

Subject index

Africans 230–4, 239, 243–4, 254
Afro-Caribbeans 230–55
alienation 11–13, 17, 191, 213
Anglicans and anglicanism 18, 58, 73, 111, 132, 219
anglicisation
  of Jews 207–9, 214–19, 222–4; of South Wales 193–203
Anglo-Jewry 209–24
animals 39–41
anti-semitism 210
armed services 158–70
army 58, 160–1, 164, 189, 258
Arsenal (Woolwich) 144–57
Asians 241–5
assimilation
  of Jews 208–11, 218, 220; of Pakistanis 272; of Scotland 184, 190
Auxiliary Territorial Service 159–60, 162, 164–9

ballads 178, 181
Baptists 26–7, 85
black identity 230–55
Black Panthers 273
books 10–17, 54–6
bourgeoisie 6, 208, 222
Britain
  character of 193; Christianity of 18; concept of 236–8; countryside of 12–15, 40; history of 14; idealised 10–14; industrialisation of 127, 176, 191, 195, 198, 202; multi-racial 17; and Pakistan 285; racism in 230, 233, 235, 237–45, 271, 273, 280–1; return migration from 237–8, 244, 251–2; subcultures in 258; tradition of 19; urbanised 17; women in 158; in World War II 158
British
  hatred of 100; ideals 281; identity 224; middle class 26, 33, 260, 281; nationalism 174; patriotism 39, 144, 146, 153–4, 158, 169, 177, 276; separateness 282; tolerance 285–6; upper class 39–42, 261; working class 235–7, 245, 261–2, 282
Britishness 178, 198–200, 285–6

C-stream classes 43–56
Campaign for Nuclear Disarmament 20, 82–3, 86
Catholics and catholicism
  English 18–36; Irish 94–119; nurses 58, 64, 73
chapel life 81–93, 94, 106
chauvinism 234–5, 238, 250
childhood 1–36
children and parents
  black 230–55; Catholic 18–36; Pakistani 270–87;

upper class 39–42; working class 43–56
Christianity 18, 211
church
Anglican 111; buildings 105–6; Catholic 20–1, 94–5, 103–4, 111; and chapel 94; of England 59, 73, 85; hierarchies 28; and nursing 64; and state 20
citizenship 180, 210, 222
class
bourgeoisie 6, 208, 222; and difference 3–8, 9–17, 33, 37–78, 148–9, 261–3, 266, 282; and gender 263; identity 158, 262; middle 26, 33, 260, 281–2; and race 231, 233, 237, 281; upper 39–42, 261; war 47–54; working 3–17, 26, 43–56, 63–4, 84, 88, 158, 199, 223–4, 235–7, 244, 261–2, 281–2
coal industry 195, 199, 202
colonialism 202, 248
colour and difference 230–55, 270–87
coloureds 230–5
Conservatives 181, 190–1, 244
Tories 21, 137, 174, 180–1, 185
consumerism 15–17
countryside 12–15, 40
Crimean War 57–78

democracy 193, 200, 202
difference
class 3–8, 9–17, 33, 37–78, 148–9, 261–2, 264; gender 123–70, 263; language 43–56, 193–203; national 173–203; racial 207–29, 230–55, 270–87; regional 3–8, 9–17, 43–56; religious 18–36, 81–119, 150; sexual 256–69
Dissenters 81, 83, 85
domesticity 126–7, 154
drink 84, 99, 275

education
C-stream classes 43–56; Catholic 18–36; eleven-plus examination 43–6; Jewish 214–15; and language 194–202; and religion 18–36, 215, 217; teachers 47–8, 50; of women 131, 133, 137; see also schools
eleven-plus examination 43–6
England
Church of 59, 73, 85; idea of 236; identification with 284
English
Catholics 18–36; Jews 207, 212–13, 218, 220, 222, 224; language 193, 196, 216; non-conformity 92; social hegemony 189
Englishness 39, 41
equality
class 68, 70–1; gender 163; racial 210, 220
Evangelicalism 126–7

family 136, 142, 278
black 230–55; Catholic 18–36; Pakistani 270–87; upper class 39–42; working class 43–56
feminists and feminism
Astell, Mary 130–7; Catholic 35; early 123–39; and history 123–31, 137; and pacifism 145; and radicalism 132; present-day 130–1; and socialism 121
femininity 158–70
Francophobia 7
French 7–8, 178

gender and difference 123–70, 261
Geordies 49, 51

hierarchies 10, 28, 58, 86, 191, 230–5, 278
history
British 14; of the family 142; and feminism 123–31, 137; of Jewish immigrants 207–8; and men 123, 128, 135; social 137, 142, 199, 208; of the Welsh 194; and women 123–5, 128, 137, 140–3

Subject index

Home Guard 163–4
homosexuals and homosexuality 256–69
hospitals 58, 60, 64, 71–2

I-spy game 9–17
identity
  assimilation 184, 190, 208–9, 218, 220, 273; belonging 39; black 230–55; British 224; Catholic 18–36, 94–119; citizenship 180, 210, 222; class 3–8, 9–17, 37–78, 158, 262; feminine 149, 158, 160; homosexual 256–69; Irish 94–119; Jewish 207–29; language 43–56, 102–3, 193–203, 214, 216, 218, 223–4, 239, 260; lesbian 264–6; national 104; 123; Pakistani 270–87; patriotism 18, 21, 39, 144, 146, 153–4, 158, 174, 177, 182, 211–13, 218, 222, 276; reform movements 185, 190, 218, 261, 263–4; regional 3–8, 9–17, 43–56; religious 81–93, 94–119; resistance 48–50, 53, 162, 199, 239–40, 267; Scottish 173–92; socialisation 208; solidarity 88, 96, 104; Welsh 193–203
immigration
  Afro-Caribbean 233–8; Indian 243; Irish 21, 94–5, 99, 102; Jewish 207–29; return migration 238, 245, 251–2; Welsh 196
Indians 13, 242–3, 254, 285
Indonesians 13
industrialisation 127, 176, 191, 195, 198, 202
industry 125–6, 174, 185–6
  coal 195, 199, 202
internationalism 5, 19, 82
Irish 21, 23, 94–119, 150
Islam 211, 276–9, 281
island chauvinism 235, 239, 249–50
Italians 101

Jamaican language 239
Jews and Judaism 22, 150, 207–29

labour, sexual division of, 144–57, 160
Labour
  movement 145, 199; Party 21, 92, 153–4, 244
'ladies' 31, 57–78, 149
land 12–15, 40, 180
language
  and difference 43–56, 193–203; and education 194–202; English 193, 196, 216; homosexual 260; Irish 102–3; Jamaican 239; Latin 18, 22; minority 197; of power 199; and religion 102; Welsh 193–203; Yiddish 214, 216, 218, 223–4
Latin 18, 22
lesbians and lesbianism 257, 264–6
liberalism 199

marginalisation 17, 193, 195
marriage 131, 133–4, 136, 150, 220
masculinity 158, 160–2, 169, 265
men
  aggression of 161; education of 134; friendships of 257; and history 123, 128, 135; homosexual 256–69; masculinity 158–62, 169, 265; middle class 261; militarisation of 161; orderlies 58; priests 25, 28, 103–4, 107, 110–11; prostitutes 258, 263; sexuality of 265; soldiers 5–6, 113, 146, 161; superiority of 133
Methodists 81–93, 97, 106
middle class 26, 33, 261, 281–2
military life
  armed services 58, 158–70, 189, 258; Home Guard 163–4; nurses and nursing 57–78, 161; pacifism 82, 145; soldiers 5–6, 113, 146, 160–2, 166; war 57–78, 144–70, 198, 222

minorities 205–87
  black 230–55; Catholic 19, 21,
  112; Irish 112; Jewish 207–29;
  language of 197; national
  173–92, 193–203; non-
  conformist 81–93; Pakistani
  270–87; religious 213; rural 195;
  sexual 256–69
missions 95, 103, 106–7, 110
mothers 33, 142, 161
mulattoes 230, 232

national differences 171–203
  black 230–55; Irish 94–119;
  Jewish 207–29; Pakistani 270–87;
  Scottish 173–92; Welsh 193–203
negroes 13, 231, 239, 250
nonconformists 19, 81–93, 211
novels 174, 182–4, 266
nuns 28–9, 31, 33
nurses and nursing 57–78, 161

oppression
  racial 244; of women 129, 135,
  142, 248

pacifists and pacifism 82, 145
Pakistanis 242, 270–87
parents and children
  black 230–55; Catholic 18–36;
  Pakistani 270–87; upper class
  39–42; working class 43–56
patriotism
  and belonging 39; British 177,
  276; Catholic 18, 21; Jewish
  211–13, 218, 222; and patriarchy
  158; in Scott's works 174, 182;
  of women 144, 146, 153–4
philanthropy 64, 72, 214, 217–18
pigmentocracy 231–2, 248
poetry 181–3
political Zionism 218, 222–4
politics
  Catholic 20–1; Party 92; and
  religion 35, 186; and women 75
poverty 40, 94, 221, 280–2
power relations 70, 191, 199, 208,
  218–20

prejudices
  class 43–56, 57–78, 148; gender
  144–57, 158–70; racial 207–29,
  230–55, 270–87; religious
  94–119, 207–29; sexual 256–69
priests 25, 28, 103–4, 110–11
prostitution 258, 263
Protestants and protestantism
  94–8, 107, 109, 127
Puritanism 132

race
  anti-semitism 210; and class 231,
  233, 237, 281; and difference
  207–29, 230–55, 270–87;
  equality 210, 220;
  pigmentocracy 231–2, 248;
  relations 96, 234; and religion 95,
  211; white people 231–7, 274; *see
  also* names of individual groups,
  e.g. Afro-Caribbeans, Indians,
  etc.
racism 230, 233, 235, 237–45, 272,
  274, 281–2
radicalism 7, 132, 215
Rastafarianism 239, 253
reform movements 185, 190, 218,
  261, 263–4
regional difference 3–8, 9–17,
  43–56
religion 32, *79–119*, 210, 217–21,
  278
  Anglicans and anglicanism 18,
  58, 73, 111, 132, 219; Baptists
  26–7, 85; and behaviour 35;
  Catholics and catholicism
  18–36, 58, 64, 73, 94–119;
  Christianity 18, 211; and
  difference 18–36, 81–119, 150;
  and education 18–36, 215, 217;
  Evangelicalism 126–7; Irish
  94–119; Islam 211, 276–8, 281;
  Jews and Judaism 22, 150,
  207–29; and language 102;
  Methodists *81–93*, 97, 106; and
  nationality 95; non-
  conformists 19, *81–93*, 211; and
  politics 35, 186; and prejudice

94–119, 207–29; Protestants and protestantism 94–8, 107, 109, 127; and race 95, 211; Rastafarianism 239, 253; Sectarianism 105–11, 132; and social status 95; and women 137
resistance
of homosexuals 267; in schools 48–50, 53, 199; to women soldiers 162
return migration 238, 245, 251–2
Russians 211, 214–15

St John's House Training Institution for Nurses 59–60, 64, 67, 71
Scandinavians 13
schools
Catholic 27–9, 95, 108–10; grammar 45; and homosexuality 257; and racism 241; resistance in 48–50, 53, 199; secondary modern 46–7; Sunday 81, 84–5, 88; teachers 47–8, 50; and Welsh language 194–202
Scotland 173–92
Scots 5, 150, 185
Sectarianism 105–11, 132
secularisation 219, 221
separateness
alienation 11–13, 17, 191, 213; of the British 282; class 3–8, 9–17, 33, 37–78, 148–9, 261–3, 266; exclusivity 19, 32; gender 123–70, 263; homelessness 252; language 43–56, 193–203; marginalisation 17, 193, 195; national 173–203; oppression 129, 135, 142, 244, 248; outsiders 8, 83; racial 207–29, 230–55, 270–87; regional 3–8, 9–17, 43–56; religious 18–36, 81–119, 150; sexual 256–69; subcultures 16, 258–64; superiority 60, 72, 75, 133, 282; tribes and tribalism 12, 16, 211

servants 39, 63, 66–7, 70, 74–5, 126, 146
sexuality
and Catholic education 33–5; and difference 256–69; female 35, 166, 265–6; femininity 158–70; homosexuality 256–69; and ignorance 280; lesbianism 257, 264–6; male 265; masculinity 158, 160–2, 169, 265; and non-conformists 90–2; prostitution 258, 263; stereotypes 128–9, 259–60
slavery 230–1, 233
social control 15, 198, 208, 219, 222, 224, 256
social difference
class 12, 26, 33, 37–78, 148–9, 261–3, 266; gender 123–70; language 43–56, 193–203; national 173–203; racial 207–29, 230–55, 270–87; regional 3–8, 9–17, 43–56; religious 81–119; sexual 256–69
social history 137, 142, 199, 208
socialists and socialism 5, 7–8, 41, 131, 219
soldiers 5–6, 113, 146, 160–2, 166
solidarity 88, 96, 104
state 19–21, 136, 154, 199
stereotypes 128–9, 259–60
subcultures 16, 258–64
superiority 60, 72, 75, 133, 282

teachers 47–8, 50
temperance 84–5
Tories and Toryism 21, 137, 174, 180–1, 185, 245
tourists 3–5, 182
trade unions 145, 152, 158, 216
tribes and tribalism 12, 16, 211

upper class 39–42, 261

war
Boer 198; class 47–54; Crimean 57–78; First World 144–57, 222; Second World 158–70; and

women 144–70; work 144, 146, 164
Welsh 193–203
West Indians 230–55
westernisation 219, 224
Whigs 136
white people 231–6, 273
women 121–70
  in armed services 158–70; Catholic 28, 35–6; and class relations 58, 63; defencelessness of 161; domesticity of 126–7, 154; education of 131, 133, 137; equality of 148, 163; fear of 166, 278; and female identity 149, 158, 160; feminism 35, *123–39*, 145; femininity 158–70; and friendships 257, 265–6; and history 123–5, 128, 137, 140–3; inferiority of 134; Irish 102, 150; 'ladies' 31, *57–78*, 149; lesbians 156, 264–6; and marriage 131, 133–4, 136, 150, 220; mothers 33, 142, 161; and national identity 123; nuns 28–9, 31, 33; nurses 57–78, 161; oppression of 129, 135, 142, 247; and patriotism 144, 145, 153–4, 169; and politics 75; professional 266; prostitutes 263; and religion 137; and sectarianism 132; sexuality of 35, 166, 265–6; stereotypes of 128–9; subordination of 128, 133–4; and Tories 137; and war 144–70; at Woolwich Arsenal 144–57; and work 63–4, 75, 126, 144–57, 160
women's magazines 165–6, 168–9
women's movement 35, 123–5
work
  war 144, 146, 164; and women 126, 144–57, 160
working class 84, 88, 158, 199
  British 235–6, 244, 261–2, 282; Caribbean 234; Catholic 26; childhood 3–17, 43–56; Jewish 223–4; Pakistani 281; women 63–4
World War I 144–57, 222
World War II 158–70

Yiddish 214, 216, 218, 223–4

Zionism 218, 222–4